Unruly Immigrants

Unruly Immigrants

Rights, Activism, and Transnational
South Asian Politics in the United States

MONISHA DAS GUPTA

Duke University Press   Durham and London   2006

© 2006 Duke University Press

All rights reserved

Printed in the United States of America on acid-free paper ∞

Designed by Heather Hensley

Typeset in Adobe Jenson by Keystone Typesetting, Inc.

Library of Congress Cataloging-in-Publication Data appear
on the last printed page of this book.

For my mother, Karabi Das Gupta,
who helped me take my first steps in feminism

CONTENTS

ix   Acknowledgments

1   INTRODUCTION: Encounters

27   CHAPTER 1: Terms of Belonging

56   CHAPTER 2: Contests over Culture

82   CHAPTER 3: Law and Oppression

109   CHAPTER 4: "Owning Our Lives": Women's Organizations

159   CHAPTER 5: Subverting Seductions: Queer Organizations

208   CHAPTER 6: "Know Your Place in History": Labor Organizations

255   Conclusion

261   Notes

275   Works Cited

299   Index

ACKNOWLEDGMENTS

This book is the product of the insights, commitments, passion, and vision of the activists whose work makes social justice possible. My heartfelt gratitude goes to all those who participated in this project and sustained it with their unwavering belief in its importance. My comrades and friends in South Asian Women for Action have lived this project with me. I owe my politics and my thinking on social change to these incredible women—Serena Sundaram, Riti Sachdeva, Ramani Sripada-Vaz, Kalpana Subramanian, Hardeep Mann, Sameeta Ahmed, Sunu Chandy, Latha Ravi, Lina Sheth, Karen Vasudavan, Sunita Mani, Falu Bakrania, and Maya Rege. The circle of love with which they surrounded me in Boston has traveled with me. While Laurie Prendergast was not part of SAWA, she hung out with us, and I am glad she did. I have benefited immensely from her love, care, wisdom, and her superb indexing. The friendship that Bhairavi Desai has extended to me has been an unexpected gift. I have learned much from her about organizing. She and the New York Taxi Workers Alliance Organizing Committee taught me one of my most important lessons— the place of compassion in political work.

A number of activists based in the academy have also supported my work. Becky Thompson committed herself to seeing this book in print. She gave me my first tutorials in publishing, and my dissertation was reborn as a book in her living room. Each chapter has benefited from her valuable feedback and constant encouragement. Linda Carty's rigorous attention to questions of political economy has profoundly informed my analysis, and her life as an activist in the academy has instructed my career. M. Jacqui Alexander inspired me with her politics. Ben Davidson, who I met my first semester at Brandeis University, and Greg Riley have continued to clarify for me the stakes in the process of writing. Piya Chatterjee, Gayatri Gopinath, Kamala Visweswaran, Julia Sudbury, and Colin Danby have greatly strengthened my work with their suggestions and their intellectual-political commitments. I am immensely grateful to the reviewers of the manuscript for their very helpful comments. My partner and intellectual companion, Richard Rath, has shared my every thought, every doubt, and every moment of exhilaration and despair. We have wrestled together with conceptualizing and working on this project. His contributions to this work defy enumeration.

At the University of Hawai'i at Manoa I am fortunate to be part of a community of scholars who have pushed my analysis in new directions. Cynthia Franklin, Linda Lierheimer, Laura Lyons, Kieko Matteson, Naoko Shibusawa, and Mari Yoshihara have with care, patience, and attention read countless drafts of my chapters. Without their emotional support, depth of knowledge, political clarity, and deadlines, this book would not have moved forward at the pace that it did. Jorge Fernandes's thinking on migrancy and his unstinted generosity that extended even to tech support have been indispensable. He is sorely missed. Esther Figueroa raised difficult yet key questions with much love and humor. A number of my chapters are stronger as a result of valuable comments from Candace Fujikane, Jon Okamura, S. Charusheela, Davianna McGregor, and Robert Perkinson. I thank the College of Social Sciences and all my colleagues in Ethnic Studies and Women's Studies for their support. Jon Goldberg-Hiller and Noenoe Silva have given me useful advice throughout the course of my work. Many thanks to Jodi Mattos at Hamilton Library, especially during the trying months after the flood, and to Peter Tsuru in the College of Social Sciences. A grant from the University Research Council was of considerable help.

I am immensely grateful to the editors and staff of Duke University Press. Ken Wissoker brought his keen understanding to the project. His enthusiasm and skill have been critical, as has Courtney Berger's help with the practical details of putting together a book along with her reassuring e-presence and promptness. Himanee Gupta, Charlene Tuchovsky, and Payal Banerjee have been outstanding research assistants who also supported me in many moments of panic. I thank the Sociology Department at Syracuse University for assigning Payal and Charlene to me and for the other forms of support for my research.

The faith my family has shown me has helped me every step of the way. My parents, both dedicated professors, helped me take the leap into graduate studies abroad. Though we live our daily lives apart, I have felt their encouragement and belief in me every day. My uncle, Ashoke, has been like a sheltering canopy over my head. Ruchira, my sister, who pushed me to return to school, has sustained me with her love, understanding, and determination. In my extended nonbiological family abroad I have been nurtured by Rajiv Gulati, David Pauley, Edgar Young, Michael Kane, Lyn Bigelow, Sudipta Sen, and Claudia Klaver. I also want to thank Janine Wrzesniewski, Rosemary Adam-Terem, and Terry Needles for restoring me to health. Finally, I am grateful to the land, seas, and skies of the islands of Hawai'i for feeding my eyes and soul.

A section in chapter 6 was first published in "The Neoliberal State and the Domestic Workers' Movement in New York City," *Canadian Woman Studies/ Les Cahier de la Femme*, 22 (spring/summer 2003): 78–85. My analysis of the Taxi and Limousine Commission's passengers' bill of rights in chapter 6 has been informed by my essay "Of Hardship and Hostility: The Impact of 9/11 on New York City Taxi Drivers" in *Wounded City: The Social Impact of 9/11*, edited by Nancy Foner (New York: Russell Sage Foundation, 2005), 208–41.

Encounters

*T*he wait at the immigration office has already eaten up half of my day. I arrived at the office before 7 AM to join the lengthening queue of women and men. At that hour of the morning, our eyelids are heavy and our voices thick with sleep. Once inside the waiting area, the sharp questions at every turn and the blink of ticket numbers leave no room for torpor. As I wait, I scan the faces of the immigration officials behind the glass partition, hoping to get someone reasonable. All I need is a temporary permit to allow me, as an "F-1" international graduate student, to work twenty hours off-campus in order to support myself. As a foreign national, admitted to the United States as a non-immigrant alien, I am legally restricted from being employed outside the university I attend.

Low grumbles reach my ear. A family—a couple and their preschool child—was just turned away because they needed one more piece of documentation, which, of course, they did not have with them. A white woman sponsoring her Middle Eastern spouse loudly demands to know what is delaying the paperwork for her husband. The officer first tries to ignore her. But the woman insists that she has a right to know, and the officer is forced to answer her question. Emboldened by this exchange, a few of us sitting in the third row who are also waiting to hear our fate turn to each other with a flurry of INS harassment stories. Things then quiet down, and I wait.

An officer's bark breaks through the low hum of the waiting area.

"How did you live?" Her tone, directed at the man at her counter, is sharp.

"What do you mean?" the man asks in confusion. He is South Asian, probably North Indian judging from his accent.

"How did you live?" The decibel rises.

"I lived with a family."

"How did you make money, pay your bills?" The officer is shouting now. In my place in the third row I can hear her clearly.

"I sold books on the pavement," he says with a nervous laugh.

"How did you reenter the country?"

"I came in through the border."

"When did you get married?"

The man stumbles on the date, and the officer sends him scurrying.

The ticket numbers change. I fear that I have lost track, so I move up to the front row. An elderly Haitian woman is at the window in front of me. She has lost her resident alien (green) card, which is holding up her application for citizenship. She wants to know how she can get a replacement for her card. Instead of answering her question, the officer begins to grill her. A younger woman accompanying the older one starts translating the barrage of questions. The officer cuts the younger woman short, then turns to the older woman and says, "Don't you know you have to speak English to pass your citizenship test? What do you need a translator for?" These are rituals of humiliation—so uncalled for yet so necessary for national identity. A poster on the wall shows a multiracial crew of INS officers, like the crew in this Boston office. It announces how well they live up to their responsibility of gatekeepers. Another poster states in big, bold letters: "You deserve to be treated with professionalism and respect." I look around the room. Most of us here are immigrants of color. A deep sense of injustice courses through me. I am ready to explode.

These are notes from one of my many trips between 1994 and 1997 to the Immigration and Naturalization Service (INS) office in Boston for the annual renewal of my work permit.[1] As a graduate student researching immigration and immigrant communities, I kept these notes to record in ethnographic detail the emotional content of what on the surface appears to be an impersonal bureaucratic process. Amid the forms, supporting documents, mug shots, passports, and checks that exchanged hands, the "U.S. gatekeepers" and the "foreign nationals" often encountered each other with mutual feelings of anxiety, tension, frustration, and suspicion. In the process, the gatekeepers created nationalist rituals while interpreting immigrant rights through elaborate classifications of entry to and residence in the United States, and the "foreign nationals" tried to negotiate those rights. Had it not been for these encounters, I probably would have sailed through graduate school accepting the legal mantle that these naturalized state practices wear. I probably would have been less receptive to the innovative rights claims posed by the immigrant subjects of this book—the South Asian survivors of domestic violence and their advocates; domestic workers; taxi drivers; and queer activists. These subjects claimed rights that are ordinarily thought to be out of bounds for border-crossing people like themselves because of the ways in which their status as immigrants is codified by the nation-state.

A few years later, I am in a plane traveling to the United States, where I now work and am a permanent resident. I am returning from my mother's funeral in Kolkata, India. On the way there and back my mind endlessly churns up wishes of togetherness made impossible by distance; by the need I felt to send dollars home rather than spend them on a ticket, since dollars were worth so much more after an International Monetary Fund–sponsored devaluation of the Indian currency; by U.S. family sponsorship laws that would not permit me to bring my mother into the country; and by the lack of affordable health insurance even for a short visit to the United States. During a stop at Amsterdam's Schiphol airport, where I am processed for my connecting flight to Newark, I am interrogated about my place of employment (an upstate New York university) and the work I do there. Why, I ask, am I being asked these questions long before I arrive at the U.S. border? Federal Aviation Administration rules, I am told. I consider the transatlantic reach of the U.S. Department of Transportation. The person at the desk persists with her questioning, in spite of my papers spread in front of her—passport, green card, university identity card, pay stub, and a letter from my departmental chair. "What do you teach?" she asks. "Sociology," I answer. "What in sociology?" At that moment, my grief-stricken body registers an immense irony. I realize that I live what I teach.

Global migration, transnationalism, border controls, neoliberal reform, and economic deregulation are not just reified structural forces operating, as sociologists would say, at the macro level. They also leave their traces in lived experiences, erupting dramatically at crisis-ridden encounters like those I describe above. In this book, I flesh out the everyday lived, nontechnical, social, and existential meanings of the legal term "immigrant." Legally, the term marks certain entrants into the United States as resident aliens. Yet in the lived sense, a person can be treated as an immigrant whether she or he is a naturalized citizen, a citizen by birth, or technically a non-immigrant—that is, someone who has been allowed into the United States on the understanding that she or he will leave after a specified period of time. This has become painfully evident in the shadow of the events of September 11, 2001.[2] Existentially, then, the term "immigrant" encompasses conditions of migrancy—a constellation of risks, crossings, in-betweenness, fragmentations, otherness, insecurities, survivals, resistances, and creativity—that characterize what the Chicana feminist Gloria Anzaldúa (1987) calls border consciousness. Migrants live their lives transnationally.[3] The fluidity as well as the tautness of their cross-border experiences confounds the static and bounded notions of belonging enshrined in the legal categorization of immigrants. Here I use the constant interplay between these legal definitions that are central to nation building and the agency exercised by certain groups of immigrants in order to capture the rise of transnational social change organizations and transnational conceptualizations of rights.

Unruly Immigrants

This book is about South Asian immigrants in the United States whom I characterize as "unruly" in view of their struggle for rights in the face of their formal/legal and popular codification as noncitizens. The study analyzes three types of organizations—feminist, queer,[4] and labor—in contemporary South Asian communities. These organizations provoke us to question the near-monopoly of citizenship on rights. The organizations' members claim rights as immigrants, not citizens, in order to challenge the various forms of exploitation unleashed in this current phase of globalization. In keeping with their realities as stretched across borders, these immigrants construct what I call "a transnational complex of rights," in which rights are mobile rather than rooted in national membership.

Once we learn about the work of these organizations, we can no longer take for granted the link between rights and citizenship. The organizations confront the contradictory forces of capital, nations, and states that attract immigrants but then render them vulnerable and exploitable through border-policing mechanisms. They mobilize survivors of domestic violence, lesbians and gays, domestic workers, and taxi drivers who live and work in spaces where they do not enjoy the protections of citizenship because of their gender, sexuality, economic standing, race, and nationality. Indeed, these structurally marginalized men and women represent "new political actors" (Sassen 1998).

To understand why these immigrants organize to change existing social and political arrangements when most organizations in South Asian communities desire to be incorporated, I interviewed seventeen core members of seven organizations in New York, New Jersey, and Boston. The organizations include Manavi; Sakhi for South Asian Women; South Asian Women for Action (SAWA); South Asian Lesbian and Gay Association (SALGA); Massachusetts Area South Asian Lambda Association (MASALA); New York Taxi Workers Alliance (NYTWA), formerly known as the Lease Drivers Coalition (LDC); and Andolan (see figure 1). In addition to conducting formal open-ended interviews, as an invited guest I attended general meetings, speaker events, festivals, film screenings, workshops, potlucks, and drag shows.

My choice of these organizations emerged from the relations I had already developed with them in my work as an activist. In 1992, six months after arriving in the United States, I started attending meetings held by a group of mostly second-generation South Asian women in Boston who went on to form what was to become SAWA. Over time, I became a core member of the group. Through my work with SAWA, I became immersed in the larger South Asian activist community in New York, New Jersey, and Boston. The organizations I studied were a defining part of this larger network; they navigated the racial landscapes and urban politics that are particular to immigration patterns on the East Coast. I was tempted to extend my study of South Asian organizations to the differently configured contexts of the Midwest and the West Coast, especially during the time when I was campaigning against the 1996 anti-immigrant legislation. But, because I did not live in those South Asian communities I would have been an outsider looking in.

Since my research project developed organically from my prior political involvement, by the time I was ready to conduct my fieldwork in 1996 I was somewhat familiar with the orientation of these groups and with their fascinating internal debates over how to do justice work. For my project I wanted to

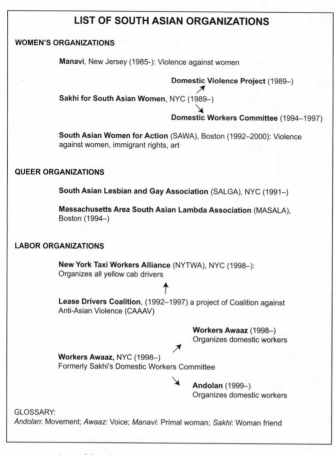

LIST OF SOUTH ASIAN ORGANIZATIONS

WOMEN'S ORGANIZATIONS

Manavi, New Jersey (1985-): Violence against women

Domestic Violence Project (1989–)

Sakhi for South Asian Women, NYC (1989–)

Domestic Workers Committee (1994–1997)

South Asian Women for Action (SAWA), Boston (1992–2000): Violence against women, immigrant rights, art

QUEER ORGANIZATIONS

South Asian Lesbian and Gay Association (SALGA), NYC (1991–)

Massachusetts Area South Asian Lambda Association (MASALA), Boston (1994–)

LABOR ORGANIZATIONS

New York Taxi Workers Alliance (NYTWA), NYC (1998–): Organizes all yellow cab drivers

Lease Drivers Coalition, (1992–1997) a project of Coalition against Anti-Asian Violence (CAAAV)

Workers Awaaz (1998–) Organizes domestic workers

Workers Awaaz, NYC (1998–) Formerly Sakhi's Domestic Workers Committee

Andolan (1999–) Organizes domestic workers

GLOSSARY:
Andolan: Movement; *Awaaz*: Voice; *Manavi*: Primal woman; *Sakhi*: Woman friend

FIGURE I. List of South Asian organizations in the study.

focus on organizations that had an agenda for social transformation and that carefully attended to issues of gender, race, class, and multiracial coalitions. These guiding research criteria were coming out of my involvement with SAWA at a time when we were working through the implications of identity-based politics in the 1990s and our effort to provide a radical alternative within our South Asian communities.

As South Asian initiatives, the two labor organizations in this study are the only ones of their kind in the United States. Over time, the NYTWA has blossomed into a multiracial organization. The emergence of these working-class organizations represents a turning point in the history of post-1965 South Asian immigration, the squarely middle-class character of which during the period

1965 to 1985 tended to dominate narratives about South Asians in the United States. Fortunately, there are many more South Asian women's and queer organizations across the United States that are devoted to addressing issues of isolation, domestic violence, gender and sexual discrimination, and inadequate services for immigrants (see Vaid 1999/2000). Manavi, Sakhi, and SALGA represent the oldest South Asian social change organizations on the East Coast. They have inspired other new groups across the country to mobilize their communities.

Although the personal stories of the activists themselves are interesting, my research documents the politics, identities, and visions of the organizations themselves. In order to get a sense of how the organizations defined themselves and their issues through internal debates, I chose the participants in this study on the basis of their long-term and active involvement in their groups. A number of the participants were members of more than one group, and as such they offered valuable comparisons. While each organization was held together by a common set of issues, ideologies, and shared identities, none of them was free of internal conflict. Working-class women clashed with middle-class women; second-generation activists sometimes had a different agenda from that of the first generation; taxi drivers felt divided from each other along national-linguistic lines or on the basis of whether they were lease drivers or owners; lesbians confronted straight women and gay men; and urban Indo-Caribbeans parted ways with some of their upwardly mobile South Asian comrades.

Raising questions about internal conflicts, however, was not easy. I knew from my experience in SAWA that we often groped for tools that would allow us to articulate our internal problems. To their credit, my participants spoke thoughtfully about the contradictions that sometimes pried apart the organizations' philosophical commitments from their actual practice. Much to my consternation, as I was ending my fieldwork in summer 1997 some of these debates exploded. This strife led Sakhi to splinter and, later in the year, it pushed LDC to break off from the Coalition against Anti-Asian Violence. The expulsion of Sakhi's Domestic Workers Committee, (DWC) and the contradictory accounts of what led to it, left the South Asian activist community stunned. While I was able to follow the development of the NYTWA because of the openness of the organization (and chapter 6 reflects my involvement with it until 2002), I was not able to do the same with Sakhi. When I approached my participants from

Sakhi to clarify the situation, they asked for time to reflect on the conflict and to heal from it. Workers Awaaz, which comprised Sakhi's DWC members, was also wracked by disagreements over the organization's structure and goals. This led to the further split that created Andolan. Not until 2001 was I able to explore the 1997 crisis in Sakhi when a member agreed to talk to me. At this time, I also contacted the founder-member of Andolan, Nahar Alam, who was one of the first members of Sakhi's DWC. Alam enabled me to document Andolan's work as an autonomous labor organization.

Thus, the focus in my research on organizational life caused anxiety-producing, though immensely instructive, fractures in my fieldwork that reflected the conflicts, crises, and reorganizations that the groups had survived. Though such conflicts are part of any organization's life course, they are rarely publicly analyzed because, as Audre Lorde (1984, 114–23) notes, we are taught to fear difference in the name of unity. Through this work I have learned that rather than being signs of failure, disintegration and discord mark the vigor and evolution of collective action.

The textures of my account reflect the capacity in which I was involved in each type of organizing. My daily involvement during a six-year period in the details as well as the overarching concerns of women's organizing made it at times difficult to question the philosophies, methods, and commitments that I had come to value through SAWA. I had to teach myself to listen to those activists who, for example, advocated providing services, or who, in the case of queer activists, felt that their organizations were primarily social spaces that did not screen members for their politics. The self-definition of the two queer organizations meant that I had to make sense of the key role of affect and sociability in analyzing their politics. This left me with the challenge of reconstructing their collective and affective life largely from the sources of one-to-one interviews conducted in cafes, offices, or homes—outside of communal spaces—and from my notes on the general meetings, workshops, and celebrations because, as a person in a heterosexual relationship, I had decided not to intrude on SALGA and MASALA support groups, socials, and retreats. I relied on those events and on my participants' accounts to give me an intimation of how the two organizations breathed affect into politics.

My rendition of labor organizations is shaped by the multiple opportunities I was given to volunteer for the NYTWA, which, more broadly, provided me with a window into South Asian working-class struggles. Such mundane tasks as entering into a database the tickets issued to drivers for traffic violations opened my eyes to how New York City constructs these workers as repeat offenders. Handing out flyers to drivers at gas stations exposed me to their distrust of conventional trade unionism, thereby deepening my understanding of the betrayals that working-class people have suffered and their consequent efforts to build alternative structures.

The seven organizations in my study surfaced at a particular moment in post-1965 immigration history—the mid-1980s and the 1990s—when the inadequacies of India-centered, elite, accommodationist politics, or what I call *place-taking politics*, became apparent. Such politics could not acknowledge, far less address, the systemic problems of violence against women, as well as homophobia, racism, xenophobia, and poverty within South Asian communities. In contrast, the organizations oriented toward social change create structures and resources that transform daily life into an arena of political contest, through what I call *space-making politics*.[5] They recognize that passports, visas, work permits, green cards, citizenship papers, deportation notices, the jurisdiction of courts across nations in domestic violence cases, and the need to earn dollars to send home mark the daily realities of immigrant life. Away from the electoral arena, these new organizations struggle to transform oppressive institutions and systems through collective action and empowerment.

The organizations simultaneously address the inadequacies of the state, their communities, and the larger social movements of which they are a part. The women's organizations frame immigrant women's abuse in their families and workplaces within various forms of institutional violence produced by the state and by capitalist arrangements. In demanding justice, they not only confront family members and employers but also an unsympathetic community, often-insensitive legal and social services, law enforcement and immigration agencies, and public policy makers. Queer immigrants, stigmatized by their communities, marginalized within the mainstream lesbian, gay, bisexual, and transgender (LGBT) movement, and policed by the state, intervene in those practices and build alternative communities. Unlike many mainstreamed LGBT communities, the South Asian queer organizations mount a critique of racism, transnational capital, and heterosexist U.S., Indian, and Pakistani nationalisms. Domestic workers, who make as little as $200 a month as live-ins, organize against their exploitation as do yellow cab drivers in New York City who work twelve-hour shifts seven days a week in an industry with one of the highest homicide rates. They make rights claims even though they are not legally recognized as "labor." As service providers, they battle against the surveillance regimes of consumer capital. Their work represents new directions in labor struggles.

All of the groups adopt a "South Asian" identity over nation-based identifications. Their pamphlets, in explaining who can join, welcome immigrants from India, Pakistan, Bangladesh, Sri Lanka, and the South Asian diaspora.[6] In actuality, the process of constructing a South Asian identity on which they base their politics is more complicated than simply affording a gathering space to members from different South Asian nations. Instead, the process is transnational. This book looks at several different ways in which the organizations negotiate the coming together of immigrants who are defined as originating from a geographic region and sharing a common culture.

The process of identity formation requires straddling wars, religious disharmony, and national and regional antagonisms rooted in a history of colonization, partition, and independence struggles. For example, in organizing Pakistani and Bangladeshi drivers, the NYTWA had to confront the legacy of Bangladesh's war of independence that made it difficult for the two groups to work together (see chapter 6). When the organizations encounter South Asians from Malaysia, the Caribbean, and East and South Africa, they have to delve into the suppressed histories of indenture and a previous era of massive labor movements. This reckoning takes place when Indo-Caribbeans attend SALGA parties but shy away from its general meetings (chapter 5). Articulating a South Asian identity in a substantive way also requires that these organizations tackle India's postcolonial hegemony in the region. As the sociologist Naheed Islam (1993) cautions us, the act of claiming a South Asian identity does not automatically ensure an equal voice for the immigrants from the less-powerful countries in South Asia. Rather, it is necessary to confront these unequal relations of power to build struggles based on the common experiences of racism and marginalization in the United States (see also Mohanty 1993).

The emancipatory politics communicated through the organizations' South Asian identity depends in part on the rejection of postcolonial and U.S. nationalisms. To say that identities are transnational does not necessarily mean that they escape bounded notions of identity and territory. Transnational practices can and do promote national identifications (Basch, Schiller and Szanton Blanc 1994; Puar 1998). Indeed, the transnational flows of donations to India and of narrow Hindu versions of Indian culture to the United States bolster Hindu nationalism at home and abroad (Prashad 2000; Mathew and Prashad 2000; Mathew 2000). Activists publicly perform the interventionary powers of a transnational South Asian identity at such events as the India Day and Pakistan Day parades in Manhattan. None of the nations that the parades celebrate—the United States, India, or Pakistan—embrace women, queers, or working-class people who break the silence around their treatment. Often refused a place in these parades, domestic workers, taxi drivers, survivors of domestic violence, and queers protest the upsurge of exclusionary patriotism expressed for the homeland and for a (mythical) fair and meritocratic United States.

In its rejection of nationalism, a transnational South Asian identity in the United States should not be confused with or celebrated as cosmopolitanism. A cosmopolitan subject enjoys class and race privilege that most of my research participants do not. In recent years, the idea of cosmopolitanism has been recuperated to combat what liberal American scholars see as the endless and dangerous proliferation of provincial identifications with nation, race, ethnicity, and religion (see Calhoun 2003; Hollinger 1995).[7] A number of scholars have felt it necessary to qualify the footloose world citizen of liberal cosmopolitanism with open-ended formulations that make an effort to accommodate vernacular cultures, group membership, multiple-level allegiances, the existential reality of transborder movements, and the critical consciousness that comes with traversing not only geopolitical but also epistemological systems (Appiah 1998; Calhoun 2003; Mignolo 2000; Pollock 2000; Cheah and Robbins 1998). However, the more fundamental problem embedded in this revival of cosmopolitanism, according to the political scientist Jorge Fernandes (2002), is whether postcolonial immigrants—not just Euro-Americans—can be cosmopolitan.

South Asian bodies, food, vernacular English, and remix music certainly cosmopolitanize the urban landscapes of New York City and Boston. However, unlike cosmopolitans South Asians are not allowed to be at ease everywhere. Nor can they posit themselves as world citizens. The racially marked bodies of South Asian queers, taxi drivers, and women who seek social services provoke varying degrees of alarm among citizens. The routine act by social service providers of turning away South Asian survivors on account of their "cultural difference," the regular brutal beatings of taxi drivers in the hands of passengers and police, and the assaults on gay men and lesbians in their neighborhoods or outside of clubs prevent them from inhabiting public spaces with cosmopolitan ease and confidence. "South Asian," for these immigrants, stands for socially located identities that are full of seams. Their politics thus aim at changing their transnationally constructed social locations.

Crisis in Rights: Migrancy and Citizenship

The politics and spaces crafted by the seven organizations fundamentally question the modern subject of rights—the patriotic, contributing, and consuming "good" citizen who is usually imagined to be white, heterosexual, self-supporting, and male (Evans 1993; Lowe 1996; Narayan 1997; Pateman 1988). Cross-border flows have increasingly uncoupled core analytical categories that anchor modernity: nations, states, nation-based citizenship, and rights (Agnew 1999; Darien-Smith 1995; Jacobson 1996; Mandaville 1999; Sassen 1996; Soysal 1994). Unlike other studies, this book examines the role that immigrants play in this transformation—as opposed to the role played by domestic courts, international law, human rights agencies, and corporations. Undoubtedly, the effects of globalization on nation-states have provided strong guarantees for global financial markets in the form of economic citizenship (Sassen 1996), in contrast with the crisis in rights experienced by migrants—especially those who cross borders without papers (Maher 2002). But such a crisis, induced by the tensions between cross-border flows and the salience of states and nations in the lives of immigrants, has also produced new ways for migrants to seek rights.

In this book I pay steadfast attention to the reconstitution of states, nations, and rights through cross-border flows in order to understand how certain groups of immigrants fight against multiple techniques of subordination through claims that do not rely on citizenship. Such attention requires several theoretical-methodological shifts. First, this work serves as an important corrective to a one-sided understanding of transnational processes as deterritorializing the nation-state. Borders are actually central to reorganizing gender, race, sexual, and class hierarchies that determine social, political, and economic entitlements. Second, I open up the kind of analysis undertaken by the sociologist

Evelyn Nakano Glenn (2002), who looks at the shaping of U.S. citizenship, through the organizing principles of race, class, and gender, to a transnational approach that traces the insistent reinscription of borders and revivals of nationalism in sending and receiving countries in response to migration. Third, I treat the nation-state as a central analytic that has been missing in the race, class, and gender approach that has dominated U.S. feminist thinking since the sociologist Patricia Hill Collins's foundational work on intersectionality (1986, 1991). To do so, I build on the contributions of radical Third World feminists who map the political economy of racialized and gendered patterns of contemporary labor flows from Third World postcolonial countries to the First World (Alexander 1994; Alexander and Mohanty 1997; Bannerji 2000; Carty 1994, 1999; Chang 2000; Guerrero 1997; Jayawardena 1986; Sudbury 1998; Yuval-Davis 1997).

Migration, from a radical Third World feminist perspective, is a direct result of displacement induced by structural adjustment programs and neoliberal policies forced on the Third World. Such a standpoint denaturalizes the operation of nation-states in the First World. As a result, we are compelled to question the right claimed by First World nation-states in the name of sovereignty to police its borders, criminalize certain forms of entry, and create systems of intolerable inequality.

In her work on globalization, Saskia Sassen (1996, 1998) has noted the deep contradiction in state practices that actively facilitate the movement of capital but aggressively police borders to contain the movement of people. Going a step further, I note that the state creates and maintains this contradiction in order to ensure the supply of skilled and unskilled workers who are chiefly exploited through their designated immigration status and the conditions laid down for naturalization. The ways in which the state itself makes the deviant subjects it then punishes becomes amply clear from the contradictory operation of U.S. policies governing immigration, labor, sexuality, gender oppression, asylum, and welfare in the lives of the South Asian immigrants in this study (chapter 3). By using its constitutive feature of sovereignty, the state hierarchically orders rights by codifying immigrants into the categories of illegal, legal but nonresident, legal and resident but noncitizen, naturalized citizen, and native born. The legal nature of these distinctions normalizes the hierarchy, thereby making common sense the differential treatment of immigrants in these categories.

The hierarchy of rights institutionalizes a highly discriminatory system that has been rightly characterized by some scholars as apartheid on a global scale because of these immigrants' grossly differential access to rights (Richmond 1994; Sharma 2002). States deny immigrants their basic entitlements by defining them as temporary workers with no legitimate place in the national body, even as they bring them in to perform crucial productive and reproductive work. Production in late capitalism depends on the flexibility of capital (Harvey 1990). Capital can be flexible and competitive because of what the sociologist Richard Appelbaum (1996) calls the "hands of color, of women, of impoverished Third World people," that is, laborers made super-exploitable in the United States through their legislated immigration status. The process is demonstrated in the treatment of South Asians in New York City's taxi and domestic work industries. With regard to reproductive work, the state in its retreat from welfare commitments subsidizes caretaking on the backs of poorly paid immigrant women while denying them access to social welfare programs and citizenship (Chang 2000; Stasiulis and Bakan 1997). Thus the conflicting regimes that administer the movements of capital and labor in fact serve the interest of First World states and global capital, thereby strengthening the nexus between them.

Citizenship for immigrants in no way guarantees their place in the national community or their rights. A cultural project of constructing the ideal citizen always accompanies legal definitions consolidating the differential access that migrants to the United States have to civil, political, social, and economic rights (Glenn 2000; Lowe 1996; Maher 2002; Narayan 1997; Yuval-Davis 1997). As a result of such representations, whether migrants become citizens or not, state mechanisms of intimidation usually discipline both categories of people into fearful compliance that facilitates their exploitation.

The contingency of citizenship, particularly for East and South Asian Americans who are constructed as perpetual outsiders, has been well documented by Asian American scholars (Chan 1991; Chang 1999; Glenn 2002; Lowe 1996; Takaki 1989).[8] In this book, however, I depart from the typical narration of Asian American rights struggles as demands for full citizenship. That narrative fails to see citizenship as an organizing principle that constitutes difference. The unruly South Asian immigrants do not pin their hopes on the idea of full citizenship and their struggles cannot be read through the familiar framework of second-class citizens asking for first-class status. At the same time, like the nineteenth-century Chinese laborers and the Filipina nurses working today, they are only too familiar with the ceaseless nature of policing and delegitimation designed to keep intact the power relations between ideal citizens and outsiders who are contingently allowed inside the nation.

The activists' refusal to invest in citizenship intervenes in efforts to rework that framework to confer rights on marginalized groups, including immigrants. The literature on transnational politics suggests that migrants, with their cross-border participation in homeland elections, are beginning to acquire some clout at both sites (Basch, Schiller, and Szanton Blanc 1994; Schiller and Fouron 1999; Itzigsohn 2000; Laguerre 1999). Reterritorialized labor-exporting nation-states are increasingly being convinced to extend political and economic rights to those residing in the diaspora through dual citizenship. To encourage the inflow of investments and technology, for example, India introduced a bill in 2003 to permit nonresidents based in North America to hold dual citizenship. Aimed only at tapping the social and economic capital of affluent nonresident Indians, however, the bill does not allow an "overseas citizen of India" to vote. Thus, even the privileged migrants have weak political guarantees.

For South Asian feminist, labor, and queer organizations, the demand for dual citizenship has not been a basis for rights claims. The constituencies of these organizations are not considered ideal citizens of either nation, and thus they cannot count on either to serve their interests. As Glenn quite rightly argues, dual citizenship "is not equally available to all" (2000, 11). While proponents of dual citizenship see it as a way of enhancing the accountability of both the sending and receiving states toward migrants, in actual practice the power imbalance between nations in the global North and South makes labor-exporting states less effective in demanding the humane treatment of their citizens abroad (Stasiulis and Bakan 1997, 113–14).

Feminists working to address the limits of citizenship have encouraged scholars to thoroughly revise that notion of national membership in the context of transnational migration and its gendered, racialized, sexualized, and elite definition. They have found it more appropriate to consider the dual operation of nation-bound notions of rights and human rights (Glenn 2000) or a flexible, multilayered citizenship that responds to the fact that people in a globalizing world no longer have an exclusive relationship with the state but rather participate in various communities at various levels (Yuval-Davis 1999). Instead of a fixed concept of citizenship, these feminists have proposed a relational one that reflects migrants' negotiations with the state for rights (Stasiulis and Bakan 1997). In addressing feminists who continue to reproduce the idea that contributing, politically active nationals epitomize citizenship, the philosopher Uma Narayan has asked them to imagine "what states might owe to all their ongoing members" (1997, 65) in light of the fact that many immigrant women are unable to exercise their civil, political, and welfare rights. Again, as in the case of dual citizenship, South Asian activists have preferred to explore the possibility of accessing rights through methods other than expanded notions of citizenship.

A Transnational Complex of Rights

In a project that began with tracing the relationship among identity, culture, and politics in social justice struggles, the question of rights came up insistently as I analyzed transcripts of my interviews, reread the notes I kept on scores of activist events, and reviewed my collection of the organizations' brochures, posters, and newsletters. It became apparent that the women's, queer, and labor organizations all respond to the crisis in migrant rights by constructing a transnational complex of rights. They inventively draw on rights regimes that are local, national (laws of more than one nation can be involved), and international in order to claim entitlements for their constituencies, who are otherwise treated as practically without rights in their nation of residence. Within this complex, migrants, not citizens, claim and bear rights.

This process institutionalizes the organizations as transnational spaces. Just as global capital has led to denationalized "global cities" within national borders (Sassen 2001), so the migrant struggles for justice in their homes, workplaces, and communities in the United States have led to new spatial expressions—the creation of transnational social justice organizations. While the activists in my story face racialized, sexual, and gendered regimes of subordination particular to their location in the United States, they battle against them with strategies crafted in a constant inter-reference between their homelands and their country of residence.

Here I wish to stage my arguments about transnational organizations and transnational rights with the story of Nahar Alam. Alam, a former member of Sakhi and a founding and current member of Andolan, organizes South

Asian domestic workers in New York City. She migrated from Bangladesh to the United States in order to escape from her abusive husband, a powerful police officer.

On arriving in New York City, the increased difficulty in finding work through which she could support herself pushed Alam into working as a live-in domestic. In this situation, she was again abused. This time it was in the hands of her employers who overworked and underpaid her. Alam came to Sakhi both as a survivor of domestic violence and as a domestic worker outraged at the conditions under which she and other women like her were forced to work. Sakhi helped her access international mandates on gender asylum, which are adopted on a case-by-case basis by the INS. This allowed Alam to regularize her immigration status and work legally in the United States.

Alam's story tells us that the process of seeking justice in New York City in the face of domestic violence experienced in Bangladesh and labor exploitation experienced in the United States was transnational even though Alam, trapped in the United States because of her immigration status, could no longer circulate across borders. Sakhi and Alam remained "localized." What circulated and crossed borders were the international and national statutes to form the basis on which Alam could demand her right to safety, her right to reside and legally work in the country to which she had fled, and the right to economic justice and dignity for domestic workers like her.

These claims to rights collapse the very symbols of scale and scope that the anthropologists James Ferguson and Akhil Gupta (2002) argue allow states to imagine themselves. In the convergence of different rights regimes—each of which is associated with scale and hierarchy—activists deploying the transnational politics of social change confound the order of what is local, national, international, and supranational rather than simply jump scales from local to state government, and national to international levels, as some geographers would argue (Mitchell 1997, 127–29, 135; Smith 1992). We can easily overlook the transnational character of organizations like Sakhi that seem small, grassroots, and local if we understand transnationalism solely in terms of the literal cross-border movement of people, votes, investments, donations, remittances, and cardboard boxes crammed with gifts. The language of levels caught in scalar thinking can miss the emergence of a plethora of agencies—certainly not simply committed to social justice work—that operate alongside the state, sometimes in a statelike fashion, as a result of the state outsourcing to them many of its functions in keeping with neoliberal governmentality (Ferguson and Gupta 2002).

Today, Alam and other members of Andolan struggle for the enforcement of existing wage-hour protections for domestic workers guaranteed by national and state laws. Andolan fights to win recognition for the household as a workplace so that domestic workers have a legal right to organize. The National Labor Relations Act still does not recognize the right of domestic workers to collectively bargain since it understands domestic service to be a one-to-one arrangement. In light of this, Andolan draws on the 1990 U.N. Convention on Migrant Workers, which came into force in 2002 and recognizes undocumented workers' rights to mobility, family reunification, and economic security.

While the legal limitations on work for those who have become undocumented have stumped both mainstream domestic violence organizations and many Asian American ones, South Asian organizations like Sakhi and Manavi have contended with exactly these challenges to find ways to ensure their members' rights (see chapter 4). Often, in order to forge cross-border rights South Asian women's organizations working with survivors of domestic violence have to deal with not only U.S. domestic violence and immigration laws but also the jurisdiction of laws governing divorce, custody, and women's property rights in India, Pakistan, and Bangladesh. The organizations thus constitute sites of legal innovation in that they demand rights for noncitizens like Alam who are otherwise treated as practically without rights in their nation of residence. They successfully pry apart the taken-for-granted link between citizenship and rights and posit an alternative and, I would argue, more effective regime of rights.

Four elements of the transnational complex of rights emerge from the organizations' justice work. First, the activists who mobilize this transnational complex contend with the nation-state as a central actor in determining migrant rights. They do not bypass the nation-state; in fact, they utilize nation-based guarantees like minimum wage laws that explicitly unhinge rights from citizen/noncitizen distinctions. The deployment of the complex of rights by no means signals a decline in the salience of borders and nation-states. For immigrant activists like Alam, the nation-state becomes a crucial site of engagement *because* many of them became politicized through viscerally feeling the punitive power of not only the American state but also the postcolonial sending states. The work of these social change organizations thus allows mapping the political economy of global flows that simultaneously deterritorialize and reterritorialize the nation-state.

Second, the complex enables rights claims beyond citizenship. In the decade that followed the spurt in post-1965 South Asian immigration to the United States, certain elite, mostly male, immigrants fought for equal rights through the route of full citizenship that requires a universal subject of rights. Their racialization as Asians and their representation as model minorities helped these earlier immigrants to claim citizenship as successful, self-sufficient, and tax-paying subjects (see chapter 1). Since the unruly immigrants whom I study fall out of these gender-blind, heteronormative, and elite definitions of citizenship, they have had to develop an alternative language and an alternative route to rights. They have felt the need for politics that can respond to the particular needs of migrant (low-wage) workers, women, and queers.

Third, the complex of rights brings together local, state, national, and international laws, protocols, and conventions. I argue that such a move on the part of activists goes beyond an expedient cobbling together of different rights regimes. The complex represents a theoretical intervention in rights talk because rights are claimed not on the basis of universal concepts of liberal citizenship or human rights concepts of universal personhood. The migrants demand rights because they are members of social groups: immigrants of color, women, survivors of violence, migrant workers, or dependents of migrant workers who are particularly vulnerable to rights abuse. They respond to their realities as border-crossing men and women caught between massively contradictory systems of globalization and reterritorialized nation-states. They trust neither in the promise of development held out by postcolonial nations nor in the humane intentions of their host country, the United States, which in a limited way grants human rights only to wear such freedoms as a badge to further its culturally imperialist project as the moral police of the world. Thus, these organizations' turn to human rights is cautious, contextual, and pragmatic.

Fourth, in this transnational complex migrants want rights to mobility rather than to rootedness and citizenship. They want rights to move with them. Like citizens, they too want to materialize themselves as subjects of rights. The immigrants in my study can inhabit spaces in the global North because they are made into temporary workers, whose temporary status rests on not being afforded the social standing and political rights that come with citizenship. This stark realization divests citizenship of its lure. In demanding their rights, the immigrants constitute transnational organizations and call upon multiply dispersed actors and rights regimes. These organizations have the capacity to imagine rights claims to protected mobility across borders and protected residence within them. The justice work of each organization illustrates one or more dimensions of the complex of rights and their different conceptualizations of it.

Telling a Different Tale

The story of South Asian immigration to the United States has not been framed transnationally until recently. It has been narrativized instead within a conventional and nationalist framework of assimilation and cultural pluralism, characterized by the race theorists Michael Omi and Howard Winant (1994) as the ethnicity paradigm. This paradigm, which continues to dominate sociology, preoccupies itself with the making of immigrants into Americans whether through various modes of assimilation (Alba 1999; Gans 1992, 1979; Handlin 1951; Matute-Bianchi 1991; Park 1950; Portes and Zhou 1993; Prashad 2001; Waters 1999) or through pluralism, which looks at the ways in which immigrants maintain multiple cultural identities within the bounded space of the United States (Alba 1990; Fuchs 1990; Glazer and Moynihan 1970; Gordon 1964; Hansen 1987; Kallen 1956; Novak 1979; Waters 1990). Until recently, the nationalist ideologies through which immigration has been filtered have gone unquestioned (Gabaccia 1997; Gerstle 1997; Hollinger 1997). As a result, not only is this framework too impoverished to grasp the transnational constitution of immigrant identities, experiences, and issues but it also limits research questions to modest ones about identity. Larger questions such as those raised in this work about the relationship between post-1965 immigrant experiences and capitalism, nationalism, state formation, and rights are absent. It is ethnicity not race, culture not power, sex roles not gender and sexuality, groups and individuals not institutional structures that are the focus of efforts to model the emergence of an "American" identity.

Most scholars of the Asian Indian community have subscribed to this nationalist framework uncritically, though not unselfconsciously, in defining their research questions around cultural adaptation (Agarwal 1991; Bacon 1996; Dasgupta 1989; Fisher 1980; Helweg and Helweg 1990; Leonard 1997; Rangaswamy 2000; Saran 1985; Sheth 2001). They paint a vivid picture of the immigrant success story that reconfirms basic U.S. mythologies about a democratic nation that offers equal opportunity to those willing to struggle. Interruptions to the story posed by racism, sexism, and class-based inequalities are noted but inadequately framed, and the authors seem to share their research participants' hesitancy in naming these instances of differential treatment as discrimination. Anthropologists such as Arthur Helweg and Usha Helweg (1990), for example, mention organizations like Sakhi and Manavi. But in the absence of sustained analyses of the family as an institution and of the systemic nature of domestic violence, they represent them as social work groups that provide services to unfortunate women who suffer from aberrational incidents of abuse. In these works, the communities' attempts to control gender relations and sexuality are mistaken as efforts at cultural retention or generational conflict. Some ethnographers (Khandelwal 2002; Lessinger 1995), though still writing within the ethnicity paradigm, are starting to correct the social-psychological approach by calling attention to the intersections between ethnicity and race, incidents of race- and gender-based discrimination and violence, and the emergence of a working class as a result of labor market segmentation rather than individual failure.

In embarking on this research, I wanted to break out of the paradigm's nationalist investment in cultural identity. In and through SAWA, I was meeting women and men who were politicizing their experiences as immigrants in the United States and also organizing around these experiences. Together, we were articulating an identity tied to social change politics that could not be run through the mill of assimilation, accommodation, acculturation, and cultural pluralism. These politics spoke of differences in class, nationality, gendered interests, and sexuality among South Asians whose immigrant bodies attract a kind of xenophobia that is not easily recognized as racism. I was in the process of discovering identities, interests, actions, and visions, the richness of which often remains hidden even in the more recent accounts on South Asian immigrants.

The world of South Asian organizing, then, opened up new narrative possibilities that provoked me to tell a different tale. In this tale, South Asians are political agents and not simply cultural actors. Their political engagements are enacted outside of the electoral arena. In this tale, South Asians have heterogeneous interests and politics because of their particular social locations in transnationally reworked hierarchies of gender, race, class, and sexuality. Unlike the historian Vijay Prashad (2000), who concludes that South Asians need rather than possess a critical consciousness even after he establishes a genealogy of South Asian radicalism, I do not collapse the heterogeneity of the communities' interests, identities, and political positions. This means recognizing that immigrants from South Asia, even though they are racialized in the United States as people of color, will not be equally invested in or attracted to progressive politics. Place-taking politics will continue to conserve and consolidate its constituencies' privileges, while space-makers will seek to transform the conditions that exploit them.

The efflorescence in the early 1990s of South Asian feminist writing, both testimonial and analytical (Women of South Asian Descent Collective 1993), started to open up decolonized discursive spaces that attended to the politics of naming culture. These works documented how tradition is used to control women's gender roles and sexuality. They situated articulations of a separate South Asian identity within the racism directed at the group. Poetry, fictional prose, autobiographies, and critical essays, following the footsteps of earlier works by women of color such as *Home Girls* (Smith 1983), *This Bridge Called My Back* (Moraga and Anzaldúa 1983), and *Making Waves* (Asian Women United of California 1989), gave voice to daily yet insidious experiences of racial difference that had so long been difficult to frame within the dominant white-on-black framework of racism. These explorations started to lay the groundwork for issue-based coalitions with other people of color also fighting intersecting oppressions. The remapping of pressing issues within South Asian communities inspired other collections about women's self-definitions, race relations, lesbian and gay experiences, and complexities of identity, home, and belonging (Ratti 1993; Maira and Srikanth 1996; Das Dasgupta 1998; Gupta 1999; Shankar and Srikanth 1998).

Academically, these developments have opened up new modes of ethnographic writing by and about South Asians that clearly move away from the dominant concerns of the ethnicity paradigm (Abraham 2000; Maira 2002; Mathew 2005; Prashad 2000; Purkayastha 2005; Rayaprol 1997; Rudrappa

2004; Visweswaran 1997). This critical literature interrogates the gender and race neutral accounts of immigrant experiences, the separation between the public and private spheres, conventional sites of resistance, access to citizenship as an unqualified boon, and the success story itself. Three new studies on South Asian community-based organizing directly and provocatively engage questions of U.S. race relations, capitalism, and citizenship, setting a new tone to what can be legitimately asked of South Asian immigrant experiences (Mathew 2005; Prashad 2000; Rudrappa 2004). I place my investigation of what necessitated space-making politics and how they are articulated within this growing body of literature.

I begin in chapter 1 with historicizing law, race, citizenship, and rights—central categories in my overall analysis—in a moment in the late 1970s and early 1980s when "Asian Indian" first appeared as a racial category in the census. I track how newly arrived Indian professionals navigated the state-crafted relationship between race, citizenship, and rights to secure a minority racial category to protect themselves from job market discrimination. In the process, their politics were shaped by a racial classification system that wedged South Asians in between whites and blacks; skepticism about their claims as middle-class immigrants to minority rights; and the immigrants' own lack of fluency in reading U.S. configurations of race and racial discrimination. At the same time, the immigrants themselves embraced the ambiguous terms of racial identity. They did so because those terms were compatible with their desire for full citizenship with its promise of a universal subjectivity, which would renaturalize their sense of leadership and excellence. A liberal discourse on citizenship, then, facilitated place-taking politics that operated within the dominant terms of belonging. These terms demand evasion of gendered and racialized difference. Chapter 1 sets up the inadequacies of such politics for those who cannot posit themselves as citizens.

The next two chapters serve as a bridge between place-taking politics and space-making politics crafted by feminists, queers, and workers—that is, actors who are out of place. Chapters 2 and 3 map the terrain inside and outside of South Asian communities on which these actors wage their battles, refusing to be silenced by the punitive discourses on authenticity and law. Chapter 2 focuses on the contests over culture within immigrant communities. Internal discourses on cultural preservation and public discourses on model minorities intersect to deny the existence of poverty and various forms of violence, including domestic abuse and homophobia within South Asian communities. I document how the space-making organizations disrupt mainstream South Asian attempts to silence in the name of culture the realities of immigrant women, queers, and low-wage workers. By recuperating other genealogies, the organizations mount counterclaims, reappropriating and polyvocalizing elite, male, and homophobic versions of South Asian culture in the diaspora.

Chapter 3 maps another terrain of struggle—the law. In this chapter I examine structural forces that create these marginalized immigrant realities and then drive them underground. It illustrates my argument that the barriers to the mobility of labor in contrast to the hypermobility of capital benefit the state because they allow it to create the anticitizen subjectivities necessary for state and nation building. The realities of battered women made dependent on their husbands for legal status, queer immigrants' daily experience of the heterosexism of the state, and the super-exploitation of working-class South Asians whose poverty is glibly written off to the "poor quality" of recent immigrants emerge from laws that oppress these groups instead of protecting them.

The last three chapters of the book are devoted to the three types of space-making organizations—women's, queer, and labor—that enable South Asians to speak their realities and transform them. These organizations emerged to address multiple gaps: the failures of South Asian place-taking politics; the racism within predominantly white feminist, queer, and labor organizations; and the inadequacies of alternative space-making politics that also end up marginalizing certain actors on the basis of their class, sexuality, or gender.

Chapter 4 on women's organizations analyzes the work of Manavi, Sakhi, and SAWA. In building on each other's work they specify the challenges faced by immigrant women and provide suitable services. Recognizing that family violence often jeopardizes women's immigration status, they secure women's rights through a transnational process. Each organization redefines "domestic" violence by contextualizing it in interlocking public structures of classism, xenophobia, and racism. The chapter places Sakhi's decision to organize working-class women as one such revision of the domestic violence movement's standard understanding of the public/private divide. In keeping with my analytical focus on state structures and capitalism, I argue that the implosion in Sakhi over domestic workers resulted from its incomplete understanding of commodified reproductive work, which in a neoliberal state creates a dependence of middle-class women on immigrant women's cheapened labor. While the three organizations have similar political commitments, a comparison among them reveals very different approaches to institutionalizing antiviolence work, social change, and pan-ethnic and multiracial coalitions. Thus, their work instructs us on building social justice movements.

Paralleling the rationale behind the autonomous South Asian women's and labor organizations, SALGA and MASALA crystallized in response to the severe shortcoming of the larger LGBT movement. In chapter 5 I read the two organizations' emphasis on queer visibility and community, the clarion calls of the LGBT movement, against the grain of the cautionary tales in queer theory, which bemoan the complicity of queer politics in consumer capitalism. Rights claims, the theorists warn, are increasingly based on presenting queers as constituting a market for goods and services. I argue that these critiques are better suited to the white affluent gay politics than to those articulated by immigrant queers of color. The accounts of SALGA and MASALA members clearly show that their need for community and visibility arises from the orientalizing impact of racism on them in mainstream queer social and political spaces. Racism in the LGBT movement and the exclusionary politics of South Asian communities explain the complex intersection of the social and political in the work of the organizations. Queer exclusion from South Asian communities, dramatically performed during Manhattan's India and Pakistan Day parades, has produced rights claims in which SALGA positions itself as a transnational rather than a national entity. This public performance of transnational community reveals the way in which states employ sexuality to constitute subjects of rights. The social elements of community building in the day-to-day work of the organizations, however, lead to political limits. To escape these limits, some members begin to work with feminist, labor, and antiracist groups. These collaborations open up new avenues of engagement for SALGA and MASALA by expanding their definition of queer politics.

In chapter 6 I look at low-end service providers—namely domestic workers and taxi drivers—who are so essential to consumer capitalism. Though the two types of work are clearly gendered, where one is done in the privacy of homes and the other on streets, Andolan and NYTWA reveal the common forces of economic restructuring that have created the conditions under which domestic workers and taxi drivers work. Both industries are structured by postindustrial transformations of the U.S. state and economy, which have relied on cheapened immigrant labor to solve the fallout from weakened welfare state commitments to labor and families. In this environment, they are deprived of the right to unionize and they are exposed to various state-sponsored disciplinary mechanisms in the name of their employers' and riders' consumer rights. Their organizing strategies for economic justice emerge from the specific ways in which their restructured workplaces construct their rights. While Andolan fights the conversion of a proposed standard contract aimed at protecting domestic workers into a consumer rights bill, the NYTWA contests the city's multifaceted efforts through consumer rights campaigns to criminalize drivers and represent them as racists. The two organizations consciously depart from the hierarchical bureaucratic practices of labor unions to bring back labor militancy and, in the case of NYTWA, mass-based organizing. Flying in the face of their legal definitions, the organizations invent domestic workers and taxi drivers as subjects of rights. Andolan draws on local, state, national, and international statutes to do this work, while the NYTWA fights various "local" policies, which in fact manifest and consolidate global economic restructuring.

In analyzing the work of South Asian organizations oriented toward social change, I have framed their struggles as a transnational process through which they search for rights that are *not* contingent on citizenship. These struggles are specific to the social location of those who wage them. The struggles emerge in the cusp of simultaneous and multiple encounters produced by what is being increasingly recognized as the contradictory process of globalization. As the needs of capital make borders of labor-hungry states more and more permeable, the same states redouble their efforts to socially and legally seal the pores. As soon as efforts are made to free rights from confining notions of citizenship, a resurgence of patriotism and nationalism resanctifies the citizen. Neither states nor national ideologies are in decline; they are transformed. Liberatory movements are not crushed; they change their shape, form, membership, and tactics. The struggles for immigrant rights, then, are best understood as constant, versatile encounters with these co-constituted contradictions rather than their resolution. Alive to the ever-shifting terrain of power relations, even when those relations seem oppressively settled, the organizations anticipate, straddle, and work within the contradictions, knowing that efforts to stifle their struggles will introduce new issues and therefore new sites of contestation.

CHAPTER I

Terms of Belonging

In October 1994 at Boston's Northeastern University a group of South Asian students organized a forum titled "Shades of Brown." An organization to which I belonged, South Asian Women for Action (SAWA), had been invited to the forum, and I volunteered to attend along with another SAWA member. We arrived at the event expecting to discuss our gendered experiences of the value placed on skin color by our families and communities. As feminists, we were eager to hear from other South Asian women, especially those who, like my SAWA friend, had grown up in the United States.

To our surprise, the forum generated a heated debate about the image in the United States of South Asians as model minorities—that is, people of color who had been portrayed as being successful in the United States because of their cultural values and their determination to work hard. The image seemed to appeal to many participants, most of whom were from the area's elite universities. Most followed in the footsteps of their professional parents, preparing for careers in medicine, law, or the sciences. These students saw a number of merits in being stereotyped "positively." Wasn't it better to be a model minority than a demonized one? One student confessed that she liked being complimented on her long dark hair and burnished skin. Emboldened, another participant explained that the model minority image could and did inspire South Asian youths to be better than their white peers. The image provided him with an incentive to preserve South Asian values, which he felt fueled the group's success in the United States.

A few of us in the room strenuously disagreed. Buying into the model minority image, we argued, erased those South Asian immigrant experiences that deviate from this myth of success. A Northeastern University student pointed out that some South Asian students on that very campus were the children of motel owners. For them, the model minority image had been elusive. My friend and I, as community representatives, talked about how the image pitted South Asians against African Americans and Latina/os, thereby impairing our chances to build alliances with them when doing progressive issue based work.

At one point, a dark-skinned Harvard medical student burst out: "I'd rather be a model minority than have a white woman passing me clutch her purse." For a minute, we all sat there speechless. Pulsing in the room was his desire to deracinate himself; to distance himself from a loaded history of racialized, sexualized, and gendered constructions of criminality; to somehow escape the treatment meted out routinely to young black men and sometimes to inner-city South Asian youth—as SAWA members knew from their brothers' brushes with the criminal justice system. My friend and I glanced at each other across the room. We had to intervene. But confronting South Asian racism toward other minority groups, couched in such pleas as this young man's, was not easy. The conversation petered out. Walking out into the dusk on Huntington Avenue, I wondered how we South Asians had come to be wedged between blacks and whites. And what enabled some of us in that room to resist the model minority image and others to hide behind it?

At this time as part of my research I was looking at a 1976 testimony to the U.S. Congress by a representative of the Association of Indians in America (AIA) who requested the addition of a separate category in the census for immigrants of Indian ancestry. The document struck me as extraordinary in that it represented these immigrants' ungainly wrestling with U.S. racial categories. As such, it disturbed me greatly; in those pages I heard the echoes of the Harvard student's simultaneous awareness of and retreat from race. In my role as an activist in the 1990s in the process of reconceptualizing my identity as a woman of color and collectively framing anti-racist South Asian politics, I wanted to connect the two moments to understand the processes that racialized

South Asians. Thus began an excavation. I pored over government documents —congressional hearings, censuses, interagency and Civil Rights Commission reports, notices in the Federal Register, and circulars from the Office of Management and Budget. I tracked down the AIA testifier, Manoranjan Dutta, and conducted multiple phone interviews with him to grasp the urgencies that informed the AIA's framing of race and rights.

Between 1975 and 1979 the AIA, committed to fostering habits of good citizenship among newly arrived immigrants, mobilized certain sections to confront race- and nationality-based discrimination in their new home. Many immigrants were both puzzled and outraged at their first encounter with discrimination. In India, they had been the beneficiaries of full citizenship on account of their class, caste, and, in some cases, male privilege. Their unequal treatment in the United States, they felt, relegated them to second-class citizenship. For them, full citizenship meant equality in the political sphere and in the realm of rights. Their treatment in their new homeland as abstract liberal citizens would mean that particularities of race, color, gender, and national origin could not interfere with their enjoyment of rights.[1] Consequently, the immigrants embarked on a campaign to demand protection against their mistreatment.

Safeguards against the forms of discrimination they faced were ensured by the civil rights legislation of the 1960s, the implementation of which explicitly tied group rights to racial categorization. On finding out that U.S. residents from the "Indian subcontinent" had been classified as white in the 1970 census, some immigrants campaigned to see themselves as a separate group in the 1980 census and thus officially be recognized as a minority. At no time before the 1970 census were immigrants of Indian descent in the United States categorized as white.

The AIA-driven redesignation of these immigrants as nonwhites in the 1980 census has been mischaracterized as a moment when they were converted into "instant ethnics" who gained access to minority rights (Espiritu 1992, 126); or as a case of mistaken identity (Fisher 1980, 129); or as an example of the political expediency of this new group, which quickly learned to manipulate group rights (Helweg and Helweg 1990, 155). In this chapter, I offer a rereading of the legal-bureaucratic minoritization through the lens of race, rights, and citizenship—three historically shaped and tightly intertwined categories (see Glenn 2002; Kerber 1997; Lowe 1996). What emerges from my analysis of congressional hearings, census categories, and government documents on racial and ethnic classification in the 1970s reveals a messy process, which paradoxically interfered with rather than enhanced the immigrants' claims to full citizenship. The black and white paradigm of race, race relations, and civil rights in the United States—unfamiliar to the new immigrants—was largely responsible for the complications. In the United States, black and white histories and experiences continue to provide the yardstick against which all experiences of racial oppression and privilege are measured, thereby obscuring the many modes through which groups entering the United States are in fact racialized (Aguilar-San Juan 1994; Martinez 1998; Moran 1998; Okihiro 1994; Omi and Takagi 1998; Ong 2000; Shah 1994).

The paradigm demanded that the new immigrants of Indian descent establish their rights claims through examining their closeness to or distance from the two dominant categories, white and black. The immigrants had to consider whether they were *actually* white, since they were contesting their assignment to that category. Entrapped in the incoherence that underlies racial thinking and the racial classification system itself, as well as their own ambivalence about racialization, the immigrants, despite their efforts to take control of the process, accepted their liminal place in the racial order.

The AIA's participation in the black-white racial logic of the state, as well as its belief in liberal democracy as elite postcolonials who had been served well by its principles in India, limited the political possibilities of that moment to place taking. The acceptance of racially ambiguous terms of belonging to the U.S. national body led to a troubling indeterminacy about the status of South Asians as minorities and their entitlement to civil rights protection. Racial ambiguity meant that the immigrants' admission to full citizenship rested on *not* being reliant on group rights (such as affirmative action) or welfare protections for which they had fought. Such a paradox interfered with recognizing the racism directed at South Asians, the legitimacy of South Asian rights claims, and the ability of South Asian immigrants to form alliances with other U.S. minorities on the basis of their day-to-day experiences of discrimination.

Historical Context: Of Race and Rights

In order to establish the relationship between race, rights, and citizenship, I begin by connecting two seemingly disparate periods—the pre–World War II era when immigrants from the British colony of India were excluded from U.S. citizenship and the post-1965 chapter when immigrants from partitioned and independent nations in South Asia were eligible to enter the United States and, in due course, apply for naturalization. In both periods, race was salient in determining what rights the immigrants could enjoy. Early-twentieth-century Indian immigrants, like other Asian immigrants before them, found their rights greatly curtailed when they were denied citizenship on the grounds that they were not white. In the post-1965 period, a new wave of immigrants, though eligible for formal citizenship, had to establish their minority racial status to become entitled to group rights that would protect them from institutional discrimination.

Until 1923, Indian immigrants seeking to naturalize as U.S. citizens argued that they were Caucasian and, therefore, white. This claim to whiteness was a way for them to access rights, and most U.S. courts accepted the argument. By relying on a combination of ethnological arguments and interpretations of the legislative intent of the 1790 law that restricted naturalization to a "free white person," the courts ruled that South Asians were white because they were Caucasians and, therefore, naturalizable (Haney-López 1996; Jensen 1988). In 1922, the U.S. Supreme Court in a landmark case denied a Japanese national, Takao Ozawa, American citizenship by arguing that the court understood that "white" was synonymous with "Caucasian" (Haney-López 1996, 85). But in 1923, the court reversed its understanding in Bhagat Singh Thind's case when it decreed that not all Caucasians were white, thereby disqualifying Indians from whiteness and citizenship. Now classified as aliens ineligible for citizenship, Indians joined Chinese and Japanese immigrants. The ruling came amid the escalating xenophobia that had already succeeded in putting in place an Asiatic barred zone in the 1917 Pacific Immigration Act that excluded immigrants from British India. The *Thind* ruling had immediate effects on the immigrants' rights. California lost no time in applying to South Asians its alien land law (which was passed in 1913, amended in 1920, and already governing Japanese immigrants) and began to deny South Asians licenses to marry white women under its anti-miscegenation law (Chan 1991, 47, 95; Jensen 1988, 259; Leonard 1985). Between 1923 and 1927, sixty-five South Asians were denaturalized— among whom were men who had won their citizenship after years of litigation (Jensen 1988, 264).

While the court ruled that Indians, regardless of whether they were Caucasian, did not enter popular understandings of "white," it did not specify what sort of nonwhites they were. They could not be deemed black. Legally, that category referred to native-born persons of African descent who were citizens under the fourteenth amendment.[2] Within the black-white framework, then, early Indian immigrants were racialized as a group that was neither white nor black so that they could be deprived of rights enjoyed by whites and formally granted to blacks—who could not, however, exercise them in practice in the Jim Crow South. These race-based denials of rights continued until 1946. That year, despite some opposition, residents of Indian descent in the United States were made eligible for citizenship in recognition of British India's efforts in World War II.

In the four decades following *Thind*, the census consistently categorized Indians as nonwhite but kept changing the group's nomenclature. Tracking the changes in the categories specified in the census race question reveals how this legal-bureaucratic process reconstructed race.[3] Indians appeared in the census of both 1920 and 1930 as "Hindu" and were counted under "All other" races (U.S. Bureau of the Census 1921, 29, table 1 n.1; 1933, 32, table 4 n.1). Rather than referring to religion, "Hindu" in public discourse was a racialized term that implied that these immigrants were backward and unassimilable—in short, the irreducible racial other (Haney-López 1996, 87–88, 93; Leonard 1992, 24). The 1940 census listed "Hindu" separately along with Chinese, Japanese, and Filipino (U.S. Bureau of the Census 1943, 5, table 1). After 1940, the term "Hindu" lost its currency until 1960. The 1950 U.S. census summary (1953) made no reference to Indian immigrants. But the 1950 California census, in its definition of "race and color," replaced "Hindu" with "Asiatic Indians" and counted them among "all other" races (U.S. Bureau of the Census 1952).[4] The U.S. 1960 summary (1964, xlii) in its definition of terms called immigrants of Indian descent "Asian Indians," and stated that they would fall under the residual category of "'all other' races." The term "Hindu" reappeared in the Census Bureau's instruction to enumerators in an attempt to distinguish "Asian Indians" from Native Americans. The instructions read: "*Indians*—For persons originating in India (except those of European stock), mark 'Other' and specify as 'Hindu.' If there is an entry of 'Indian' on the Advanced Census Report be sure you know whether the person is an American Indian or an Asian Indian" (1964, cxiii). In 1965 Congress lifted racial quotas imposed on immigration.

TABLE 1. Racial designation of South Asians in the U.S. Census, 1920–2000

1920	1930	1940	1950	1960	1970	1980	1990	2000
"Other" if Hindu	"Other" if Hindu	"Hindu"	"Other" if Asiatic Indian	"Other" if Asian Indian or Hindu	"White" if Indo-European	"Asian Indian"	"Asian Indian" under APIs	"Asian Indian" under Asian

Sources: U.S. Bureau of the Census 1921, 29, table 1 n.1; 1933, 32, table 4 n.1; 1943, 5 table 1; 1952, xvi; 1964, xlii and cxiii; 1973, app. 15; 1982, 21; 1992, B-12; and the census form distributed to households for 2000.

This event inaugurated a new period of inflow that overwhelmingly came from Asia, with India being a top sending country.

The 1970 census departed from all previous censuses by counting immigrants of Indian descent under "white." This reassignment from nonwhite to white at a moment when the state was installing measures to protect minoritized groups from the discrimination they historically faced blocked the new immigrants' access to new civil rights provisions like affirmative action. The definition of terms in the 1970 U.S. census summary specified that "persons who did not classify themselves in one of the specific race categories on the questionnaire but entered Mexican, Puerto Rican *or a response suggesting Indo-European stock*" (1973, app. 15; emphasis mine) were to be reassigned to the category "white." This recategorization erased the decades-long history of race-based discrimination against Indian immigrants, galvanizing the AIA into action. By 1970, immigrants from India and other South Asian countries formed a critical mass for self-advocacy. The number of "Asian Indians" admitted to the United States had jumped from 1,973 between 1951 and 1960 to 27,189 between 1961 and 1970 in the wake of the 1965 immigration amendments (Gall and Gall 1993, 411, table 515).

The state in the post-1965 period tried to bridge several contradictions. Its racialism and renewed labor importation (overwhelmingly, this time, with skilled workers from Asia, Latin America, and the Caribbean) sat uncomfortably with its recommitment to welfare and racial equality based on group rights in the domestic sphere. In fact, the 1965 reform of the Immigration and Nationality Act (INA) was a piece of civil rights legislation that eliminated race-based exclusions that governed immigration. The reform was clearly informed by the double imperatives of the cold war in the international arena and a welfare state in the domestic arena charged with correcting racial injustice toward minorities. Starting in the 1950s, those who favored immigration reform framed the racial quotas controlling immigration as a dimension of legalized racial discrimination and argued that this gravely undercut the image of the United States as a leader of democracy in a cold war world (Tichenor 2002, 203–18).

The amended INA reintroduced large-scale labor importation after a forty-year hiatus to materially address the cold war–welfare state imperatives.[5] The new immigration policy was geared toward recruiting highly skilled foreign labor that could, on the one hand, help the United States outstrip the Soviet Union's aerospace and weapons development and, on the other hand, supply health practitioners for Medicaid and Medicare programs established under the Lyndon Johnson's "Great Society" plans (Hing 1993, 38–39; Khandelwal 1995, 92; Prashad 2000, 72–75). Nonwhite immigrants dominated the labor flow. Though nonwhite, the process of state selection for skilled labor had already set them up to be relatively successful. Would these nonwhite entrants have access to the benefits of the welfare state and civil rights protections? And if so, on what grounds?

The state answered these questions in part by ideologically constructing the new entrants as minoritized migrants who had no need for welfare and civil rights protections. Even though it did not legislate differential access to social entitlements for noncitizens as it would do in 1996, it achieved some of the same effects through ideological work.[6] It defined as anti-citizens those who relied on welfare or group rights for social mobility.[7] It achieved this through the racialized image of model minorities. In 1966, a year after the INA was reformed, the *New York Times Magazine* and the *U.S. News & World Report* popularized sociologist William Petersen's discussions of Japanese and Chinese Americans as "model minorities" who were the antithesis of state-reliant African Americans (Chang 1999, 54–55). South Asian professionals migrating mostly from India were quickly absorbed into this construct (Prashad 2000, 168). This hegemonic image enabled the state to actively produce a racially ambiguous identity for South Asians who were amenable to be represented as nonblack, though also definitely not white.

Although most new immigrants at this time were professionals, many were underemployed, underpaid, and hit the glass ceiling (Dutta 1980, 469–83; 1982;

Elkhanialy and Nicholas 1976b, 48). Their "alien" and "nonwhite, nonblack" appearance, their nonnative dialect of English, and their lack of professional networks blocked their upward mobility (Dutta 1982, 80). A mid-1970s survey conducted on behalf of the India League of America (ILA), a Chicago-based pan-Indian organization, revealed that 44 percent of those polled reported that they had been either denied jobs for which they were qualified or were overlooked for promotion (Elkhanialy and Nicholas 1976b, 47). Indian women, despite their high rates of labor force participation, were considerably underpaid (Kanta Marwah's 1978 study, cited in Dutta 1982, 82). The predicament of these immigrants paralleled that of other newly arrived Asian Americans who were facing similar barriers (U.S. Commission on Civil Rights 1980). Clearly, they were confronting what the legal theorist Robert Chang (1999) calls nativistic racism, a potent combination of xenophobia and racism directed specifically at immigrants, and thus began their search for rights.

Enacting Citizenship

In 1974, the AIA decided to intervene in the system that federal agencies used to classify the U.S. population by race, because the organization's members felt that none of the existing official categories matched the immigrant group's geopolitical and cultural identities. At that time, the AIA was one of a handful of civically oriented Indian immigrant organizations that operated at the national level. To execute the project of gaining visibility for immigrants of Indian descent, the AIA had to get its members involved in addressing their reality in the United States, which was marred by the unequal treatment that many of them faced. The organization appealed to immigrants by urging them to start acting like citizens or to prepare themselves for citizenship by taking an interest in processes such as the census and the congressional debates on it. At the same time, the AIA approached various government agencies in charge of racial classification to persuade them to recategorize immigrants of Indian descent as nonwhite. An effort to recover the scope of the AIA's double task shows that it cannot be reduced to a convenient cashing in on civil rights "benefits."[8]

Formed in 1967, the AIA was the oldest national-level organization with chapters across the country. In the 1970s, along with the National Federation of Indian Associations in America and the National Association of Americans of

Asian Indian Descent, the AIA stood out among the array of regional, linguistic, and religious immigrant organizations because it focused on political issues that immigrants, as residents and citizens, confronted as a result of being in the United States (Leonard 1997, 89–90). The AIA's membership included post-1965 immigrants as well as earlier immigrants. Some of its members were U.S. citizens, while others were permanent residents. The AIA's Web site states that its goal since the founding of the organization has been to help its members "become part of the mainstream of American life" through fostering their "Indian heritage" and "American commitment." This means that the AIA has urged immigrants to imagine themselves as politically active American citizens.

The AIA's campaign to change the official designation of the immigrant group and to secure a separate category was in keeping with its larger mission of encouraging political participation. In describing the connection between the AIA's founding mission and the reclassification campaign, Manoranjan Dutta, the AIA president during the campaign, told me that "the most important idea was that this organization was set up on the basis of their [AIA members] being in America. Their concerns were, therefore, the American government, the American Census: . . . [that is,] how they could interact with America and American establishment. Other associations did not see that. This was a new initiative on part of the AIA."[9]

The task of getting new and would-be citizens to shift their allegiance, interest, and involvement to the United States was not an easy one. In explaining the difficulties of mobilizing immigrants who were preoccupied with homeland politics, Dutta gave me the example of an eminent Indian immigrant who mistook the AIA's meeting with the U.S. Bureau of the Census for a meeting with the Indian Census Bureau chief, who he assumed was visiting the United States. Challenging this indifference to U.S. institutions and practices, the AIA argued that these immigrants needed to exercise their right to be counted because they lived in and paid taxes to the United States.

The AIA brought this sense of civic duty to the congressional hearings in 1976 on the 1980 census. Testifying to the House of Representatives, Dutta connected the need for all U.S. residents to participate in the census with the need for accurate data, which in turn would lead to a fair redistribution of resources. As he declared: "The political and economic future of thousands of people rests on the [Census] Bureau's demographic data. For the administration of many

Federal and local governmental programs involving affirmative action, and allocation of funds in the areas of employment, education and health services, accurate census enumeration of all minority groups is mandatory. We all have a stake in proper enumeration of the census" (U.S. House of Representatives 1976, 34–35). The AIA understood how, in the post–civil rights era, inaccurate census data on minority groups interfered with their ability to receive a proportional share of federal revenues and to benefit from federal antidiscrimination programs. But the organization also stressed the importance of participating in the census as a civic duty. The "stake" that Dutta alluded to in his testimony was a bid for full citizenship and its concomitant rights and responsibilities.

Along with encouraging immigrants to transfer their habits of democratic citizenship to the United States, the AIA also began expressing its concern to various government agencies about job market discrimination. Its first battle on this score was with the Federal Interagency on Culture and Education (FICE) ad hoc committee, which in 1974 was standardizing racial and ethnic categories that would be adopted by the Office of Management and Budget (OMB). These categories would then be used to collect data to track civil rights compliance. The FICE committee, chaired by a Census Bureau official, became the architect of the five racial and ethnic categories enshrined in what is commonly known as the 1977 "Directive 15." This ethno-racial pentagon (Hollinger 1995) has been credited with "inordinately shap[ing] the very discourse of race in the United States" (Espiritu and Omi 2000, 45).

The FICE in its deliberations classified people from South Asia as white (Federal Interagency Committee on Education 1975, 3–5). In coming to this conclusion it was faced with many of the same quandaries as were the early-twentieth-century courts. Were immigrants from South Asia white because they were "Caucasians"? Or were they "Asian" because "they came from Asia and some are victims of discrimination in this country" (4)? After much debate, the FICE limited the minority category "Asian" to "peoples with origins formerly called 'Oriental' and to natives of the Pacific Islands." People from the "Indian subcontinent," it decided, were "Caucasian/White," not Asian (3–4) on the grounds that "while evidence of discrimination against Asian Indians exists, it appears to be concentrated in specific geographical and occupational areas" (5). Thus the FICE chose to go along with long-discredited ethnological claims that people from South Asia were "Caucasian" and therefore "White." In dismissing "geographical" and "occupational" discrimination as valid reasons to claim minority status, it returned to biological notions of race. By stating what it did, the FICE suggested that minority status rested on typologies of "race" rather than on a group's experience of racism.

In its efforts to place immigrants of Indian descent in the ethno-racial pentagon, the FICE came up against the limits of a black-white formulation of civil rights (Ancheta 1998; Chang 1999; Moran 1998; Perea 2000). This framework treats minoritized groups that are not African American as "whites-in-waiting," an association that raises suspicions about their claims to minority rights (Perea 2000, 347). Because the pseudobiological category "Caucasian" had contingently absorbed Indians and not East Asians at certain points in history, the former group's claim to minority status was suspect. The legal scholar Rachel Moran (1998) has shown how the civil rights model, rooted in historically specific white-on-black relations of oppression, does not translate easily to other groups. These groups have different histories of racialization and they need civil rights to protect them against distinct forms of discrimination such as nativistic racism.

In January 1975, the AIA protested the FICE's decision by submitting to it a statement on discrimination faced by immigrants of Indian descent in order to prevent the OMB from adopting the committee's recommendations. It identified affirmative action in white-collar jobs, protection against social discrimination, and access to federal contracts and loans for immigrant-owned small businesses as priorities for the community. In the statement, the AIA clearly asserted that "Indians are disadvantaged, we believe, for reasons of racial discrimination" (quoted in Fisher 1980, 129). It placed the disadvantage squarely in the racial coding of Indians as nonwhites who faced skin-color and phenotype-based discrimination. It voiced its concerns about family members who were entering the United States in the midst of the economic recession in the 1970s under family reunification preferences (Koshy 1998, 304). Unlike their sponsoring family members, these immigrants were not coming in to fill a labor market shortage. They, the AIA argued in its statement to the FICE, would be competing "with other ethnic groups for the kinds of jobs [to] which affirmative action programs are particularly applicable" (quoted in Fisher 1980, 131). Without affirmative action, these family-sponsored immigrants would be at a disadvantage in a market skewed in favor of white, middle-class, American-born men.

The AIA succeeded in convincing the Equal Employment Opportunity Commission (EEOC) of the FICE's folly. The EEOC filed a notice on government-wide standard racial and ethnic categories in the *Federal Register* on 4 April 1977, to announce the addition of "the Indian subcontinent" under "Asian or Pacific Islander" (Equal Employment Opportunity Commission 1977, 17900). On 12 May 1977, the OMB followed suit in its "Directive 15" (Office of Management and Budget 1977).

The negotiations among the AIA and the various state agencies demonstrate the contradictory ways in which access to rights for immigrants from Asia have been thoroughly mediated in all periods of immigration by "institutionalized, legal definitions of race and national origins" (Lowe 1996, 10). These definitions have determined the state's decision to withhold or grant citizenship rights as it saw fit at different times to different groups racialized as "Asian." It is not surprising that for the AIA, claims to full citizenship and equal rights became tied to questions of racial classification and discrimination on the basis of racialized alienness, the quintessential racial formation to which Asian Americans are subjected. Far from exploiting affirmative action policies set up for established minority groups (Fisher 1980, 117, 129; Helweg and Helweg 1990), the AIA was attempting to locate immigrants of Indian descent in the U.S. racial landscape on the basis of their treatment and to articulate the stakes they should have as U.S. citizens.

In Search of a Name

While the federal recognition of people from the "Indian subcontinent" as "Asian" was a major victory, the AIA still had to get them removed from the category "white" in the census. The organization still needed to argue for a separate census label. In order to fit into the post-1965 relationship between race and rights, immigrants of Indian descent needed to transform their national, regional, cultural, religious, and linguistic identities into a racial one. The search for a name highlights the artificiality of racial labels for immigrants who have multiple systems of making sense of their identities. At the same time, the labels start to define the parameters, in this case for legal-bureaucratic purposes of distributive justice, within which immigrants have to articulate themselves.

The AIA's aim was to secure a separate category in the race question of the short form, which is distributed to all U.S. households, so that the Census Bureau could gather a 100 percent count of the community. The organization thus approached the larger Indian community beyond its membership to ascertain how the community would prefer to appear in the census. To do so the AIA used ethnic radio, ethnic newspapers, and meetings with other Indian organizations to generate a debate about an appropriate census descriptor for the community. Ethnic newspapers provided an active forum for community members to discuss the merits of minority status that the naming would achieve (Fisher 1980, 127, 131).

The AIA in its outreach reinforced the point that, historically, immigrants of Indian descent had not been treated as white. It invoked the 1917 Asiatic barred zone to remind the immigrants that they had been treated as "Asians." Indeed, that law itself was preceded by such measures as renaming the Japanese and Korean Exclusion League as "Asiatic" so as to include immigrants from British India who were just as unwanted (Song 1998, 90–91). Despite this treatment, as Dutta observed, Indians had suddenly appeared in the 1970 census as "a footnote to whites."

During the 1970s internal debate over an appropriate label, community members proposed regional (Tamil, Gujarati, Punjabi etc.), religious (Hindu), and nationalist (Indian or Bharatiya) identities in lieu of the racial terms used by the Census Bureau. According to Dutta, the AIA recommended "Indian," a term that it eventually based on cultural heritage rather than on national origin, and it expanded the term to diasporic Indians. Caribbean and British Indian immigrants approached the AIA on reading its memorandum and self-identified as Indians. Ugandan refugees of Indian origin also agreed to identify as "Indian" as a gesture of appreciation for the AIA's role in petitioning the Congress to accept fifteen hundred refugees in 1972. The ILA of Chicago proposed the term "Indic," based on its discussions and survey, at an October 1976 symposium to which it invited the Census Bureau and the EEOC (Elkhanialy and Nicholas 1976a, 7). It asked the Census Bureau to list in brackets "the countries of the Indian subcontinent" (7) so that those not familiar with "Indic" could check the right box.

Immigrants participating in the community-wide debate rejected the labels "White" or "Black" because they felt that in their case skin color did not line up with those racial categories (Fisher 1980, 119–20, 127–28).[10] The protests against a test run of the Chicago-based ILA's survey that asked participants to identify themselves racially as white or black indicate the immigrants' refusal to submit to U.S. terms (Elkhanialy and Nicholas 1976b, 45). The mismatch between official designations and self-perception is exactly what opens up a contested terrain allowing communities to act on their own behalf and intervene in their racialization. In the final ILA survey, the categories that the participants themselves proposed for the census were "Oriental, Asian, Indian, Asian Indian, Indo-Asian, Indo-Aryan, Indo-American, Aryan, Dravidian, Mongol, Dravido-Aryan, Hindu, Hindustani," and so forth (47). This range reflects their perceptions and interpretations of "race" and ethnicity. Thus, the rejection of U.S. racial categories, on the one hand, could be read as resistance on the part of South Asian immigrants and an assertion of their ethnic identities (Koshy 1998, 301). On the other hand, their refusal to engage with those categories promoted their racial ambiguity within the dominant ways of understanding race in the United States (Kibria 1998, 71–72).

The ILA strongly supported a separate census category that would allow an autonomous identity to Indian immigrants who saw themselves "as racially different from White, Black and Oriental Americans" (Elkhanialy and Nicholas 1976a, 6). However, the group was conflicted about the demand for minority status, even though its own survey showed that three-fourths of the respondents supported the initiative (1976b, 49). While the ILA president at the time, Chandra Jha, was careful not to dismiss reports of discrimination, he did raise doubts about the extent and seriousness of such practices (1976a, vi-viii). The ILA felt that minority status was probably unnecessary given the blanket protection afforded by Title VII of the 1964 Civil Rights Act. According to the organization, raising immigrants' awareness of such legal safeguards would be a more effective strategy. The ILA's report underlined its willingness to support minority status if, after informed debate, immigrants and their representative organizations favored such a move. But in an *India Abroad* interview several months after the symposium, the ILA again expressed its reservations when its president argued that such a status for South Asians could alienate "truly disadvantaged minorities" if employers were to comply with civil rights requirements by hiring relatively privileged Indian immigrants (quoted in Fisher 1980, 132; Fornaro 1984, 30).

Other sections in the Indian community also opposed minority status. Some rejected the effort because they did not want to embrace a minority identity that in their minds was stigmatized. Minority status for them was associated with disadvantage. Commenting on this association, the sociologists Yen Espiritu and Michael Omi point out how minority status is often seen as giving up on principles of individual achievement instead of being understood as "group demands for recognition and collective empowerment" (2000, 57). Those who held this position, which was similar to that of the ILA, were afraid that "preferential treatment" accorded to Indians, whose mean and unadjusted incomes were higher than those of whites, would provoke a backlash against them (Fisher 1980, 131–32). The Asian Americanist Susan Koshy (1998, 304) suggests that the support and opposition to minority status were class based. More secure and higher-ranking professionals—doctors and engineers—were invested in a colorblind approach that would promote the "model" image of the community. A minority status would, according to this section, damage that image. In contrast, those who were locked into technical jobs and were having difficulty advancing in their positions felt that eligibility for affirmative action programs would help them get out of the rut.

Undeterred by the multiplicity of positions among immigrants, the AIA carried its proposal to the Census Bureau. In March 1976 the AIA's insistence on the inappropriateness of the category Caucasian/White for South Asians and its alignment with other Asians were rewarded. The Census Bureau invited the AIA to a conference aimed at ascertaining Asian American concerns about the proposed categories for the 1980 census. The invitation suggested that the Census Bureau considered immigrants of Indian descent to be a part of "Asians." The Asian American advisory committee that emerged from this meeting made space for the AIA thereby opening up a category associated with East Asians to Indians. This merger is significant because it marked the beginning of a strategic alignment of Indians, and more broadly South Asians, with Asians. Thus, according to Dutta, when the Native American advisory committee requested that the qualifier "Asian" be added to the label "Indian" to "end Columbus' confusion," the AIA readily agreed to this modification as it got ready for its congressional testimony.

Immigrants and immigrant groups continued to challenge the AIA and its position well into 1977. This occurred even as the AIA was speaking for them in its meetings with federal agencies. Curious about why the other Indian organizations were not present at the federal-level debates, I asked Dutta to explain how the AIA emerged as the voice of the community. Dutta claimed that the AIA was the only group with a formal petition to the Census Bureau and with a clear set of strategies. This explanation is plausible given that state practices favor and reward professionalism in minority leadership (Espiritu 1992, 11). It is likely that one reason for the AIA speaking for all immigrants was the endorsement it received from federal agencies as a result of its willingness to follow bureaucratic procedures methodically. Petitioning, letter writing, and caucusing were class-based skills that the AIA brought to its campaign.

"Not All Caucasians Are White"

The AIA was invited on 1 and 2 June 1976 to present its case to the U.S. House of Representatives' Subcommittee on Census and Population, which had been convened to address the problem of undercounting in minority communities. The buildup to the 1980 census represented an intensely contested moment since racial categories had become institutionally relevant (Espiritu 1992, 9–14). Mexican Americans, African Americans, and Korean Americans, like the AIA, wanted to address their concerns about category construction, undercounting in minority communities, and the resultant impact on distributive justice. The AIA was part of the Asian American delegation, and it appeared with the chairs of the Advisory Committee on the Spanish Origin Population and the Advisory Committee on the Black Population. The AIA in its testimony demanded that, instead of treating "people of Asian Indian heritage" as white, the Census Bureau should create a separate category for them under "Asian American" in the form distributed to every household.

The AIA's 1976 testimony before Congress shows how the black-white paradigm operated to frustrate its efforts to complicate existing racial identities (U.S. House of Representatives 1976). The bipolar frame actively produced racial ambiguity. The AIA had hoped to challenge the existing system and still be able to make a case that would underline the ethnic group's eligibility for protections granted to minoritized groups. In the process of navigating the black-white framework that only permits groups to ask whether they resemble blacks or whites, the AIA shifted among essentialist, power-evasive, and power-cognizant discourses on race that Ruth Frankenberg (1993, 137–42) identifies as the dominant repertoires of thinking and talking about race. The AIA, confounded by the black-white terms of belonging, was unable to consistently provide historically and experientially grounded reasons for minority status. At certain points, it attempted to deracinate Indians by evading power relations. Unable to fully disrupt the terms of racial classification, the AIA lost the opportunity to establish the specific forces that had worked to racialize immigrants of Indian descent. This lack of articulation interfered with the AIA's ability to relate meaningfully the immigrants' experiences to the minoritization of other groups, even though they all had common concerns.

Convincing the subcommittee that the Census Bureau's conflation of Caucasian ("race") and white ("color") was erroneous became the AIA's biggest task. It placed the severe undercounting of immigrants of Indian descent in the 1970 census squarely in the Census Bureau's merger of race and color. The AIA's inquiries into the 1970 census had revealed that the Census Bureau had added to the category "Whites" those who had written in "Indian" for the "Other" races category (see figure 2). Some respondents, on not finding an appropriate identity, had checked "Indian (American)" because it was the one category where the word "Indian" appeared. Others had checked the category "Black." According to the AIA, the Census Bureau's construction of the race questions and its method of handling these responses led to a paltry count of 78,000 Indians in 1970 (U.S. House of Representatives 1976, 33–35).

In confronting the problem of undercounting, the AIA parted ways with the other undercounted groups. At the testimony, black, Latino, and some Asian American community leaders had cited as barriers to data collection such factors as illiteracy, language problems, isolation in inner cities, lack of census enumerators from the community, and immigration status (U.S. House of Representatives 1976). These problems, the AIA claimed, did not affect the (highly educated and relatively well-to-do) Indian immigrants. Instead, the problem lay in the group's miscategorization. This discursive move distanced Indians from other minoritized groups that had been ghettoized and not fully counted as a result of the Census Bureau's inability to respond to their needs. The breach in the AIA's otherwise-used language of solidarity with minority groups could have been avoided had the AIA related the departures in the profiles of recent South Asian immigrants to immigration provisions and connected its concern about racial categorization to similar legal-bureaucratic impositions suffered by all the other groups with which it was testifying.

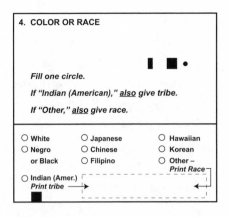

FIGURE 2. In the 1970 census, immigrants of Indian descent had no separate category of their own. Their choices on the question on race included the following: "White," "Negro or Black," "Indian (Amer.)," or "Other." This image was reproduced from the census form. (Source: U.S. Bureau of the Census 1973, app. 53)

At first the AIA used historical precedent in insisting that immigrants of Indian descent were not white and fit best as Asians. Using this power-cognizant strategy, it went over the early-twentieth-century legal history to emphasize the way in which the *Thind* ruling used "race" to exclude immigrants from the Indian subcontinent. The AIA's use of these precedents to talk about a group's "race" points to its understanding of race as a product of history and an exercise of power rather than objectively observable physical characteristics. In tying the treatment of Indians in California to the 1917 legislation of an Asiatic barred zone, the AIA underscored the history of exclusion and discrimination that Indians shared with other Asians in the United States. Given this history, the AIA argued, "It is important to note that exclusion of immigrants of Asian Indian heritage from the category Asian American is arbitrary" (U.S. House of Representatives 1976, 35). What made immigrants of Indian descent "Asians" in the United States, then, was a common history and not biology. This formulation of race closely paralleled Canta Pian's testimony on behalf of the Chinese community advocating a panethnic "Asian and Pacific Islander" category based on a shared history of "discrimination," and "ethnic stereotyping" (U.S. House of Representatives 1976, 41).[11] This discursive move attempted to shift the attention of the Congress and the Census Bureau from phenotype as a basis of group definition to that of the group's treatment. By prying apart race and color to argue that color often has little to do with racial assignment in the United States, the AIA could have shown that white and black are not transparent references to phenotype (Davis 1991; Lyons 1997; Nobles 2000). Rather, the two racial categories structure unequal relations between two groups.

Yet, in picking its way through "race" in an effort to separate "white" from "Caucasian" (termed "Indo-European stock" in the Census Bureau's 1970 instructions), the AIA ended up treating "Caucasian" in essentialist terms: as a biological reality, draining whiteness of its history of domination. By casting the problem with the category as one of inaccuracy, the AIA's argument shifted from history to pseudobiology, sapping the interventionary power of its position. To convince the Census Bureau of its error, the AIA reverted to the ethnological terms that had played such a major role in the court cases of the early twentieth century. "Caucasian" appeared in its narrative as a race to which some "Indians" belonged and others did not, thus authorizing the category as a scientific reality instead of an ideological construct to justify colonialism and slavery. At one point the testimony claimed: "The fact is that some Indians are Caucasian, and others are not. In addition, we wish to emphasize that not all Caucasians are white. It is erroneous and misleading to equate the two terms, 'caucasian' and 'white,' as if they are synonymous, and use the term Caucasian to describe all Asian Indians" (U.S. House of Representatives 1976, 35).

If race were not considered the same thing as color, according to the AIA, then where did immigrants of Indian descent fit in the U.S. racial schema? The tensions between understanding race as a social construct and race as a phenotypical descriptor coursed through the AIA's testimony as it argued that "the misspecification of the census model in relation to the race/color question must be corrected so that Asian Indians are able to identify themselves accurately. The present category of race/color is an unscientific amalgam of race and color questions. Physiognomic criteria of race classifications remain controversial among the leading authorities in the field of anthropology. Cultural anthropologists rightly emphasize the importance of self-perception in any classification of race. The AIA submits that race and color are not coterminous. The category of color, if it must be included, should be a separate one. It must include not only black and white, but also brown, copper and others as well" (36). The AIA, in this excerpt, first rejected biological race by invoking self-definition or subjective understandings of one's racial identity. It then treated color, which has had a long history in organizing racial hierarchy in the United States, literally as a reference to skin color and proposed other color categories such as "brown" and "copper."

By trying to separate race and color in this way, the AIA lost sight of the power relations that the color categories configure and shifted to presenting Indians as having no race. As Frankenberg points out, reference to variations in color, a power-evasive repertoire, is "a euphemism or strategy to avoid race: it shifts attention away from color differences that make a political difference [in this case black and white] by embedding meaningful differences in nonmeaningful ones" (1993, 38). The insertion of "copper" turns racial categories such as white into benign signifiers of skin color, thereby converting the AIA's power-cognizant argument into a deracinated power-evasive one. Unable to keep the politics of race at the center of its challenge as a result of the obscuring effects of the black-white paradigm, the AIA continued to miss the opportunity of naming the distinctive ways in which Indians were racialized and of laying the grounds on which they could ally themselves with black and Latino struggles. Nearly two decades later, this willful indeterminacy haunted another generation as the participants in the Boston forum described above floundered with the language of race and its implications for race relations.

The AIA's discussion of color and its use of discredited ethnological terms like Caucasian, Mongoloid, and Negroid in proposing an alternative to the Census Bureau's categories (U.S. House of Representatives 1976) demonstrates the collision between the arcane history of race in the United States and the understandings of race that these postcolonial immigrants brought with them. This encounter between South Asian and U.S. ways of articulating identity can be read as the process of racialization at work. In postcolonial South Asia, notions of race, though not as relevant as in the West, are filtered through a colonial lens.

The AIA's notions of race are continuous with nineteenth-century colonial constructions of the Aryan theory of race (Koshy 1998), modern Indian history, and postcolonial immigrant ideas about race (Mazumdar 1989b). The Aryan theory floated by European orientalists and Indologists proposed a common Aryan stock for people of Indian and European origins. High-caste Hindu nationalists appropriated this theory in the pre-independence and postcolonial eras, as did non-Brahmins in South India to challenge Brahmin hegemony (Koshy 1998, 294–301). The South Asian studies scholars Sucheta Mazumdar (1989b) and Susan Koshy (1998) both note the grip that these now-defunct theories have on predominantly Hindu post-1965 immigrants. This could explain the facility of these immigrants with terms such as "Caucasian," "Aryan," "Dravidian," and

"Mongol" and their treatment of these terms as objectively valid. Furthermore, for these immigrants not only was color not the same as race, but also "unlike racial identity in the West, color does not constitute a primary social or political identity in the subcontinent the way that caste, religion, language, region, gender, and class do (although it may be loosely configured within some of these categories)" (Koshy 1998, 295). Thus, the AIA's awareness of the racism directed at early-twentieth-century and post-1965 South Asian immigrants; its refusal to accept U.S. racial categories as universal; and its solidarity with U.S. minorities existed throughout in severe tension with its uncritical acceptance of race as a classificatory tool that existed outside social relations.

"Where Does Race Stop?"
Contentions within the Establishment

Confusion about what exactly constituted race for the Census Bureau plagued not only the AIA but also Congress. The state's race work unfolded in the exchanges between the congressional subcommittees on the census and the Census Bureau. Indians figured as a group whose lack of fit with existing racial categories called into question the utility of the census race item. The arguments against the Census Bureau's categorization system, however, restored the salience of black-white ways of making sense of race, because Indians did not fit only in reference to that bipolarity. Once again, power-evasive understandings of race—this time focused on how racial categories violate individual self-identifications—shifted attention away from the power-laden, and in that sense political, processes of constructing race. From the Census Bureau's defense of its practices it becomes clear that its attempts to implement the post-1965 relationship between race and rights through standard racial categories were embedded in the production of indeterminacy for groups like South Asians and other Asians, thereby compromising their rights-claims as minorities.

In 1977, a year after the AIA's testimony, the Census Bureau was cross-examined at a congressional hearing by Rep. William Lehman, the presiding member, about how it defined race (U.S. House of Representatives 1977, 153–68). Lehman repeatedly challenged Census Bureau officials to justify the collection of data by race and ethnicity. He questioned the reliability of data collected under boxes that might not match people's self-perceptions (153). To highlight the limits of the Census Bureau's racial categories given the diversity in self-identification, Lehman used the example of an exchange student from India whom his family had hosted. This student had insisted that his correct "racial" identification was "wheat." In trying to make sense of such a self-description, Lehman actively implemented the black-white framework, creating a racially ambiguous body. His remark that the Indian student "didn't think he was brown; he didn't think he was black; he didn't think he was white" (165) did not lead to an examination of the dissonance the black-white system creates for those who do not fit and are not socialized in it. Lehman's understanding that "wheat" is a common racial distinction in India and his recommendation to the Census Bureau that it include a plethora of skin color variations in its race item to accommodate such responses stabilized the bipolar system by absorbing the challenge historically posed to it by Indian immigrants.

In responding to the congressman's doubts, the Census Bureau used its adoption of self-definition as a method to defend itself against criticisms about the narrowness of the race categories, their homogenizing function, and their confusing intersection with ethnicity. When Lehman asked the census officials, "Where does race stop and ethnicity stop, or vice versa?" they argued that the Census Bureau was "not attempting to make either an anthropological or physiological determination" (160–61). The Census Bureau clarified that census takers allowed "the respondent to indicate and to answer or to check whichever one of the specific categories" (161) because it recognized that racial identification was subjective. If the specified category did not describe the respondents, then they could write down the race to which they thought they belonged. This method, according to the Census Bureau, gave "the maximum latitude to the respondent to decide both on race and ethnic origin" (161).

In the census officials' testimonies, identifying oneself racially appears as a benign and routine process that allows for ample individual choice. It is important to note that self-identification, rather than being a routine technique, was established as a valid method for data collection through political struggle. In documenting the "Hispanic" community's protracted encounter with the Census Bureau over better data, the sociologist Harvey Choldin (1986, 406–7, 409–10) notes that census staff resisted self-identification because it feared introducing a subjective element into an objective process. Not until 1960 could respondents choose their racial category. The enumerator still reserved the right to classify the respondent in case of confusion. In 1980, enumerators for the first time could no longer decide the race of a respondent by observation (Lee 1993, 78–79). All that self-identification comes to mean is that those filling out the census forms have the agency to identify with the categories already provided by the Census Bureau instead of having an enumerator decide the appropriate category.

The Census Bureau's answer about using self-identification did not satisfy Lehman. This time, the Census Bureau's construction of the label "Asian and Pacific Islanders" (API) was brought up as a perfect example of how this racial category collapsed "substantial differences between these people" (U.S. House of Representatives 1977, 161). In this case, API was cited as a prime example of how standardized racial categories imposed homogeneity. The Census Bureau's response to why it constructed such a category exposed its implemented understanding of race. While the Census Bureau argued that it clustered groups such as Japanese, Chinese, Filipino, Asian Indian, and Samoan under APIs to respond to those communities' demands for inclusion in that category and to conform to Directive 15, the following exchange shows that the Census Bureau had clear ideas about which groups were properly Asian or Pacific Islander when Lehman asked whether an Iranian would be considered "Asian." To this, the Census Bureau's chief of the ethnic and racial statistics staff, Mrs. McKenney, rebutted, "Generally, for the Asian and Pacific Islanders, we have used guidelines which have been prepared by the Office of Management and Budget to determine which groups come under this specific category, and *the category would not include all persons from Asia.* It primarily would include Japanese, Chinese, Filipino, Korean, Guamanians, Samoans, Hawaiian, and persons from the Indian subcontinent" (162; emphasis mine).

Lehman's attempt to clarify the liminality of Iranians under the existing classifications and the Census Bureau's categorical exclusion of Iranians from what it understood to be "Asian" gestures to the ways in which "race has always been an inescapably geographical concept" with regions being associated with "racial" types (Lewis and Wigen 1997, 120). Also, the history of U.S. military intervention in and occupation of the Philippines, Hawaiʻi, Guam, Samoa, Korea, and Japan has informed how Asia is demarcated in the United States. McKenney's reply was an attempt to fill in "Asia" which in and of itself is "an empty and arbitrary signifier" (Bahri 1998, 27). It intimates the Census Bureau's underlying ideas about cartography and racial classification, thereby contradicting its earlier assertion that it did not attempt "anthropological or physiological determination" (U.S. House of Representatives 1977, 160–61). In reality, the Census Bureau's implicit understanding of who belongs to what race circumscribes the "maximum latitude" that a respondent has to specify his or her race.

Doubts about the Census Bureau's conception of who can be deemed Asian did not stop with this presentation. In 1979, Ratnam Swami, a representative of the Concerned Asian-American and Pacific-American People's Task Force and a self-identified "South Asian" testifying at a House of Representatives oversight hearing in Los Angeles, demanded to know if the Census Bureau would consider Afghanistan (which was included in the 1917 Immigration Act's demarcation of an Asiatic barred zone) and Iran as part of Asia (U.S. House of Representatives 1979, 69). Exasperated with the Census Bureau, he exclaimed, "I am willing to take a bet that no two people in this room will come up with the same definition of Asian-Pacific. I have tried it. The Census Bureau cannot give me a definition. . . . Just what is Asian-Pacific?" (69).

The question "Just what is Asian-Pacific?" underlines the indeterminacy that results from the state's race work—its reinscription of ethnicity, class, map making, and U.S. foreign relations as race within a black and white framework. The implications of this racial indeterminacy are troublesome because the group's race-based rights claims are consequently clouded with confusion. As Robert Chang, in commenting on the ambiguous racialization of Asian Americans, observes, "When we try to make our problems known, our complaints of discrimination and calls for remedial action are seen as unwarranted and inappropriate and may spark resentment" (1999, 55). South Asians in the United States suffer from the same paradoxical delegitimation.

At the end of these debates, the 1980 census form printed "Asian Indian" as a separate category (see figure 3). Unlike the EEOC and the OMB, it did not specify a summary category "Asian or Pacific Islander." The term "Asian Indian," with little currency outside of scholarly and bureaucratic usage, thus emerged. Unlike such subcategories as "Chinese" or "Korean," which referred to national identity, "Asian Indian" was supposed to allude to immigrants from all South Asian nations and the diaspora. It has failed to operate successfully as a transnational term because it repeats India's geopolitical hegemony in the region. Many South Asians such as Pakistanis or Bangladeshis or Sri Lankans do not

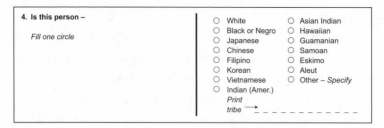

FIGURE 3. In the 1980 census "Asian Indian" appears as a separate category. None of the Asian and Pacific Islander categories are grouped. This image was reproduced from the census form. (Source: U.S. Bureau of the Census 1982, 21)

identify as "Asian Indians" and do not check that category. This means that the South Asians in the United States continue to be undercounted in the census.

In hindsight, what did the AIA win for immigrants of Indian descent after its six-year struggle with government agencies? By the AIA's own admission the utilization of the direct gains from the group's reclassification as a minority were modest. South Asian academics and professionals filed court and EEOC cases to challenge promotion and tenure denials and rejections from medical residency programs (Chopra 1995, 1332–35; Leonard 1997, 90; Motihar 1996, 19). Business owners benefited to some degree from their eligibility as minorities to federal funds and contracts. However, in 1980, a U.S. Supreme Court judge, affirming the second circuit court's determination in *Fullilove v. Klutznick* that a 10 percent set-aside for minority businesses in public works projects in New York was constitutional, skeptically asked, "The inclusion of Orientals troubles me—what discrimination can be shown against them?" (Chopra 1995, 1338). This statement is emblematic of the invisibility from which South Asians and Asian Americans suffer within white-on-black understandings of racism. Such erasure renders as mere formality state recognition of those groups as minorities. To contest the erosion of rights, the National Association of Americans of Indian Descent persuaded the Small Business Administration in 1982 to recognize the eligibility of Asian Indian business owners for its minority programs by showing they had suffered from "the effects of discriminatory practices," "prejudice or bias" and "economic deprivation" (Small Business Administration 1982). Again, these efforts had limited success. That "Asian Indians" could be systematically discriminated against continues to be questioned (Omi 1996, 181).

Conclusion

The focus of this chapter has been on the relationship between state practices and Indian immigrants' engagements with them to reveal the terms on which the first post-1965 wave of immigrants could belong to the United States. Rather than accepting the AIA's bid for minority status as sheer opportunism, I have argued that the AIA was attempting to articulate the post-1965 immigrants as racialized Americans in need of full citizenship with the promise of equality that came with that role. Consequently, the organization was caught in the central contradiction of a racialist state—that is, between sameness and difference. The state reinscribed several distinctions that were on the point of being destabilized by its new immigration, civil rights, and welfare policies when it demanded that Indians make their identity (difference) decipherable within the hegemonic terms of black and white to become eligible for sameness (equality guaranteed by civil rights). Their racialization as ambiguous entities stabilized U.S. national identity by drawing the distinction between model self-reliant Asians and troublesome state-reliant blacks and between citizen-workers and noncontributing anticitizens. Thus, the newly named "Asian Indians" were granted a slippery toehold in the United States as long as their belonging was contingent on their willingness to assimilate and contribute economically without demanding anything in return. In other words, the state was ready to offer citizenship with its responsibilities of economic contribution and political participation (see Marshall 1950 for the three stages of citizenship) but without the substantive right to protection against marketplace discrimination that would ensure the group's social and economic security.

Further, the AIA was willing to accept these assimilative terms charting what I call place-taking politics. The AIA's acceptance of these terms of belonging brought the community important victories. These gains could be secured because of its ability to act effectively in national political processes by utilizing the discourse of engaged citizenship that assumed an abstract subject equivalent to all other citizens. The AIA's elite membership's cultural and political capital, such as facility in English, familiarity with democratic methods of lobbying, and ease with media publicity, were central to its success. The immigrants transferred skills learned in independent India to their new environment, a transnational process used in this case to promote a sense of belonging to the United

States. Even though they faced discrimination in the United States, this did not shake their faith in abstract liberal citizenship. In India, they were its primary beneficiaries. Having never had to examine their class, gender, and caste privilege, they represented themselves as the universal. On coming to the United States where they were confronted with their racial and national difference, the immigrants sought to restore their habitual power to name everything while remaining unnamed themselves—a practice that Sakhi cofounder and feminist activist Annanya Bhattacharjee (1992) correctly diagnoses as the habit of ex-nomination. This desire facilitated the state's production of racial ambiguity and made these immigrants perfect candidates for place-taking politics.

The AIA in many ways modeled assimilative politics—participation in U.S. democratic structures through democratic methods. These modes of participation were being hailed by ethnicity theorists such as Nathan Glazer and Daniel Patrick Moynihan (1970) as ways for immigrant groups to become American without abandoning their distinctive cultural practices. For South Asians, the AIA blazed the path that made cultural pluralism compatible with U.S. nationalism. It struck the accommodating medium between the reinfusion of U.S. society with culturally different immigrant workers and their (tentative) absorption in the national body through their participation in conventional politics. The place-taking politics of the AIA set the tone for the South Asian mainstream's political involvement.

At the same time it left another legacy: unmet community needs and a lack of fluency among South Asians about U.S. race relations. The rise of South Asian social change-oriented organizations such as Manavi in New Jersey and Trikone in San Francisco by 1985 testifies to the severe limitations of place-taking politics. Such politics could not meet the needs of noncitizen immigrants, immigrant women, sexual minorities, and low-wage workers. The rhetoric of citizenship that the AIA used constructed race and gender inequality as a mere impediment to full citizenship rather than being central to it. The AIA uncritically accepted that citizens are the privileged subjects of rights, and to earn that standing South Asians needed to contribute to their new homeland and become politically active. The same limiting valorization of the nation-state and its promise of full citizenship with social and political equality can be found in the civil rights model (Lee 2000, 99) within which the AIA worked.

The feminist philosopher Uma Narayan's (1997) critique of hinging citizenship on the criteria of contribution and political participation—a critique shared by many of the activists in South Asian social change organizations—offers a way of understanding the inadequacies and dangers of the AIA's position. To predicate rights on conventional modes of political participation for which citizenship is a prerequisite leaves out those who neither have nor want citizenship (55–64). While the United States no longer excludes resident aliens from citizenship on the basis of race, not everybody can become an American citizen. Years of residence, immigration status, income, fluency in English, political history, criminal record, and family members' ability to sponsor new immigrants determine a person's eligibility for citizenship. Many immigrants do not meet these criteria and are therefore excluded from the circle of citizenship rights.

The notion of citizenship as requiring a contribution, even when expanded beyond labor force participation to such work as raising future citizens, is fraught with danger because, as Narayan notes, it "locate[s] individual dignity and worth in capacities to be 'autonomous, self governing and self-supporting,' a view which suggests that the only rights such citizens need are 'negative rights'" (53). The image of contributing self-sufficient citizens pathologizes the actual relations of dependency that suffuse society. Recognizing these dependencies is the basis of positive rights that can respond to social needs (for Narayan's positive rights, see 52–53). From the analysis I offer, we can see that the notion of the contributing citizen fits snugly with the independent, self-supporting image of the model minority. It has the deleterious effect of delegitimizing certain immigrant and native-born minorities' need for state-led antipoverty and antidiscrimination programs.

The departure of space-making politics from place-taking politics in South Asian communities comes with the recognition on the part of social change organizations that gender, class, sexual, and racial inequalities *constitute* citizenship, which in turn organizes those axes of difference (for a historical analysis of this relationship, see Glenn 2002). Space makers understand citizenship as a social and cultural institution created by the nation-state. They do not rely on it to address the multiple and intersecting systems of oppression, which, in part, that institution creates. Through their engagements with oppressive systems, they take up the project of succinctly naming their communities' racial formation, the project at which the AIA not only failed but also created the painful legacy of ambivalence that I witnessed during that fall afternoon in Boston.

CHAPTER 2

Contests over Culture

The 1980s and 1990s saw a change in the context within which place-taking organizations like the Association of Indians in America surfaced. The continued immigration from different parts of South Asia along with the family formation made possible by family reunification preferences in the 1965 immigration law have increasingly diversified the group along national, religious, generational, and class lines. This demographic and class diversification has led to the emergence of distinct, often conflicting, needs and interests on the part of immigrants from South Asia.

These divergent experiences gave birth to space-making organizations. By creating alternative structures for collective action, these organizations started to voice the problems underlying the divergence: misogyny, class exploitation, racism, narrow nationalism, and homophobia within and outside their communities. The organizations tackled these issues with the intention of transforming unjust social relations. These new forms of organizing profoundly challenge the accommodationist place-taking politics in South Asian communities, but each poses a unique threat to the place takers.

In this chapter, I look at the ways in which culture becomes a potent site at which the place takers and space makers confront each other. Which immigrants and what practices and values can be considered truly South Asian? Place takers rework notions of culture to restore the social privileges they enjoyed at home. Space makers intervene in these social hierarchies by reaching for emancipatory strands in their homeland histories. Both processes are transnational, involving a back and forth movement among different national and regional cultural landscapes.

In these competing accounts of cultural authenticity, place takers do the work of conservation while space makers do that of redefinition. Place takers construct the ethnic group as a monolith held together by a common culture, identity, and political goals. Without the cultural work that has to go into producing a singular identity, they cannot portray themselves as problem-free immigrant-citizens who can be trusted to uphold the existing social order in their new country of residence and in their homelands. For them, charity and social work, not struggles for social transformation, represent acceptable channels of civic involvement. To produce discourses on cultural authenticity, place takers have to erase women's oppression within their families, sexualities that challenge monogamous procreative heterosexuality, and the labor of working-class South Asians. Through culture making, place takers present domestic violence within the community along with those who dare speak out against it as antithetical to South Asian culture. Similarly, they see homosexuality as a Western influence corrupting core South Asian values. They distance themselves from the lives of poor South Asians because those experiences depart from the immigrant success story.

To counter these constructions, space makers produce their own narratives of authenticity. Women's, queer, and labor organizations excavate alternative genealogies in which cultures of women's dissent, homoerotics, and working-class militancy have a legitimate place. The members of these groups project themselves as valid South Asians and demand recognition as such. Though all three types of organizations—feminist, queer, and labor—redefine cultural belonging for their members, they present different specters for the South Asian mainstream.

Cultural Politics of Model Minorityhood

The deployment by place takers of cultural authenticity merges two processes. Their attempts to silence "inauthentic" subjects and realities mesh well with the portrayal of South Asians as model minorities. The hegemonic belief that certain minorities do well despite their race powerfully vindicates the immigrant success story. In the previous chapter I described the contortions through which South Asians were inducted into the U.S. racial order as model minorities, an image that initially was concocted for East Asians. This image of an evenly successful, self-reliant, and almost-white immigrant group helped the first wave of post-1965 immigrants to represent themselves as deserving full citizenship and it continues to appeal to mainstream South Asians. When we shift our attention from the legal-bureaucratic arena to the cultural one, we see that the place takers' versions of cultural authenticity feed this image.

The South Asian mainstream's use of culture to distance itself from co-ethnics who speak of domestic abuse, alcoholism, drug addiction, racial discrimination, poverty, and homosexuality is well illustrated by the Manavi founder-member Sujata Warrier. In discussing the investment of New Jersey's ethnic organizations in a problem-free model minority image, she said: "The community has a very hard time talking about incest or sexual abuse or racial discrimination because we are in a sense considered to be the model minority. [pause] It also means that certain things don't happen to us. Alcohol, substance abuse is not a concern for us [according to the community]. In fact, in the early years we [Manavi] actually worked with a couple of men with alcohol problems. When men have been pulled over by the police and treated very badly they have called *us* for information and have not talked to any of the mainstream social/cultural organizations. They just won't support them. . . . It gives them a bad name."[1] Mainstream organizations steer clear of the problems that Warrier enumerates because they fear that rallying around these issues would portray the immigrant community in negative ways. Putting up a wall of denial is their way of countering the racism inherent in treating immigrant communities of color as potentially troublesome.

The connection between the promotion by place takers of the model minority image and its discourses on culture reveals that the success story fundamentally relies on violent elisions of gender, sexual, and class oppression *within* those communities. The gendered and sexual dimensions of the model minority myth have not been discussed by Asian American critics, who see the myth as a class-inflected racially divisive project.[2] In the last two decades, they have amply critiqued the ways in which the project manipulates class to construct good and bad racial subjects. The project contrasts Asian Americans, depicted as upwardly mobile despite racial prejudice, with "unsuccessful" African Americans and Latinos who fail to overcome such barriers. The scholars have shown how the myth damages Asian Americans by erasing socioeconomic disparities within and among distinct ethno-racial groups clustered under the rubric. But they have failed to examine how the myth permits mainstream sections of Asian Americans to control gender and sexuality through heteronormative and patriarchal imperatives to present themselves as models.[3] From an anti-racist, feminist point of view, the enthusiasm with which the South Asian mainstream embraces the model minority image is reprehensible not only because it accepts antiblack and anti-Latino racism but also because this acceptance is tied to patriarchal oppression and compulsory heterosexuality in the name of culture.

Within South Asian communities in the United States, the conservative politics of authenticity is mobilized by South Asian families as well as regional, national, and religious associations. The conservative sections represent a constellation of institutions and individuals preoccupied with the work of cultural preservation and professional or business promotion by tapping into ethnic and national ties. Even though national, regional-linguistic, and religious differences divide them, their need to conserve traditions to maintain privilege cuts across these divides. Together, they function as gatekeepers. They name what is true to homeland traditions. Those who do not conform to the standards of authenticity are cast out into "America." Through this act of naming who or what is South Asian, the communities' mainstream sections reproduce the idea that ethnic traditions are fundamentally antagonistic to U.S. values and practices. Yet, at the same time, their culture work reaffirms the American dream and its tropes of meritocracy, individual achievement, fairness, and cohesion.

The conservative politics of authenticity set to work seemingly contradictory processes. On the surface, the mainstream community's emphasis on maintaining "traditional" ways and its refusal to accept "Americanized" immigrants within its fold can be interpreted as resistance to assimilation. In the assimilation model, ethnic values and practices fall away as immigrants convert themselves into Americans who then step out of their enclaves to participate fully in the economy and society. Ethnographers have found intriguing the Indian community's ability to assimilate at the economic level while protecting their cultural identities from being tarnished by U.S. society (Agarwal 1991; Bacon 1996; Dasgupta 1989; Saran 1985). As an explanation, they have turned to sociologist

Milton Gordon's (1964) concept of structural assimilation, which allows minority groups to integrate into American social networks and educational, political, and economic institutions while retaining their cultural distinctiveness.

But if we examine the values that place takers uphold, we see that the processes of retaining ethnic identity and integrating (somewhat) into U.S. schools, workplaces, civil society, and political institutions are interconnected and not separate or contradictory. The traditions that community leaders and families valorize bear a strong resemblance to values that white society finds acceptable, making it possible for exceptional minority groups to access some privileges held by the majority. The South Asian mainstream's aggressive promotion of traditional families feeds into the model cultural values of family solidarity, diligence, and obedience. Familial relations that romanticize the strength of kinship and the stability of marriage are filtered through notions of "family values" and the accompanying attack on public assistance made popular by the U.S. Right. These dovetailed culturalist arguments about self-help, the sanctity of marriage, and intact families reinforce the widely held belief that for their advancement "functional" minorities depend on themselves and on each other, not the state.

The cultural project that lies at the heart of the model minority image holds out the enticement of assimilation even as it writes difference. The project presents some differences as more manageable, palatable, and therefore more assimilable than others. The South Asian scholars Vijay Prashad (2000, 109–32) and Sharmila Rudrappa (2004, 132–46) have also noted the simultaneous operation of assimilation and ethno-racial difference. Multiculturalism, they argue, brings together these two processes because it specifies what whites would like to see and hear about minoritized, culturally different communities. Rudrappa powerfully argues that South Asians produce culturally authentic selves not to recapture their sense of belonging to their homelands but to belong to U.S. national culture as citizens. As we will see below, these modes of belonging are available to place takers more than they are to space makers who occupy quite different social locations and have different needs. Moreover, those South Asians who claim such "cultures of citizenship" (Rudrappa 2004) must silence "misfits"—other South Asians—even as they themselves are silenced when their public self-presentation departs from the fixed repertoires of multiculturalism.

The seven South Asian social change organizations provide a space where those who cannot be model minorities, or do not want to be, can speak and reconceptualize themselves as part of their ethnic cultures. These organizations open up a critical space in which they effectively unsettle the homogenizing model minority myth. They enable accounts of culture as contentious rather than static. To them, cultures are not hermetically sealed but are made porous through colonization, migration, and contemporary transnational flows. Consequently, they disrupt discussions of ethnic culture that turn on the binary oppositions of "traditional" and "Western."

In my earlier work I analyzed the reliance of immigrant communities on tradition through claims of authenticity as a dynamic and transnational culture-making process that is deeply gendered, heterosexual, and classed (Das Gupta 1997). Developing that analysis further, I show that immigrants respond to their multiple displacements not just through oppressive discourses on authenticity. Authenticity can also be employed to build alternative cultures. These cultures let survivors of domestic abuse, single mothers, divorced or single women, queers, domestic workers, and taxi drivers feel that they too are South Asians and that their stories are also part of the immigrant story.

"Homebreakers": Domestic Violence and Its Survivors

To do their antiviolence work, Manavi, Sakhi, and South Asian Women for Action (SAWA) had to unlearn and decode the dominant discourses on culture. In my first months as a member of SAWA, I embarked with others on this process of unlearning. At first when we introduced ourselves we referred to our families in normative two-parent terms, even though many of us came from single-parent, female-headed households. After all, we were in an ethnically marked space and did not want to relive the painful experience of being discredited. I remember the moment when one of our members broke our collective silence to talk about the shame she felt around her father's abandonment of her family after they immigrated. To support her and her sibling, her mother had to run a clothing store. This member's experience had no place in a community that upheld as the norm the two-parent, professional, and successful immigrant family. Her story unlocked our silenced experiences. We started to talk about how many of us felt ostracized at the slightest indication that we deviated from standards set by and for immigrant families. We carried our fear of being found out to all ethnic spaces. Only after we realized that in SAWA we were articulating a critique of these acts of disempowerment did we start naming ourselves as survivors of abuse and incest, members of female-headed households, lesbians, divorcees, single women not interested in marriage, and women who do not speak in their native tongue or relate to "traditions" their parents tried inculcating in them.

Thinking critically about families was the starting point for Manavi, Sakhi, and SAWA in decoding the conservative politics of authenticity. This process uncovered the emotional, economic, sexual, and physical abuse of women in their families. Abuse within the domestic space, the organizations were soon to learn, was not restricted to spousal violence. Women who worked for pay as domestics in South Asian homes reported forms of violence similar to marital abuse. In response to gendered violence within homes that were also workplaces for working-class women, Sakhi started to organize domestic workers. Such manifestations of violence reveal the range of disciplining mechanisms that construct domestic space. These mechanisms often function through discourses on culture that normalize hierarchical gender and class relations within the privatized space of home.

South Asians who raise the issue of violence against women within their communities immediately come up against the idea that it is inconsistent with a culturally moored upbringing. These communities do not deny that violence should be condemned—rather they deny that such practices actually exist within South Asian families. Warrier captured this viewpoint quintessentially when she sketched the stance toward domestic violence that Manavi first encountered in the community: "The general attitude was, 'We are a civilized, peace-loving people. A people with a five thousand-year civilization. . . . In our community these things don't happen.'" From the community's perspective, violence against women is barbaric. According to community members, cultural sanctions against it are so strong that it could not possibly occur under the communities' watch.

When activists confront their communities with the evidence of violence, it is the activists and the survivors of violence, not the batterers, who become the targets of their ire. They are portrayed as women who betrayed their culture and who no longer deserve community membership. A cofounder of Sakhi,

Anannya Bhattacharjee (1992), analyzes how place-taking organizations denounced Sakhi as a "homebreaker" at such public cultural events as the South Street Seaport Diwali festival. According to place takers, organizations like Sakhi, Manavi, and SAWA infiltrate their communities with feminist ideas that are foreign to South Asian values. They accuse women's organizations of creating dissension within the family and of interfering in issues that could otherwise be resolved internally. In their eyes, by making domestic violence an issue they encourage women to act like "Americans,"—that is, to leave their families. Ethnic communities, through such harmful views, revictimize women who take measures to ensure their safety (Bhattacharjee 1997b, 36; Luthra 1993).

Women who speak out against abuse are considered to be at once antifamily, antitradition, and antinational. The deep entanglement of family, tradition, and nation goes back to nineteenth-century anticolonial struggles in South Asia. Nationalists imagined restoring their country's freedom through imposing restrictive (Hindu) notions of chastity, domesticity, and self-erasure on women who were charged with maintaining the integrity of their family and the nation. Contemporary nationalisms in India, Pakistan, Bangladesh, and Sri Lanka continue to utilize women's sexuality and labor to circumscribe their role in the family in order to bolster their particular visions of the nation. These symbols are reworked in the diaspora, where, as Bhattacharjee has shown in the case of the immigrant Indian bourgeoisie, women's bodies become the "site for the preservation of India" (1992, 31). South Asian immigrant families and communities find women's compliance with patriarchal dictates indispensable to establishing their cultural identity and purity (Das Gupta 1997; Mani 1993). Immigrant families and communities ceaselessly demand culturally attuned child rearing, care work, and community service—all gendered forms of labor done for free—from women in the name of duty. In this way they re-create their nation away from home, which can be nested safely within U.S. national ideologies. Since place takers, as the self-appointed guardians of culture, ensure national integrity at the cost of women's bodily and psychological integrity, they quickly discredit anything that disrupts the idealized notion of woman as a sign of the family and nation.

Manavi, Sakhi, and SAWA publicly question whether a domestic unit in which violence takes place can be called a "family." According to them, what makes such a unit home and family is women's safety in that space. They openly challenge their communities' idealization of the family as a tight-knit unit where members take care of each other, especially when they are in trouble. Such characterizations obscure women's abuse by family members or employers in domestic spaces and prop up the model minority myth. Warrier speaks passionately about Manavi's survivor-centered approach to domestic violence. In rejecting antiviolence efforts that prioritize keeping families intact, she said: "When the community says you're breaking up families, I always ask, 'Is that a family to begin with?'" According to Manavi, it is violence—not the survivors and their advocates—that shatters homes. The organization thus redefines family by putting women and their safety at the center of its analysis. This position on women's basic right to be safe in their homes is shared by SAWA. Sakhi extends the analysis further by exposing how employers use the language of familial relations to exploit domestic workers.

The organizations offer counterdiscourses that enable survivors to reconceptualize themselves as culturally valid subjects. Activists in these organizations place the survivors' struggles within South Asian feminist traditions, thereby dismantling the opposition between feminism and a culturally grounded ethnic identity. They situate women's strength and resilience in their cultural reservoir of resistance, not in their self-sacrifice. They demand that their communities redefine their cultural beliefs so that women are valued apart from their duty to the family, community, and nation. They also reject as culturally unsuitable individualistic methods adopted by mainstream domestic violence shelters, including the Chicago-based Apna Ghar, the first battered women's shelter in the United States to employ and serve South Asians. These mainstream methods are compatible with place-taker demands of model minorityhood because they inculcate immigrant survivors with U.S. ideologies of individualism so they can become disciplined workers who then can quickly move toward self-reliance (see Rudrappa 2004 for Apna Ghar's definition of "good" clients). Instead, the space-making organizations rely on the culturally familiar concepts of relationality and interdependency to move South Asian survivors toward collective empowerment.

Even when certain immigrant communities in the United States come to terms with the existence of domestic violence and are provoked to do something about it, some idealizations of national/ethnic cultures accompany such acceptance. Caitrin Lynch (1994), who volunteered for Apna Ghar, shows how the shelter mobilizes community support by arguing that domestic violence does indeed go against traditional South Asian family values. In this formulation, both Apna Ghar and the Chicago Indian community attribute domestic violence to the pressures that families face as a result of immigration. According to the shelter, the stresses of immigrant life such as women being employed while men are underemployed lead to men's alcoholism, sexual promiscuity, and violence against women. These reasons deftly shift the responsibility for abuse from the "Indian social system" to its dissolution in the United States. As Lynch puts it, this displacement helps the community to make the case that "battered women in the diaspora serve as an example of why traditions need to be preserved" (433). Consequently, the local community does not perceive Apna Ghar to be anti-national or anti-traditional.

The transnational framework within which the three space-making organizations do their work counters the deliberate amnesia promoted by such discursive moves that displace domestic violence on male traumas of migration. Each of the reasons cited for abuse in immigrant families exists in South Asia. Women in lower castes and class have always worked outside the home. In the postcolonial periods, middle-class women in urban and semi-urban areas have entered paid employment in considerable numbers. In contemporary South Asia, male unemployment is very high in urban and economically depressed areas. Alcoholism and male sexual promiscuity are rampant problems that cut across class and, in the case of Hindus, caste. While urban middle-class Indian women have remained silent about these issues, working-class and rural Indian women have organized the strongest anti-liquor movements in South Asia. Manavi, Sakhi, and SAWA thread their knowledge of these developments in South Asia, including histories of women's resistance, into their antiviolence work. In that sense, like place takers they too authorize themselves to speak about "home"—South Asia. But they do so to remind their communities that certain groups of South Asian women have spoken up against gender violence and that resistance refutes the construction of a violence-free homeland.

Looking toward South Asia does not mean that the three organizations do not differentiate between violence against women in South Asia and the United States. They pay careful attention to the ways in which violence within immigrant families are shaped by their new geopolitical context. But in doing so they do not attribute domestic violence to the loss of tradition, a supposed consequence of migration. For Manavi, Sakhi, and SAWA, the situational dimension of domestic violence requires a careful examination of the legal, social, economic, and political structures that make immigrant women vulnerable to abuse (see chapter 3). Women are often noncitizens who are legally dependent on their husbands, ineligible for public assistance, and unfamiliar with the way things work in the United States. If they do not have legal immigration status, they are often held hostage by their husbands or employers. It is these structurally induced vulnerabilities, not cultural degeneration, that is the source of abuse. Thus, the three organizations hold individual abusers, ethnic communities, immigration authorities, legislators, and courts collectively accountable. When they attend to the specific challenges that South Asian survivors of violence face in the United States, they do so not to make their communities feel safe about naming domestic violence. On the contrary, they want women to feel safe in domestic spaces.

With the diversification of immigrant communities along national and class lines, another set of cultural arguments that elaborates the pathological nature of working-class and Muslim families has become available to the conservative sections. In her 2004 ethnography of Apna Ghar, Rudrappa documents the way in which certain shelter workers articulate deeply internalized chauvinistic views that promote the superiority of Hindu culture and the gentility of Hindu middle-class families by attributing domestic violence to lower-income and Muslim families (18–19). With the appearance of working-class and Muslim immigrants, the elite Hindu character of that mythical woman who guards her family and nation against contamination can be resuscitated. Domestic violence no longer has to be portrayed as a wholesale violation of South Asian cultures. Through the prism of Hindu nationalism, it can be displaced on "undesirable" South Asians and their cultural proclivity toward violence. The pitfalls of Apna Ghar's placatory stance show how risky it is to frame antiviolence work within place-taking discourses on culture.

Regardless of the particular strategies that South Asian communities use to displace domestic violence, it is characterized as aberrant and thereby erases the systematic nature of women's physical and emotional abuse within families. This representation enables these communities to manage their admission of domestic violence by seeing survivors as charity cases. The value placed on charity as an appropriate response to social problems preserves the status quo and can deeply distort the orientation toward social change in antiviolence organizations. For example, affluent South Asians sometimes use these organizations to recruit domestic workers (see Rudrappa 2004, 32, 58–60). They justify this practice as a way to help unfortunate battered women by providing them with employment and a roof over their heads. This form of charity keeps exploitative class relations intact by locking women into dead-end low-paying jobs. It compromises domestic workers' radical redefinition of "domestic violence" to encompass gender violence in paid housework and care work.

While the three space-making organizations provide alternative structures and cultural discourses, they claim that they too are a part of their communities. Over time, they have developed an arsenal of strategies to establish themselves within their communities, despite resistance. These communities have also changed their attitudes over the years. It is no longer unusual for local communities to extend material and symbolic support to them. But in extending this support, they often try to blunt the transformative thrust of these organizations by casting their activities as social work. Such negotiations between mainstream sections of the community and the space-making organizations have served to redefine community, which is best understood as incorporating a range of actors who have interests that are not easily reconcilable.

In discussing the relationship between Manavi and the New Jersey South Asian community as it has developed over time, Warrier says: "Because we never took money from anybody else [until 1996], it is also the community who supported us because they are the ones who were giving [pause] grudgingly because some of us bulldozed them into giving the fifteen dollars a year [the membership fee]." Recalling Manavi's relationship with the community in its earliest days, Warrier observed with amusement: "In the early stages we had a very tenuous relationship. As you know, Manavi means primal woman. We used to be called Danavi [female demon/s]." Yet, five years after its birth, an article in Manavi's newsletter reported that the organization had been able to "rise from a state of complete anonymity to one of grudging recognition" (Manavi 1990, 1). The same report, however, notes that the community continued to trivialize Manavi's work as well as question its authenticity and make fun of its members. Writing a few years later, another founder-member, Shamita Das Dasgupta, notes a more accepting, if not supportive, community: "I suppose the community has also learnt that we will not go away. To a certain degree, our tenacious existence has proved to the community that much of the model minority image is a myth" (Dasgupta and Das Dasgupta 1993, 127). By 1997, when I interviewed Manavi members, they talked about the community's gradual recognition of Manavi as a much-needed resource.

The two other feminist groups have had a more oppositional relationship to the mainstream in their communities. Through marches and demonstrations, Sakhi publicly confronted New York City's South Asian communities with the realities of domestic violence and abuse of domestic workers. At the same time, the group raised money within these communities without compromising its feminist perspective. Unlike the Apna Ghar's charity shows that conjured away the ugly realities of domestic violence for its community audience (Rudrappa 2004, 31–32), Sakhi staged film festivals featuring South Asian women directors and used the venues to raise consciousness about domestic violence. By 1997, it could set up a table without controversy at the South Street Seaport Diwali festival, which had previously excluded it. Sakhi has also been able to conduct workshops on domestic violence in a few places of worship, both Hindu and Muslim. It now marches in the city's India and Pakistan Day parades. But parade organizers, in granting Sakhi the permission to march, have tried to dilute its mission by presenting it as a service provider (P. Shah 1997). Despite being critical of the community's methods to misrepresent their work, Sakhi members deem these advances as significant breakthroughs (see also Abraham 2000; Bhattacharjee 1992; P. Shah 1997).

The strongest allies of SAWA in the South Asian communities around Boston traditionally have been older women who understood the extent of women's abuse in their families and the urgency of addressing the problem. For years these women had served in their personal capacities to support abused women in their communities, and in 1996 many of them joined to establish a group, which they called Saheli, to better serve suburban survivors. Like Manavi and Sakhi, SAWA also felt hijacked when drawn into events organized by mainstream groups that redefined it as an organization that "helped" women. These experiences led SAWA to restrict its interactions to the progressive sections of Boston's South Asian community.

The repertoire that mainstream South Asian immigrants create and draw upon to deny or manage domestic violence puts culture in the service of nation building at the expense of women's safety. When survivors of domestic violence and their advocates depart from the script of obedient and dutiful women or abject women to be rescued or victims of violent Muslim and working-class men, they lose their membership to community, culture, and nation, thereby becoming alien to their mainstream compatriots. Antiviolence advocates intervene in the diasporic constructions of authenticity by displaying *their* cultural knowledge to remind their communities of the forms taken by domestic violence in their homelands as well as the homeland-based struggles against it. They draw on the rich tradition of secularism in South Asia to intervene in religious nationalism.

"A White Disease": Homoerotics and Queerphobia

The South Asian immigrant mainstream's discourse on sexuality rests on a cultural argument that labels homosexuality as a Western phenomenon. According to this discourse, immigrants learn to be homosexual after coming to the West where they are exposed to all kinds of "sexual promiscuities." The erasure of indigenous traditions of same-sex erotic relationships accompanies a cultural project that utilizes heterosexuality to rewrite the difference between "Western" and "South Asian" in irreducible terms. The historian Nayan Shah accurately describes this project when he says: "South Asian heterosexists have often denied the authenticity of queer-identified South Asians by labeling homosexual relationships a 'white disease,' insinuating that our presence in the U.S. or Britain has 'contaminated our minds and desires.' . . . They perceive queer identities as a threat to the cultural integrity of South Asian immigrants" (1993, 119). Shah pinpoints how the conservative politics of authenticity defines itself against what it names "Western." Homosexuality is not only Western and non-indigenous but also is racialized as "white." Thus, to identify as gay, lesbian, bisexual, transgender, or queer is a sure sign of assimilation into a dominant white society and an abandonment of one's cultural roots. Within this framework, one cannot be South Asian and queer, thereby making the term South Asian queers an oxymoron. In this negation, immigrants show no awareness that the normative status of heterosexuality is itself a "Western" conception (119).

Members of the New York City–based South Asian Lesbian and Gay Association (SALGA) and the Boston-based Massachusetts Area South Asian Lambda Association (MASALA) link their efforts to create or find a South Asian queer space to their desire to escape from the conventional heternormative world of their parents and peers. The MASALA member Kavita Goyal recalled her inability to relate to her South Asian friends in college who were busy chasing what she called the American dream. As she noted, "I wasn't into the yuppie thing that most of my South Asian friends in college were into: be professionals, achieve high economic status, have a family, get married, raise kids. . . . Social injustices just did not seem important to the people I knew."[4] Her friends' aspirations reveal the normalization of the stable procreative endogamous family in the community's definition of achievement. Such a family perpetuates homeland culture while also supplying workers who adjust well to U.S. cultures of capitalism, coupling the process of cultural preservation and assimilation. In this context, Goyal's assertion of a queer subjectivity and her passion for social justice profoundly threaten the cultural work that goes into representing South Asian success and ensuring that it is founded on heterosexuality.

The same national project that requires chaste and domesticated women to signal cultural purity in the diaspora also banishes queerness outside national borders. The body politic of diasporic nationalisms outlaws queer sexualities through cultural discourses about authenticity. Female queer sexuality, articulated by women like Goyal, becomes particularly troublesome because, as the literary critic and queer theorist Gayatri Gopinath (2005, 15–20) has pointed out, it is rendered "impossible" in the heterosexualized configuration of woman, family, tradition, and nation. While the disciplining discourses on "domestic violence" chain women's bodies and (unquestionable) heterosexuality to the nation, those about queer sexuality, especially female homoerotics, expel these bodies from the cultural borders of the nation (see also Gopinath 2005, 18–19). Diasporic communities battle queers with xenophobic fervor as they would foreign enemies. The consignment of SALGA to the borders of Manhattan's India Day Parade between 1992 and 1999; and more recently the Pakistan Day Parade, symbolizes this process of border patrolling (see chapter 5). The exclusions resemble the consolidation of Hindu nationalism in India through "xenophobic queerphobia" defined as "a particular form of queerphobia that justifies itself by constructing the self-identified Indian queer as originating outside the self-same nation" (Bacchetta 1999, 143). Just as evocations of foreign enemies whip up patriotism, so does place-taking politics in the diaspora use queer bodies to construct a genuine cultural identity in the diaspora.

Unlike domestic violence, which place takers rhetorically denounce, homophobia is not considered a social ill. It is essential for ethno-national integrity. The moralistic backlash in the United States against gay and lesbians in the last two decades further justifies the conservative sections' tenacious and public disavowal of South Asian queers. The two queer organizations in this study unequivocally express dissident sexual identities that they place within, not outside, South Asian cultures. Since both have consciously stayed away from service provision, their work is less amenable to depoliticizing reinterpretations. In short, queers and queerness become unmanageable for place-taking politics.

National integrity and cultural authenticity in the diasporic communities come at the cost of fragmenting queer subjectivities. Within ethnic spaces South Asian queers cannot maintain the integrity of their religious, cultural, national, and sexual identities. The MASALA founder-member Imtiyaz Hussein speaks eloquently about his efforts since he was a teenager to bring together his "distinct lives" by trying to integrate his gay identity with his faith as an Ismaili of Indian origin who was raised in a large, close-knit, expatriate Tanzanian community in Toronto. On moving out of this community that he took for granted and found stifling at times, he started to realize how deeply his identity had been shaped by his cultural and religious upbringing. In founding MASALA in Boston, he expressed the hope that, "For myself, I can begin to know my Indianness again . . . maybe meet other gay Muslims."[5] A SALGA founder-member, expressing the painful fracturing that he experienced in ethnic spaces, said, "When we go to South Asian events we can't take our gay selves" because the community defines cultural identity and homosexuality in mutually exclusive ways.[6]

As immigrants living in a Eurocentric society, queer South Asians need familiar contexts where they can live their cultures without having to explain, translate, hide, or apologize for them. But in mainstream South Asian spaces they have to trade the erasure of their sexual identities for that sense of ease and community. As the conservative discourses on authenticity would have it, queer South Asians have already abandoned their culture to become whitewashed. Why would they need any connection to their ethnicities? Contrary to this racialized narrative, South Asian queers experience racism and cultural imperialism in white-dominated LGBT spaces. They are simultaneously exoticized and Westernized. In these spaces, their bodies are valued for their difference, but their "sexual liberation" is read as a sign of Westernization and a rejection of their "repressive" homeland culture. Once again, South Asian queers feel the pressure to split off their sexual and cultural identities.

To contest these multiple fractures and delegitimations, South Asian queers create cultures that are transnational in scope. Creating and redefining culture is a core part of diasporic queer politics that traverses the United States, Britain, and Canada through a host of productions in different media (Cvetkovich 2003, 132–55; Gopinath 2005). The visibility of queer activists–cultural workers like Pratibha Parmar (United Kingdom), Urvashi Vaid (United States), Shyam Selvadurai (Canada), and Shani Mootoo (Canada) have infused the public domain with complex expressions of queer migration integral to which are lesser-told stories of the legacies of colonial indenture for South Asians in Africa and the Caribbean, of British and U.S. racism, and of war-torn South Asia. In conversation, SALGA and MASALA members mentioned the inspiration they derived from these public figures whom they invited to their organizations or heard at alternative South Asian cultural festivals. The new modes of cultural belonging remember queer bodies, desires, and subjectivities splintered by the intersecting forces of heterosexism, racism, imperialism, and cultural chauvinism. In doing so, these cultural spaces and cultural forms sever the knot that ties heterosexuality to cultural reproduction. They demonstrate that displacements resulting from migration do not have to be managed through homophobic discourses of authenticity.

Counterdiscourses of authenticity have also entailed excavating South Asian history to recuperate alterior sexualities. Queer South Asians in South Asia and the diaspora share this project. Such counterclaims in the diaspora, as explained by the SALGA member Javid Syed, refuted the cultural casting of homosexuality as alien and the justification of homophobia as a natural response to cultural violations. This rewriting of community memory, he pointed out, is also accompanied by an erasure of social movements in South Asia around sexual autonomy. While reflecting on these transnational contests over culture, he said: "There is another culture that has not been talked about a lot; a culture that was more pluralistic for sexual minorities, that was more egalitarian, and that was not so heterosexist and was not invested in this form of nation-building. This [erasure] is really a strategy for calling certain things as culture. It [the calling] supports certain power structures."[7] To recover homoeroticism in South Asian history makes it part of South Asian culture, which then can be formulated as polymorphous. Evidence of indigenous forms of homoeroticism would make it difficult to deploy queerphobic xenophobia to construct national identity at home or abroad.

Such alternative narratives of authenticity are controversial within the U.S. South Asian queer community because they too are seen as relying on a mythic past and a homogenous Indian culture that stands in for South Asia. Nayan Shah (1993, 120–23) cautions against the projection of modern sexual categories into the past. Such an exercise, he warns, takes away from a historically situated and culturally specific analysis of multiple operations of erotics, which might have held different meanings and valences at different times in different places in South Asia. Also, the recovery of a "gay and lesbian" history, given the material archived, could reproduce elite histories paralleling mainstream efforts at recreating a high-Hindu past. Attention to historical specificity has actually generated nuanced accounts of precolonial discourses on same-sex sexuality on the subcontinent not only in the classical languages of Sanskrit and Urdu but also in vernaculars. In the process, scholars have also traced the normalization of heterosexuality in colonial times (see Vanita 2002).

In writing about the dangers of organizations like SALGA reinforcing Hindu nationalism and Indian hegemony in the acts of recuperation, the feminist queer theorist Jasbir Puar shows that they invoke India (rather than South Asia or the diaspora) and Hindu texts, motifs, deities, and temples. These invocations achieve dangerous "intersections of nationalism and communalism, resulting in an unfragmented and uncontested version of Hindu India" (1998, 406). Indeed, Puar's critique hits home when one reads an action alert dispatched on the Internet on 12 August 1999 to announce SALGA's protest against its exclusion from the India Day Parade. In listing one of the goals of the protest, the dispatch stated that SALGA wanted "to demonstrate and celebrate the diverse range of sexualities that has been part of our tradition in South Asia. From the Babar Nama (Book of Moghul King Babar) to the Temples of Khajuraho, there have been numerous depictions of men loving men and women loving women, as well as gods and humans that have aspects of both genders—hijras and ardhanarishwara (transgendered people)" (South Asian Citizens Web 1999). The Hindu imagery, despite being attenuated by references to India's Muslim heritage, is hard to miss.

But these problematic Hindu references coexist with SALGA's recognition of events like the India Day Parade as potent sites at which the Indian community's place-taking leadership deploys a Hindu nation. What SALGA brings to such events is its understanding of a queerphobic Hindu nationalism in the diaspora that is missing in the analyses offered by its progressive South Asian allies. Its allies do not clearly grasp the dependence of nationalism on queer bodies and focus more on the harnessing of heterosexuality. SALGA's critique, developed in its years of protest, allowed it to ally itself with the Delhi-based Campaign for Lesbian Rights to mobilize against the Hindu nationalist backlash in late 1998 against Deepa Mehta's feature film *Fire* about the erotic relationship between two Indian sisters-in-law. Thus, SALGA's turn to a queer South Asia cannot be easily written off as another version of religious nationalism.

Furthermore, the transnational construction of South Asian queer culture, compared to nationalist versions of culture, consciously opens itself up to distinct histories of colonization, decolonization, and racialization in East Africa, the Caribbean, Canada, and Britain. When singular presentations of culture that privilege India surface in queer retellings (as they sometimes do in SALGA in ways that I describe in chapter 5), they collide with these other trajectories. Since the emphasis of culture making in queer spaces is not on purity and fixity, the possibility of reproducing Indian nationalism is continuously destabilized. Whereas diasporic subjects with longer histories of migration to the Caribbean, Africa, Britain, and Canada are dismissed by place-taking post-1965 South Asian immigrants to the United States as culturally adulterated, they gain legitimacy in South Asian queer spaces like SALGA and MASALA. These organizations are committed to considering them even when such considerations are initially difficult and halting. This configuration of transnational culture departs from conservative renditions in that it authenticates culturally situated queer subjectivities without establishing monolithic traditions or a single origin that is in danger of being lost.

Compared with the case of women's organizations, the homophobic community-building strategies of place takers make SALGA and MASALA less eager to claim membership in the larger South Asian communities. While SALGA and MASALA see outreach in the mainstream sections of their communities as crucial in fighting homophobia, they have been cautious. When they do participate in events organized by mainstream sections, they concentrate on reaching out to queer South Asians who have had to check their sexuality at the door.

Otherwise, they ally themselves with local South Asian women's, youth, labor, and anti-racist organizations. In addition, SALGA works within New York's large Indo-Caribbean community, which is marginal to the city's South Asian community.

The trauma of moral and sexual policing in the name of culture in South Asian conservative spaces explains SALGA and MASALA's cautious approach. The MASALA member Goyal felt that the rift between mainstream sections and South Asian queers was so deep that it would take a generation to heal. As she noted, "I think I cut off myself from a lot of South Asian things, people, events and I see very good reason for that. I think we [MASALA] can go back in . . . but it might not happen in our generation. We have a lot of bitterness and a lot of anger toward that structure, so we may not be the ones to do it." Another MASALA member, Anushka Fernandopulle, felt that any strategy to play a "bigger part" in Boston's South Asian community would have to be crafted in the context of MASALA's primary goal to provide a safe space for its members. As a trained public speaker who visited schools, offices, and various organizations to speak about homosexuality, Fernandopulle laughed at the thought of addressing a South Asian audience: "To speak about being gay in front of South Asians? Forget it!"[8] For her, the work of undoing heterosexism and homophobia through sharing very personal narratives was unthinkable in a mainstream South Asian context because much of the pain in such testimonies had been inflicted in families and other ethnic institutions. Instead, members have tried other tactics such as wearing their MASALA T-shirts to the Boston area's South Asian events to attract those looking for a queer space.

The engagement of SALGA with New York's South Asian community has taken the very public form of protesting its exclusion from the India Day and Pakistan Day parades. Though members understood the symbolic value of the yearly protests, they also questioned whether the organization was really interested in marching in a nationalistic and homophobic parade. The protests that have been staged, however, have brought the organization to the ethnic media's attention. The SALGA member Tim Baran pointed out that *India Abroad's* unsolicited coverage of the organization before the 1997 protest signaled a new legitimacy within the community.

Mainstream sections have been not been successful in domesticating the sexual identity–based politics of the queer organizations. Place takers continue to produce discourses of sexual deviance that reduce a plethora of genealogies to a univocal culture. The counterdiscourses of SALGA and MASALA expose the work that queer bodies are made to do in the cultural coding of sexual deviance. Queer bodies become powerful transnational sites of meaning-making to consolidate distinct but interrelated projects: religious nationalism in South Asia and the diaspora and the myth of immigrant success in the diaspora. A transnational queer culture provides creative ways for queer South Asians to reconceptualize themselves and their "community." By doing so, they redefine South Asian culture and society.

Failing to Make It:
Service Workers and Small Entrepreneurs

The initial hardship, struggle, and eventual success reflected in upward social and economic mobility are key motifs that lend authenticity to the immigrant story. The sociologists Richard Alba (1990) and Nazli Kibria (1997) have noted the power that this story line holds for immigrants. When South Asian professionals sit in the back of cabs driven by compatriots, an awkward silence hangs between those who ride and those who drive. How does the professional negotiate the obvious and unavoidable difference in class status, especially in New York where 60 percent of the taxi industry is composed of South Asian drivers? Does the taxi driver fall all over himself to clarify that he is an owner-driver, and therefore is at least as well-to-do as his passenger? If he is a lease driver, living from lease to lease, does he invoke the class status he enjoyed back home and fervently underline that this existence is temporary? Class difference among South Asians becomes particularly troubling in the immigrant context. The immigrant story is painfully disrupted as the narrative veers away from success and advancement and as the cast of characters changes. The fear and the shame that sit between passenger and driver revolve around the anxiety that working-class immigrants "destroy" the communities' "cherished professional image" (Varadarajan 1998).

A strong belief in meritocracy, a fair and open system, and individual endeavor—potent U.S. mythologies—feeds the South Asian mainstream's politics of authenticity to discredit working-class South Asians. Such a discourse departs in interesting ways from those who discipline unruly women and unruly sexualities. The politics of authenticity, when deployed to exclude and vilify working-class South Asians, centers on the story of immigrant success. Those who lapse can lay no claim to being authentic immigrants. They are imposters and "spoilers" (Varadarajan 1998) who are ill-qualified to enter the labor market as skilled workers. The appearance in the 1980s of working-class South Asian immigrants has been linked both by scholars (Helweg and Helweg 1990, 69, 149 fn 4; Khandelwal 1995, 179; Mogelonsky 1995; Sheth 1995) and by South Asian immigrants themselves (see Lessinger 1995, 14, for views of affluent immigrants) to the shift to family reunification–based migration. They assume that those who immigrate on the basis of the family reunification are less qualified than those admitted under merit-based occupational preferences.

South Asian professionals play into the cultural racism inherent in model minority discourses when they attribute their success to the supposed value that South Asian cultures place on education, discipline, and respect for authority and hierarchy. This reliance on cultural traits resembles the narratives of second-generation Chinese and Korean immigrants in the work of the sociologist Nazli Kibria (1997). Kibria shows how the success story, which resonates with the model minority image, is vitally linked with her participants' understanding of Confucian values. In the case of affluent South Asians, the cultural narrative extolling ethnic values combines inventively with "American" cultural idioms that use the language of individualism and personal merit.

When barriers to upward class mobility among South Asians have been noted, scholars have discussed them in the context of the glass ceiling (Barringer, Gardner, and Levin 1995; Dutta 1982; Fernandez 1998; Sheth 1995; Woo 2000). While the glass ceiling continues to be a severe and often invisible problem, it pertains to professional fields. Scholars have remarked on the presence of South Asians in the secondary labor market, but the analysis has been less systemic than that of the glass ceiling. The shift to family reunification, with the resultant decline in the quality of immigrants, has been the standard explanation, when, in fact, family reunification has been a key labor recruitment strategy since the 1980s (Reddy 2003).

Secondary labor market workers appear even in studies that tell the Asian Indian success story (Helweg and Helweg 1990; G. Alexander 1997). Unemployed Indians, hot dog vendors, janitors, clerk-typists, messengers, dishwashers, and maids working for successful Indian immigrants populate these accounts. The nod to a growing split "between the very rich and the very poor, in spite of the appearance of general prosperity indicated by the statistics" (Helweg and Helweg 1990, 191) among Asian Indians does not alter the success story. As these working-class men and women have become difficult to ignore, mainstream South Asians, along with a group of scholars, have come to characterize them as "failures"—that is, incompetent South Asians who did not "make it."

Rather than looking for explanations in factors such as merit and skill, the South Asian presence in the secondary labor market needs to be understood as a product of the labor market's segmentation into primary and secondary sectors (Bonacich 1972). The secondary market thrives on the labor of immigrant and disadvantaged minorities, and it is characterized by poor pay, poor job security, minimum benefits or none at all, hazardous working conditions, and minimal opportunities for promotion (Cabezas and Kawaguchi 1988; Min 1995). The primary labor market favors those who are native-born and who traditionally have held better-paid and more secure positions. Highly restricted mobility between the two markets maintains the segmentation (Cabeza and Kawaguchi 1988, 155–56). South Asians can be found in both markets, but scholarly and community attention to professionals spotlights the primary labor market.

By the 1980s, South Asian faces became common at newsstands, taxi stands, and roadside food stands in New York City. Indian restaurants have always been staffed with South Asian workers, both men and women. South Asian ownership of motels and franchises like 7-Eleven has become a stereotype. Away from these public spaces, South Asian domestic workers, all women, carry on the reproductive work of caretaking, which frees up their employers to become productive members of the U.S. workforce. These domestic workers manage the daily running of the household and take care of children and the elderly in affluent South Asian homes. Organizing South Asian domestic workers began as an antiviolence project of Sakhi and evolved into Workers Awaaz and Andolan, which define domestic space as a gendered workplace. In making the connection between immigrant success and the exploitation of women's labor, an organizer of Workers Awaaz in New York City observed: "I don't think that these people could have succeeded without the cheap labor they hire at home. Those who are established here—got a new house, established themselves maybe as doctors—are usually able to pay for the house and all that by paying people like domestic workers so little. I don't think these people could have succeeded in their jobs outside if they didn't hire anyone to do the work cheaply at home" (Samar Collective 1994, 14–15).

South Asian immigrants in low-paid service, agricultural, or industrial sectors work twelve to fourteen hours a day, six to seven days a week. Even though these immigrants are among the most hardworking—a powerful trope in the success story—they fall out of it because, most often, they do not make minimum wage. They find upward mobility elusive. Intimidation in the hands of employers who often use the workers' immigration status to exploit them makes escaping these work situations difficult. While the educational qualifications and work experience of these working-class South Asians range widely, many get trapped in the secondary sector because they cannot apply for jobs in the primary labor market without retraining to acquire U.S. certifications to replace their devalued South Asian degrees. Retraining requires money that many of these immigrants—working the jobs they do—cannot save. Furthermore, retraining does not guarantee employment because of anti-immigrant hiring procedures in the primary labor market (see chapter 3).

Another case involves those who are not paid for their work. Small businesses, which depend for their viability on the unpaid labor of relatives, increasingly have offered South Asians avenues for self-employment. Many of these businesses, romanticized as mom-and-pop stores in U.S. lore, are set up by salaried male professionals—doctors or middle-level executives—who continue to hold their salaried jobs (Lessinger 1990, 80). Expropriating the labor of family members, particularly wives, becomes necessary for the day-to-day functioning of the business. Historically for Asian Americans self-employment has been a way to cope with the racial segregation and stratification of the labor market (Espiritu 1997, 77–84; Kwong 1997, 139–59). As the anthropologist Sylvia Yanagisako (1995, 289–90) points out in the case of Japanese Americans, a family-business economy becomes possible once women's labor is available. Like other immigrant women, those from South Asia are expected to run the family business as part of their spousal duties along with cooking, cleaning, and child rearing. As a result, these women work extremely long hours constantly negotiating the fluid boundaries between work and home (Dhaliwal 1995). Ethnic businesses—which capture the South Asian mainstream's endorsement for embodying the entrepreneurial immigrant spirit—are built on the backbreaking yet invisible labor of these women, who because of the overlap between home and work suffer extreme isolation. Rarely do they get the chance to retrain for another job or improve their language skills. Once again, gender subordination is harnessed to the story of immigrant success, which in turn forms the bedrock of the model minority myth.

The New York Taxi Workers Alliance (NYTWA) and Andolan—labor organizations founded by South Asians—assert a visible and well-organized working-class presence. Both organizations fight for economic justice for the working poor, even though neither domestic workers nor taxi drivers, who currently are considered independent contractors rather than wage earners, fall within the types of labor that are allowed to unionize.[9] As first-generation immigrants, who in their lifetime witnessed and sometimes participated in antipoverty, trade union, and democratization movements in South Asia, they bring the critiques of state practices and the militancy of those struggles to their immediate political concerns (see chapter 6).

In their campaigns both organizations analyze the systemic forces that need to be transformed in order to end their exploitation. Drivers and domestic workers trace the institutional patterns of exploitation through personal accounts of their everyday material reality. These fine-grained stories, shared at their organizations' meetings as well as at public hearings, authenticate their experiences as working-class people. When domestic workers demonstrate in front of the homes of abusive employers, they publicly expose the gendered, class, and sexual oppression on which the model minority myth is built. When the NYTWA claims a public presence for a South Asian majority workforce or contests the public perception of racist South Asian drivers who refuse to give rides to black New Yorkers (see chapter 6), it reorganizes racial and class terms of place-taking discourses. In these ways, domestic workers and taxi drivers reveal the forces that trap them into extremely poorly paid and hazardous jobs. They rewrite the hegemonic story of success and failure to foreground the structural location of the workers.

Conclusion

The South Asian mainstream, the state, and the space-making organizations make multiple calls on culture in constructing what is authentic. The South Asian mainstream calls upon culture to preserve its class and heteropatriarchal privilege. The state executes its project of racing, gendering, and sexualizing immigrant bodies through the cultural hegemony of the "American dream" which feeds the model minority image so dear to the South Asian mainstream. The space makers ask who claims culture and to what effect, thereby insisting on the intersection of culture with politics. In resignifying culture and retelling history, they too lay new claims on authenticity.

These contestations have turned culture into a privileged site of struggle. Questions of identity and community are thus part of the space makers' political agenda. Whereas the cultural work of mainstream South Asians supported by the state has centered on excluding survivors of domestic violence, queers, and working-class folk from regional, national, religious, and dominant diasporic definitions of identity, the work of space makers has involved decentering those definitions of identity and culture. The Asian American literary critic Lisa Lowe identifies culture as a "material site of struggle" for Asian American immigrants because their experience of the failures and inconsistencies of the liberal democratic project "erupts in culture" (1996, 22). South Asians seeking social change disrupt the state-endorsed place-taking politics within their own communities. The construction of South Asian identities and spaces becomes part of alternative cultural projects that enable us to center marginalized immigrants as key subjects whose narratives rewrite the immigrant story to expose the contradictory workings of the liberal state.

CHAPTER 3

Law and Oppression

Along with immigrant discourses on cultural authenticity and success, the state through its laws creates and shapes the realities of South Asian domestic violence survivors, lesbians and gay men, and low-wage workers. Just as culture operates in not readily visible ways to normalize patriarchy, heterosexism, and elitism, so the traces of law in structuring immigrant lives are difficult to detect because law creates the very realities it reviles and punishes. The state increases the vulnerability to exploitation of immigrant workers, survivors of domestic violence, and queers through legislating various forms of dependency. It criminalizes them when they cannot meet the conditions required for legal immigration status.

The immigration law's codification of immigrant bodies works with labor laws and laws that govern domestic violence, welfare, and marriage to drive underground the realities of oppression that they create. The basic premise that immigrants do not belong to the national community (R. Chang 1997; Lowe 1996) underlies the surveillance of their legal status and rights. While each form of oppression arises out of legally enforced disentitlement, it remains unspeakable within the discursive construction of South Asians as model minorities.

Critiques of liberal law by critical legal scholars, critical race theorists, and feminists have shown that law has not protected or served people of color, women, and the poor. Asian American scholars like Lisa Lowe (1996), Yen Espiritu (1997), Robert Chang (1999), and Erika Lee (2003a) have laid bare a legislative history of nativism and exclusion that has shaped gender, class, and racial formation in Asian American communities. Looking at the experiences of South Asian immigrants through the lens of the post-1965 laws reveals how these legislative measures increase women's vulnerability to spousal violence; coerce gays and lesbians to submit to the will of a heterosexist state; and expose workers in low-paid service sectors to extreme exploitation. These vulnerabilities are interrelated because assumptions about gender relations, sexuality, and class shape the laws that govern these immigrants (see also Volpp 2003). Thus the South Asian women's, queer, and labor organizations are equally concerned with state restrictions on employing immigrants. They all understand the impact of laws that treat immigrants as potential public charges and how this treatment penalizes those affected by unemployment, disability, illness, and violence at home or in the workplace. Similarly, the women's and queer organizations together mount a trenchant critique of the institutionalization of marriage and dependency through immigration laws.

The Subordination of Women and Domestic Violence

When a South Asian survivor of marital violence speaks of abuse, the advocates of the survivors of domestic violence along with law enforcement agents and the courts often see the abuse as a product of the "traditional" place of men in the survivor's society of origin. They assure her that domestic violence is punishable by law in the United States and that she does not have to accept the tolerance of such abuse in her culture.[1] In this argument, U.S. law stands as the unwavering guardian of individual rights.

However, when we examine another set of laws—those pertaining to immigration—it becomes clear that the state in fact strengthens patriarchy by legislating an immigrating spouse's dependence on her husband's status as citizen or permanent resident for her own legal status. The subordination of women in their families is not just the result of individual patriarchs but also of a patriarchal state that privileges marriage and produces, in this case through immigration laws, norms that govern that arrangement. Manavi, Sakhi, and South Asian Women for Action articulate this dual face of patriarchy. They move beyond the battleground within families and communities to hold the state equally accountable for the ways in which it impairs immigrant women's right to safety.

Patterns of post-1965 immigration from South Asia show that most women immigrate to the United States as dependent wives (Abraham 2000).[2] While immigration reforms initiated in the 1930s and put in place in 1952 corrected the gender bias in sponsorship by allowing both women and men to petition for their spouses, these laws did not have a leveling effect on South Asian spousal sponsorship (Abraham 2000, 52–53; Bhattacharjee 1997a, 314). Immigration patterns skew further in favor of men the gender relations in an already patriarchal institution—the heterosexual family—because the law requires that the immigrating wives get their legal status through their husbands.[3]

Under the family unification preferences set up in 1965, a woman who enters the United States on the basis of her marriage is defined as a beneficiary of her husband's immigration status. She does not exist in law as an autonomous person. Immigration law deprives her of her agency because she cannot, under ordinary circumstances, petition the INS for immigration status on behalf of herself. This provision has been correctly identified by the sociologist Margaret Abraham (2000, 50–51) as enacting the doctrine of coverture through which the husband is granted legal power over his wife and children. State-legislated dependence of immigrating women on their husbands' legal and economic status as well as state scrutiny of these marriages is not new. We find continuities in immigration officials' interrogation and surveillance of Asian women who entered the United States in the late nineteenth century and the first half of the twentieth century (Gee 2003; Lee 2003b; Luibhéid 2002; Young 2003). In another configuration of concerns over proper familial relations, sexuality, and class, those exclusion-era screenings enforced white middle-class notions of respectability, morality, and the racial inferiority in order to control family formation among these immigrants.

The 1965 Immigration and Nationality Act amendments, the 1986 Immigration Marriage Fraud Amendments (IMFA), the 1990 waivers for battered spouses, the 1994 Violence against Women Act (VAWA), and the 1996 Illegal Immigration Reform and Immigrant Responsibility Act (IIRIRA) have all, in different ways, placed onerous burdens on all South Asian women immigrating to join their husbands. The imbalance in power, structured by law into immigrant marriages, becomes exceedingly dangerous for women with abusive husbands who use the provisions of U.S. immigration law as another instrument of terror. An examination of the force of law in these women's lives reveals how U.S. legal requirements, far from protecting immigrant women from abuse, interlock with so-called traditional relations to subordinate women. Women's bodies and psyches bear the marks of state and spousal violence because of what the critical legal scholar Kimberlé Crenshaw (1995, 359) has called "double subordination" in her discussion of marriage fraud provisions of immigration law.

In 1986, the Immigration Marriage Fraud Amendments (IMFA) protracted the period of dependency by making the sponsored spouse's residency conditional for two years. Under the IMFA, which is still in effect, immigrant spouses can no longer become permanent residents immediately. Instead, they are granted conditional residence for two years after which the couple jointly repetitions the INS. The INS then reassesses whether the marriage was contracted in "good faith," which means ascertaining that the sponsored partner did not get married in order to immigrate to the United States. During the two-year period of conditional residency, the sponsored spouse has no way of changing that immigration status to one that is permanent under ordinary circumstances.

The two-year waiting period was supposed to curb what legislators sponsoring the bill claimed to be the rampant misuse of marriage as an avenue to get immigration status—that is, a green card. In fact, the amendment not only reinforced the power of sponsoring men over their immigrant spouses but also privileged the rights of U.S. citizens over the rights of immigrants. The IMFA, in determining who was most vulnerable to such fraudulent marriages, sets up a hierarchy in which nonresident immigrant women's right to protection is outweighed by the rights of women who are U.S. citizens. The U.S. Civil Rights Commission (1992, 178 n.153) draws on the Immigrant Women's Task Force report to the National Lawyers' Guild to discuss how the media campaign around fraudulent marriages exaggerated the numbers and stirred up public panic and xenophobia over foreigners exploiting citizens for legal status. For immigrant women, who could be and indeed are in abusive marriages, the two-year waiting period meant that they were locked into the abuse for at least two years if they wanted to remain legally in the United States.[4] This reveals the gender bias in the law in two ways. First, the predicament of immigrant women who find themselves in these situations disappears in the concern over saving citizen women (racialized white in the public imagination) from exploitative immigrant men. Second, the state's concern for citizen women remains patriarchal at its core because it treats them only as victims.

In an immigrant context, the disappearance of immigrant women as subjects who also need to protect their rights to safety parallels the historical development of imperialism, which privileged Western women's interests over colonized women. The IMFA protects citizen women by imperiling other women; that is, immigrant women. If they are from the global South, they are overwhelmingly racialized as women of color on their entry into the United States. Both categories of women—U.S. citizens and immigrants—should have the right to protect themselves from abuse, whether it is abuse from a sponsored partner who abandons a marriage after his immigration needs are met, or whether it is physical, sexual, and psychological abuse in the hands of a sponsoring husband. Yet, noncitizen immigrant women risk losing their right to work, their public support, and their residency if they resist their mistreatment during the conditional period.

Conditional residency allows an abusive husband to control his sponsored spouse in several ways. The paperwork for conditional and, later, permanent residency can be filed only with the husband's cooperation. To induce fear and anxiety, abusers often withhold from their partners all information about the petition process. Like employers of domestic workers, husbands hide or destroy their wives' immigration papers and their passports. As a result of the power that the state puts in her husband's hands, a battered immigrant woman can lose legal status in the following ways. Her husband may refuse to petition the INS in time to adjust her status from a conditional resident to a permanent one—which, according to South Asian women's organizations and the U.S. Commission on Civil Rights (1992), is a common strategy of abuse. Many times, a husband who is responsible for the woman's loss of legal status in this way may threaten to report her to the INS and in some cases even does so. Alternatively, he may petition on time but declare during the review process that the marriage was fraudulent, in which case the INS initiates deportation proceedings against the woman. As Crenshaw observes, "When faced with the choice between protection from their batterers and protection against deportation, many immigrant women chose the latter" (1995, 359).

When a woman becomes undocumented she loses her right to work legally. In other words, she loses her right to self-sufficiency. It exacerbates her economic dependence on her husband and, if she decides to leave, greatly reduces her options. Sanctions against employers hiring undocumented workers—put in place by the Immigration Reform and Control Act (IRCA), which was passed the same year as the IMFA—adds another layer of vulnerability in an immigrant woman's life. As a result, her husband, her current or potential employers, and the INS all exercise power over her. The punitive mechanisms of the state thus reinforce marital abuse.

The "good faith" clause, which is supposed to guard a marriage against fraud, introduces fear and instability in the lives of women and children who are in abusive situations. The Sakhi cofounder Anannya Bhattacharjee (1997a, 314-16) astutely points out the clause's double standards. The moral determination that marriages should be affective and not instrumental underpins the clause. Yet when a sponsoring husband violates this affective dimension of family life by abusing his partner, the INS does not examine the sponsoring husband's "good faith." His abuse is not seen as a violation of what a family ideologically represents. The intense surveillance by the INS of the intimate details of domestic life that otherwise are considered private does not extend to the sponsoring husband's motives behind marriage or his actions in the marriage. It does not matter to the INS that the husband might have brought in the woman "to get free domestic help or a free sex partner" (315). Only the woman's intention—whether or not she entered a "green card marriage"—is scrutinized. When the wife's short-term legal status expires as a result of the husband's inaction, the INS starts proceedings against her and not her husband. She is the one who is then considered "illegal" and is deported.

Advocates in the domestic violence movement have made efforts to legally respond to the penalties that immigrant women suffer as a result of the IMFA and to routinize the process through which battered women can apply for deportation waivers. The two initial waivers in the IMFA—which were granted to women who could prove that their legal status had lapsed through no fault of their own or that deportation would cause them "extreme hardship"—were revised in 1990 as part of the Immigration Act. While the 1990 revisions no longer required the women to file for divorce or prove that during the waiting period the marriage had ended for a "good cause," they still needed to establish that they had entered the marriage in good faith. Women who asked for a deportation waiver on the grounds of domestic violence had to produce evaluations signed by a licensed mental health practitioner to prove "extreme cruelty" and battery (Abraham 2000, 63–64; Das Dasgupta and Warrier 1997, 45).

Activist efforts to address these flaws culminated in the 1994 Violence Against Women Act (VAWA).[5] As a piece of landmark legislation for immigrant women, it allows survivors to self-petition and petition for their children. It establishes them for the first time as autonomous legal entities. While the series of corrective legal provisions do make a difference in women's lives, their effect is limited. The legislation and the INS, as the enforcing agency, do not account for the ways in which structural barriers shape these women's access to the resources required to qualify for waivers. They assume that the women have already tried leaving their batterers and that they have access to legal and social services to assist them to document their abuse and apply for the waiver. These assumptions also impact native-born survivors—but, for immigrant women, access to these services becomes critical to their right to live and work in the United States.

South Asian women's organizations that address domestic violence confront in their day-to-day work the pressures that the evidentiary requirements for the waivers create for immigrant women. The organizations know from their dealings with the INS that, compared to personal affidavits, official documents such as medical reports, police reports, restraining orders, and records of shelter residency have greater credibility. The greater value attached to such official documentation, of course, stems from an anti-immigrant stance, which treats with intense suspicion all efforts by immigrants to adjust their status so that they may remain and work in the United States.

For immigrant women, the steps that would produce such documentation are enormous and very difficult. Their lack of familiarity with the police, courts, and counseling systems in the United States and the isolation enforced by their partners and by a culture that treats them as alien go against them (Abraham 1995; Das Dasgupta and Warrier 1997). They may also face language barriers, which undermines their confidence, cuts them off from resources, and increases their isolation. These women may not consider going to a shelter as their first option. They may also be reluctant at first to file a police report against their husbands, get a restraining order, or consider divorce.[6] Manavi and Sakhi, in designing their services, consider exactly these barriers to ensure that South Asian survivors can exercise their right to safety and residency (see chapter 4).

Survivors of domestic violence, who are criminalized for retaliating against their husbands or not being able to protect their children from abuse, run the risk of being automatically deported under the 1996 IIRIRA and the Antiterrorism and Effective Death Penalty Act. A Manavi workshop for service providers and community organizers conducted in the summer of 2000 highlighted the ways in which the INS has unabashedly used the provisions of these two laws to detain and remove residents with minor criminal charges even after they have paid the penalties or served time. In domestic violence cases, husbands have been known to bring criminal charges against their wives for defending themselves or their children from abuse. Child welfare agencies also end up criminalizing survivors when they are unable to intervene in their children's abuse or cannot prevent their children from witnessing violence. In such cases, social workers try to protect children from abuse by removing them from their mothers. If the children are removed, it is a mark against the women who then cannot fulfill the "good moral character" requirement of VAWA (Pendleton 1998, 5).

Along with acceptable evidence of abuse, the women who ask for deportation waivers need to prove that they cannot go back to their country on the grounds of "extreme hardship" (Das Dasgupta and Warrier 1997, 45-46). At present, South Asian women's organizations, such as Manavi, provide the women who use their services with three to four affidavits from experts testifying to the class, caste, religion, and region-specific status of women, as well as the state of domestic violence legislation and services for battered women in their countries of origin. Thus, to take advantage of VAWA, which is an improvement over the 1986 and 1990 waivers, an immigrant woman must have access to a range of services that can facilitate her negotiations with the police, courts, lawyers, and immigration officials. These services must also be familiar with the transnational social contexts in which the immigrant woman is embedded in order to strengthen her case to remain in this country. Sakhi in New York City, Manavi in New Jersey, Asha in the DC-Maryland-Virginia area, Apna Ghar in Chicago, Saheli in Austin, and Maitri in the San Francisco Bay Area provide some or all of these services. However, they and other South Asian women's organizations, mostly concentrated in urban areas, can serve only a fraction of the abused women scattered all over the country.

Apart from limited accessibility, the reforms do not hold the abuser responsible or prevent abuse. No changes have been made to the underpinnings of the IMFA, which writes into law the dependency of immigrant women on their sponsoring husbands. The abuser can continue to use the punitive powers of the INS, along with physical and sexual assault and emotional abuse, to intimidate his wife and keep her from taking any action to change her situation. Furthermore, VAWA applies only to women who are married to permanent residents or citizens. The relief does not extend to other categories of women with dependent visa status such as wives of students, exchange scholars, or men who have temporary work permits like H-1B visas. Unlike the women who have conditional residency, these women do not have the right to work and have no legal means of becoming economically independent.

The safety options available to immigrant women were severely curtailed by the 1996 IIRIRA and the Personal Responsibility and Work Opportunity Reconciliation Act.[7] These laws were driven by racist fears that immigrant women migrated with the intention of abusing publicly funded services. The new immigration laws disqualified all permanent residents from two federally funded public assistance programs—food stamps and supplemental security income (SSI)—with the narrowly defined exception of battered women and their children who were adjusting their immigration status under VAWA (Ayuda 1996; Davies 1997; Mandell 1997; National Health Law Program 1996; U.S. Department of Justice 1997). Those survivors and their children who were defined as "qualified aliens" under the Immigration Act had to prove that the batterer was no longer living with them as well as obtain a determination from the attorney general that their need for public assistance was connected to abuse (National Health Law Program 1996). Under the old welfare law, permanent residents after a five-year restriction used to be eligible for Aid for Families with Dependent Children (AFDC), Medicaid, and food stamps. Under the new law, the federal government left it up to the states to permit permanent residents to apply for Temporary Assistance for Needy Families (TANF), which replaced AFDC, Medicaid, Title XX block grants, and other state and local public aid programs (Ayuda 1996; Mandell 1997). The lack of standard policies across states greatly interferes with the kinds of decisions women need to make in order to be safe (Davies 1997).

The immigration and the welfare laws together create a sense of disentitlement that discourages immigrant women from accessing even the emergency assistance for which they qualify by inducing fears about losing their legal status. While permanent residents and undocumented immigrants can still access emergency Medicaid, prenatal care, supplemental food programs for women, infants and children (WIC), domestic violence shelters, immunization for children, school nutrition programs for children, and testing and treatment for communicable diseases, they are severely discouraged from doing so (Center for Immigrant Rights 1998). Permanent residents fear that their legal status would be jeopardized if they were found to be "public charges" for availing of public assistance. Undocumented residents are intimidated into not using these services because welfare agencies now have to report to the federal government those persons "known to be unlawfully present in the United States" (Ayuda, 1996, 2; Center for Immigrant Rights 1998, 1). This state of disentitlement is similar to the INS misinformation that prevented eligible immigrant women and their children from accessing public assistance when they were seeking amnesty under the 1986 IRCA (Chang 2000).

Immigration law that legislates immigrant women's dependence on their abusers for legal status and economic support thus undercuts the domestic violence laws that allow women to take action against their abusers. This situation is similar for workers, who out of fear of deportation do not report their exploitation even though labor laws entitle them to minimum wage regardless of their immigration status. The effectiveness of laws put in place to redress exploitation and these laws' ability to deliver justice depends on the gender, race, immigration status, and economic power of those who come under its purview. It is not surprising, therefore, that South Asian women's organizations have identified these severe contradictions within the legal system as points of intervention. Their work in the legal arena is not simply reformist because challenging the so-called neutrality of law requires radical analyses and radical agendas. By finding ways to advocate the rights of immigrant women, these organizations contest the state's continual disempowerment of these women on the grounds that they are noncitizens.

The Heterosexual Contract

The right through marriage to permanent residency and citizenship in the United States is a heterosexual privilege. The categories "heterosexual" and "homosexual," far from being fixed and immediately perceptible to legislators and immigration officials, are actually produced through immigration controls, as the immigration scholar Eithne Luibhéid (2002) has shown. By regulating immigration through determinations about applicants' sexual identities and desirable sexual arrangements, the state legislates heterosexuality and homosexuality. It contains heterosexuality within the institution of marriage through the family unification imperatives of immigration law and punishes those who refuse to enter the heterosexual contract through marriage. Even legislative proposals to allow citizens or permanent residents to sponsor their same-sex permanent partners require these partnerships to closely resemble monogamous heterosexual relationships. Heterosexuality or its approximation thus becomes intimately tied with the rights of immigrants to live and work in this country, reflecting what M. Jacqui Alexander (1997) terms the colonization of citizenship by heterosexuality. Heterosexuality lies at the center of the state's definition of itself because it is used as a criterion for membership to the nation.

A number of laws such as the Immigration and Nationality Act (INA) of 1952 and its amendment in 1965, the 1987 introduction of HIV screening for permanent residents, and the 1996 Defense of Marriage Act (DOMA) discriminate against lesbian and gay immigrants. Each of these measures reinforces heterosexual marriage and family. The 1994 revision of the 1980 Refugee Act is the sole piece of legislation that does recognize the human rights of lesbian and gay immigrants, thereby making it possible for them to seek asylum. However, the severe limitations of the provision put this option out of the reach of many. Another measure that favors lesbians and gays is the bill introduced in Congress in 2001 to grant sponsorship rights to citizens or permanent residents who have "permanent" same-sex partners. The bill has languished, however, and it is not likely to be passed under the current Bush Administration.

Sexual minorities were not allowed to immigrate to the United States until 1990. The 1965 INA, usually hailed as a key civil rights law because it removed the racially discriminatory national origin quotas, explicitly specified "sexual deviation" as a medical condition that disqualified an applicant from entering (Davis 1999, 19). In doing so, it went a step further to clarify what was implicit in the 1952 McCarthy-era INA, which barred the entry of "aliens afflicted with psychopathic personality," a designation that in practice was extended to homosexuals (Foss 1994). The Public Health Service was charged with certifying the physical and mental health of applicants, and Luibhéid (2002, 77–101) shows how these practices constructed sexually deviant bodies. Even after the American Psychiatric Association removed homosexuality from its list of mental disorders in 1973, Congress did not vote until 1990 to remove this exclusionary and pathologizing clause, thereby demonstrating the acute invisibility of the civil liberties of sexual minorities.

In 1987, the INS started to screen applicants for permanent residency for HIV, and in 1993 it was authorized to bar all HIV-positive entrants, even those applying for tourist visas. All applicants for a green card have to pay an INS-certified health practitioner to do the mandatory test. The state's anxiety about the threat to public health posed by HIV-positive residency applicants and the strains that immigrants living with AIDS would put on the health care system has to be called into question because of its blatant neglect of the domestic AIDS epidemic as a public health crisis throughout the 1980s. The privatization of prevention and treatment and the Reagan-Bush Administration's aggressively homophobic, moralistic, and behavioral approach had led to approximately 100,000 deaths by 1990 (Eisenstein 1994, 146). That HIV/AIDS continues to be seen as a gay disease makes lesbian and gay applicants particularly vulnerable to harassment. The state's anxiety and surveillance is not, however, translated into a responsible public health response. The INS-designated practitioners do not counsel the persons being tested and take no responsibility for referring them to resources if they are found to be HIV positive.

For lesbian and gay permanent residency applicants, the HIV screening has specific implications for their access to a waiver that permits those who are HIV positive to continue with their application. The stipulations of the waiver re-inscribe heterosexual family arrangements. According to the Lesbian and Gay Immigration Rights Task Force (LGIRTF), to avail of the waiver, HIV-positive applicants must have citizen or permanent resident relatives who are eligible to sponsor family members. Lesbian and gay immigrants are least likely to qualify since immigration law does not recognize same-sex partners. These immigrants might not have other eligible family members in the United States or, if they do, they might not be "out" to them. These requirements, therefore, reinforce normative ideas of what a family should be and how it should function. Applicants who do have sponsors have to provide certification that they pose a minimal danger of spreading the virus, proof of health insurance, and documentation that the U.S. government would not incur any costs for allowing the person to stay in the United States. In setting up these difficult criteria, the state absolves itself of its welfare responsibilities, denying queer immigrants of the social right to a safety net. Lesbian and gay immigrants who apply for permanent residency through their employers and test positive have no recourse because waivers are not granted to employment-based applicants (Lesbian and Gay Immigration Rights Task Force, 2001).

Since access to permanent residency is heavily weighted in favor of heterosexuals through spousal sponsorship and spouse-based waivers, some lesbian and gay immigrants have to "pass" as straight and enter into "green card marriages." As the Malaysian–South Asian documentary maker and activist Grace Poore asks, "Is the risk of rape or domestic violence any less for a lesbian married to a paper husband? Is the cost of paying for a green card sponsorship all that different from paying a dowry? Even if the sponsoring 'husband' were a friend where no payments exchanged hands, is a green card marriage not also an arranged marriage?" (1996, 22). For those who left their country of origin to escape forced marriages and compulsory heterosexuality, submitting to the coercion of the U.S. state in order to survive materially is perhaps the most galling. The submission to marriage—even if only for the short term—takes an enormous toll on those who have to live this way to avoid deportation, thereby inducing what Poore calls "internal eviction" (22).

More commonly, gay and lesbian immigrants secure permanent residency by finding an employer who would be willing to sponsor them. While such sponsorship would require that the immigrant be a skilled worker, the power imbalance that informs the relationship between a domestic worker and her employer also suffuses the relations between the skilled worker and her employer, especially if it is a nonprofit or a small organization that does not have the resources of a corporate sponsor. The process of gaining residency often involves paying a lawyer and takes anywhere between two to ten years, during which time the immigrant cannot travel outside the United States without securing what the INS calls a "parole." Two of my participants who worked for nonprofits had spent several years waiting for their green cards. Heterosexual immigrants are also subject to the same process when their employers agree to sponsor them. Their heterosexuality, however, protects them from the sanctions applied to gays and lesbians. While all applicants for residency have to be screened for HIV and criminal charges, these requirements are particularly daunting for lesbian and gay applicants. Through these violating procedures, the state can "out" an immigrant to his or her employer, colleagues, and family.

In 1994, the attorney general recognized that gays and lesbians constituted a social group that could ask for asylum on the basis of the persecution they face in their home countries (Lesbian and Gay Immigration Rights Task Force 2001; International Gay and Lesbian Human Rights Commission 1997). This extended the 1980 Refugee Act to lesbians and gays. The Refugee Act was designed to grant asylum to those who could establish "persecution or a well-founded fear of persecution based on race, religion, nationality, political opinion, or membership in a particular social group." However, as a result of cold war politics, it was narrowly applied to admit people who were fleeing communist regimes. A number of legal precedents dating back to 1986, when a gay Cuban man asked for asylum to escape group membership–based persecution, led to the extension of the definition of a "particular social group" to lesbians and gays in 1994 (Davis, 1999). Asylum for foreign gays and lesbians promotes the international image of the United States as guarantor of all kinds of freedoms. Ironically, thirteen states in the United States had antisodomy laws on the books until a Supreme Court ruling in 2003 invalidated them. Thus, the self-presentation of the United States as a bastion of liberty erases the domestic persecution of sexual minorities.

Legal controversies over how group membership could be established for asylum-seeking lesbians and gays were resolved in a way that makes it difficult for them to meet the evidentiary requirements. Courts came up with two standards for group membership. One standard defined the group as members who shared "common immutable characteristics" (Reed 1996, 107; Davis 1999). This standard defines homosexuality as fixed and biological rather than socially constructed and fluid. Most INS courts follow this restrictive standard (Reed 1996). The other standard asks the applicant to show voluntary association as proof of membership to the persecuted social group. In countries where homosexuality is illegal such membership would be hard to prove.

Lesbian and gay asylum applicants have to prove a "well founded fear of persecution" along with group membership. The LGIRTF points to the difficulties involved in establishing the direct persecution of lesbians and gay men in countries that do not use Western categories to index same-sex relations. As with gender asylum applicants and domestic violence survivors asking for deportation waivers, area studies experts often have to be called in to establish the status of homosexuals in the relevant country. According to the LGIRTF, asylum seekers from India and Pakistan always need expert witnesses. Concerns about the problematic nature of the evidentiary requirements were brought up and discussed in a legal workshop on immigration issues sponsored by the Massachusetts Area South Asian Lambda Association (MASALA). The workshop demonstrates this community's interest in the particular ways that South Asian lesbian and gay immigrants are affected by these laws.

In addition to the limits placed on asylum for lesbians and gays through the evidentiary requirements, the INS in 1998 restricted the procedure for seeking asylum by imposing a one-year application deadline. This new qualification meant that an asylum seeker would have to apply for asylum within a year of his or her entering the United States (Lesbian and Gay Immigration Rights Task Force 2001), thus disqualifying those immigrants who have lived in the United States for more than a year yet who had not availed of asylum because of a lack of knowledge or resources. Through this stricture, the INS effectively limited the number of eligible applicants, thus causing much alarm and concern among members of the South Asian Lesbian and Gay Association and MASALA. Between 1994 and 1997, the INS had accepted only one hundred sexual orientation-based asylum applications (Davis 1999, 20). New immigrants are less likely than those who have lived in the United States for a few years to know about such laws. Moreover, they would not only have to be aware of the possibility of seeking asylum but also would need to have institutional connections through which to find immigration lawyers who handle cases for lesbians and gays and have access to expert witnesses. The asylum project advances the rights of immigrant gays and lesbians in very limited ways. But it shores up an immense amount of moral authority that consolidates the idea that the United States rescues foreign nationals from their repressive countries of origin to grant them sexual freedom. The project does not erode the heterosexual premise of spousal sponsorship. It also promotes the notion that sexuality is immutable, thus naturalizing both heterosexuality and homosexuality. This tendency runs counter to the challenge posed by queer politics and queer studies that destabilizes both categories in order to insist that sexual identities and desires are socially shaped.

The 1996 Defense of Marriage Act (DOMA) explicitly instituted heterosexuality as a cornerstone of the family unification provisions of immigration law. Congress passed the act preemptively to prevent legally married same-sex couples—citizens and noncitizens—from enjoying the benefits extended to married heterosexual couples in anticipation of Hawai'i's effort to legalize same-sex marriages.[8] One such benefit is the sponsorship that a citizen or permanent resident partner extends to an alien spouse. The declaration by DOMA that federal agencies restrict the terms "marriage" and "spouse" to heterosexual couples (Reed 1996, 128–29) directly impacts immigrant lesbians and gays. Under DOMA, the INS, a federal agency, does not have to recognize same-sex civil unions such as those legalized in Vermont.

As a result of DOMA, changes in state laws allowing gay marriage will still not allow citizen or permanent resident partners to sponsor their immigrant same-sex partner. When evaluating the issue of gay marriage, immigrant lesbian and gay activists consider the fact that immigration is a federal subject while marriage is legislated by states. During the intense mobilization to legalize gay marriage in the wake of the 2004 Massachusetts Supreme Court order to the state legislature to recognize same-sex unions and the subsequent issuing of marriage licenses by some cities, immigrant activists called into question the campaign's disregard for noncitizens, whose immigration needs would continue to be unmet. For example, the Queer Asian Pacific Alliance in Boston, which works closely with MASALA, issued a warning on its Web site asking foreign lesbians and gays to not assume that same-sex marriage would allow them to adjust their immigration status. The recognition that gay marriage will not benefit noncitizens to the same degree as citizens (who, in fact, will still not have the right of spousal sponsorship) has also pushed activists to become more critical of the institution of marriage itself. This marks a shift from the ringing endorsement of gay marriage at a MASALA immigration workshop, held before DOMA, at which almost all gays and lesbians present enthusiastically raised their hand when asked whether they would get married if it were made legal.

Advocates of lesbian and gay immigrants, despite DOMA, continue to seek ways to legalize sponsorship by same-sex partners. The Permanent Partners Immigration Bill was introduced in the House of Representatives in February 2000, and then reintroduced the following year, to amend the INA by allowing gay and lesbian U.S. citizens and permanent residents to sponsor their partners for family-based reunification. The bill aims at aligning the rights of same-sex couples with those enjoyed by married heterosexual couples. To circumvent

DOMA, the bill defines permanent partners as those "who are unable to contract with that person a marriage cognizable under this Act [INA]" but are in an "intimate relationship" with the intention of a "lifelong commitment" and are financially interdependent (U.S. House of Representatives 2001).

While the language of "permanent partnership" moves toward disarticulating domestic partnerships from marriage, the bill demands that same-sex couples resemble the normative heterosexual nuclear family with the same arrangement of monogamous cohabitation and financial dependence. This is evidenced by the likelihood that same-sex "permanent partners" would have to show the same kind of documentation required of heterosexual married couples. The bill assumes that the norms that govern domestic partnerships are universal and that same-sex relationships are really similar to heterosexual marriage. More troubling, the proposal does not challenge the legal dependence that is enforced by conditional residency in the existing rules that govern heterosexual sponsorship. Marriage, dependency, and immigration thus remain intertwined. No changes have been made to break that intimate connection in public policy. Moves to advance the rights of binational same-sex partners remain within the constraints of a heterosexual imagination that can grant rights to lesbian and gay immigrants but only through domesticating homosexuality.

The Exploitation of Immigrant Workers

Academics, policymakers, and South Asian immigrants have turned to individualized and merit-based explanations for the ethnic group's class composition. Such explanations obscure the structural forces that operate to create an elite at one historical moment and a working class at another. Immigration law tightly controls who enters the labor market, as well as when, where in the occupational structure, and under what conditions. Furthermore, immigration law, by setting up a distinction between documented and undocumented entrants, also creates a steady supply of super-exploitable labor to the host of services and light industries in urban centers such as New York City, San Francisco, and Los Angeles (Bonacich 1996; Bonacich and Appelbaum 2000; Chang 2000; Hondagneu-Sotelo 2001). The emergence since the late 1970s of a visible South Asian working class, then, has to be situated at the interface between immigration laws and labor market needs.[9]

The 1965 amendments to the INA introduced a seven-tier system for admission with two occupation-based preferences (the third and sixth) to permit foreigners to enter the United States to fill labor shortages. The legalization of a new era of skilled labor importation was qualified, however. In responding to the concerns of the U.S. labor movement about foreign workers glutting the market and depressing wages—an old anxiety that had driven nativist anti-immigrant legislation in the late nineteenth century and the early twentieth—the law charged the Labor Department with determining sectors short of domestic labor so as to eliminate competition from immigrants (Reimers 1985, 72–74).

Under the new preference system, South Asians wanting to move to the United States could avail of occupation-based visas rather than family sponsorship because Asian exclusion in the past meant that few had family members in the United States who would sponsor their immigration. Immediately after 1965, most Indian and Pakistani immigrants came under labor certifications for third-preference occupations for professionals and scientists. In the early 1970s, 80 to 90 percent of occupation-based Indian immigrants were professionals (Khandelwal 1995, 179).

But by 1980, 90 percent of all nonrefugee immigrant visas issued to entrants from Asia went to family members (Min 1995, 12). What explains this dramatic shift from occupation-based to family-based immigration? Three pieces of legislation—the 1976 Health Professions Education Assistance Act, the 1977 Eilberg Act, and the 1986 Immigration Reform and Control Act (IRCA)—curbed the flow of occupation-based immigrants. In reaction to the economic recession in the 1970s, the 1976 act removed physicians and surgeons from its list of sectors in need of immigrant labor (Chan 1991, 147). As a further disincentive, it required that surgeons and physicians intending to enter the United States pass the National Board of Medical Examiners or take an equivalent visa-qualifying exam. As a result, by the early 1980s the number of health professionals entering the United States, most of whom were Asian, dropped to one-tenth of its 1977 peak (147). To discourage third- and sixth-preference hires, the Eilberg Act made employers of foreign workers responsible for a Labor Department certification. Under the old system, the Labor Department, on reviewing areas of labor shortage, would directly certify an occupation-based visa applicant. Faced with extra paperwork, expenses, and legal issues related to labor certification in the new system, employers started to turn to the domestic labor market. All of these measures caused the number of employment-based immigrants to plummet.

Within a decade, the work authorization provisions of the 1986 IRCA made foreign applicants even more unattractive to employers, who were now penalized for hiring workers without proper documentation. While the law required employers to verify the work authorization of all applicants, and while it was supposed to eliminate the employers' incentive to exploit workers, the law in fact promoted discrimination. Employers managed to pass along the risk of the IRCA sanctions to their employees. In keeping with the neoliberal and privatizing turn taken by the state in the 1980s, the state farmed out its policing functions to employers, and the employers, in turn, transferred the costs and responsibility to employees. This relegation has produced a legally vulnerable group of workers who bear the responsibility of documentation. In addition, the bias against immigrant workers—both citizen and noncitizen—in the process of verification is amply documented by a study conducted by the General Accounting Office in 1990. The study reported that "a widespread pattern of discrimination has resulted against eligible workers . . . [and] it is more reasonable to conclude that a substantial amount of these discriminating practices resulted from the IRCA than not" (U.S. Commission on Civil Rights 1992, 148–49). According to the Commission on Civil Rights, employers perceived all Asians and Asian Americans as workers who had a high probability of being unauthorized, and therefore they were not eager to hire them.

As a result of all of these labor-related measures, doors to professions that had opened for the first wave were shut to those coming in after 1976. State policies no longer encouraged the entry or hiring of professionals, but immigration under family-based preferences rose. The first of the post-1965 South Asians, many of whom quickly became citizens, were established enough to sponsor their relatives who, in turn, brought in others. Family reunification became a new, though clandestine, way for the state to recruit immigrant labor for a restructuring economy hungry for low-wage, part-time, flexible labor while also restricting direct labor importation to appease domestic unease (Reddy 2003). In the late 1970s, South Asian family-sponsored immigrants entered a postindustrial economy in recession. Despite the fact that they were documented, barriers to finding work in the better-paying sectors of the labor market pushed many of the newer immigrants to settle for the lower-paying nonprofessional sectors of the market. This dynamic between immigration policies and the labor market explains the appearance of self-employed and working-class South Asians. Just as the occupational preferences of the 1965 immigration law responded to the economy's needs for professional labor, its family reunification quotas serve the interest of a service economy seeking low-wage and deskilled labor amid corporate downsizing.

Undocumented immigrants—created through the post-1965 immigration policies that specified who is legally permitted to work and, by extension, who is not—supply urban areas and the agricultural sector with the cheapest and most exploitable source of labor. Legislators, policymakers, and immigration officials understand the value of undocumented labor in agribusiness and in the low-wage sectors of the postindustrial economy and are reluctant to strictly regulate them. Debates over immigrant agricultural labor dragged on for sixteen years before the IRCA was passed (Reimers 1985, 232–40). A 1980 statement made by the head of the Los Angeles INS office quoted in the *New York Times* warned that 90 percent of the city's restaurants, car washes, and light industries would close down if the agency raided them for undocumented workers (222).

Similarly, lawmakers recognize the utility of cheap immigrant labor in agriculture. Through the special agricultural worker clause in the 1986 IRCA, undocumented Indian, Pakistani, and Bangladeshi agricultural laborers were able to apply for amnesty and legalize their status (Leonard 1997, 71). The central role of this type of labor is also reflected in resuscitated proposals for a temporary workers program similar to the 1943–1964 Bracero agreement between the United States and Mexico every time Congress is poised to crack down on undocumented immigrants. Even as the House of Representatives was getting ready to pass the 1996 IIRIRA, which virulently targets undocumented immigrants, agricultural interests in the Southwest were lobbying for a guest worker program (Schmitt 1996). Since the IRCA amnesty program in 1986, no sustained policy effort has been made to legalize the underground army of undocumented workers. The undeniable reliance of the U.S. economy on undocumented immigrant labor is instead being addressed through a Bracero-style temporary workers' program. A 2005 bipartisan bill in Congress has proposed three-year visas for immigrants to work in the health care, hotel, restaurant, retail, and construction industries. Thus, immigration law ensures rather than deters the supply of cheap labor to the domestic secondary labor market. The conditions of entry that cheapen the labor of immigrants are also those that prevent these workers from availing the few legal labor protections due to them under labor laws.

Domestic workers, recruited from South Asia to work in the homes of their professional compatriots, become undocumented when their employers bring them in under tourist visas that do not allow them to work. South Asian activists organizing domestic workers note that these women often move to the United States not knowing that they had entered into agreements or signed contracts that are considered illegal by immigration authorities (Alam 1997, 16). The employers, who sometimes knowingly put these women at risk, use the threat of INS intervention, arrest, and eventual deportation to hold the women hostage to situations that are intolerable. Domestic workers do not receive minimum wage, time off from work, or health benefits. The average monthly income of South Asian live-in nanny-housekeepers working seven days a week is $200 per month. The role of immigration law in driving down their wages and structuring their deplorable work conditions bears out the feminist scholar Grace Chang's (2000) argument that U.S. policies deliberately create and maintain this low-wage, super-exploitable labor force. A domestic worker, explaining how her undocumented fellow workers are caught in a cycle of exploitation by coethnics, noted, "We go to South Asian families because American employers [non-South Asian, possibly white professionals] want work permits and legal papers" (Samar Collective 1994, 14). These women's need to work, combined with a lack of permission to do so, produces an undocumented labor force—"illegal aliens"—who are snared in an underground economy.

Neela Trivedi, an organizer who used to work for Sakhi's domestic workers' project, described how immigration status traps women into domestic work. Even when women change employers, their undocumented status prevents them from finding work other than as domestics or restaurant workers. Underlining how being undocumented affects the women's life chances, she said, "I feel that most of the domestic workers are doing the babysitting job because they are undocumented. They are not doing it by choice; [for the majority] . . . to look for another job. . . . for a better job—better than a baby sitter/housekeeper job—they need better immigration status."[10] For domestic workers, better immigration status means asking an employer to sponsor them for a green card. Employer sponsorships are, however, concentrated in the professional fields. In these cases, the employer processes the paperwork but the employee pays for an immigration lawyer. Domestic workers do not have the material resources to pick up such costs and thus have to rely on their employers. If they find an employer willing to sponsor them the process takes eight to ten years, and during this time they are tied to the employer.

The workings of immigration laws stymie hopes for a decent job and expose immigrant women to extreme exploitation and physical and mental hardship. Though the 1974 revision of the Fair Labor Standards Act entitles domestic workers to minimum wage (NOW Legal Defense and Education Fund 1997), it is rarely enforced. Workers learn about these entitlements and start to insist on them once they are educated about their rights and supported by organizations like Sakhi, Workers Awaaz, or Andolan. Even though the women are often injured in the workplace and develop chronic health problems because of poor living conditions in their employers' home, their employers rarely pay health insurance or cover their health costs. Further, without the backing of the labor organizations they are not able to file for workers' compensation for work-related injuries. Domestic workers report that often they are not paid, and their passports and belongings are taken away or destroyed by their employers. The organizations help aggrieved members file cases for back pay and take legal action against employers who tamper with their documents. As with survivors of spousal abuse, the legal/illegal distinction set up by immigration law enables these forms of abuse.

Like paid domestic work, the yellow cab industry in New York City depends on undocumented immigrant labor. South Asians comprise 60 percent of the cab drivers in New York City's taxi industry. The switch in the early 1970s from a commission system to leasing eliminated benefits for drivers and required them to work twelve-hour shifts. This reorganization of the industry was accompanied by a flight of native-born workers and a shift to predominantly Third World drivers, who lease their taxis from garages. Under this arrangement, drivers can work the day shift or the night shift seven days a week. Drivers who lease their car and medallion (which makes the vehicle into a taxi) need to make at least $130 to $145 per day in order to pay for the lease, which ranges between $100 and $115 a day. Added to the lease are the costs for gas, maintenance, and repair, as well as for tickets from the New York Police Department, the Department of Motor Vehicles, and the Taxi and Limousine Commission.

Given the nature of the industry, some days a driver makes as little as $10 for an entire shift. As one taxi driver–organizer observed, "It's not even a guaranteed wage, forget about sub-minimum wage." In order to raise the money for the next week's lease payment, a lease driver ends up working all seven days of the week. When I asked drivers why they did this grueling and extremely hazardous job the answer was, "No one asks you for paperwork." Many drivers' lack of legal status and their need to support themselves and their families have pushed them into this industry. Many drivers, documented and undocumented, took up taxi driving as a temporary job, but the inability to make an adequate income has locked them into the industry. Some get through each day hoping that they will be able to go or return to school, get a degree, and find better work—goals that are not attainable, however, because of the way in which their work is structured.

Despite their exploitative working conditions, drivers have difficulty seeing themselves as workers because they are defined by the industry as independent contractors—or in other words as self-employed business people. In explaining how this definition works in tandem with the model minority myth, the New York Taxi Workers Alliance (NYTWA) organizer Bhairavi Desai, said: "The way it has been constructed, it's about being a small businessman. This form of employment is constructed as something a self-employed person can do. . . . You look at Gujaratis who are in the motel business or the small groceries business. Then you look at the Punjabis who are in the taxi cab industry, and most of these guys don't see much of a difference. That's one of the ways in which capitalist, racist America has contributed to how people make the choices people make. They're stereotyped. These economic categories are set up for us based on those stereotypes and they reinforce each other."[11]

Since the taxi industry in New York City defines operators as independent contractors, even lease drivers who are at the bottom rung of the industry can conceptualize themselves as self-employed. Many entered the industry from even more unattractive workplaces like gas stations in the hope of being able to own their car and eventually a medallion. Yet, the material reality of a car owner and lease driver is that of a worker, not a business owner. They need wage-hour protections, health insurance, and social insurance for unemployment and temporary disability. But their legal definition as self-employed entitles them to none of these benefits. While the perception of self-employment can help taxi drivers maintain their dignity, as Desai pointed out, the contradiction between their status as independent contractors and lived experience makes them feel they have no rights. For example, despite high rates of workplace injury, drivers rarely claimed workers' compensation, the one social insurance program to which they are entitled, until the NYTWA started to organize them.

Working-class people, who are so maligned by the first-wave post-1965 immigrants, are as much the creation of immigration law and its intersections with a race- and gender-stratified labor market as the professional first wave. Yet, the first wave's elite character is touted as an immigrant success story. To explain the contrast between the elite first wave and later working-class immigrants, scholars studying South Asian immigration commonly point to family reunification, which does not screen entering immigrants for skills (Helweg and Helweg 1990, 69, 149 n.4; Khandelwal 1995, 179; Mogelonsky 1995; Sheth 1995). Working-class post-1976 immigrants are considered to be less educated and less qualified. The anthropologists Arthur Helweg and Usha Helweg epitomize this viewpoint when they say, "One can see when immigration legislation gives primacy to family unity, the channels soon become blocked with relatives and little room is left for the 'talented and skilled' on their own. Thus the average level of education of Asian Indians entering America is declining, and because they have relatives to make their way easier for them, they might not be as determined or innovative as the original sojourners" (1990, 69). The INS too shared this view. In 1990, at a time when working-class South Asians were becoming an undeniable presence, *India Abroad* reported an INS official as saying that applying brothers and sisters were "obviously not as qualified" (Dutt 1990, 15). That reuniting family members are less qualified becomes common sense through such reinforcement. Contrary to impressions that reuniting immigrants abuse state benevolence, the state has consistently used family reunification as a method to recruit labor that it can then deskill and underpay (Reddy 2003).

Empirically, if education is taken as an indicator of the qualifications with which immigrants enter the country, then family-sponsored immigrants continue to have higher levels of education than do those who are native born. An analysis of census figures between 1980 and 1990 shows that 42 percent of Asian Indians immigrating between 1985 and 1990 held a bachelor's degree compared to 20.3 percent of the total U.S. population (Sheth 1995, 177). The assumption that immigrants screened for skills necessarily do better than family-sponsored

immigrants, and that family reunification has negative effects on the employment possibilities and mobility of the new immigrants, also has been called into
question. A study using an INS-released dataset between 1977 and 1990 (Jasso
and Rosenzweig 1995) found that, over time, sponsored male spouses showed
occupational upgrading while male employment-based immigrants showed occupational downgrading. Among these men, those who became naturalized
citizens did better than those who did not, thus underlining the correlation
between immigration status and social mobility.

Structural forces rather than individual failings, then, determine the slots in
the economy that the newer immigrants occupy. The anthropologist Johanna
Lessinger, one of the few scholars who considers structural factors, discusses
several barriers that Asian Indians working in New York City's newsstands
faced despite being well educated. Among the reasons for these men accepting
such poorly paid and high-risk jobs were the nonrecognition of the scientific
degrees they had from smaller or provincial Indian universities, family pressures
to help with the business or become self-supporting soon after immigration,
age, and the economic recession in the late 1970s and 1980s that exacerbated
racism and nativism (1990, 81).

South Asians with tenuous immigration status often have to rely on ethnic
networks to find work. Members of the same ethnic group exploit their own or
poor immigrants from other minority groups, which leads to complex class and
racial formations that depart from the "black-white made-in America model of
racialization" (Appelbaum 1996, 312–14). In an ironic twist, the same ethnic
solidarity that the model minority myth extols locks many members of that
group into low-paying, dead-end jobs created by their better-off compatriots
(see Kwong 1997 for the similar predicament of the Fuzhounese in New York
City's Chinatown). The racism that creates the glass ceiling leads to a proliferation of ethnic businesses. In turn, these businesses rely on exploited labor—
family labor, women's labor, and undocumented labor—made available through
the regulation of immigration preferences. The anthropologist Nancy Abelmann and the sociologist John Lie (1995, 179), in discussing Korean American
entrepreneurship, remind us that in an age of corporate capitalism, small family
businesses are hardly the key to success. Though resilient, their survival is
contingent on the unpaid labor of family members or the extremely cheap labor
extracted from one's own ethnic group or from the poorest men and women of
another racial group.

At the turn of the twenty-first century, intracommunity class struggles play out in affluent homes, motel businesses, taxi leasing companies, restaurants, groceries, gas stations, and a host of other small operations. Conflicts in class-based interests between professional and working-class immigrants within the same ethnic group were noted as emerging issues by the South Asian scholars Sucheta Mazumdar (1989a) and Jyotsna Vaid (1989) in analyzing the incorporation of Asian American and South Asian women's labor in the U.S. economy. These struggles pose new problems for labor organizers (see Cho 1994). Labor organizations that have sprung up to address the exploitation of South Asian workers confront a complicated landscape in which South Asians exploit other South Asians within larger economic arrangements that stratify occupations by race. Labor activists face the challenge of organizing within so-called ethnic occupational enclaves. To do this they contextualize their class analysis in the cleavages that divide South Asian communities and in structural racism. As complex relationships between class and race emerge, so do new labor tactics.

Conclusion

I have outlined above the political economy of immigration as created by a heteropatriarchal state in which capitalism advances through its dependence on transnational flows of labor that become undocumented and driven underground. Undocumented immigrants, far from being public charges, serve a number of critical functions. They not only supply the cheap, exploitable labor that forms the foundation of a service economy but also serve as bodies that the state uses for its ideological projects. The invisible labor of undocumented workers bolsters the myth of ethnic entrepreneurial success. Through exceptional measures such as VAWA and asylum programs for those facing persecution on the basis of their gender or sexual orientation, the state feels secure in its paternalism and consolidates its cultural imperialism by presenting itself as the ultimate democratic system (see Grewal 1998). Concurrently, the state promotes the ideology of the heterosexual nuclear family as a haven by instituting heterosexual marriage as one criterion of residency and guarding it against fraud.

The state masks these advantages by inventing and ordering two naturalized categories—"legal" and "illegal" immigrants. It presents the policing of its borders as its natural right. It justifies penalties against "illegal immigrants" as the logical consequence of legal violations. In contrast, labor organizers, advocates of domestic violence survivors, and queer activists denaturalize the legal/illegal distinction to show how immigration law creates undocumented immigrants and their resultant hardships. There is nothing natural or logical about the ways in which these people become criminalized. In many cases, they lapse into the category.

Weaving together a transnational rights complex becomes central to the work of South Asian space-making organizations along with cultural politics, collective empowerment, and identity building. Rights as a terrain of struggle opens up because these organizations denaturalize the process through which immigrants become undocumented and lose many of their rights. They recognize the importance of challenging the notion that immigrants, particularly undocumented immigrants, have no rights and no rightful claims on the state in their new, perhaps temporary, homeland. As people cross borders, so must their rights. In an effort to secure immigrant rights that are not attached to nation and citizenship, space-making organizations engage with local, state, federal, and international legislative processes and with public policy. However, the analyses and methods they bring to their interventions differ greatly from place-taking tactics that rely on petitions, debate, and appeals to legislative representatives. Instead of playing by the rules of liberal democratic participation, space makers craft a politic that can respond to the invisible, underground, and silenced realities of their constituencies.

CHAPTER 4

"Owning Our Lives": Women's Organizations

The groups Manavi, Sakhi for South Asian Women, and South Asian Women for Action (SAWA) all emerged to express the realities of immigrant women in order to change the social conditions that oppress them. They are part of a trend seen since the late 1980s when South Asian women's organizations started to proliferate all over the United States (Abraham 2000; Shah 1994; Vaid 1999/2000). However, the commitment of Manavi, Sakhi, and SAWA to transformation—beyond providing much-needed social services or social spaces for otherwise isolated South Asian women—sets them apart from many of the other organizations formed during this period. All three groups strive to transform relations through which families, workplaces, and the state subordinate women. I selected these organizations because each forged distinctive approaches to social change as it wrestled with the immediate and overwhelming needs of underserved South Asian immigrant women. The debates within these three South Asian women's organizations over issues in institutionalization and alliance building hold important lessons for immigrant and feminist communities in the United States.

Although in their literature Manavi, Sakhi, and SAWA avoid using the word "feminist" to describe themselves, feminist principles do inform their work. Such a practice resonates with what scholars have found in U.S. and British organizations for women of color who engage with a multiplicity of issues that knit together self, family, and community (Barnett 1995; Collins 1991; Pardo 1995; Sudbury 1998). These scholars, in fact, have urged researchers to develop a cognitive eye to perceive what the sociologist Bernice Barnett calls "feminist values, practices, and outcomes" (1995, 202) in organizations that depart from the standard categories used to identify feminist organizations.

Manavi, Sakhi, and SAWA expand notions of what "feminist" issues in the United States could be by addressing racism, immigrant rights, neo-imperialism, nationalism, and the religious Right. The organizations embrace and further Asian American feminism, which has insisted on tackling the persistence of anti-immigrant brands of racism in Asian American women's lives as integral to the second-wave feminist agenda (Yamada 1983). All three groups enable women to speak out about what it means to live in the United States as immigrants. Naming these realities has broken the silence that surrounds the severe mistreatment of women both inside and outside of their communities. In the words of one Sakhi member, breaking through the denial of the various forms of violence to which women are exposed empowers them to "own their lives." For many women, these organizations provide them with the first-time opportunity to discuss issues of violence, sexuality, racism, and class in the context of their lives as South Asians.

Autonomous South Asian feminist spaces came out of the resistance that South Asian activists faced from predominantly white second-wave feminist organizations, as well as identity-based organizations for people of color, to their efforts to articulate the struggles of immigrant women. By chronicling the emergence of these autonomous organizations and their reformulation of feminist concerns, I see myself contributing to the sociologist Becky Thompson's (2001) attempts to conceptualize the feminist movement in the United States as a multiracial enterprise rather than one initiated by white women or one that evolved through conflicts between white and black feminists. In this chapter I correct the tendency to reduce alternative accounts of U.S. feminism to a black-white framework (see, e.g., Breines 2002) that erases the interventions and innovations of feminists from other minoritized groups. I also contest the observation, noted by Pierrette Hondagneu-Sotelo, that the feminist movement has remained on the whole unresponsive to the immigrants rights movement "partly because immigrants, as a group, have not been a popular or powerful group around which to rally" (2000, 111). While a feminism that upholds the sanctity of national borders and sees immigrants as "trespassers" must be challenged, here I would like to center immigrant feminists and their organizations as part of the feminist movement in the United States. These organizations productively redefine central concerns of the movement. Thus, a far more complex story of the feminist movement surfaces when we veer away from conflating feminism with what Chela Sandoval (1991) calls hegemonic feminism and start taking into account the efforts of activists, such as those noted in this chapter, who have spelled out and organized around their particular and unmet needs.

The work of Manavi, Sakhi, and SAWA shows that they emerged to intervene on multiple fronts. First, they offer alternatives to white feminist organizations and dominant feminist understandings of issues such as domestic violence. Second, they confront people of colors' perception of South Asians as model minorities. Many members formed or gravitated toward autonomous South Asian women's groups because they felt marginalized or delegitimized among African American, Latino/a, and East Asian activists. As I demonstrate here, these organizations provide more solid grounds for coalitions through their nuanced examination of the differences and similarities between South Asians and other people of color. Finally, these organizations offer what is missing in their own ethnic communities—a safe space for women whose realities do not fit their communities' idealizations of womanhood.

While these South Asian spaces represent a sisterhood based on members' shared experiences of living as South Asian women in the United States, they are by no means seamless. As Sucheta Mazumdar (1989a, 15) reminds us in her discussion of the conflicts within Asian American communities, the impact of gender is felt differently even within the same ethnicity or class. Manavi, Sakhi, and SAWA all faced the challenge of organizing across difference. Generational differences, inflected with issues around immigration such as time of arrival, time spent in the United States, and citizenship status, separate the interests of first- and second-generation immigrant women. As immigrant communities diversify along class lines, South Asian women's organizations have had to determine how they are able to incorporate working-class women and their concerns. In a survey of such organizations as they were emerging in the 1980s,

Jyotsna Vaid (1989, 399) found them to be predominantly middle class and professional in character. In the 1990s, I found that confronting questions around cross-class organizing in middle-class South Asian spaces had become imperative. Questions around whether these organizations can attend to the needs of lesbians and transform their struggles accordingly have become similarly urgent. The organizations, in their resolve to be "South Asian," have to negotiate divisions along national lines not only in terms of diversifying their membership, which tends to be majority Indian, but also grappling with the changes that such inclusion brings about in defining issues. The generational, class, and occupational characteristics of members, as well as members' sexual orientation, set Manavi, Sakhi, and SAWA apart from each other. But these same distinctions also play out within each group to produce debates and conflicts over how South Asian women's groups can respond to these differences.

In doing their work, Manavi, Sakhi, and SAWA have been faced with three interrelated questions: How do they politicize domestic violence? How do they contend with the problem of institutionalization? How do they understand immigrant rights? In the first case, each organization has had to reconceptualize domestic violence to reflect immigrant women's experiences and their particular predicaments, thereby changing the ways of thinking about violence against women. Second, the problems of institutionalization and funding raise questions about the organizations' autonomy and ability to function nonhierarchically. Concerns surface about how nonprofits can affect social change in the midst of providing services for which they need funding. These are familiar dilemmas that have long vexed feminist organizations (Ferree and Martin 1995a). Less familiar are the ways in which immigrant feminists have dealt with these questions in their organizations' missions, campaigns, day-to-day functioning, and efforts at building coalitions. Third, each organization—in learning from and building on each other's work—has had to articulate the rights to which immigrants are entitled, often having to claim rights without the benefit of citizenship, and in the process, putting together a transnational complex that becomes a basis for demanding safety, gender equity, and economic justice.

The three groups differ from each other in terms of their membership, structure, funding, and goals. Formed in 1985 in suburban New Jersey, Manavi, which means primal woman in Sanskrit, was the first initiative in the United States to bring South Asian women together so that they could organize around the issues they faced as immigrants to the United States. Founded by six first-generation Indian women who immigrated in the 1960s and 1970s, Manavi is dedicated to ending violence against women. Since it is based in New Jersey, its regular attendees are mostly suburban professionals of Indian origin who are U.S. citizens or permanent residents. At the time I did my fieldwork, Manavi had a local membership of 150. Another 150 to 200 members are spread across the United States, Canada, and South Asia. Manavi began as an all-women's space, but in 1987–1988 it voted to include men in the day-to-day running of the organization, as long as the men did not work directly with survivors. All members pay a small yearly fee. These fees along with fundraisers within South Asian communities were, during the group's first eleven years, the only sources of funding. Manavi accepted its first large grant from the state government in 1996. At present, Manavi carries on its day-to-day work with a small paid staff and is registered as a nonprofit. It deals with an average of fifteen to twenty cases a month. About thirty volunteers work directly with the women who come to Manavi for help. Before the volunteers start working with women, they go through a two-day training session that introduces them to crisis intervention appropriate for South Asian women. In 1997, Manavi offered South Asian women and children the first transitional home in the Northeast.

Sakhi for South Asian Women was founded in New York City in 1989 by a group of young professional first-generation women who came to the United States in the 1980s.[1] Their goal in establishing the organization was to combat violence against women in their communities. Sakhi means friend in Sanskrit and in Sanskrit-derived languages. Within a year of its founding, Sakhi registered itself as a nonprofit with a formal board that meets frequently. The board operates as a policymaking and budgetary body so as not to undercut the general membership's role in making decisions. Sakhi's membership is open only to women, who are referred to as "volunteer-members." In 1996, most of its seventy-five active volunteers were of Indian origin, but the group also included seven Pakistanis, five Bangladeshis, and one Sri Lankan. The organization also represented the religious diversity characteristic of South Asia. Compared with the other groups I studied, Sakhi struck me as being more nationally and religiously diverse, which could be a reflection of its location in New York City and its recruitment policies. Volunteers, who do most of Sakhi's advocacy, sign up to undergo ten to twelve hours of training at orientations conducted two or three times a year. Each year, between fifty and seventy-five women are trained in issues of domestic violence. Apart from advocacy, many Sakhi volunteers are also involved in the organization's committee work. In 1994, Sakhi established the Domestic Workers Committee (DWC) to organize women who were being severely abused by their employers. The DWC functioned as a part of Sakhi until 1997, when conflict between the domestic violence and domestic workers' projects lead to the dissolution of the DWC. In the wake of the split, Sakhi reorganized itself. While it no longer has a separate labor project, its definition of violence against women continues to encompass economic exploitation.

South Asian Women for Action (SAWA), initially called Indian Subcontinent Women's Alliance for Action, was formed in Boston in 1992 to provide a space for women interested in feminist and anti-racist work. It has not been active since 2000. The founders of SAWA were mostly young second-generation women, as were most of its members. Compared to Manavi and Sakhi, SAWA was a small, relatively unstructured group with no external funding. Seven core members (of which I was one) were involved in the everyday work of the organization. Its monthly meetings attracted fifteen to twenty women and it had a mailing list of sixty names. There was no membership fee. Instead, members put time into the organization, and it functioned as a nonhierarchical collective where decision making was by consensus. At the core of SAWA's mission was a commitment to multiple issues, one of which was domestic violence. Its members maintained SAWA as an all-women's space because they strongly felt that, as women, they needed to find their voice and devote their energies to the issues that were important to them.

Manavi: Addressing the Spectrum of Violence against Women

Through its work with survivors Manavi has developed an analysis of violence against women that connects the abuse women face at home with the racism, sexism, and discrimination against poor people and immigrants that survivors encountered in the outside world. By integrating women's abuse in the domestic sphere with the institutionalized dimensions of oppression in the public sphere, Manavi transforms the battered women's movement's understanding of violence as simply "domestic." In keeping with this broadened understanding, Manavi has charted alternatives to the ways in which the battered women's movement supports and empowers survivors. Along with directly meeting immigrant women's material and psychological needs, it educates courts, the police, and social services about the specific obstacles that immigrant women face in their journey toward a violence-free life. Through transnational networks, it ensures that the rights of these women, many of whom may still be citizens of their countries of origin, are safeguarded. In this way, Manavi enhances the gains of the battered women's movement.

Six first-generation Indian immigrant women, "all runaways from mainstream feminism" (Dasgupta and Das Dasgupta 1993, 126), came together in 1985 to form a study group that was soon to become Manavi, a pioneer among South Asian women's organizations. Disappointed with the mainstream feminist movement's inability to deal with problems faced by immigrant women and its demand that the Indian women follow rather than cooperatively set the movement's agenda, the six women decided to start their own organization. In recalling the founding moment, Sujata Warrier, a founder-member, recounted how Manavi's original intention of operating as a study group quickly changed when, soon after its inception, it was called in to help a young Indian woman who was being battered. Since then, Manavi has dedicated itself to working with South Asian women to ensure their right to self-determination and to a violence-free life.

Older first-generation women, rarely credited with activism, have been the most active members of Manavi. As the first post-1965 wave of professionals or wives of professionals, they are assumed to have been preoccupied with establishing the first immigrant families and building cultural institutions. Clearly, some of them were moved to act collectively and politically on women's behalf, laying the groundwork for South Asian contributions to U.S. black and Third World feminisms.

Though Manavi's membership is predominantly Indian, the organization presents itself as South Asian. This self-presentation keeps open the possibility of recruiting members who trace their origin to South Asian nations other than India and thus makes the space hospitable for all South Asian survivors of violence. This commitment takes an active form in its opposition to religious nationalism. Manavi was among the handful of progressive immigrant organizations that were vocal during the massacre that followed the Hindu Right's attack on Babri Masjid in Ayodhya, India, in December 1992. Unfortunately, the Hindu Right's communal politics and violence against Muslims find widespread support among Hindu immigrants. Manavi's secular approach (also found in Sakhi and SAWA) is critical in drawing to it South Asian women across religious lines.

In order to protect Manavi from pressures to dilute its agenda within and outside the South Asian community, members have been very cautious about accepting external funding. Organizational autonomy is one of Manavi's guiding principles. As Warrier puts it, the organization refuses to let funding agencies, whether South Asian or the state, "dictate what we can and cannot do." In 1996, Manavi accepted its first grant under the Violence against Women Act (VAWA) from the state of New Jersey. State funds released under VAWA has made it possible for many women's organizations, previously wary about the state and its role in reproducing gender inequality, to accept money from the government (Abraham 2000, 189). In the last few years, Manavi has also received grants from private foundations. So far, Manavi has been able to use external sources of funding without compromising its autonomy.

REDEFINING VIOLENCE, TREADING NEW PATHS

Defining violence against women as "all social conditions or individual action that keep women subjugated" (Manavi 1992, 5) enables Manavi to center the multiple impacts of racism, imperialism, poverty, and homophobia along with the effects of sexism and patriarchy in the lives of immigrant women. Manavi's work encompasses a wider range of experiences of abuse than solely domestic violence, usually understood as partner abuse. In correcting my characterization of Manavi as a domestic violence organization, Warrier points out that the organization saw "domestic violence as representing *one* piece of the larger spectrum." The impoverishment of immigrant women through legal strictures on work, racist attacks, elderly women's abuse in the family, and the objectification and devaluation of South Asian women all qualify as issues that Manavi recognizes as violence against women. Such a broad definition of violence against women complicates and enriches the mainstream domestic violence and feminist movement's focus on gender as the sole axis of women's oppression, a limitation that has been noted by scholars who study women of color (Abraham 1995, 2000; Crenshaw 1995; Chow 1993).

Addressing the range of violence in women's life would mean transforming the social structures that perpetuate systemic violence. Through its one-to-one work with individual women, Manavi targets structures of oppression to bring about fundamental change. In outlining the way in which activism was different from charity or social work, the favored modes of engagement among elite and middle-class South Asian immigrants, founder-member Shamita Das Dasgupta noted in a public lecture that working on violence against women means taking steps to end it.[2] Elaborating on this goal, Warrier states that such an approach essentially aims at "dismantling these systems so that an organization like Manavi does not need to exist." The radicalism of Manavi's vision lies in its recognition that what matters is not its own survival but the elimination of problems that require such organizations.

Understanding the needs of survivors from the South Asian immigrant women's standpoint has meant that Manavi has had to develop its own definition of what steps would empower a woman whose status as an immigrant makes it difficult for her to choose options open to native-born women. Tracing "the new paths that suit our methods of traveling," Shamita Das Dasgupta states: "We have had to redefine terms such as 'empowerment' for our South Asian context. The accepted modes of empowering women as elaborated by the mainstream feminists—speaking out, marches, rallies, living alone, finding your 'identity'—do not necessarily apply for us. Forcing individuals to make decisions without informational, financial, practical and emotional resources correspond to virtual abuse" (Dasgupta and Das Dasgupta 1993, 128).

For independent living, advocated by the mainstream domestic violence movement, to be a real option for South Asian women, they would need skills to negotiate life in the United States, a country that is alien to many of them. Underlining the importance of skills development, Manavi's handbook on domestic violence notes: "For example, an Asian Indian woman may not be fluent in English, able to drive a car, be familiar with banking facilities, job search systems, shopping in super markets, and other institutions of this country. Thus, to ask an Asian Indian woman to seek employment, find housing, and start living on her own without helping her first to build necessary skills is to disempower her even further" (Das Dasgupta and Warrier 1997, 39). Manavi's efforts to formulate a culturally appropriate model of empowerment and service sets it apart from shelters like Apna Ghar that, as Rudrappa (2004, 25, 53–72) argues, use skills development to discipline South Asian women into American ways of functioning. Unlike Manavi, Apna Ghar does not question mainstream domestic violence paradigms, and thus it ends up implementing Americanization programs that, as Rudrappa points out, are reminiscent of those directed at reforming early-twentieth-century Eastern and Southern European immigrants.

Providing services to immigrant women who otherwise fall through the cracks forms an integral part of Manavi's political stance against violence. Unlike Sakhi or SAWA, it does not see providing services as a function that could compromise its commitment to transformation. It offers survivors counseling, English classes, job training and placement, legal aid, translation services, interest-free loans, and a transitional home. Its volunteers provide women with transportation. They accompany them to police stations, doctors' offices or hospitals, social service agencies, and courts. They translate for those women who are not fluent in English. Manavi has found volunteers who speak the major South Asian languages, and in its outreach work it uses brochures in Bengali, Urdu, Hindi, Tamil, and Gujarati. Urdu is spoken in Pakistan and parts of northern India, while Bengali is the national language of Bangladesh.

Manavi's acknowledgment of the need for culturally sensitive service provision came early in the life of the organization, when it received a call for help from a mainstream shelter. A woman who came to the shelter after being severely beaten by her husband had not eaten for three days and had not changed her clothes and the shelter workers were worried that she was suffering from depression (Dasgupta and Das Dasgupta 1993, 127).[3] When Das Dasgupta arrived, she found out that the woman was a strict vegetarian and could not eat any of the food that was being served at the shelter. The survivor had also not felt comfortable wearing the Western clothes that shelter workers gave her, and thus chose to spend the three days in a long nightgown because it was the item closest to a sari. This incident impressed upon Manavi the need for shelters that could respond to survivors' dietary and cultural needs. South Asian women speak many different languages and they might not always be fluent in English. Their notions about family, duty, privacy, sexuality, state agencies, and so on depend on their class, caste, religious, and regional backgrounds, and also their experiences with state authorities in South Asia. To respond to these specificities Manavi—in alliance with another New Jersey-based group, Women Aware—established in 1997 a transitional home named Ashiana, an Urdu word for nest or a refuge (Sekhri 1996, 1). Manavi's aim in Ashiana is to create a culturally familiar and safe environment in which women can "get back on their feet by learning English, developing marketable skills, finding a job and permanent housing," according to the Ashiana brochure. The residents cook their own food and share in housekeeping. While Ashiana can house women for a maximum period of eighteen months, it is a small facility with only eleven beds.

Since Manavi's resources are limited and the organization has to depend on mainstream shelters and social workers to meet the needs of South Asian women, it has utilized some of its grant money to offer cultural sensitivity workshops called Bridging the Gap. These workshops are also attended by South Asian organizations working with survivors so that they can learn from Manavi's experience. At the workshops, Manavi explains survivors' cultural contexts but resists cultural relativism by always contextualizing them in structures of inequality. The workshops cover South Asian family structures, religious issues, modes of negotiating with authority, forms of and attitudes toward sexual assault, the development of immigrant communities in the United States after 1965, and the role of immigration law. For example, Manavi asks service providers to keep in mind that marital violence needs to be situated in a South Asian woman's immigration status and the complex matrix that ties her and her family to her husband's family. Given the gendered power relations within a marriage, an immigrant husband is more likely to bring over his own family. Thus, as in South Asia, the husband's entire family could be implicated in the abuse, including sexual abuse by male members of the husband's family. The abuse can also be transnational, with the husband's family in South Asia pressuring the woman's family with financial demands or threats of social disgrace, thereby disabling her from taking action to end her abuse. Without being able to turn to her family-of-origin networks in the United States, she might be rendered more vulnerable. Manavi's treatment of the place of religion in women's lives is another good example of how it politicizes culture. At the workshops, it shares with participants its women-centered interpretations of Hinduism and Islam to help survivors keep their faith by reclaiming those aspects of their religion. For Manavi, therefore, providing culturally sensitive services reduces a woman's disorientation at a time of acute crisis and thus enables her to take steps toward safety.

CROSS-BORDER RIGHTS

Much of Manavi's social change work illustrates the process through which space-making South Asian organizations put together a transnational complex of rights by using international mandates for gender asylum, U.S. federal laws on domestic violence, and gender equity laws in survivors' home countries. Manavi has developed strategies to advocate the rights of women whose residency in the United States is endangered because courts and the INS define them as violators. Manavi challenges the construction of "illegal" immigrants by exposing the ways in which U.S. laws become an instrument of abuse in the hands of the abuser. It also shows how these laws revictimize women. As I discussed in chapter 3, domestic violence laws, child protection laws, and immigration laws often work at cross purposes, thereby trapping immigrant women in a legal nightmare. Manavi has effectively intervened in numerous cases to contest the criminalization of survivors by the INS or child protection agencies in order to prevent the women's deportation.

Manavi's Project Zamin responds to the fact that immigrant women often navigate multiple legal regimes. *Zamin* means land to which one has rightful claim. In this case, the term alludes to immigrant women's right to residency in the country to which they have migrated and the protection of their rights in their country of origin as well as in the United States. Project Zamin is a legal clinic that brings together attorneys, scholars, and activists who can offer their expertise in helping survivors file for residency. Manavi utilizes the provisions available to survivors under VAWA as well as international human rights protocols that deem oppression on account of one's gender as the grounds on which a woman can seek asylum. Along with international and U.S. laws, Manavi has to familiarize itself with the jurisdiction of Indian, Pakistani, or Bangladeshi laws. Even as a survivor of domestic violence petitions for legal residency under U.S. laws, her divorce, her children's custody, and her property rights might need to be re-adjudicated under Indian, Pakistani, or Bangladeshi laws.[4] The U.S.-based South Asian organizations thus wrestle with the interface between U.S. laws and laws particular to South Asian nations in order to ensure that women's rights are guarded at both locations. They work with South Asian feminist legal experts, social workers, and activists as well as with human rights protocols to release many women from the tyranny of U.S. courts, the terror of deportation, and the fear of being cheated out of their custody and property rights in South Asian courts.

In reflecting on the right of survivors not to be displaced through such measures as deportation, which exposes them to further material and social violence, Das Dasgupta asks if deporting survivors might be an attempt by the state to construct an immigrant community that can present itself as violence free. She astutely points out that the state literally erases these women, "tainted by domestic violence," from the national body by deporting them (2000). Simultaneously, these removals enable South Asians to represent themselves as problem-free citizens or would-be citizens of the United States. The erasure of gendered violence through such practices and representations powerfully demonstrates the inadequacy of place-taking tactics and the need for organizations like Manavi that are able to separate rights from the confines of citizenship.

As Manavi grows, its members see new challenges. Manavi's acceptance of external funding and its changing membership present new issues that demand attention. Members feel that Manavi needs to closely monitor the relationship between its agenda and funding requirements in order to maintain its autonomy. In terms of Manavi's membership, one member remarked that the gradual entry of second-generation women and women from Pakistan and Bangladesh was transforming what, in the 1980s, used to be an "India-heavy," first-generation-dominated organization. Second-generation members, who live in working-class New Jersey communities, anticipate that the changes are not simply a matter of numbers but require Manavi to reexamine its suburban character, which had so far informed its work. They also feel that Manavi will have to confront issues of class and urban living in unprecedented ways, which perhaps will result in a new organizational culture.

In tracing Manavi's growth and reflecting on its implications, Warrier remarked that the organization has always paced its expansion and changes, moving slowly to develop new programs and to foster a more diverse membership. So far, its self-conscious and regulated growth, its expansion of programs only when it is ready, and its adherence to core principles as it responds to changes within the organization has lent Manavi a strength and stability that is remarkable in the midst of the demands of crisis intervention.

Sakhi: Putting a Public Face on Violence against Women

Sakhi for South Asian Women, formed four years after Manavi, considers its work with survivors of domestic violence to be part of a larger struggle to end violence against women. Two innovative approaches distinguish Sakhi. First, it brings visibility to the issue of domestic violence in South Asian communities by publicly protesting women's abuse. From its early days, it has claimed space at public community events to highlight issues of violence against women. Over time, it has developed tactics that publicly hold perpetrators accountable, along with the communities in which they live. Second, Sakhi has radically challenged the battered women's movement to rethink "domestic violence" by extending the definition to the exploitation of domestic workers within the confines of a space that is usually treated as noneconomic, nuclear, familial, and affectual. Sakhi's incorporation of working-class women, however, was short lived as the organization splintered over the goals of the domestic violence and domestic workers' projects. The split raises crucial questions about the possibilities of cross-class organizing within South Asian communities and within the women's movement.

The women who started Sakhi in New York City began by attending Manavi meetings in New Jersey; contrary to their expectations, New York did not have any South Asian women's organization. Even though Manavi's work with survivors of violence inspired them, the difficulty in traveling to meetings in New Jersey alerted them to the need for establishing an organization accessible to women who lived in the city. In addition, it was apparent to Sakhi's founders that South Asian women in the city had a distinct set of issues that stemmed from urban life and politics. In explaining the need for a group like Sakhi, one founder, Anannya Bhattacharjee, noted, "New York has a very large [South Asian] population that cannot be handled by New Jersey. The City has its own laws and logistics. This was a big enough community that it needed its separate organization."[5] Sakhi thus was born out of the desire for a South Asian women's space that could address South Asian women's needs in New York City.

Like Manavi, the founders of Sakhi immediately identified domestic violence as their organization's issue. They found it to be a "concrete way to begin," given that domestic violence was one of the most urgent, yet unaddressed, issues that faced women in South Asian communities. For its founders, Sakhi provided a progressive way to become active within their ethnic communities. While some of the founders had been politicized through various social movements in the United States, Sakhi was their first opportunity to work with South Asians. Bhattacharjee, tracing her history as an activist, said that until Sakhi, she had never worked "as a South Asian." She had been involved in the solidarity movement against U.S. intervention in Central America, "but it came to a point where people would say, 'How interesting that you're working in black/Latina communities.' [In working with South Asians] we were legitimate actors within our communities. We knew the culture; we could speak with confidence. We wanted to make a difference within our community—[it was] a logical place to start." Sakhi thus became a space for South Asian women in New York City to articulate a politics rooted in their communities.

Compared to Manavi and SAWA, Sakhi quickly formalized itself as an organization. Its founders—professional women in law, film, finance, and computer science—made this formalization possible by bringing their resources and skills to the organization. These women's professional networks expedited acquiring office space, furniture, and staff for the organization, in addition to formal nonprofit status. Sakhi was able to start fund-raising as well as grant writing at an early stage because of the founders' skills and contacts. Bhattacharjee explained that a clear internal structure and clear guidelines about how the organization was to function were aimed at promoting a democratic process within the organization.

Deciding on appropriate sources of funding has been a matter of debate among Sakhi volunteers, many of whom are afraid of co-optation. Scholars who study feminist organizations have noted that external funding often raises questions about whether an organization can maintain its autonomy and oppositional stance (Acker 1995; Martin et al. 1992; Matthews 1995; Reinelt 1995). In Sakhi's case, its founders decided that for advocacy the organization should rely on volunteers, despite their turnover, so that its work could continue regardless of its funding and staffing situation. At present, most of its funding comes from private foundations and the rest comes from the state government, corporations, and the South Asian community. Until 1997, Sakhi avoided applying for state funding because it did not want to work within the limits that the state might set for it (Abraham 2000, 189).[6] This parallels Manavi's cautiousness about state-sponsored funds, even though debates over funding have been far more contentious in Sakhi than in Manavi. Sakhi, in its efforts to broaden its funding base, accepted corporate sponsorship for a few of its events, a move that many of its volunteers did not endorse. Its decision to raise money within South Asian communities also came after much deliberation, during which this tactic was seen as a legitimate way of demanding the communities' support and driving home the importance of fighting violence against South Asian women.

One cofounder, Tula Goenka, pointed out the bridging role of staging high-profile fund-raising events such as premiers of films directed by South Asian women. The film shows attracted local South Asians who would otherwise not attend Sakhi events.[7] Once they came to the events, Sakhi exposed them to its mission, the problem of domestic violence, and the necessity of its antiviolence work. These events served the dual function of fund-raising and outreach.

Sakhi's work began with developing a domestic violence program. During this time the organization also received numerous reports from domestic workers about workplace abuse. Its critique of the sanctity of domestic spaces—a critique that it shares with the larger domestic violence movement—pushed it to integrate into its work exploitative domestic employer-employee relations. This step redefined domestic violence as all forms of violence taking place in the privatized space of the "home." In 1994, Sakhi started its domestic workers' project, and between 1994 and 1997 it ran both the domestic violence and domestic workers' projects. Each project responded to the particularities of the problems that the women faced, and each developed the strategies required to address them. In addition, Sakhi had committees to direct literacy programs, fund-raising, policies, organizing, and political education.

As part of its domestic violence project, Sakhi volunteers provide one-to-one advocacy for South Asian survivors, who can also join a support group to draw strength from each other's experiences. While Sakhi volunteers are mostly young professional women who are middle class to upper middle class, many of the women who approach it for help come from low-income families or are low-wage workers. Unlike suburban areas, the city has a critical mass of immigrants in small businesses and low-end service sectors. The socioeconomic gap between the volunteers and the women that Sakhi serves reflects the class stratification to be found in the city's South Asian communities. As Sakhi's domestic violence and domestic workers' projects developed, a few survivors and all domestic workers became part of its volunteer base, presenting the organization with critical questions about how to negotiate the differences in class and experience.

SOCIAL CHANGE AND SERVICE

Like Manavi, Sakhi enables women, who come to it for help or call its hotline, to find counselors, pro bono legal help, shelters, and public assistance. The organization also receives calls for help from South Asia, thereby making its reach transnational. Using strategies similar to those of Manavi, Sakhi secures women's rights through a transnational complex of international law, U.S. federal law, and state laws. Nahar Alam, who, as I related in the introduction, had fled to the United States to escape from her abusive and powerfully placed husband in Bangladesh, was the first Sakhi member to win gender asylum. As a domestic worker at that time, she contributed to and benefited from Sakhi's training about immigrant workers' rights under New York state labor laws. These innovative ways of ensuring women's right to resist abuse and exploitation later became templates for the many cases that Sakhi handles.

Its awareness of the constellation of issues that immigrant women face led it to develop a literacy program, a job training program, a court interpreters campaign, and a South Asian women's health project focused on gynecological and reproductive health, mental health, and nutrition. Its literacy program was designed as a place for survivors of family violence as well as domestic workers to build their skills and, in the process, become politicized around women's rights. In 1998, Sakhi merged its literacy and job training programs into an economic justice project. As part of its health project, it generated a referral list and worked to educate physicians and other health care workers in issues of abuse and cultural sensitivity. Since 1998, it has tackled the inadequate translation services provided in court for South Asian women. It has been negotiating with New York City's coordinator of court interpreters to draw attention to the gender bias introduced by the court's selection of predominantly male interpreters as well as a dearth of interpreters fluent in each of the many South Asian languages (see also Abraham 2000, 164–65). Even when an interpreter can be found, that person is often unsympathetic to the woman's claims and can distort the woman's story to the attorney and the judge and the court's instructions to the woman. Sakhi's efforts to put together necessary and appropriate resources and to empower women through political education arise from an understanding of the ways in which stereotypes about South Asian women—especially those women who are newcomers and not fluent in English—exclude them from social services and their entitlements within the civil and criminal justice systems.

This part of Sakhi's work can be read on the surface as providing services to manage crises in women's lives rather than organizing to change the conditions that pitch women into crisis. Articulating the place in Sakhi of these two kinds of work and the links between them has been at the core of the processes through which the organization's identity has evolved. In recounting Sakhi's original vision, Bhattacharjee said that the volunteer-members wanted to organize survivors so as to challenge the very bases of patriarchy. But, as its work evolved the volunteers, according to her, were confronted with "the need for [domestic violence] organizations to provide services because immigrants and people of color need urgent things to get on with their life." The volunteer-member, who served on Sakhi's board, elaborated on why the group believes that it is necessary to provide services: "I think when a woman is in crisis one cannot talk about organizing without acknowledging her reality: her need for one-to-one advocacy. . . . Throughout the progressive movement there is a tendency to put service down and organizing up. . . . When a woman needs a service—her need for a job comes before any organizing. . . . As part of our ideology and political vision, we do a thorough job of recognizing that piece."[8] This member also pointed out that activists often created a false opposition between service provision and social change work by treating the two types of work in isolation. Within Sakhi, the greater value placed on organizing caused tensions.

To illustrate the connections between service and Sakhi's philosophy of change, the member analyzed how the literacy classes functioned. Women not fluent in reading or writing English came to these classes, where they used material that touched their own lives, such as writings about women's rights, labor issues, racism, and their communities and neighborhoods (Shah 1996, 7). Underscoring the political content of the literacy classes, the member noted: "The discussion [in the literacy classes] is political. It [the literacy program] provides a safe space for women to come out of their homes without saying that she is in a domestic violence situation or that she wants to be political. She can say she is going to Sakhi for literacy classes. This is not controversial." Thus, the literacy program—ostensibly a service—provides an acceptable reason for a woman to leave a domestic space and enter a semipublic one without having to identify as an abused and/or a politicized person. Within the structure offered by the literacy class, women can safely discuss exploitation, abuse, and their own rights.

At the same time that Sakhi empowers survivors of violence it also politicizes its volunteers. Its general meetings, domestic violence training for its volunteers, and the volunteers' advocacy work are all sites of politicization. In talking about what the organization has done most successfully, Bhattacharjee pointed out that Sakhi trained innumerable women who were radicalized in the process. She underlined the political transformation that members experience when she remarked, "Women who came into Sakhi without identifying themselves as feminists left with identifying as feminists in a way that made sense to them as South Asian women."

The board member quoted above expanded on the way in which Sakhi offers a space where members can make sense of their experiences as South Asian women. She recalled the difference between her prior involvement with a very white pro-choice organization and her experience in Sakhi. According to this member, going through Sakhi's training gave her the tools to understand women's issues in a South Asian context. "With Sakhi, I started to think of domestic violence in a political way," she said. "It was completely amazing that domestic violence was being tackled in a South Asian context." She also pointed out that Sakhi "takes the woman as a whole" instead of separating her various needs—a compartmentalization that she had encountered in her work with white women's organizations. Through Sakhi, she learned to treat survivors as socially located entities, who, when evaluating their options, needed to consider their ties to their families and communities.

HOLDING COMMUNITIES ACCOUNTABLE

Beyond one-to-one and group work with survivors and members, Sakhi mobilizes its members to act collectively in public spaces. Its activist agenda utilizes public demonstrations to draw attention to the privatized and therefore invisible suffering of women in domestic spaces. Sakhi has adopted public protests and marches as a tactic that confronts South Asian communities with its secrets. Through these demonstrations, it publicly demands accountability on the part of families, employers, and the community. For example, in 1996 group members demonstrated in Jamaica, Queens, in front of the house of a man who had severely abused his wife for three years and then tried to kill her by dousing her with gasoline. Sakhi members chanted: "Wake up fathers. Wake up brothers. If you abuse, you will lose" (Bhattacharjee 1996, 2). Through the invocation of familial relationships that in South Asia extend to unrelated persons in the community, Sakhi called upon men in the affected family as well as men in the community to stop the abuse of women.

Sakhi adopted public shaming is a transnational tactic. Women's movements in India have effectively mobilized members to hold their communities publicly accountable for the abuse that individual women suffer in their families (Bhattacharjee 1997a, 39–40).[9] The strategies of public protest shame not only the batterers or the exploitative employers of domestic workers but also those who condone the abuse through their silence. Sakhi, in the diaspora, was drawing on this method of struggle. The sociologist Margaret Abraham (2000, 186), who is also a member of Sakhi and has chronicled its work, assesses public shaming as an "extremely effective alternative strategy [to legal routes] in the South Asian community where 'honor and shame' are an integral part of the value system." However, the boundary between public and private is far more rigid in the United States, especially in an urban space like New York City, than in those Indian communities where feminists have deployed this tactic. Protesting Sakhi members can be seen as libelous or as infringing on the abusers' right to privacy, thereby opening up organizations with small budgets like Sakhi to litigation, which could threaten their very existence. As a solution to this serious risk, Abraham, rather than abandoning the tactic, calls for accountability on the part of members when deploying it. She takes this position because this tactic empowers women and brings public visibility to issues that are usually swept under the carpet.

Since its founding, Sakhi has approached a number of cultural organizations established by different South Asian ethnic communities and places of worship, many of which have been resistant to the visibility that Sakhi brings to domestic violence. Sakhi has consistently and powerfully intervened in ideal representations of national culture and identity staged by organizations such as the Federation of Indian Associations (FIA) on such occasions as Diwali (Festival of Lights), India's Independence Day Parade, or the Pakistan Day Parade. These representations glorify a self-sacrificing, chaste, and virtuous womanhood, leaving no space for survivors or their advocates to speak up about abuse (Bhattacharjee 1992; Shah 1997). Over the years, Sakhi has encountered opposition or, at best, grudging inclusion in response to its requests to participate in these events as a South Asian anti-violence women's organization. It faced further resistance for supporting SALGA, the city-based gay and lesbian group, which was routinely excluded from participating in India and Pakistan Day parades between 1992 and 1999 (see chapter 5). Sakhi's presence at these events, as well as its support for other transnational activist groups, intervenes in the nationalism promoted by the organizers of these parades, for whom, in the words of Purvi Shah, "the notion of 'South Asian' is itself dangerous because it threatens the national-cultural boundaries that these parades attempt to reify" (1997, 53). Through public protest, Sakhi reclaims South Asianness for survivors of domestic violence and their advocates.

ORGANIZING DOMESTIC WORKERS
AND CLASS POLITICS

Sakhi's vigilance with regard to monitoring the political content of its work came from its awareness of the turns taken by the domestic violence movement in the United States. The movement, while it has mobilized hundreds of women to become active, has also become "institutionalized as a social service industry" (Scott 2000, 785). According to Bhattacharjee, "Domestic violence organizations have a certain history. They helped us to the extent that the path had been traveled before and we are aware of the critiques [of the movement]. The organizations have become professional and service oriented. We wanted to avoid that trap." Yet she also notes that, over the years, "what has happened reasonably well is advocating on behalf of individual survivors. . . . Sakhi has promoted the visibility of domestic violence in a mainstream way."

Despite its original vision, few survivors of domestic violence have been involved in Sakhi's organizational work or even in its general meetings. In reflecting on why survivors were difficult to organize despite Sakhi's philosophy and its commitment not to replicate the client-provider model found in many domestic violence organizations, Bhattacharjee said, "The position of a victim is a painful one. Women want to leave the organization and start over again." Even though in her explanation Bhattacharjee highlighted survivors' personal motivations, she also gestured toward a structural problem that created a hierarchy, which positioned survivors as victims or clients.

The domestic workers' project became a way for Sakhi to implement its vision of social change, which it understood as changing the power base instead of simply managing a social problem. It was also a way for the organization to concretize its commitment to issues of working-class women and economic justice. The DWC wanted to "stay away from one-to-one advocacy . . . [and] favored collective group work," according to Neela Trivedi, a former DWC organizer. Though the domestic violence project and the domestic workers' project were characterized by a DWC member to be as inseparable as a person's "two arms," the difference in the principles driving the two kinds of activism led to a painful and difficult split. In April 1997, Sakhi's board members decided to dissolve the DWC. Subsequently, many of its domestic worker members formed their own organizations, which I discuss in chapter 6.

Between 1996 and 1997, Sakhi was powerfully confronted with questions about its identity and orientation to social change. In those turbulent years, Sakhi had to examine its mission, its organizational structure, its philosophy, and its membership. It is worth noting that Sakhi has weathered a number of contentious internal debates on the practical and ideological dimensions of funding and its sources and relations with mainstream community organizations. These issues, in turn, spawned controversies over tactics and quandaries over alliance building such as those relating to boycotting the India and Pakistan Day parades in solidarity with SALGA (see chapter 5). But internal contradictions imploded around the place of the domestic workers' project in the organization.

In building a project centered on poor working-class women Sakhi undertook a bold experiment tried by no other South Asian women's organization. The incorporation of women who were being abused within a domestic space as a result of an exploitative economic relationship overturns the understanding of "domestic" as an affectual and familial space. Sakhi's experience with the domestic workers' project also holds important lessons for progressive politics within South Asian communities. As South Asian communities diversify along class lines, not only will working-class people organize on their own behalf but also predominantly middle-class South Asian social change organizations, ideologically committed to addressing class issues, will have to examine what it means to organize with working-class members. In order for South Asian activists to learn from Sakhi, I believe, it is imperative to understand why the domestic workers' project was such a flashpoint.

As tensions in Sakhi emerged, it established processes through which the disagreements could be addressed. In the last three months of 1996 when I interviewed members of Sakhi, the group had organized retreats and discussions to rethink its mission and figure out how the working-class members of the DWC could be better integrated in all parts of Sakhi's work including the board's activities, fund-raising, and the domestic violence project. It was clear from my conversations that Sakhi was searching for a framework to understand the differences between the two projects. The existing academic analyses of the debates (Abraham 2000, 175–79, 181–86; Bhattacharjee 1997b) differ in terms of how the authors locate the problems that led to the split. One study confronts the issue of class inequality, while the other sees class-based differences among the membership as incidental. One proposes that, organizationally, service provision is ameliorative instead of transformative. The other argues that, in cases where individual women are empowered to join a group like Sakhi, service is transformation.

On the one hand, Bhattacharjee, writing as a founder of Sakhi and a member who was a driving force behind the domestic workers' project, connects Sakhi's difficulties with the domestic workers' project to the parameters of the U.S. domestic violence movement. The mainstream approach within the movement emphasizes personal empowerment—an individualized solution to larger structures of power. From Bhattacharjee's perspective, efforts to reflect on the place of the DWC in the organization boiled down to problem solving on the part of Sakhi "without ever delving into the systematic roots of class exploitation" (1997b, 33). She attributes the split to Sakhi's failure as a middle-class women's organization to work through fundamental questions of class-based inequality of which Sakhi itself was a microcosm.

On the other hand, Abraham, a Sakhi member who was actively involved in the organization at the time of the conflict, sidesteps class issues to frame the conflict as an ideological clash that pitted organizing against service provision. She argues that service also has transformative potential through empowering individuals and providing services to immigrant women who are systematically excluded from them (2000, 178). Deploring the degeneration over time of the debates over the role of the two Sakhi projects into personal power struggles, she sees the language of "class" as a rhetorical strategy that certain members used to divide the membership. She warns against the polarization of views on what social change work entails and calls for moderate and pragmatic politics because, in her view, the ideological debates within Sakhi led to factionalism, acrimony, and certain members' self-aggrandizement.

Though I was an outsider to these painful debates because as a researcher I had agreed to access Sakhi's workings only through interviews, I was invested in understanding the roots of the split as a South Asian activist involved in another women's organization doing similar work. Trying to sort out the conflict in Sakhi was a difficult task. The Sakhi participant who was on the board at the time it made the decision to disband the DWC was not ready to talk about it because she herself had not fully processed what had happened. Others had either left the organization or were abroad. The analysis that I offer here has emerged from conversations I had with current and former members of Sakhi in 2001, public accounts of the split (Abraham 2000; Alam 1997; Bhattacharjee 1997b), and discussions with other South Asian activists, all of whom were seeking to understand the lessons to be learned from the DWC's expulsion.

Since privileged members of South Asian communities enter into exploitative relations with poorer coethnics, in my analysis of the split I want to center the implications of the structural, not personal, dependence of middle-class professional women on paid reproductive labor, which increasingly is provided by poor immigrant women of color (Chang 2000; Glenn 1992). Whether employed middle-class women like it or not, they rely on a range of mundane services from take-out food to dry cleaning to babysitting, and thus they need to recognize their dependence on working-class women. Any struggle to address the exploitation of women's paid reproductive labor must come from an acknowledgment of this structurally induced relationship. While middle-class Sakhi volunteers perceived domestic workers to be in need of leadership training in order to organize, they did not consider themselves to be in need of everyday lessons about the gendered dimensions of class exploitation. Eager to organize working-class women, Sakhi volunteers paid little attention to the role of commodified reproductive labor that enabled women like themselves to work outside of their homes. This failure to grasp how their workplaces were structurally related to those of working-class women obscured the more fundamental injustices: the lack of socialized care work and the perpetuation of the unequal gendered division of household labor by outsourcing it to another set of less-privileged women who are a part of a global trade.

If we are to build organizations that can transform existing social relations, we must ask who owns them. The class question that confronted Sakhi was specifically about middle-class women setting the agenda and goals for domestic workers while disavowing their dependence on them as a class to do the gendered work of caretaking, cleaning, and cooking in private as well as commercial settings. The central role of middle-class women in shaping the DWC is evident from the account that Bhattacharjee leaves of the decision to start the domestic workers' project: "At varying levels of conviction, we [Sakhi volunteers] believed that this should be an 'organizing' project with the goal of having domestic workers as part of the leadership of the project and that it should not be about providing direct services" (1997b, 41). Middle-class women defined what should constitute collective action when the project was set up, during the time the project developed, and when volunteers tried to resolve the conflict between service and organizing in terms of resource allocation and organizational identity. The emphasis on collective action and the decision to stay away from providing services—or setting up organizing and service as competing activities —did not evolve organically from domestic workers. These priorities were decided at the outset by a middle-class volunteer body. By assuming that middle-class women with access to more resources could empower a less privileged group, when in fact they as working women were structurally dependent on it, reproduced transnational hierarchies that marginalized working-class women from leadership and decision making.

Had domestic workers owned the project, a radical social change agenda, which incorporated service, might have been possible. As I show above, from the internal discussion about social change and service provision such a position was available within Sakhi. Indeed, the autonomous organizing efforts of domestic workers after the split indicate that the workers themselves wanted service and social change to go hand in hand (see chapter 6). Social change is most effective when a group of people come together to empower themselves in order to collectively identify the conditions under which they live and then take steps to change them. In Sakhi's case, this would have meant that domestic workers set the agenda and give direction to the organization.

What, then, is the role of middle-class organizers, who along with having political commitment also have the skills, contacts, and resources that provide the material base on which such organizing can be meaningfully built? In cross-class organizing, middle-class organizers need to see themselves as facilitators and participants, who require long-term exposure to and political education about the working conditions of the people with whom they organize. Being doctrinaire, as was the attitude of some middle-class Sakhi members about defining social change, violates politics rooted in lived reality. Just as volunteers working with survivors of violence undergo training to understand violence against women and accumulate experience through their advocacy work, so too do middle-class volunteers organizing with working-class activists need to develop a praxis through long-term engagement with working-class experiences.

One of the valuable resources that middle-class organizers have to offer to working-class movements is volunteering their time. But what are the class and gender politics of volunteerism and how are they related to the politics of transnationalized paid reproductive labor? Unlike the denizens of the time-starved society that the sociologist Arlie Hochschild (1997) depicts in *Time Bind*, where workers walking the work-family tightrope disengage from civic activities, Sakhi volunteers make the time to devote to a social cause while working at demanding professional jobs and juggling the demands of care work at home. These domestic demands lead to a reliance on paid labor for childcare and a range of services that are increasingly provided by women who cross borders into the global North to look for work. Sakhi by no means exists outside the structural dependence of one set of women on another created by the state's and employers' mounting disinterest or inadequacy in providing support for care work. Had Sakhi members, who raised questions about Sakhi volunteers' class position, treated this interdependency within unequal power relations as a structural rather than a moral issue, Sakhi could have offered insights on the gendered dimensions of volunteering and care work within advanced capitalism. Such a political economy organizes women's professional work in a way that they enter into exploitative, class-based relationships with other women, who at this moment are predominantly immigrant. For Sakhi, that would have meant taking on the larger question of devalued reproductive work and the current gendered and racialized international division of reproductive labor.

Sakhi, in its present form, does not have a separate labor project, though it continues to work with those domestic workers who approach it. In the wake of the split, Sakhi reiterated its commitment to movement politics in a December 1997 letter to its members and to the activist community by stating, "We at Sakhi . . . believe in a multi-pronged approach to social change: one that combines education, advocacy, leadership development, and community action, and that does not place undue emphasis on one mode of organizing. We believe that support services are an essential component to organizing and empowering battered women and domestic workers." In an effort to integrate its work with battered women and victims of economic exploitation, Sakhi reconceptualized its literacy program into an economic justice project. This project helps low-income women to develop skills that would make them more marketable and help them move out of the lowest-paid sectors of the service economy. Sakhi's new mission statement as of July 1997 continues to define the organization as one that is "committed to ending the exploitation and violence against women of South Asian origin." It continues to recognize that this violence is multicausal and multidimensional. This standpoint informs the services it provides to immigrant women, who are rendered vulnerable in a society that is often blind to their particular needs.

SAWA: Multi-issue Organizing

South Asian Women for Action (SAWA) emerged in Boston in 1992 out of a need that its founders felt for a politicized South Asian women's community that identified with the struggles of women of color in the United States. Instead of seeking out a constituency to serve, it recognized its members as comprising a community of women who, according to SAWA's mission statement, needed to be able to voice, understand, and get support concerning their experiences of living as South Asian women in the United States. Like Manavi and Sakhi, SAWA was moved to address the pressing problem of domestic violence. But to tackle the multiple ways in which oppressions work, it developed parallel projects that focused broadly on immigrant rights, thereby expanding the scope of feminism. Its desire to be identified with struggles of women of color drew it to work in coalition mostly with other Asian American groups. It realized that to be strong these alliances had to be built on issues that emerged from a politics of location.

In the late 1980s and early 1990s, Boston was witnessing the growth of identity-based women's groups. However, attempts at creating a South Asian feminist space had been short-lived, thereby leaving a gap that needed to be filled. In the words of Riti Sachdeva, a SAWA founder, "Personally for me, having grown up in the Boston area . . . and not having any sort of South Asian contact or community, just seeing a lot of organizing happening around ethnic women's spaces made me really want that."[10] After a friend told her about an older South Asian woman living in the area—Hardeep Mann, a socialist who had grown up in Britain—Sachdeva and Mann organized a discussion on *Mississippi Masala*, a film that had just been released. The event opened up a space to talk about relations between South Asians and blacks in the United States and stereotypes about South Asian women, both taboo topics within mainstream South Asian communities. A number of South Asian women left the discussion wanting to meet again on a regular basis.

The women who joined Sachdeva and Mann founded SAWA during the next few months. As a metropolitan area with scores of universities and colleges that attract South Asians, Boston presented SAWA with the challenge of organizing a community away from the campuses. South Asian groups on campuses served student interests and often felt no connection to local issues beyond campus life. Women who had been involved in previous attempts in creating a space for South Asian women strongly advised the founders to organize independently of college-going South Asians. Having grown up in the Boston area, Sachdeva was acutely aware of the "separation between South Asians who go to school here and those who live here." The South Asians who lived in the Boston area were not visible, even though in the 1990s they constituted the second-largest Asian group after the Chinese (U.S. Bureau of the Census 1993, 20).[11] The founders of SAWA were thus interested in constructing an agenda around the local, everyday issues that South Asian women confronted living in a racially segregated city and in suburbs where South Asians were dispersed and, therefore, isolated. Over the years, SAWA's efforts have put South Asians on the map for East Asian, black, and Latina/o activists and for the various social service agencies that work with women.

As an organization SAWA began as the Indian Subcontinent Women's Alliance (ISWAA), which is how Sonia Shah (1994, 153) chronicles it in her essay on community-based Asian American women's organizations. In naming the organization, the founders debated whether it should be based on a geopolitical identity or on progressive ideology because, fundamentally, they were trying to attract women interested in feminist political work. But to not claim the space they were creating for women of South Asian descent, as Sachdeva put it, "would be denying why we were coming together." The founders eventually settled for "Indian subcontinent" as a reference to the geographical sweep of the organization, even though at least one founder pushed for "South Asian" as a more politicized label. This discussion continued as new members joined the organization. In 1993 the group's members by consensus took the "political decision" to change the name ISWAA to South Asian Women for Action (SAWA 1993, 1).

Renaming ISWAA served two purposes. First, the new name intervened in the default use of "Indian" to describe a region divided along national, linguistic, ethnic, and religious lines. By rejecting the fantasy, shared by colonial masters and postcolonial Indian nationalists alike, that South Asian nations could be subsumed under the single reference of "Indian subcontinent," SAWA members hoped to build a politically informed space that could contain the complex of South Asian histories. Second, it inserted South Asia into the received U.S. understanding of Asia as East Asia. In renaming the organization, the members expressed the desire to "align ourselves with the growing Asian community in the U.S." (1). While SAWA members identified as Asians in the U.S. racial schema, many had their presence questioned in Asian American organizations (see also Sinha 1998). As a result, one of SAWA's objectives was to carve out a visible space for South Asians within the local Asian American movement. In claiming a presence within Asian America, SAWA did not accept an ambiguous place in the racial landscape in the way that the Association of Indians in America did in the 1970s (see chapter 1).

The founders of SAWA and its members were mostly second-generation immigrants, a fact that set it apart from Manavi.[12] The organization attracted and retained women who had spent most of their lives in countries outside of South Asia and felt they had little in common with immigrants from South Asia. Many of the second-generation immigrants had grown up in different parts of the United States, Britain, Switzerland, and Malaysia. One member, Kalpana Subramanian, in remarking on the diverse immigration histories of SAWA members, noted that she met women who were "South Asian, but in so many different contexts!"[13] Subramanian herself had spent her life in changing contexts, having immigrated to the Washington, D.C. area as a child and then spending her teenage years with her relatives in Chennai, India. Thus, from the very beginning, SAWA embodied a sense of the diaspora in terms of cultural hybridity and diversity of experience, thereby setting the tone for its membership. First-generation women like me joined SAWA because we were seeking communities receptive to progressive and feminist politics. As a newcomer to the United States, I joined the group in September 1992 in my search for a feminist immigrant community away from the more readily available conservative regional-linguistic spaces.

The organization could offer an alternative because its members' biographies departed from the ideal immigrant mold. A core member of SAWA, Serena Sundaram, who is bi-racial, said that in SAWA she met women who had a different set of experiences and goals than did the sheltered, conservative, straight, and upper-middle-class South Asians with whom she had gone to school. SAWA members were consciously creating a community of women who refused the immigrant dream of success and assimilation. Like its founders, SAWA's members strongly identified with and as women of color. In explaining why its members developed an engagement with racism, Sundaram said: "All the members of SAWA, whether they were young or old, had quite a few pretty serious hard knocks in their lives. They had been battered around in this country. . . . Every one of us has stories to tell, whether it's stories of [pause] sexual and physical abuse within homes, stories of being beaten up in a schoolyard for being brown, for being nonwhite, feeling alienated and ignored and invisible in Asian settings. . . . I think members of SAWA had experienced all these forms of racism. There was a sense of relief in finding home, to find other people who also experienced it and knew that this stuff happened and knew that we had to find ways of articulating the outrage."[14] The SAWA members' desire to be linked to black, Latina, and East Asian women's activism emerged directly out of experiences of violence and racism as South Asians in the diaspora.

Creative resource-sharing through coalition politics has been a way for SAWA to make an impact despite the fact that it had no funding, budget, office space, or staff. For example, it organized events for cosponsors in exchange for their material support. As an organization SAWA worked effectively in alliance with local Asian groups, queer organizations, and coalitions against domestic violence. This kind of resource sharing, SAWA members felt, left the organization free to decide its agenda and priorities. The agenda that SAWA developed evolved in response to the needs of its membership, constituency, and allies. Its first members proposed that summer 1992 (the year of a presidential election) be devoted to registering South Asian voters to encourage them to make a difference in electoral politics. However, the collective soon saw the limitations of such a project. In recalling the first agenda-setting meetings, Sachdeva noted,

"Considering that so many of us weren't even citizens and weren't eligible to vote, it was hard to really feel that was going to be an agenda that we could get into and sustain." Thus, early on in its work, SAWA was provoked to think about a political platform that did not hinge on citizenship.

The group then decided that its agenda should emerge in the course of public discussions about what South Asians in the greater Boston area perceived as the most pressing issues. Like Manavi and Sakhi, SAWA was drawn to domestic violence work because those who attended the community meetings testified to the devastating effect of abuse in South Asian women's lives. Along with violence, local women exchanged connected experiences of alienation, "cultural schizophrenia," isolation, racism, and economic struggles. To respond to this range of needs, SAWA decided to define itself as an organization devoted to multiple issues. To do so SAWA used advocacy, political education, and community building in its work. From time to time, its members debated steering the organization toward providing services. The core membership, however, always favored developing a voice that demanded services for South Asian immigrants rather than directly providing them.

From the beginning SAWA was envisioned as a feminist space that would provide its members with support and a base from which to act. Speaking about her vision for SAWA, Sundaram said, "I really saw SAWA as an alternative community, a space where a survivor [of abuse] was supported as a South Asian woman . . . who had actively taken steps to be safe." She pointed out how a survivor found that her ethnic community "shut the door on her" when she got out of an abusive situation. At that point, Sundaram explained, "There is no community for her and she is in a country which is often hostile to her as an individual. To have to choose one's racial identity, cultural background, and community or one's physical safety is too much to ask!" So that women would not have to make such awful choices, SAWA was seen as a home where the South Asian women's realities of violence, homophobia, and economic injustice were validated, thereby moving members to political action.

The community that SAWA's members created was a warm, loving, playful space where women developed political comradeship and trust in each through sharing and naming their experiences and exploring their identities. In her "manifesto" for a progressive South Asian politics, Sachdeva captures the energy of such a space: "We delve into the depths of our identities, beyond our subservient savage selves. We dialogue, argue, laugh, sing, gossip, eat, drink, plot revolution with each other" (1993, 5). In a similar vein, Subramanian, in describing what attracted her to SAWA, reminisced: "We were talking about our experiences, the way that people saw us, the way that we were seeing things around us, . . . and how our perspectives of ourselves are so reflective of many political things that are happening around us. We were spending time identifying what those were and our struggles as South Asian women in various ways: in our workplace, our sexuality, in talking about our identities as feminists, and talking about not only how other people see us but how our own community looks at us, how our families see us." Like Sakhi, SAWA provided a space for members to find a language and politics that made sense to them as South Asian women.

The sharing that went on in SAWA, especially during the first few years, led many members to define it as a support group. Since the women who founded SAWA left the state or the country within a few months of its establishment, the remaining members were free to recast the organization. It was not until I interviewed Sachdeva, who returned to Boston in 1994, did I realize that at no point did the founders conceive SAWA simply as a support group. Of course, arriving at frameworks that help women understand the ways in which oppressions work in their lives, and building a space that affords them relief from a sexist, racist, and competitive world, are themselves political acts, especially for women of color (Sudbury 1998, 59–73). But from the very beginning SAWA was drawn to issues such as domestic violence, which demanded that it do much more than what would be possible in a support group.

DOMESTIC VIOLENCE AND ADVOCACY

Domestic violence, the severe isolation of survivors, and the lack of resources for immigrant women came up powerfully and repeatedly in the two community forums that SAWA organized in September 1992. Survivors told their stories at the meetings. Older, suburban women talked about feeling burned out from trying to personally support battered women in their communities year after year. They urged SAWA to come up with ways in which survivors could be supported in a sustained way. In response, several members underwent domestic violence training offered by local shelters and domestic violence coalitions in the following year. But these trainings had little to offer in the contexts South Asian women faced. To learn about how to approach problems specific to

South Asian survivors, SAWA members attended conferences and workshops organized by Manavi and Sakhi. During this period, SAWA started receiving calls for help from abused women. Even as individual members who were trained in domestic violence provided a range of support to some of these women by accompanying them to appointments with their lawyers, to courts, and to social service agencies, the organization struggled to find systematic responses appropriate for a small group with no funding.

The role of SAWA as a voice for South Asian women in Boston's domestic violence movement emerged in 1995 as a result of seeking answers to the problem of sustained support for survivors. Members felt that instead of reinventing the wheel, SAWA should utilize existing shelters and services in the Boston area by making them safe and resourceful places for South Asian survivors. The task, then, was to get these institutions to see and hear South Asians. To do this, SAWA focused its domestic violence project on sharing its knowledge with these institutions and collectively working on resource building by generating lists of pro bono lawyers, doctors, therapists, and social workers who would best serve the interests and needs of South Asian women.

SAWA selected the Asian Shelter and Advocacy Project (ASAP) as an institution with which it wanted to work closely. It learned about efforts to set up the shelter from its allies Asian Sisters in Action (ASIA) and the Asian American Resource Workshop (AARW). Once ASAP was inaugurated, members felt that they could now refer to it South Asian women who called SAWA seeking shelter and services. ASAP received funding under a pan-Asian umbrella, and this further encouraged SAWA to approach it. As Yen Espiritu (1992) points out in her work on Asian American panethnicity, Asian American social service agencies frequently use a pan-Asian identity to attract funding. However, SAWA was soon to discover that South Asians were not seen as an integral part of that pan-Asian identity. The scattered residential patterns of South Asians in the Boston area as well as the variations in their legal status as immigrants made South Asians invisible to ASAP, which was more familiar with native-born East Asian women or first-generation Southeast Asian refugee women. To correct the invisibility, SAWA entered a long period of negotiations with ASAP so that South Asian clients approaching it could feel that they were being heard and supported.

In its last few years of operation, SAWA made efforts to ensure that ASAP in particular, and the Boston domestic violence movement in general, served South Asians. Along with advocating the needs of South Asian women as a group, SAWA educated providers on the politics of violence in South Asian women's lives. Simultaneously, it demanded that South Asians get a proportional share of domestic violence programs, especially if they are funded under a pan-Asian mission. In practical terms, this meant that shelters and service providers have staff who are sensitive to South Asian survivors' cultural and immigration needs and are equipped to do outreach in greater Boston's South Asian communities. Since refugee women from the Vietnamese, Cambodian, and Laotian communities have a separate (though just as complex) set of issues from those of immigrant women, SAWA educated service providers about the constraints that immigration procedures place on South Asian women and their children struggling to end violence in their lives. For example, South Asian women who entered the United States as dependents needed work permits before they could be counseled to work. Thus SAWA offered Manavi's work as a model to agencies confounded by the immigration restrictions that South Asian women faced in finding work and in making the transition to independent living.

In doing this work, SAWA encountered the damaging effects of the model minority image of the South Asian community even within the domestic violence movement. In the eyes of East Asian advocates and those elite South Asians who served on the boards of domestic violence organizations, South Asian survivors appeared better off on account of their suburban residence and their spouses' professional status. SAWA members used their experiences with survivors to make visible the impoverishment of South Asian women and children who leave their abusers. In reality, these women often did not have the legal permission to work and depended on court-mandated support from spouses. From SAWA's experiences with court hearings, it found that the survivor often did not know the amount of her household's monthly expenses because her abuser kept the information from her as a form of control, and thus in asking for financial support she underestimated the actual expenses. As a result, women with suburban homes could not keep up with mortgage payments, pay their other bills, or even adequately feed and clothe themselves and their children.

In its commitment to end violence against women, SAWA has had to chart its own transnational feminism. In 1995, it was invited to help organize a conference on bride burning related to demands for dowries in India with an organization founded by a male South Asian immigrant. The goal of the conference was to mobilize international outrage against the practice. While SAWA members welcomed the opportunity to work with a local South Asian organization on a feminist issue, they struggled against the organizers' problematic representations of Indian women as victims of a backward culture. As South Asian activists located in Boston and called on to participate in an antidowry campaign, they felt responsible for keeping the spotlight of the conference on the responses of the Indian women's movement to dowries and bride burning. Such a focus intervened in the tendency of non-South Asian participants as well as immigrant South Asians to dictate a path of action without taking into account the long struggle of Indian women themselves on this issue. Keeping the Indian women's movement as a reference point enabled SAWA members to identify how their feminist perspective—shaped by their daily encounters with racist, orientalist views of South Asia and South Asian women in the diaspora— could strengthen a position in which Third World women had to be contended with as agents.

UNDOCUMENTED IMMIGRANTS AND RIGHTS

All aspects of SAWA's work explored immigration. For its members, immigration represented a constellation of conditions—emotional, racial, economic, and legal. In January 1996, when it became evident that Congress would pass the most restrictive and xenophobic immigration bill in the post-1965 period, SAWA joined the Massachusetts Asian Pacific American Agenda Coalition (APAAC) in its effort to mobilize Asian communities to oppose the legislation. The bills in the House and Senate proposed measures that attacked undocumented and legal immigration. The anti-immigrant discourse that informed the legislation constructed family reunification and state-sponsored social services as policies that encouraged the explosion in Third World immigration. In order to control this undesirable development, the bills pushed increased enforcement against undocumented immigrants. The legislation proposed that undocumented immigrants and their children be denied the few public services they could access and that legal permanent residents be made ineligible for federal public assistance programs. It also proposed to revise all four preferences for family reunification set up by the 1965 Immigration Act. The immigration of adult children of permanent residents and adult children, siblings, and parents of naturalized citizens was in danger of being eliminated.

Immigrant rights were defined by SAWA in the broadest possible way in designing its campaign. Unlike the member organizations of APAAC that took up the cause of legal immigrants, SAWA found it imperative to advocate the rights of legal and undocumented immigrants in its outreach within the Boston-area South Asian communities and in its letter writing campaign to legislators. Like Manavi and Sakhi, SAWA recognized the disastrous effects of the so-called reforms on survivors of domestic violence. In deliberating over how to define the project, SAWA members felt that a focus on the rights of all immigrants could only expand the issues that could become part of a feminist agenda and could only deepen feminist understandings of the way in which immigrant status reinforced existing power relations.

Members of SAWA began their outreach work in South Asian groceries and restaurants. The outreach team immediately sensed concern and fear on the part of South Asians about the political atmosphere surrounding immigration. Those approached wanted to know what the bills would actually legislate. What would happen to relatives who have been waiting for years to emigrate? Why was Congress passing these stringent measures? During its outreach, the SAWA team was struck by the anger over "illegal" immigrants voiced by South Asian professionals and small business owners. These relatively privileged South Asians felt that "illegal" immigration was not a South Asian problem, a conclusion that was fed by the media's and legislators' obsession with the flow of Mexicans and Central Americans across the southwest border. So why as legal immigrants were they being made to pay for the "nefarious" activities of "illegal" immigrants? This view was ironic because SAWA members also talked to grocery store employees, cooks, and waiters—many of whom did not appear to have legal immigration status—in the same establishments where the owners or customers had expressed such hostility against undocumented immigrants. This initial experience strengthened SAWA's decision not to participate in the silence around undocumented Asians, a silence that promoted the Asian American communities' model minority image. Moreover, its domestic violence work had already alerted it to the many ways in which immigrants become undocumented.

The local Asian American activist organizations argued against the proposed legislation by protesting the treatment of legal immigrants. They claimed that the bills violated the right of legal immigrants to equal protection. They also pointed out that legal immigrants were valuable, law abiding, taxpaying, and hardworking members of U.S. society. The state needed to recognize and reward these attributes instead of punishing legal immigrants. The petitions to representatives, senators, and the president that APAAC distributed to Asian American communities for signature campaigns maintained that it was unfair of the government to restrict the rights of citizens and "lawful" permanent residents to family reunification because legal immigrants contributed $25 billion more to the U.S. Treasury than they used in social services. The language in these letters—such as "I have worked hard and played by the rules," or "Although described as bills dealing with 'illegal immigration,' S1664 and HR 2202 have many provisions that will hurt legal immigrants"—served to distance legal immigration from undocumented immigration. This distinction bought into the state's representation of undocumented immigrants as a drain on and threat to the U.S. economy and polity.

In contrast, SAWA's members strongly felt that the xenophobia driving these pieces of legislation could not be effectively confronted without advocating in the same breath the rights of legal and undocumented immigrants. No meaningful social change or alliances with other immigrants of color could be forged if Asian Americans played into dominant ideologies that denied the U.S. state's impoverishment of Mexican, Central American, Latin American, Caribbean, and Asian economies and the crucial role of undocumented labor in the U.S. economy. While SAWA agreed with the coalition's position that the immigration bills fundamentally violated legal immigrants' right to family and put sponsorship of relatives out of the reach of many Asian Americans by increasing the income eligibility of the sponsoring immigrant, it wanted in its educational material and in its petitions to legislators to register its concern about using undocumented immigrants as scapegoats.

Members also agreed that all immigrants, legal or undocumented, deserved social services. They wanted to openly contest the idea that immigrants slipped through the borders to take advantage of state-sponsored programs, which, in the members' analysis, were woefully inadequate. The critique by SAWA members of U.S. public aid programs came out of their lived experiences with social services in Western welfare states such as Britain and Canada as well as Third World social democracies such as India where members were taught to treat the state provision of social services as an entitlement rather than a benefit.

The draft petitions to Congress that SAWA distributed during its outreach asked for a vote against all measures restricting immigration and denying social services to immigrants. Unlike the APAAC petitions, which registered their protest against measures directed at "legal immigrants," SAWA used the word "immigrants" in an attempt to move away from privileging the rights of legal entrants. However, its petitions did not explicitly support undocumented immigrants because members felt that such a move would discourage people who were already fearful and unwilling to take public action.

In response to SAWA's letter writing campaign, form letters from the senators John Kerry and Edward Kennedy as well as from the office of President Bill Clinton stated their opposition to clauses that intended to put a stop to family-based immigration yet promised, as a way of reassurance, to crack down on "illegal" immigrants. These promises of stepped-up terror against undocumented immigrants only impressed upon SAWA the urgency of putting forward a progressive Asian American position at a public forum. In a letter to APAAC on 6 March 1996 SAWA expressed its distress over the "specious distinction" in the debates between "illegal" and legal immigrants. Stating that the South Asian community in the Boston area had its own share of undocumented workers— overworked, poorly paid, and vulnerable—SAWA added: "As a grassroots organization, we feel that we need to oppose further harassment and attacks on 'illegal' immigrants, even as we raise consciousness within our communities about how the Bills are going to affect legal immigrants." However, in the last few weeks of mobilization against the bills, APAAC did not follow up on SAWA's request for a meeting to bring together the different Asian communities and activists. On 21 March the House of Representatives voted 333 to 87 in favor of what was going to become the Illegal Immigration Reform and Immigrant Responsibility Act of 1996 (see Lacey 1996). The legislation approved increased INS vigilance to curb undocumented entry and stringent civil and criminal penalties against "illegal aliens." While severe cuts in immigrant visas were averted and proposals to restrict family reunification were rejected, permanent residents were made personally responsible for their own upkeep and that of their sponsored relatives, thereby cutting them off from public aid programs. As discussed in chapter 3, these measures have severely impacted survivors of domestic violence.

In the course of the campaign, SAWA learned two important lessons that called for innovative strategies in the long run to mobilize immigrants to influence policymaking. First, the opportunity to link the struggles of Latina/os with Asian Americans—both ruthlessly targeted by the bills—demands strategies that intervene in the association of Latina/os with undocumented aliens and Asians with legal immigrants. What prevented an effective intervention in the dominant discourse around undocumented immigrants was the intense fear that the state promotes among immigrants around issues of immigration status —a fear to which SAWA and APAAC submitted, though in varying degrees. This terror makes advocating the rights of undocumented immigrants appear illegal. To robustly challenge the state's construction, activists, who themselves might suffer from the tenuousness of immigration status, need to develop tools so that individuals can feel safe when collectively protesting the excessive power that the state has in their lives.

Second, exhorting immigrant communities to speak up and make a difference requires methods that go beyond the democratic process of petitioning, letter writing, and signature campaigns because their effectiveness is limited only to citizens. Many Asian immigrants are not citizens for a variety of reasons. These reasons range from the historical exclusion of Asians from citizenship to the citizenship test, which requires fluency in English, and to the post-1965 predominance of first-generation immigrants who retain allegiance to their postcolonial nations of origin. In its outreach, SAWA found permanent residents and undocumented immigrants acutely interested in the outcomes of the debates over the immigration bills. Yet in both cases immigrants felt powerless to influence the course of the debates because they were not voting citizens. Their signatures, petitions, or calls did not technically count. These immigrant realities challenge activists to formulate tactics that can give voice to a significant section of immigrants in the face of state exclusion. To develop such tactics, organizations involved in similar activities need to exchange their collective experience.

THE CHALLENGES OF COALITION BUILDING

The experience SAWA gathered in working with other Asian, South Asian, and queer organizations and its analysis of that process speaks of coalition building as a difficult yet necessary enterprise, particularly in the context of a national environment hostile to racial and sexual minorities. To forge alliances among oppressed groups in order to be able to combat backlash in the 1980s and the 1990s, black and Third World feminists—who were at the same time claiming their right to organize apart from white feminists—held up coalition building as an alternative to models of solidarity (Lorde 1984; Reagon 1983). Coalition building opens up the possibility of alliances across the differences among social and political actors rather than erasing or denying difference in the interest of unity.

In SAWA's case, coalition building was not simply a product of the organization's creativity in resource sharing. Rather, it came from a political recognition that issue-based social change work must engage with and support the struggles of other organizations. In her essay "Why Stand Alone?" SAWA core member Ramani Sripada points out the importance of ties with other women of color with whom South Asian women share a marginalized status in U.S. society. In defining coalition building as an everyday practice that does not need to be restricted only to times of crisis, Sripada states: "We build coalitions everyday in professional and personal contexts. . . . A coalition just consists of various groups coming together around specific issues or agendas. . . . This process is usually initiated in response to a crisis, but it could serve as a long-term effort to affect social and political change" (1993, 3). Not only did every SAWA project involve working with other groups, but many SAWA women were also members of allied groups such as the Massachusetts Area South Asian Lambda Association (MASALA), Queer Asian Pacific Alliance, and Asian Sisters in Action (see chapter 5 for SAWA's alliance with MASALA).

Since the recognition of difference lies at the core of coalition building, the difficulties that SAWA faced in the process had to do with how the various groups understood and negotiated difference. As Bernice Johnson Reagon reminds cultural workers and activists, coalition building is neither comfortable nor always nurturing. In comparing coalition building with a room that is no longer made up of like-minded people, she notes: "The first thing that happens is that the room don't feel like a room anymore. And it ain't home no more. And you can't feel comfortable no more. . . . You don't do no coalition building in a womb" (1983, 359). SAWA most forcefully confronted questions of difference and sameness in pan-Asian settings. Participating in these settings led SAWA members to quickly realize that there could be no "natural" alliance on the basis of a common "Asianness." In its coalition work, SAWA was often taken aback by images of South Asians as pushy when they made demands, as backward because they ate with their hands, or as uniformly affluent because they lived in the suburbs.

Specifically in its domestic violence work, SAWA encountered the lack of meaningful South Asian representation and sensitivity to South Asians in contexts that professed to be pan-Asian. For instance, when SAWA members drew the pan-Asian shelter's attention to the fact that it was not meeting South Asian women's needs, it was told that the executive director was South Asian. This implied that having one South Asian person in a decision-making position precluded discrimination against South Asian clients and staff. On another occasion, the shelter put two South Asians on its board to make it more representative even though SAWA expressed concerns about their lack of knowledge of the scope and nature of domestic violence in South Asian communities. For SAWA, the politics of the board members were more important than their ethnicity. Disturbed by the way in which South Asians were being tokenized within local Asian groups, SAWA initiated efforts to begin discussions with Asian American activists on how to become effective and accountable allies.[15]

While it was difficult to bring up the tensions that SAWA felt in working with Asian American organizations, the process brought political clarity. In reflecting on what was so difficult, Sundaram explained, "We had to figure out a way to deal with an Asian group . . . without feeling we were airing grievances and causing problems to the whole Asian movement in general, you know, trying to figure out how to fend for our needs without feeling like we were betraying the larger movement." But with the help of Asian American groups with whom SAWA had long-term relations, a critical space was opened up. Members of these groups discussed the role of Japan's colonization of Korea in shaping relations between Japanese and Korean Americans, the automatic assumption in East Asian settings that participants would speak Mandarin, and the erasure of Filipinos and South Asians in U.S. constructs of Asia. Their reflections provoked them to examine the fragility of "Asian America."

However, in keeping with mainstream understandings of diversity as benign interpersonal cultural exchange, participants in the discussion suggested educating each other on cultural differences and building stronger friendships outside one's ethnic group in order to make reliable alliances. When SAWA reassessed the needs it was trying to meet through alliance building, it realized that these solutions did not address the politics that make South Asians "Asians" in this country and yet place them on the margins of that group. If a South Asian woman ran the risk of being made fun of in a shelter because she ate with her hands instead of with chopsticks, this was not merely culturally offensive but stood in the way of the woman feeling welcome or safe at a shelter that was supposed to serve all Asian women. In stating its position in an essay, SAWA argued: "While we agree that these strategies [developing cross-cultural understanding and nurturing personal ties] are very important, we find the clarity about our political commitments to be crucial. We should be able to come together on political issues regardless of our personal friendships and be able to explore our common political concerns as they arise from our cultural specificities. Cross-cultural understanding needs to be rooted in how our politics emerge out of our position in this country as Asians from various countries and cultures" (Sachdeva, Sripada-Vaz, and Das Gupta 1996).

By recentering Asian American and South Asian identities as political rather than cultural, and pan-Asianism as a political necessity rather than a step toward inclusion for inclusion's sake, SAWA put forward issue-based grounds for alliances.[16] This move lays the substantive grounds for dealing with difference and is similar to Manavi and Sakhi's efforts at keeping their cultural sensitivity trainings focused on how entering a South Asian woman's understanding of her culture facilitates her access to safety.

To work with difference among women within and across organizations requires substantive transformation of these spaces. As SAWA's work with the Asian shelter shows, it cannot stop at mere inclusion. Yet SAWA itself is not exempt from adopting somewhat mechanical approaches to difference. The problem of overlooking heterosexism started surfacing in SAWA once its composition changed. Until 1996, almost half of SAWA's regular members were lesbian, bisexual, or women questioning their sexuality. With many of these members moving away from Boston, the group became increasingly aware of how heavily it leaned on the core lesbian and bisexual members for its sexual politics. As a group, members had done little work collectively to understand heterosexual privilege or to recruit lesbian or bisexual women, or to represent SAWA as a space that was owned equally by straight women, lesbian, bisexual, and questioning members. The dependence parallels practices in white institutions that do not have to examine white privilege as long as they have people of color to testify for their openness. This is not to say that individual straight women in SAWA were not disturbed by this realization and did not want to keep lesbian issues on the group's agenda. With the shift in membership, a few women had to be constantly vigilant about overlooking sexual politics when it came to planning a panel, setting up speakers, or talking about SAWA.

Sexual politics were not worked into SAWA's culture in the same way as race or class politics. Collectively, SAWA did not feel the impact of heterosexism in the same visceral way that it felt racism. The difficulties of SAWA with sexualities stem from the lack of a situated, ongoing analysis of sexual politics in the course of which members could make concrete connections between the personal and the political and between heterosexuality and other systems of privilege. While such connections breathed life into SAWA's discussions of class relations or racism, issues of sexuality were discussed at an impersonal, ideological level. Members of SAWA publicly articulated a radical Third World feminist stance on reproductive rights, gay and lesbian rights, and women's health. They were also very aware of the role of nation-states, international aid agencies, and corporate interests in controlling women's sexuality. However, members found it difficult to talk about themselves as sexual subjects. In referring to the "oppressive silence" maintained around sexuality in South Asian communities, Shamita Das Dasgupta of Manavi reminds us that "as activists within our communities, the majority of us are not exempt from participating in this repressive practice indirectly, if not directly," and she finds that sexuality is often considered "too intimate a subject for public airing" (1994, 3). Certain SAWA members did privatize sexuality and took a liberal stance on sexual orientation, seeing it as a matter of "choice." Yet unlike Manavi or Sakhi, which do not have a significant lesbian or bisexual presence, SAWA was uniquely situated as a women's group to develop an analysis of heterosexual privilege and perhaps even chart what "erotic autonomy" or sexual agency (Alexander 1997) could look like within a South Asian feminist context. These conversations took place not in SAWA but in MASALA, where members of SAWA who were lesbian, bisexual, or questioning felt far more comfortable discussing their sexual identities and the heteronormativity of mainstream South Asian communities.

SAWA faded into dormancy between 1998 and 2000. A number of its core members, myself included, left the area for job-related or personal reasons. Turnover in core membership was, however, nothing new to SAWA. The older members who remained continued the group's work by drawing in new members. The turnover phase that was spread over 1997 and 1998 came at a time when SAWA had a number of projects underway and was becoming a respected group in Boston's activist circles, receiving four or five invitations to speak at local events each month. In addition, SAWA was invited to sit on the state's domestic violence advisory committee to continue ensuring that South Asian survivors receive their share of resources and appropriate service. It was also a time when the group struggled internally to understand how the increased workload could be shared equitably among members without imposing an alienating accountability structure. At such a juncture, given its visibility, the group did not see as an option turning inward to regroup even as the remaining core members started to feel burned out by the pressure of doing political work with few resources. A few members proposed that SAWA formalize its operation, but SAWA members had built a culture that refused institutionalization, which would have to come with grant writing and routinizing the running of the organization. Also, SAWA's radical vision, gained over years of operating as a feminist collective, made it less open to women who were just discovering feminism. Unlike its earlier years, SAWA stopped retaining new members who were just becoming politicized. Even so, it continues to receive e-mails from women who express interest in joining the group.

Certainly SAWA is not the only grassroots activist organization that has been ephemeral. Yet, a sense of failure and shame usually surrounds discussions of why an organization folds. Underlying this feeling is the assumption that organizations should be self-perpetuating in order to be deemed successful. What, in the current political economy of nonprofits, makes social change organizations viable? Continuous grant writing, fund-raising, and the bureaucratization that accompanies these tasks seem to be the answer to the immortality of organizations. The demand to work within rule-bound capitalist logic often puts a great strain on social change organizations, as can be seen from Sakhi's experience. If we were to shift our attention from the survival of a particular organization to organizing as an activity that can shift from site to site, or attend to what the feminist historian Margaret Strobel calls "organizational learning" in her history of the Chicago Women's Liberation Union (1995), it might be easier to think of movement politics as having a lifespan beyond specific organizations.[17] Barbara Smith, in talking about the inquiries she receives about the

Combahee River Collective—which in 1977 issued a widely read statement setting the terms of radical black feminism—years after the collective's demise, frames the interest as testifying to "a practical vision that continues to inspire" (1998, 171). While SAWA did not survive, many of its members continue their political work in different arenas.

Conclusion

Manavi, Sakhi, and SAWA are the Combahee River Collectives of the present day. In a 1977 statement, the collective called out to black women to "look deeply into our own experiences, and from sharing and growing consciousness, to build a politics that will change our lives and inevitably end our oppression" (Combahee River Collective 1983, 212). A similar urgency animated the founders of Manavi, Sakhi, and SAWA to create spaces where none existed so that South Asian immigrant women could become politicized, act on their politics, and envision a full life for themselves and their families, communities, and political comrades.

These three women's organizations offer the most clear and compelling account of how nation and race intersect in the bodies of "immigrant women." They explicate the complicated ways in which these women are racialized on the basis of their cultural and legal status as outsiders to the United States. Racism, as experienced by immigrant women, is intrinsically tied to who is allowed to belong to that nation and who is not and under what conditions. Thus, these organizations have *produced* understandings of racism that U.S. black feminism and other anti-racist movements need to incorporate in their struggles. These organizations open up new methods through which racism and a racialist state can be fought. To situate South Asian women activists as producers of anti-racist knowledge moves away from the idea presented in Vijay Prashad's work (2000) that South Asians have to catch up with the anti-racist struggles of other people of color in the United States. Sections within South Asian immigrant communities—in this case women's organizations—are along with Chicana and Native American women engaged in developing critiques of the power of the nation in constructing racialized, gendered others (see, e.g., Guerrero 1997).[18]

The three groups, through their redefinitions of domestic violence, advance our understanding of the intersecting systems that devalue women and unleash the violence that women experience. In turn, the redefinitions raise questions about the efficacy of the work against domestic violence such as shelters, one-to-one counseling, support groups, legal help, police protection, and personal empowerment (see Arnold 1995, 279; Reinelt 1995, 88). Are these tools adequate or even appropriate to use in combating the many forms of oppression that the redefinitions reveal? Women of color have long struggled against the white-dominated domestic violence movement's inability to address the convergence of race, class, and gender in the lives of minority survivors. In this context, Kimberlé Crenshaw correctly argues that by "adopting policies, priorities, or strategies of empowerment that elide or wholly disregard the particular inter-sectional needs of women of color" (1995, 364) the movement ends up subor-dinating these women instead of empowering them. These very elisions and exclusions necessitated that Manavi, Sakhi, and SAWA overhaul the understand-ings of domestic violence with which they had started. Manavi was compelled to develop an alternative to the domestic violence movement's model of indepen-dent living when it connected the abuse that immigrant women face at home with the many types of violence they are exposed to in the public sphere. Sakhi, while adopting this broader definition of violence against women, further chal-lenged the public/private divide by introducing the exploitation of domestic workers within private households as a domestic violence issue. The limitations of an individualized model of empowerment became obvious when Sakhi tried to translate the movement's notion of empowerment in organizing workers.[19] In effect, SAWA attempted to confound the hierarchical service provider–client model of most domestic violence work by defining itself as a community, which included survivors, and by taking on the role of an advocate rather than a service provider. Following the reformulations that organizations offer to their logical conclusions would mean rethinking the standardized domestic violence services and methods of empowering women.

Women of color have been instrumental in increasing the domestic violence movement's awareness about the need for culturally attuned services and diver-sity in staffing (Scott 2000). These activists have confronted the movement's implicitly white, monolingual, and monocultural assumptions that marginalize, alienate, and revictimize black, Latina, and Asian women (Crenshaw 1995; Lin and Tan 1994; Scott 2000). Educating mainstream service providers about the culturally and structurally specific ways in which a South Asian woman is abused, how she decides to cope with abuse, the problems she faces in moving toward a violence-free life, and her path to empowerment is an intrinsic part of the advocacy of Manavi, Sakhi and SAWA. Here we find a critical practice of cross-cultural antiviolence work. Only too aware of the ways in which their analyses of South Asian cultures could be fetishized and essentialized, the organizations actively strategize against such appropriations. They locate the beliefs and practices of survivors in relations of power that shape women's opportunities. Their insistence on power and history, particularly immigration history and the histories of anticolonial and postcolonial struggles, opens up a strategic space from which activists doing this kind of transnational and trans-cultural work can deploy a critical multiculturalism that by definition is rooted in questions of justice rather than in cultural relativism (Bannerji 2000; Chicago Cultural Studies Group 1994; McLaren 1994).

Feminist organizations, particularly those with grassroots origins, have historically struggled with the implications of institutionalization for their survival, internal functioning, and accountability (Ferree and Martin 1995b). Manavi, Sakhi, and SAWA present us with three distinct models of dealing with the problems raised by institutionalization, particularly with regard to the relationship of funding to organizational autonomy; structure to collective functioning; and service to social change. Manavi has managed to maintain its autonomy by introducing structure gradually, by accepting funding cautiously, and by deliberately conceptualizing service provision as an integral part of altering immigrant women's life chances. In comparison, Sakhi introduced structure and grant writing soon after its inception to ensure clear organizational procedures and successful service delivery. Like Manavi, it recognizes the urgent need of immigrant women for services but also struggles to reconcile service provision with its commitment to social transformation. Thus, while Sakhi embraced certain aspects of institutionalization, it also dramatically experienced the move as contradictory. In contrast to Sakhi and Manavi, SAWA spurned all forms of institutionalization even as it clearly perceived the importance of services in domestic violence work. It chose coalition building and resource sharing in order to make sure that women received services, and its membership retained its focus on social change. Yet, SAWA was also the one organization that was not able to sustain itself beyond a point. Despite the different trajectories of the organizations, they all share a common critical consciousness about the pitfalls of institutionalization, particularly for minority groups. Historically, the rules that govern institutionalization have worked against them. Even as the three organizations felt the pressure to provide services and join the social service industry, at every step they evaluated these pressures against their agenda for social change. Rather than asking which model is the most successful, I would argue that each offers its own lessons that organizations need to take to heart while continuing to experiment with new conceptualizations of structure, decision making, leadership, and accountability.

Activists of color working on issues of violence against women have had to engage with the state because of the ways in which it regulates and polices these communities. Their debate over the relationship between feminist organizations and the state is less about what scholars like Claire Reinelt (1995) or Myra Ferree and Patricia Martin (1995a) have characterized as the choice between radical and liberal politics and more about the terms of engagement. The three women's organizations' engagement with the legal aspects of immigrant life is innovative rather than reformist. The organizations constitute sites of legal innovation in that they demand rights for noncitizens, thereby prying apart the taken-for-granted link between citizenship and rights. Manavi, Sakhi, and SAWA call into question the state's configuration, in the name of sovereignty, of a hierarchy of rights that stratifies immigrants.

The roots of the three organizations' transnational feminism lie in the ways in which they construct a transnational complex of rights and hold themselves accountable to women's movements in South Asia to act in partnership with them. To understand how their feminism is "transnational," I attend not only to the materiality of transnational flows—connections that Basch, Schiller, and Szanton Blanc (1994, 27–30) favor over evocative discussions of cross-border circulations. I also trace the activists' knitting together of various legal regimes and genealogies of struggle in the diaspora and in homelands. Such inter-reference does not necessarily require actual connections between groups or movements. Of course, those connections develop as Manavi identifies networks of feminist lawyers in South Asia, or as Sakhi takes calls from India about women trapped in abusive relationships in New York City, or as SAWA invites women's rights activists visiting from India to speak to its members and allies. Alongside these tangible links, we find Manavi's use of Pakistani feminists' women-centered reinterpretations of the Koran, Sakhi's deployment of public shaming developed by Indian feminists, and SAWA's insistence on the gains of the antidowry movement in India at a Boston conference. These less literal deployments of transnational feminism show that cross-border solidarities, in which Chandra Mohanty (1997) invests her hopes for a liberatory feminist praxis,[20] can be built through the circulation of ideas, rights regimes, and oppositional practices without direct contact. Manavi, Sakhi, and SAWA help us recognize that these "local" groups, which call themselves "grassroots," are actually transnational organizations that span borders in highly imaginative ways.

While the work of these three organizations is in multiple ways instructive about political action and vision, it also raises questions about whether women's organizations can fulfill the political desires and dreams of all South Asian women. In my discussion of the organizations, I point to a pattern that shows that lesbian and working-class women within these organizations have had difficulties with power and resource sharing and agenda setting. The proliferation of South Asian LGBT, youth, and working-class groups indicates that lesbians, young women, and poor women prefer to set up their own spaces rather than work solely within women's organizations. As I show in the next chapter, lesbian women have had to seek a host of political venues to do the work they would have liked to do within South Asian women's groups. Working-class women are also building their autonomous organizations. These developments defy the idea of a homogenous "women's interest" even within a single racial-ethnic group. They reflect the socioeconomic stratification within South Asian immigrant communities, which, as I have argued throughout this book, is key to understanding and recognizing the plurality of political struggles within those communities. In doing so, I have refused to pathologize the heterogeneity of interests and the political forms they take.

Even then, core questions remain about the sorts of political analyses, ideologies, and political culture that women's organizations need to generate in order to make sense of these developments. Will South Asian women's organizations replicate the limitations of the second wave of U.S. feminism despite the fact that they themselves are the result of resisting white women's exclusionary practices? Are conflicts between working-class women and middle-class women, or straight women and queer women, inevitable in women's movements? These fissures and limits are hardly inevitable; rather, they speak of differentials in South Asian histories and social locations that we must understand in order to envision social change. South Asian women, when moved to form autonomous women's organizations, do so because they realize that gender oppression as a pure, self-contained category cannot explain their realities. They come together out of a realization that the sexism they face is racialized, defines them as perpetual outsiders, and mobilizes assumptions about their class position and sexuality.

Recognizing the relationality of gender to class, sexuality, nationality, and race was not the starting point of U.S. second-wave feminism. Instead, it is the staring point of women-of-color movements. Given this point of departure, I would argue that these movements—of which South Asian women's organizations are a part—are particularly well situated to analyze the ways in which differences among women of color are produced through the complicated intersections of social hierarchies. Julia Sudbury, in her study of black women's organizations in Britain, suggests that women's organizations in the 1990s, which rejected an earlier emphasis on feminist Marxist analyses, are able "to speak more openly about socio-economic divisions among black women" (1998, 169), and by extension are better equipped to address those divisions. South Asian feminists have the political tools—and a political responsibility—to analyze how exclusionary practices, far from being inevitable, come out of histories of colonial, postcolonial, and transnational class formations which in turn intersect with sedimented constructions of gender, sexuality, and race.

CHAPTER 5

Subverting Seductions: Queer Organizations

It is summer 1996 and I am in a small Manhattan apartment conducting an interview. I turn on my tape recorder and ask my interviewee, whom I am told is one of the oldest members of the South Asian Lesbian and Gay Association (SALGA), how the organization started. After he first requests that I do not use his name, he begins to tell the story: "The way SALGA started is strong evidence of international connections." I furiously scribble "transnational links" in my notebook. My heartbeat quickens because I had not anticipated his story to start in this fashion, even though I had listed my interest in "transnationalism" at the beginning of the interview.

The SALGA founder-member continues his story by saying that he had come out soon after arriving in the United States in fall 1988. But what politicized him—what made him aware of himself "as an immigrant, as a minority, as an Asian"—was his work with an Asian American and Pacific Islander men's group in New York City. During this time he had seen newsletters published by Trikone (which translates as "triangle"), which began in the San Francisco area in 1986 as the first U.S. South Asian gay and lesbian group, and he had met with a Trikone member on a trip to the Bay Area. When he visited Delhi in winter 1990, Trikone connected him to a newly formed gay group in the city. In reconstructing SALGA's inception, he muses: "I met two people who were very active in organizing the group in Delhi. . . . I had several conversations with one of them. He took me to meet Giti Thadani [an Indian lesbian scholar-activist]. I had one conversation with her. The net result was that the whole thing left me very excited and energized! I thought we should start a group like that in New York. . . . Over the course of the past two years I had come across gay South Asians but they did not know each other. So, then, I thought it would just be nice for all of us to know each other. At that time I did *not* want to call it a group. I just wanted to call it a network because once you start calling it a group, it sounds grandiose and it becomes unmanageable. After I came back, I organized a meeting. . . . It was the first meeting and there were twelve or thirteen people [all men]. That's how the group started. There was a lot of enthusiasm." This informal "network," at first called South Asian Gay Association (SAGA), developed into SALGA as lesbians joined. That very first summer, SALGA marched in New York's Gay Pride Parade.

Catching himself digress, the member pulls himself back to the founding moment: "The point of the whole story *is* the fact that ideas travel. The formation of gay groups in India was catalyzed by the Trikone newsletter in San Jose. And then those two together catalyzed the formation of SALGA. Now, I don't want to give myself too much importance here because it may be that [pause] I am convinced that the circumstances were just right so something would have come into existence *anyway*. Even if it had been someone else, I am sure it would have still been the same process." In the first five minutes of the interview, this SALGA founder-member shuttled me from the U.S. East Coast to the West Coast, then to New Delhi, and then back to New York City. In doing so, he concretely laid out the process that I was trying to abstract by using the term "transnationalism." He marked the circuits as a phenomenon that he felt had little to do with himself as an individual.

Another summer evening—this time in 1994 in Boston. I had just arrived at one of the South Asian Women for Action (SAWA) meetings, in which the boundaries between doing business and socializing were fluid. As we settled into our seats, I noticed two SAWA members with a conspiratorial gleam in their eyes. "What's going on?" I ask. The two burst out, "Well, we met these South Asian queers! *Desi* queers. It was amazing!" The pleasure in their voices was unmistakable. "*Where* did you meet them?" I asked. They had seen a small ad in the classified section of *Bay Windows*, Boston's gay and lesbian newspaper, that announced a new South Asian gay and lesbian group, MASALA, an acronym for Massachusetts Area South Asian Lambda Association. They had attended the meeting downtown the previous day. Finding MASALA—a formalized South Asian queer group—was as much of a momentous event for these SAWA members as it had been for us to meet Manavi and Sakhi activists for the first time.

Two years later I interviewed the Canadian South Asian founder-member of MASALA, Imtiyaz Hussein. My discussions with him revealed another complex "flow chart," one node of which was MASALA in Boston. In the early 1970s, when Hussein was three years old, his family immigrated to Toronto, Canada, from Dar es Salaam, Tanzania. His family history in Tanzania went back four generations when his ancestors left Kutch in Gujarat, India, in the second half of the nineteenth century. His family's decision to move to Canada was related to the Africanization programs and socialist reforms of the then newly independent Tanzania, which led to the exodus of fifty thousand South Asian settlers, many of whose ancestors were brought to Tanganyika by British colonizers and given certain privileges that placed them above Africans in the racial order created during colonial rule (Nagar 2000). As the feminist scholar Richa Nagar argues, reservations about anticolonial struggles, which South Asians feared would erode their privileges, marginalized them in postcolonial Tanzania and led to their outmigration to Canada and Britain. Though Hussein was very young when he left Tanzania, his deep connections with this immigrant history emerged again and again in his interview as he talked about his identity as an Ismaili Muslim who grew up in Toronto, which had a community of twenty-five thousand Ismailis, most of whom came from East Africa in the 1970s and 1980s.

Hussein framed his history of politicization, which eventually led to the founding of MASALA, as having been part of the struggle he had engaged in since he was fourteen to integrate his gay identity with his faith, as well as with his communities of family, friends, and lovers and with his growing consciousness about being a diasporic South Asian. During his undergraduate years at MIT in the late 1980s, Hussein initiated and was involved in campaigns centered around gay and lesbian issues on campus, during which he gained considerable political experience first by organizing against ROTC's discriminatory recruiting practices that excluded gays and lesbians and then by doing HIV / AIDS education. At the same time, he was establishing ties with Boston's small Ismaili community, within which he and other younger members tried to create a space to discuss a wide range of topics involving sexuality, including abortion, premarital sex, and homosexuality.

On finishing his undergraduate degree, Hussein made several attempts to return to Toronto, where he became active in Khush (which translates as "ecstatic pleasure"), a South Asian gay men's group in which more than half of the members were Ismaili. This gave Hussein his first opportunity to "reconcile" the different parts of himself. When he came back to Boston after a year in Toronto, he felt the need in Boston for a group like Khush. In characterizing his student years in Boston as a period when he focused on the "gay piece" of his identity at the expense of his ethnic identity, Hussein noted: "As much as I was trying to integrate my life, one thing that was taking a back seat was the Indian part of me." Unlike Toronto, where he was immersed, sometimes claustrophobically, in a close-knit Indian Ismaili community, Boston offered little contact with Indian culture outside of the Jamatkhana (a place of worship and a community center). Hussein was uncomfortable in the Indian students' club on campus because, he said, "It felt that group was for the real Indians, like the ones from India or Pakistan. It wasn't for the North American–raised version of India." These spaces did not accommodate his Tanzanian Indian Ismaili Canadian upbringing. Khush, as a Canadian South Asian collective that validated Hussein's diasporic reality and his gay identity, thus served as a model for starting something similar in Boston.

Hussein started his organizing efforts as the Boston contact person for Trikone. Calls came in not only from the larger metropolitan area but also from western Massachusetts, Rhode Island, and Connecticut with queries about whether there was a group like SALGA in Boston. Responding to what he saw as a clear need, he hosted the first gay meeting in February 1994, which was followed by two more monthly meetings before he decided again to return to Toronto. This time he remained in Toronto for two months. Back in Boston, he restarted in earnest what was to become MASALA. Like SALGA, MASALA was born out of the confluence of desires, ideas, and political experience that flowed from continent to continent and crisscrossed national borders and regions to find spatial expression in Boston, thereby creating community for lesbian, gay, and bisexual South Asian migrants.

I relate Hussein's story in some length here in order to trace not only his personal story but also the trajectories of migration before, during, and after the

British colonization of India, Tanzania, and Canada. Such highly personal stories about sexual identity—often simply labeled as "coming out" narratives—are also larger social stories that archive violent episodes of colonization, racialization, and migration (Cvetkovich 2003, 118–55). Hussein and, as I discuss later, the Indo-Caribbean SALGA member Tim Baran, in narrating their queer transnational subjectivities uncover traumatic moments in history that are otherwise willfully buried in national memory as are the links between nation building and nonnormative sexualities.

In this chapter I analyze the ways in which SALGA and MASALA create transnational identities, spaces, and politics to subvert the relationship between sexuality-based rights and citizenship, which in the United States is increasingly defined through consumer entitlements. Based on the work of the two organizations, this chapter marks the ways in which they dispute the pessimistic diagnoses on the part of some queer theorists that queer politics have succumbed to the seductions of consumer capitalism. While SALGA and MASALA adopt the movement's classic though recently maligned strategies of building community and gaining visibility, and while they resemble post-Stonewall organizations in their need for community, affection, safety, and pleasure, as autonomous organizations they also rebel against the racism within the larger lesbian, gay, bisexual, and transgender (LGBT) movement. Given this departure, what do "community" and "visibility" mean to SALGA and MASALA as tools to fight for rights? How and to what end do they deploy these strategies?

As queer immigrants are legally and discursively considered noncitizens in their multiple national contexts (see chapters 2 and 3), their rights claims do not neatly fit into the model of sexual minorities, relegated to second-class citizenship, who fight to access full national membership. They assert their presence as a visible community not in the hope of becoming the rights-bearing citizens of one nation or the other but to contest the interplay of U.S. and South Asian nationalisms that disenfranchise them through context-specific techniques. In this way, they advance a transnational conceptualization of identity and rights. Such a transnational positioning allows groups like SALGA, for example, to confront the queerphobic politics of Hindu nationalism in the diaspora and its intersection with U.S. ideologies that put immigrants and queers outside the national imaginary.

If the search for sexual rights is not conducted via citizenship, to what extent can the cautionary tales about the consumeristic turn in gay and lesbian politics apply to queer immigrants of color? Since the post–World War II economic boom in the United States, the state and the economy have fused citizenship and consumerism to invent the citizen-consumer; a good patriotic citizen is one who consumes. Under neoliberalism, an era inaugurated by Ronald Reagan in the United States and by Margaret Thatcher in the United Kingdom, this relationship was further refined. Citizens are encouraged to demand rights not as clients of a social democratic welfare state but as responsible voters and taxpayers who exercise their rights mainly as entitled consumers (Cohen 2003; Evans 1993). Since the 1990s, consumerism has been one terrain on which gays and lesbians have battled for rights. Under the terms of neoliberal citizenship, lesbian and gay communities often have to make demands for distributive justice (not just for lifestyle-related goods and services) through the language of consumerism rather than that of welfare. This is because the state subcontracts to the private sector the provision and distribution of basic rights—such as those to health care, employment-related fringe benefits, and various social insurance programs—which then privileges market forces.

The new political visibility of queers as a community of consumers has recently come under attack (Gluckman and Reed 1997; Hennessy 2000; Joseph 2002). Progressive queer theorists have expressed reservations about the state of U.S. queer politics that employ visibility and valorize community with little self-consciousness about how these strategies impair the links between struggles based on sexuality and those against racism and transnational capital. The representation of gays and lesbians as entitled consumers, they warn, is harmful because it generalizes the profile of white, urban, affluent gay men to the entire queer community. Rosemary Hennessy (2000, 111–42) decries the trend in queer activism to assert visibility by queering the spaces of hyperconsumption such as malls or by presenting gays and lesbians as markets for specialized lifestyles. Miranda Joseph (2002) suggests that anti-oppression queer politics is possible only when they are critical of community. She further states that those who embrace such politics need to grasp that community does not offer an antidote to the fragmentation, alienation, and exploitation induced by capitalism. This is because community building enters into a generative relationship with capitalism; the discursive construction of one calls the other into being.[1] According to Ann Pellegrini, such cautions, despite their anti-racist impulse, tend to "narrate homosexual identity and community formation through an unmarked whiteness" (2002, 139). They erase the political contributions of queer constituencies that employ alternative structures of kinship, community, and consumption within capitalism to intervene in oppressive social relations. The severe limits that these theorists diagnose are, therefore, not symptomatic of all queer politics but of a white Euro-American affluent brand that has traditionally disavowed the privileges of race, class, and national belonging.[2]

Considering the critical practices of SALGA and MASALA demonstrates that the sweeping indictments of queer politics ignore other possibilities and trajectories that are also integral to the queer movement in the United States. Both SALGA and MASALA navigate the intersecting circuits of community, capital, consumption, and nationalisms without necessarily capitulating to consumer-based arguments for what the queer theorist David Evans (1993) calls "sexual citizenship" even as their political practice requires new spaces of consumption mediated by transnational capital. This chapter explodes monolithic representations of queer activism by marking the ways in which a group of immigrants uses community and visibility to search for rights that are not rooted in neo-liberal and religious nationalist citizenship. In doing so, it builds on efforts to formulate a queer of color critique (Alexander 1998; Ferguson 2003; Gopinath 2005; Manalansan 2003; Reddy 2003) that maps the relationship among capital, state formation, and queerness by accounting for migration, colonization, and racialization.

Queer immigrants of color, far from uncritically embracing visibility as a mode of political empowerment, inventively resist the exposure, fixity, and linearity of mainstream calls to become politicized through "coming out" and becoming visible (Gopinath 2005; Manalansan 2003). For these immigrants, visibility is fraught precisely for political reasons, as the scholarship that centers on their perspectives reveals. The "logic of visibility" (Gopinath 1998, 2005), which makes "lesbian" and "gay" the only intelligible signs of sexual alterity, pits secrecy against publicity or silence against disclosure, thereby violating queer immigrant subjectivities and their need for security. As Martin Manalansan, in talking about the *bakla* participants in his research, notes: "Public visibility, canonized by the mainstream gay community, is questioned and held at bay by these men" (2003, 33). They doubted public visibility's promise of transparency and empowerment because it negated the representational and interpretive frames that their desires, pleasures, and identities required. These men also shunned public visibility to avoid scrutiny of their immigration status and to secure their sense of class mobility and success in the United States. Though SALGA and MASALA want public visibility for South Asian queers, they adopt it critically as a political strategy. This chapter unfolds the two organizations' retooling of visibility.

As an activist myself I initially had reservations about SALGA and MASALA's political culture that celebrates visibility and community. I wondered about the extent to which they could be progressive while operating within the assimilative and consumeristic terms of the larger LGBT movement. For both organizations, providing a safe community for South Asian queers, regardless of their political orientation, is itself a political act. At first I had trouble accepting such a position because I suspected that this valorization of community was exactly what opened the door to anti-affirmative action South Asian computer engineers who were interested only in partying. My interviews with both SALGA and MASALA members were marked by my anxious questions about how they understood the political dimensions of their work. In comparison with the women's and labor organizations in this study, SALGA and MASALA's definitions of the political seemed to me to be amorphous. I worried that they were anomalous to my emphasis on radical social change as the point of departure for space-making organizations.

But, over time, I have come to examine the set of binaries within which I was operating: social/political, identity/issues, assimilation/resistance. Neither SALGA nor MASALA allows a quick and facile separation of these pairs or a greater valuing of resistive, issue-based politics. Outside of these binaries, it is possible to see how the organizations' emphasis on visibility and community contests white queer politics and U.S. and South Asian heterosexist nationalist politics. Both SALGA and MASALA share these engagements with South Asian women's and labor organizations. While the members of the two queer organizations reimagine, reformulate, and newly enact community, they are aware of the ruptures within that are caused by sexism, classism, and inadequate attention to the histories of diasporic formations in places like the Caribbean. As queers of color, they are critically conscious of the ways in which the sense of community can easily elide differences of gender, class, nation, and generation. The presence of lesbians, older immigrants, members who are not as proficient in English, second-generation South Asians, and Indo-Caribbeans who have little in common with upwardly mobile first- or second-generation South Asians constantly unsettle the sense of community even as they seek ways to act collectively.

Since I found many similarities between SALGA and MASALA, instead of describing the work of each organization separately as I do in chapters 4 and 6, I have structured this chapter around four themes. After offering brief biographies of both organizations, I examine why SALGA and MASALA embrace the terms "gay" and "lesbian" in the context of the literature on the globalization of sexual identities. In the next section, "Community and Visibility" I look at the intersection of the social and political in the organizations' work. The section "India Day Parade and Sexual Citizenship" maps SALGA's assertion of transnational rights against U.S. and Hindu nationalisms displayed at the annual parade. The last section, "Cross-Connections," focuses on the collaborative spaces that open up as a result of the political limits within SALGA and MASALA. The coalition work of individual members connects the two organizations to new issues that make it difficult for them to compartmentalize LGBT politics from other struggles such as those to end class, race, and gender oppression.

Founded in 1991, with chapters in New Jersey and Philadelphia, SALGA is a volunteer-run group that defines itself on its Web site as "a social, political and support group for lesbians, gay men, bisexual and transgender people" of South Asian descent.[3] Its fourteen-point charter lays out its goals to build solidarity and community, promote rights, and identify and address issues facing South Asian queers. General meetings draw anywhere between thirty-five and fifty attendees. Separate support group meetings are held regularly. As an organization SALGA brings together first- and second-generation members, U.S. citizens, and noncitizens. The members trace their national origins to countries in South Asia and its diaspora. Business in SALGA is done through delegating organizational tasks to committees, and decision making is by vote not consensus. Because SALGA has no membership fee, the organization is funded through donations from members, cover charges for parties and other events, and small grants from private foundations. In seeing itself as a "cause," which is fed by what the founder-member cited above called the "energy and ideas of a movement," it has consciously stayed away from offering services in order to avoid the divide between clients and providers and the pitfalls of continuous grant writing and, ultimately, professionalization.

Like SALGA, MASALA started in 1994 as a men's group but quickly extended its membership to women. Its goal, as stated on its Web site, is to "celebrate cultural events, connect with others in discussion of common concerns and provide a safe and supportive environment for South Asian lesbians, bisexuals and gays" (MASALA 2005). Its membership's demographics are similar to those of SALGA. Members pay a small membership fee and get a newsletter in exchange. They also personally fund and raise money for events. Although MASALA has a board it is not formally a nonprofit. The board is in charge of decision making by vote and allocating the organization's money. Like SALGA, MASALA does not see itself as a service-providing organization.

The Politics of Naming

When presenting this work to colleagues at meetings and elsewhere, I have sometimes been asked why the two organizations named themselves "lesbian and gay" and "lambda" (the Greek letter adopted in the wake of Stonewall in 1969 as a symbol by the Gay Activists Alliance of New York) instead of turning to terms in South Asian languages for same-sex sexualities. This question expresses legitimate concerns about the universalization of the historically and culturally specific terms "gay" and "lesbian" that cannot exhaust the operations and understandings of homoerotics in other cultural contexts. The concern over the politics of naming draws attention to what travels from where, and whether using terms that are historically rooted in sexual categorizations and social movements in the economic North—lesbian, gay, or lambda—undercuts the authenticity and self-representation of those who are not originally from that place. At the same time, the question reserves "gay" and "lesbian" identities for modern and "Western" sexual subjects and, in a nativizing move, assumes that indigenized identities would automatically reflect authentic "non-Western" configurations of desires and their expression.

The issue of naming bears on a lively debate about the globalization of gay and lesbian identities (see, e.g., Altman 1996; Champagne 1999; Gopinath 1998; King 2002; Manalansan 2003; Puri 2004). While some scholars argue that globalization has facilitated the currency in the South of originally Northern sexual identities ("gay" and "lesbian") and has sparked sexuality-based liberation struggles in that region, others contest the universalization of these categories to ask what they can encompass and what happens when sexual identities and politics flow in the reverse direction, from the South to the North.

When we wonder whether "gay" and "lesbian" are appropriate labels for South Asians, we anchor those terms in the North and in a specific moment when "the nineteenth century homosexual became a personage, a past, a case history" (Foucault 1990, 43). Manalansan calls into question this developmental narrative that secures "gay" and "lesbian" for properly evolved Euro-American sexual subjects for whom homosexuality is a political identity and not merely a set of practices. Such a narrative fixes the meanings of "gay" and "lesbian" as well as of sexual dissidence. To be included in these identities, queer subjects from the South have to resemble them. Gopinath has shown how "lesbian" represents not only an identity but also a knowledge-producing "regime of visibility" that, in cross-national contexts, renders illegible desires and pleasures that exceed Euro-American articulations. To counteract this regimentation, Gopinath suggests "a more nuanced understanding of the traffic and travel of competing systems of desire" (1998, 117) as expressed, for example, in queer diasporic appropriations and resignifications. Thus, localizing traveling sexual identities through the use of vernacular does not necessarily open up "gay" and "lesbian" identities to the kind of interrogation and destabilization that Gopinath and Manalansan advocate.

The members of SALGA and MASALA who during the interviews identified themselves as gay, lesbian, and/or queer are attuned to these discussions about Western sexual categories. They recognize that many South Asian sexuality-based organizations in North America have chosen to name themselves in South Asian languages. They know that through translation, retrieval, and re-appropriation, these organizations signal the existence of same-sex desires and practices in their own cultures, which under the influence of colonialism have been so systematically erased that South Asian languages appear not to have words for same-sex eroticism (Vanita 2002). Some organizations like Trikone and Khush translated Western symbols and identities. Others have excavated indigenous terms like Shamakami (those who desire their equals), Anamika (women who have no name), and Sangini or Saathi (female companions).

The heated debate over adopting such terms as "gay" in South Asia reverberate in the diaspora (Jenkins, Pappas, and Islam 2001; O. Khan 2001; S. Khan 2001). In naming themselves, diasporic South Asian queers struggle with class-marked and sometimes regionally specific identities such as hijra, khusra, kothi, or panthi that do not neatly line up with gay Euro-American codings of sex, gender, and sexuality.[4] One SALGA member, Javid Syed, tracked the discussions within SALGA about its appeal to transnational queers who do not identify with "gay." In talking about SALGA's effort to respond to class, language, and cultural divides within South Asian communities, he remarked that SALGA was becoming "a more accessible site for communities that are not middle-class English speaking . . . [for whom] gay and lesbian might not be an appropriate word." The organization, he observed, had become friendlier to South Asians who identified as khusra or hijra, even though some primarily English-speaking members did not relate to the cultures or distanced themselves from identities associated with a lower economic class. Elaborating on these members' discomfort with the cultural gap that also reflects differences in class status, he said: "There are some cultural things that *they* enjoy that folks who are primarily Urdu-speaking khusras *don't* understand and enjoy. And these are differences they learn to live with." This polyvocality pries open the identity categories "gay" and "lesbian" as SALGA interjects itself into New York's queer landscape and, further, has to reexamine its self-understanding when hijra and khusra identities insert themselves. South Asian queer immigrants globalize urban spaces in the United States as profoundly as discourses of gay liberation globalize spaces in the South.

The MASALA member Hussein expressed his awareness of another dimension of the debate over naming in India, where some AIDS activist groups have focused on same-sex practices in order to reach men who have sex with men but who do not define themselves as homosexuals. He linked the shift away from sexual identity (gay) to sexual practice (men who have sex with men) to a rhetorical strategy adopted in African American, Hispanic, and Asian American activist communities that "differentiate themselves from the white community in order to get resources flowing to their groups" by claiming that "our people don't label themselves gay." While recognizing the success of the behavioral approach in raising funds, he expressed his reservation about a focus on sexual practices at the expense of understanding gayness as an identity. In reflecting on the complicated homoerotic terrain that he found on his visit to India, Hussein mused, "For myself, I have always thought of myself as gay. It's not just about who I am sleeping with; it's also about how I experience the world, how I interact with it." In the transnational debate over taxonomy, Hussein positions himself as a gay man whose sexual identity structures his reality. This reality marks the unmarked—the omnipresence of heterosexuality as a system of privilege. Hussein's insistence on a consciousness about identity beyond sexual practices does not, in my mind, return us to the developmental narrative that culminates in the fully evolved "out" gay man. The reality that Hussein references is shaped by his struggle to understand his sexual identity through his religious beliefs, which in turn crosscut with his identity as a Canadian in the United States via Tanzania. Hussein's self-identification dislocates the fixity and stability of a gay identity on which its global currency depends.

Understanding the politics of naming is crucial. But demands for indigenization to reflect specificity, locality, and ethnicity invite another set of critical questions. Like the names of the North American organizations listed above, do the Sanskritized and Urdu names sound familiar to all South Asians, given that many language families in South Asia have no relation to Sanskrit or Arabic? Do they speak to those South Asians who have grown up in North America, Fiji, the Caribbean, or East Africa? Given that "local" sexual identities mark class, region, religion, and culture, which terms gain currency in the diaspora? To assume that the identities, politics, and practices that circulate out of the South should be marked through the use of vernaculars only seals the "local" from past and contemporary phases of globalization. Clearly, calling themselves "gay and lesbian" has not prevented SALGA or MASALA from being aware of the politics of globalizing the term "gay" and the way in which that deployment dislodges it from its ideological and historical underpinnings.

Community and Visibility

In describing to me the workings of SALGA and MASALA, members talked about potlucks, parties, and clubbing—social and cultural events that forge bonds of community. They reflected on the affective dimensions of their work in which comradeship, trust, affection, playfulness, sexual attraction, and relationships built a sense of community. In answering my question about MASALA's activities as a South Asian organization, Hussein wove in and out of his own and the membership's social and political definitions of the space: "When MASALA took off people were just thrilled that there were all these South Asians who were also queer with whom they could connect socially. Some people were hoping to get a boyfriend or a girlfriend out of it. That's always a big piece. . . . Remember when the first group of seven men came together? Six out of the seven did not want politics to be any part of it. . . . It wasn't about marching in Gay Pride. It was just social. We wanted to come together; we wanted to enjoy our 'dal and curry' together; we wanted to maybe go out to clubs together." His personal incentive in starting a group like MASALA, he clarified, was to create political visibility for South Asians in Boston's LGBT community. He said, "In terms of my own views on that . . . because of my contact with the white gay community in Boston, I knew that there was really an aching need to show more people of color representation." Other MASALA participants similarly expressed intermingled desires for a social space of their own, an alternative to the white-dominated gay and lesbian clubs and organizations, and a presence that would contest their erasure or marginalization as South Asian queers.

When I pushed the MASALA member Anushka Fernandopulle to give me a clearer picture of her group's agenda, she laughed and said, "Maybe we don't work on issues. We just do potlucks," referring to MASALA's decision to temporarily replace issue-oriented meetings with open-ended potlucks with the hope that a political focus would develop organically. Tackling my question seriously a minute later she gave me the example of her participation in a recent panel on activism in queer communities of color to show that progressive members of MASALA participated in various community initiatives for social change.

Though at its inception many SALGA members lobbied to define the organization as a purely social space, the founder-member said he was "determined" that the group serve the political purpose of promoting the rights of lesbians, gays, and bisexuals. In his view, as well as that of other members, SALGA's work revolved around forming a community to gain visibility and representation both in the LGBT movement and in South Asian communities.

Organizational agendas, campaigns, meetings, and rallies were far less central to the accounts of SALGA and MASALA members than to those of feminist and labor activists. How does one explain this departure? And to what extent does SALGA and MASALA's emphasis on the social, cultural, and affective to build community and bring visibility to South Asian queers echo the culturalist turn in the larger LGBT movement? From a political economy standpoint, according to Hennessy, the movement relies on visible markers of queer lifestyles and aesthetics to stand in for politics. As a result, visibility as a queer strategy fails to demystify the commodities as the embodiment of the social relations of capital

(2000, 128–29). In consumer-oriented commodity capitalism, queer activism, with its emphasis on a "gay public culture," increasingly avoids addressing issues of economic and political justice, leaving that work to individuals (Joseph 2002). Such political stances are said to foreclose robust, social-change-oriented analyses of oppressive relations of production and consumption.

Indeed, SALGA and MASALA do not simply imitate the larger LGBT movement when they articulate community and visibility as their central issues, though they are partially shaped by the terms of the movement. Community and visibility become significant for the two organizations because of the racism that South Asian queers face in mainstream gay and lesbian social and political contexts and the homophobia in their own ethnic communities. In specifying this dual goal, the SALGA member Debi Ray-Chaudhuri said the organization aimed at "gaining some recognition from the South Asian community and gay community—a two-fold redefinition of South Asian identity."[5] The organizations' understanding of the social and affective as political intervenes in Hennessy's and Joseph's dire assessments of lesbian and gay politics.

In terms of SALGA and MASALA's work, their activities point to the intertwining of the political with the affective and social. Nurturing social and emotional bonds to form community, which in turn lends these groups visibility, enables queer immigrant actors to do the political work of constructively countering homophobia and racism. Members of SALGA and MASALA enact what Ann Cvetkovich calls the "affective life of politics" (2003, 157), a formulation that contests the artificial distinction between the private world of emotions and the public and political world of activism. Love, affirmation, empathy, understanding, and protection all become central to the stories that SALGA and MASALA members relate about their organizations because they directly engage with desire. For these members, any analysis of the social edifice built by heterosexuality has to start with an examination of desire that spills out of the straightjacket of normative sexuality. Even though the feminist and labor organizing covered in this book also depends on bonds of affection and trust, these elements do not have an analytical place in organizational accounts because of heterosexist taboos on deeply exploring intimacy in all-women's groups[6] and the heterosexual construction of cogender groups, where opposite sex relations are examined only in the context of sexual harassment.

Second, SALGA and MASALA through their dance parties, drag shows, and potlucks create cultural spaces that allow "new articulations of queer plea-sure and desire" (Gopinath 1996, 123) away from the heterosexual demands of immigrant cultural formations and the racism of white queer organizations. These cultural activities break with mainstream immigrant techniques of cul-tural reproduction, which manage the anxieties and moral panics of displace-ment through disciplinary discourses that promote endogamous heterosexual marriage and family as ways to perpetuate homeland cultures (Cvetkovich 2003, 122). South Asian queers posit an alternative diasporic culture that also counters their erasure, marginalization, or objectification in white lesbian and gay spaces in New York and Boston. Finally, in considering SALGA and MASALA's goals of securing community and visibility, my discussion of "curry queens" shows that South Asian queers cannot have the same generative relationship that Joseph (2002) proposes between (mainstream) queer politics and capital. This is because in the urban queer landscape they are often treated as consumable commodities.

HOMECOMINGS

What has finding SALGA or MASALA meant for members of these groups? The two organizations meet a number of related needs. They address the isolation that South Asian queers feel in heterosexist conservative as well as progres-sive South Asian circles. In capturing the core function of queer South Asian organizations—offering South Asian gays and lesbians an organizational base that they did not have before—Debi Ray-Chaudhuri said of SALGA, "Certainly it was reaffirming to go there and know that there's people for whom the whole question of sexual identity was at least as much of an issue as it was for me. . . . Just knowing of people's [South Asian queers'] existence was in some ways not just self-affirming but a redefinition of South Asianness." For some members, these organizations offered the first opportunity to examine the effects of their cultural assimilation and explore their South Asian roots.

Members who initially had sought out the visible sites of queer culture and politics in their cities and in doing so found them very white expressed their sense of homecoming on joining SALGA or MASALA. The MASALA member Kavita Goyal's experience illustrates the gaps filled by the two groups. Goyal grew up in Buffalo and then in an affluent Philadelphia suburb where the Indian identity of her family was erased or overlooked. Her first encounter with significant numbers of South Asians was in college. Having little in common with her South Asian student peers, she made friends with East Asians and African Americans. Describing her long route to MASALA, she said:

> There was a very large South Asian society in my school. And so, I then tried to form a community for myself there. I didn't feel good about that. . . . There was just a lot of these girls with long hair who were trying to get all these guys. That was just not my interest even though I had not come out to myself yet. . . . When I moved to Boston, a lot of my friends were gay and lesbian, mostly white, but none of us were really involved in any queer politics. It really happened by accident. I was going through New Words [a women's bookstore in Boston] and I found *Lotus [of another Color]* and I was like, "Oh my god! Other gay Indians exist! Where are they?" It was around that time that I really wanted to become . . . well, it was really through *Lotus* that I wanted to hook up with other women who were South Asian—queer or not queer. It was just hitting my mind that there was a different world in the South Asian community that I have not discovered.

Goyal marks her alienation from her heterosexual and achievement-oriented South Asian peers in college. After coming out, however, she was also uncomfortable with her white lesbian and gay community, which was a striking contrast to her people-of-color circle in college. In 1993, *Lotus* (Ratti 1993), a collection of essays, coming-out stories, and poems by South Asian gays and lesbians, publicized a queer South Asian presence in South Asia and its diaspora, politicizing its readers through its "anthology-making activism" (Franklin 1997; Keating 2002, 9). *Lotus* was as formative for a generation of South Asian immigrants as *This Bridge Called My Back* (Moraga and Anzaldúa 1983) was for women of color (Keating 2002). The anthology connected people across the United States and affirmed the existence of South Asian queer communities. It alerted Goyal to a progressive community created by South Asians who believed in many of the things she believed. She sought out South Asians and found out about Boston-based SAWA and then MASALA, which was getting started at that time.

Unlike Goyal, who was aware of her Indian identity, the SALGA member Tim Baran, who immigrated to the United States from Guyana with his parents when he was ten, described himself as "totally assimilated" growing up in a mixed-race New Jersey neighborhood.[7] He had minimal contact with Indo-

Caribbeans, let alone Indians, Bangladeshis, and Pakistanis. After coming out he was "preoccupied with looking for a gay culture," but in the process he discovered "that even within gay culture there was a white community; there was a black community; there was a Latino community."[8] In reconstructing how he developed an interest in exploring his South Asian identity, he recalled feeling out of place among Caribbean immigrants. He traced his discomfort back to the colonially engineered tensions transplanted in New York between people of Indian and African ancestry in Guyana and, more broadly, the Caribbean.[9] As he stated: "In the United States racial tensions are between blacks and whites and places in the Caribbean it is Indians and blacks. And even though I was brought up in the church [in Guyana] . . . and the church often transcends that [racial tensions], over here [in New York City] I would see it." He met Jamaicans and black Guyanese at gay clubs where he enjoyed dancing to Caribbean music, but over time he "realized that culture is not only about music and food but it is also about . . . how comfortable you feel. I started not feeling as comfortable as I thought I would around Caribbeans, including Indo-Caribbeans." At that point, he noted: "[It occurred to me that] I should try and explore not only my Caribbean roots but also my South Asian roots, and that is when I discovered SALGA. That was an *incredible* eye-opener for me." The exhilaration of finding SALGA was palpable in his voice. In his search for a gay space that felt right in a highly diverse though enclaved landscape, Baran—one of SALGA's most active members and passionately committed to its work—had to navigate multiple identity claims in the diaspora: hegemonic Anglo-American, Afro-Caribbean, Indo-Caribbean, Indo-Guyanese, and South Asian. These identities collided, connected, and disconnected. Recall here MASALA founder Imtiyaz Hussein's desire for a group where he could present himself integrally instead of having to separate his cultural, religious, and sexual identities. Thus, SALGA and MASALA members' complex homecoming stories contextualize the social need for community not only in their alienation from white gay communities but also in histories of multiple diasporas forged in an earlier moment of colonialism and capitalist expansion.

The perniciousness of racism in the larger LGBT movement surfaced repeatedly in SALGA and MASALA members' responses to why they needed a South Asian space. Like the women's organizations, SALGA and MASALA came out of a struggle with the racism they faced in predominantly white LGBT groups. Explaining why an organization like SALGA had become so urgent, the founder-member said, "We don't get all our needs met in the gay community, which is predominantly white or white-oriented." According to all of those with whom I spoke, these needs were cultural. Tensions and fears around coming out had to be situated and understood within South Asian family dynamics; a healthy sexuality for lesbians and gays needed to be conceptualized by critically engaging with cultural and religious regulatory mechanisms; a gay social life had to be redefined because the South Asian gay community was solely not organized solely around bars.

Community and visibility, for SALGA and MASALA, were strategies used to turn South Asians into sexual subjects who presented an organized front. In the early 1990s, South Asians in white-dominated gay spaces were seen as aberrations. During those years SALGA and MASALA members, who moved in those spaces, often heard comments like: "I never see gay South Asians." As one SALGA member said, in expressing his exasperation at the homonormative whiteness of those spaces that erased his presence, "If homosexuality is a white thing, why am I here?!" Like the conservative segments of South Asian communities (see chapter 2), white gay men and lesbians conflated whiteness with homosexuality, though with different intent and effect. In an intersection of imperialism and racism, the developmental narrative of gay and lesbian identity (Manalansan 2003) locates sexual repression and backwardness in South Asian bodies. The narrative has to strip these bodies of their Third World markers and redo them as Westernized, modernized anomalies. The other iteration of this imperialist discourse depends on the hypervisibility of South Asians as exotic sexual partners rather than on invisibility. In this representation, South Asian queers yet again are denied their subjectivity.

GOODBYE CURRY QUEENS

The debates within these organizations in their early stages over the merits of separatism and who could be admitted to such a space is instructive of how the members conceptualized a collectivity that would free South Asians from these racist and imperialist representations and allow them to articulate a queer South Asian and people-of-color subjectivity. Like the initial debates in Trikone and the Khush electronic mailing list, MASALA and SALGA in their early stages had to resolve whether they were being exclusionary in restricting their membership to South Asians, and, since both organizations served social functions, whether they would admit their members' non-South Asian partners. Since the organizations' life revolved around social events and support groups, the admission of non-South Asian partners had to be hammered out. Members had to resolve whether they opposed the participation of white gays and lesbians and whether they would be willing to make exceptions for non-South Asians who were people of color. Those who supported an all-South Asian membership argued for a space that was free of the racism that they routinely faced as people of color. Laying out the debate in SALGA, the founder-member said:

> I very strongly wanted it to be a South Asian group, because *I* believe that there are two dangers of non-South Asian people: One is that negative types of people would walk in, like curry queens. We don't want to encourage that. We don't want SALGA to be a place where curry queens come to pick up SALGA members. That, most people in the other camp *agreed* with. They didn't want that either. Their objection was, "What about those people who can give us something. Maybe if they wanted to be educated." To that, my response was—our faction's response was—that we educate them all our lives. Can't we have two hours in a month when we don't have to educate anybody? . . . Even the most well-meaning white people—non South Asians—by their very presence distort the [group's] dynamics. Even if they are not doing anything. Because the tendency is for us Indians to become nice and solicitous toward them and start *explaining* things to them. And I absolutely hate it when that happens.

Two racial dynamics are identified here—an undesirable one in which white gay men, coded "non-South Asian," preyed on South Asians, and the other a seemingly benign one of cultural curiosity in which white gays and, I assume, lesbians by their presence within the space interpellated South Asians into becoming native-informants.

On analyzing the first dynamic, SALGA members agreed to exclude curry queens so that they could constitute a space in which they were subjects and not mere objects of an exoticizing white gaze. In this case, SALGA powerfully contests an imperial circuit of desire. Gay tourism, which has become an important development tool for nations in economic crisis and has been instrumental in globalizing sexualities (Puar 2002), establishes the imperial circuit by serving up nativized bodies made pliant, exotic, and hypersexual to North American and

European queers. As M. Jacqui Alexander (1998) points out, niche market advertising and travel guides promote this sort of contemporary imperial travel. It creates nativist ideologies that circulate in transnationalized metropoles, where the privileged white gay consumer, on encountering the queer native outside his exotic and local context, quickly recolonizes and renativizes him, thereby consuming him just as he would consume curry. Not only do European or American gays travel to the South but queers from the South also travel North. As a result of this South to North flow, the imperial economy of desire signifies South Asian queers as commodities (though there is no direct purchase) in a highly racialized queer landscape of New York City that is dotted with "rice bars" for Asians and Asian Americans or "cha-cha bars" for Latinos (Manalansan 2003, 71, 81–87).

When SALGA members move out of these objectifying contexts, they set up their own spaces of cultural production and consumption, which also are mediated by transnational capital. The Bombay film industry (Bollywood) music, British bhangra and British Asian music, and Caribbean chutney in New York clubs with a South Asian queer clientele form circuits of transnational consumption. But, these circuits interrupt the reproduction of neoliberal citizenship through consumer capitalism. The cultural products as well as their consumption for queer pleasure destabilize national belonging and invoke classed and racialized histories of migration. These cultural performances remember the trauma of migration. They engage with the lived realities of a transnational existence. Unlike the South Asian mainstream, South Asian queers in these cultural spaces do not relive the trauma through nostalgia for a mythical homeland (see Gopinath 2005). Instead, SALGA and MASALA make culture, and in the process the unavoidable questions of transnationalism erupt. Beyond the disruptive questions about which cultures are embraced and who is being represented, SALGA and MASALA have to respond to the particular national configurations of queerphobic xenophobia. Therefore, the production and consumption of South Asian transnational queer cultures, even in their ephemeral forms, "provide means by which to critique the logic of global capital itself," as Gopinath (2005, 12) has compellingly argued. In that case, the two queer organizations put community and visibility to work in ways that differ from those that Hennessy (2000) and Joseph (2002) see queer politics perform. More importantly, for the purposes of my argument, transnational queer consumption does not take recourse of the entitled citizen-consumer. This interferes with the smooth co-constitution of capitalism and citizenship.

The second racial dynamic, which involved encouraging cultural awareness among white attendees, is also nativizing, though SALGA members making that argument had greater difficulty recognizing it as such. They were willing to act as cultural ambassadors and saw no problem in admitting well-meaning white gays and lesbians. In the member's rendition of this side of the debate, the argument that allowing whites to attend SALGA meetings could contribute something to the group shifted quickly to how South Asians could enhance white people's understanding of South Asia. This slippage, which repositioned South Asians as teachers, is noteworthy. Radical women of color have long called their white feminist sisters on the racism and lack of responsibility entrenched in the demand to educate (Rushin 1983). This racist practice (not restricted to white feminists) intersects with a colonial one in which the native turned informant serves as a source of knowledge about his or her culture and people but cannot author the narrative because she or he can speak only within the terms set by the interrogator. The exasperated question / comment, "Can't we have two hours in a month when we don't have to educate anybody?" expressed the desire for a respite from the native-informant mode of interaction so as to enable SALGA to focus on meeting the needs of South Asians.

The split over admitting non-South Asians was also at issue in MASALA. According to Fernandopulle, some members, who lacked political experience, did not understand that the "concept of a separate space" was not exclusionary; on the contrary, it affirmed one's culture and identity. She strongly felt that no honest discussion about racism within the gay community could be conducted if the space were to be opened up to white LGBTs, who were bound to feel attacked and defensive. Commenting on the confusion in some members' minds between exclusion and affirmation, she said, "A South Asian space is really important. It is very rare to find such a place. When you are in the minority, there is something very tiring about not seeing South Asians. It is a relief to go into South Asian spaces. And it is not like any South Asian space is comfortable. It is really important to have South Asian queer spaces." Organizationally, MASALA resolved the debate by deciding to keep its space open to people of color but restrict voting rights exclusively to South Asian members, so that MASALA, in Goyal's words, "never becomes a place where our voice is not first." During my time in Boston, MASALA never had to exercise this provision.

Both SALGA and MASALA construct a queer South Asian space through cultural work. The life of both organizations revolves around social and cultural events like potlucks, spectacular fund-raising parties, dances, fashion shows, and cele-brations of Hindu and Muslim festivals. Newsletters from SALGA reported on events such as *Eid* (Muslim festival) parties; a Stardust party (in which Stardust refers to the widely circulated Indian film magazine); and Disco Diwali (Festi-val of Lights), a spin on the U.K.-based Pakistani singers Nazia and Zoheb Hassan's number-one 1980 hit song "Disco Diwane." Playfulness, humor, irony, affection, and erotic tension pulse through these events and activities as partici-pants resignify, reappropriate, and hybridize mainstream U.S. gay and lesbian as well as South Asian immigrant cultural forms.

Historically, the gay and lesbian movement has promoted parties as social-political tools. After Stonewall, the Gay Activists Alliance of New York dis-covered that its parties at the Firehouse, starting in 1971 in SoHo, not only helped them with fund-raising but also created community, increased its mem-bership, and lent visibility to the city's gays and lesbians. While SALGA and MASALA can be seen as following in the footsteps of this tradition, they created a *desi* culture, indelibly marked with puns, intertexts, and performances that queered South Asian icons and altered queer entertainment.

At parties, SALGA and MASALA members danced to videos of Bollywood hits and, in the process, staged the most effective critiques of Euro-American visual registers of homosexuality. Members also called into question the diasporic consumption of the authentic, therefore heterosexual, nation through these transnationally circulating popular hits, as Gopinath (2005, 93–130) has shown. In analyzing spectatorial strategies, Gopinath argues that diasporic queers con-sume these cultural products by reveling in the homoeroticism embedded in seemingly heterosexual scenes. While Bollywood song and dance sequences left most white attendees at the parties bemused, South Asian queers read pleasures that elude visual codings of "lesbian" or "gay." Simultaneously, these queer performances and gender parody displace the symbols of national identity and affiliation, which are consolidated through heterosexuality.

These cultural productions merge the social and political to do the critical work of redefinition and reinvention. As I argued in chapter 2, no queer South Asian space, community, and identity could be created without providing a viable alternative to hegemonic versions of South Asian as well as U.S.-based LGBT identities and cultures. These versions played cultural, national, and racial allegiances against homosexuality. In this context, Fernandopulle underlined the politics of MASALA's social events when she noted, "MASALA played a part in giving people a place to come. . . . Most people in MASALA are transplanted people who are in exile from their community." To address the sense of exile resulting from incompatible identities, the organizations re-created a sense of "home" by mobilizing affective resources associated with families. Commenting on the desire for home, Ray-Chaudhuri said, "Even our conception of SALGA was in some way based on the idea of family." Exile, of course, is a strong and poignant theme in the lives of sexual minorities. But with migration comes displacement and, unlike the South Asian mainstream, queer immigrants manage it with cultural formations that do not depend on discourses of assimilation or cultural authenticity.

I hesitate, however, to call these alternative formations public culture or even counterpublics. Theoretically, such publics, even when conceptualized as fragmented, contestory, and multiple (Berlant and Freeman 1992; Cvetkovich 2003; Warner 2002), remain integrally linked with the emergence and evolution of modern nations, citizenship, and national interests. To use the language of publics voids the possibility of asserting a political presence and subjectivity that does not draw its legitimacy from nation-based citizenship (Reddy 2003). Thus SALGA and MASALA performed a transnational identity and politics, not nationalism (which, of course, can also be transnationally produced).

The organizations represented transnational cultural formations not only because they bring together Pakistanis, Sri Lankans, Bangladeshis, Indians, Canadians via Tanzania, and Indo-Caribbeans but also because they deploy hybridized cultural forms. Soca, calypso, reggae, dub, chutney, and British bhangra bring Caribbean and British histories of racialization and resistance to diasporic sites in New York City and Boston. In talking about the impact of Indo-Caribbeans on SALGA parties, Ray-Chaudhuri, who was brought up in the United States on the staple of Indian classical and regional music and dance, noted that on being exposed to Caribbean music she had to redefine her notions of South Asian culture. Of course, within these transnational formations, we have to note the privileged place of Bollywood songs and visuals, which despite their immense transnational popularity and market, do stand for (north) Indian preoccupations with questions of national identity, economic development, politics, justice, and religious harmony and strife. While these very specific Indian references sometimes alienate those who grew up in the diaspora, the queer performances of Bollywood hits subvert the sexual politics of patriotism and dislocate the dominant narratives of the nation (Gopinath 1996; 1998). Such subversions work against implanting a stable Indian identity or Indian hegemony in these transnational sites.

The cultural, social, and affective work of SALGA and MASALA puts them on the political map in New York and Boston. They send out a message to the larger LGBT community on the order of, "We're queer; we're here; we're immigrant." Articulating their identities as South Asian queers has helped them lay claim to their own immigrant communities. Over the years, both organizations have gained respect and visibility that members think far surpass what their actual numbers would suggest.

India Day Parade and Sexual Citizenship

Every August since 1980, thousands of South Asians who live in New York City, Long Island, New Jersey, and Philadelphia stream into Manhattan for a day to watch, and participate in, the India Day Parade. The parade celebrates India's independence from British colonial rule and the successful economic and political assimilation of Indian immigrants in the United States. At the parade, Indian nationalism—increasingly "saffronized" in the diaspora with Hindu nationalist representations of Indian culture—combines potently with U.S. versions of ethnic pride. Efforts to transform the constitutionally secular Indian state into a Hindu nation have gained ground since the 1990s and, as Vijay Prashad (2000) has shown, hold tremendous appeal for Indian immigrants in the United States. The parade effectively communicates the heterosexist politics of this nationalist agenda.

In the India Day Parade floats stage such spectacles as a "traditional" Hindu wedding. Bollywood film stars deliver fiery speeches to rekindle a patriotic fervor to build a technologically advanced yet culturally pristine India. The spectators who line the streets are inspired to chant "Bharat mata ki jai" (Victory for Mother India) and "Jai Hind" (Victory for Hind). At the same time, there is brisk business at ethnic food kiosks and stalls promoting Indian small businesses. Next to them are the displays by huge corporations like AT&T and MCI. Ethnic pride, then, is cast within the familiar story of immigrant success and adaptation, one of the most powerful mythologies that creates and re-creates U.S. national identity. Though the organizer of the event, the Federation of Indians in America (FIA), portrays the parade as a cultural event, for the Indian community it holds considerable political significance, and it is graced by the New York City mayor, city council representatives, state and federal legislators, local Republican and Democratic Party members, and Indian politicians and dignitaries.

Members of SALGA staged their protests between 1993 and 1999 at this crucial site of material and ideological production and consumption not as aspiring citizen-consumers but as critics of the exclusionary acts performed by the nations in play. The India Day Parade became a privileged site at which SALGA explicitly articulated these critiques, which are not as pronounced in its other activities. Just as the Indian nation places queerness outside its imagination, and the rise of Hindu nationalism reworks homophobic colonial scripts to do the same (Bacchetta 1999), so do mainstream diasporic communities erect visible borders at these public performances of nationalism, culture, and identity in an effort to keep out queers and their allies—progressive South Asian organizations. Since 1995, when the FIA also excluded Sakhi, the Lease Drivers Coalition, Yaar, and South Asian AIDS Action (SAAA) for not being Indian,[10] some combination of these groups have been part of a task force to strategize around the yearly exclusion of SALGA.

Cast out by the FIA, SALGA stands on the borders of the India Day celebration. Many SALGA members appear in drag, some superbly simulating Bollywood heartthrobs. Other members hand out fliers, and over the years they have enticed curious parade participants to cross the border, talk to them, and learn about SALGA and other members of the task force, thereby disrupting the territorial integrity that the parade valiantly tries to project. An article in a SALGA's newsletter communicates the transgressive spirit, love, irony, and solidarity of the alternative spectacle: "Dressed up in our *lungis, lachas* and *cholis,* Sahira, Vinita, Javid and Chandan dragged it up in their various gender appropriate butch/femme drag. . . . A lot of younger folks were delighted by Javid's and Faraz's fab dresses and kept beckoning us to join them" (SALGA 1996, 1). Members of SALGA seduced spectators and marchers by embracing the same central symbols—Bollywood and its stars—that keep the diaspora vibrantly connected to contemporary Indian popular culture. Through this subversion of irresistible icons, SALGA members identified and navigated a Hindu nationalist discourse on membership in the ways that Gopinath (2002) proposes, namely by collapsing the distance between an authentic and essentially heterosexual India and a diaspora in which queerness can be framed as a polluting American aberration.

When I asked SALGA members about what they found "political" in their organization's work, without fail they referred to the summer activities building up to the annual parade protest. Parades symbolically reproduce the nation and provide spectacular sites for the constitution and consumption of national identities (Stychin 1998, 29–35). At the India Day Parade, SALGA and its progressive allies challenge the fascinating nesting of U.S. and Indian nationalisms that are defined through the construction of normative and deviant sexualities.[11] They unsettle taken-for-granted properties of nation-states—the right to set borders and police them; the ideology that national identity is necessarily predicated on exclusions; and the requirement that a patriot uncritically accept border setting.

Scholars working on lesbian and gay rights have argued that heteronormativity is a basic requirement for national citizenship, but they disagree over the strategies through which sexual minorities can access full citizenship (see Rimmerman 2002 for an overview of the literature). These debates center on whether the way to secure sexual citizenship is through assimilative politics that demand incorporation into existing institutions or through liberatory politics that fundamentally challenge the sexually disciplining terms of citizenship. Materialist queer theorists such as David Evans (1993) have flagged the dangers of the queer communities' pact with consumer capitalism in its quest for sexual citizenship. In a neoliberal state, citizenship is awarded to those who pay taxes, consume, and are self-sufficient (a trope that invokes its other—the welfare-dependent citizens or welfare-seeking immigrants). According to Evans, in keeping with this logic sexual minorities capitalize on their purchasing power and constitute themselves into markets to seek rights.

My reading of the parade focuses on SALGA's intervention in consumerism-oriented sexual citizenship (for other analyses, see Abraham 2000, 192–95; Gopinath 2002; Khandelwal 2002, 176–77; P. Shah 1997). By transnationalizing what seems to be local, I trace another configuration of the transnational complex of rights compared to the one constructed by women's organizations. I argue that SALGA frames its right to march in the national parade as a *transnational* entity. Its protest thus cannot be interpreted as asking for sexual citizenship, which demands that sexual minorities be recognized as equally valid members of the national body. In the United States, such demands are made quintessentially through the language of civil rights and full citizenship (Stychin 1998). The protests by SALGA at the parade provoke us to question national membership and its terms: membership to which national body and under what conditions?

The queer protestors disarticulate their rights claims from citizenship. The group addresses itself to both India and the United States but not as aggrieved second-class citizens or citizen-consumers who do not receive their due. The routine denials of basic rights to family reunification and legal employment to "alien" queers in the United States sometimes shut them out of the gay niche markets, for example in financial services or health insurance, to which affluent citizen-consumers have greater access. The multiple ways in which immigrant queers are blocked from the civil rights correctives available to heterosexual immigrants in order to access residency and U.S. citizenship (see chapter 3) prevent them from representing themselves as citizen-consumers. Members of SALGA also reject modes of belonging adopted by South Asian place takers, who project themselves as self-reliant, tax-paying citizens, whose successful assimilation depends on becoming good consumers (see chapter 1). Further, the spectacular display of Hindu nationalist versions of queerphobic xenophobia (Bacchetta 1999) at the India Day Parade have made SALGA members increasingly skeptical of seeking rights through the trope of citizenship.

The parade and the protest transform a so-called localized space into a transnational terrain on which Hindu nationalist versions of Indian culture, powerful U.S. mythologies of immigrant success through assimilation, and the profoundly disruptive queer demand for the right to march as transnational subjects jockey with each other. The protest by SALGA claims this public space. Such occupations, in the case of groups like Queer Nation, have been seen as opportunities for queers to reappropriate the nation-state and to exercise the citizenship they are denied (Berlant and Freeman 1992). But, as Gopinath (1996) has pointed out, such an analysis of counterpublics assumes citizen actors. Queer South Asians in the diaspora often do not have U.S. citizenship and thus, as Gopinath notes, they "enact a much more complicated navigation of state regulatory practices and *multiple* national spaces" (261). Members of SALGA transgress borders but not in the hope of being included in the charmed circle of U.S. or Indian citizenship.

Unlike the Irish-American Gay, Lesbian and Bisexual Group of Boston that challenged in court its exclusion from the city's St. Patrick's Day Parade, SALGA in its protest does not deploy a hyphenated ethnic-American identity to contend that its members, as U.S. citizens, are being deprived of their basic entitlement to equality. Nor does SALGA want representation in the parade as *Indian* queers. Instead, the group confronts the production and consumption of nation-based identities. The very presence of SALGA at the parade and its alliance with other South Asian progressive groups reveal how national identity co-constitutes heterosexuality, Hindu hegemony, and capitalist practices that range from U.S.-based small ethnic entrepreneurship to inroads that transnational corporations have made in India since the liberalization of its economy in the 1990s.

By inserting itself as the *South Asian* Lesbian and Gay Association in the diaspora in alliance with other South Asian groups since 1996, SALGA publicly refused to pay the price of erasure from the narratives of the Indian and American nations. It formulates, in this instance, a critique of the re-creation of elite, high-caste, and homophobic Hindu nationalist imaginings of India in the United States. When the FIA banned SALGA by stating, "That [homosexuality] is not what we should be showing to American people" (P. Shah 1997, quoting then-president Nitin Vora), it simultaneously constructed what the Indian nation wants to display in the diaspora and what "Americans" want to see. New York City officials have twice challenged SALGA's exclusion by making arguments based on human and civil rights. Indeed, city officials persuaded parade organizers to admit SALGA in 2000 in part by arguing that the ban violated civil rights protection for minorities. However, SALGA, by insisting on its transnational queerness, does not limit itself to the language of civil rights and full citizenship. It knows only too well that gays and lesbians, despite their American citizenship, are routinely deprived of their economic, political, and social rights. It secures its right to march without claiming an allegiance to India or to the United States.

In allying itself with feminist activists, survivors of violence, and working-class South Asians, SALGA refuses the representation of the immigrant community as uniformly successful, problem free, and culturally pristine, rupturing both dream India and the American dream. Over time, SALGA has utilized the India Day Parade to think through, and strategize to oppose, the multiply located project of nation building and Hindu nationalism through the lens of sexuality. Its understanding of Hindu nationalism that developed at its protests led SALGA to ally itself with the Delhi-based Campaign for Lesbian Rights, which mobilized against the Hindu nationalist backlash against Deepa Mehta's film *Fire* in 1998.[12] More encouraging are the recent debates within SALGA over the implications of its inclusion in the parade. As the SALGA member Svati Shah reports: "SALGA's struggle to participate in the India Day Parade the following year [2001] was marked by many more internal and external discussions about the politics of participating in an event that promotes an increasingly unitary, Hindu-right representation of India" (2001). In recent years, SALGA's members and allies carry posters and shout slogans such as "Down with Hindu nationalism," "Anti-capitalist Queer desis," and "Down with brown misogyny" that make connections among systems of oppression (Samar Collective 2002). Since its contingent inclusion in the India Day Parade in 2000, SALGA has paid greater attention to the economic liberalization and aggressive foreign and nonresident Indian investment that has accompanied the political project of Hindu nationalism.

Thus SALGA's demand for inclusion and its current participation in the parade cannot be read straightforwardly though a narrative of sexual citizenship that cuts deals with accommodationist politics and consumer capitalism. Its protest and, later, its inclusion exposes the link between statecraft, nation formation, and the production of a normative sexuality. It connects sexual policing with the exclusion of feminists, religious minorities, and poor and working-class people from national imaginaries. Its rights claims and rights talk emerge within a transnational framing of identity and community that is critical of narrow nationalism and of transnational corporate practices. The appropriation by SALGA of mainstream queer public protest tactics bears out Gopinath's observation that "it is precisely from a queer diasporic positionality that some of the most powerful critiques of religious and state nationalisms are taking place" (2002, 159). As it deeply unsettles the consumption of culture, tradition, and patriotism, SALGA makes crucial political contributions. Its engagement with the parade is instructive for other space-making organizations because the place of homoerotics and queerness in crafting the nation-state is only weakly grasped by anticommunal progressive South Asian activists outside of queer spaces. Its deployment of queer immigrant politics in a public space of consumption also pushes us to reconsider the critiques of queer community and protest so that we can see signs of social justice that conjoin domestic preoccupations and international crises. Until we do so, these new formulations will remain unintelligible in the critical practices of queer theory.

Cross-Connections

Multiple urgencies induced by racism, nationalism, and heteronormativity make alternative community building through collective action a primary objective for SALGA and MASALA. As heady as these experiences of finding and founding community are, both organizations testify to the fraught process of community formation. Members note problems within their organizations stemming from sexism, class inequality, language barriers, inadequate attention to immigration status, and the cultural dominance of South Asia. A critical practice, then, attends SALGA's and MASALA's community building and political action. My participants made it clear to me that they recognized the impossibility of producing a seamless and naively celebratory or romantic narrative of community even as they were deeply invested in a sense of togetherness, mutual support, and joint purpose.

In this section, I discuss lesbian confrontations of sexism in SALGA and MASALA, the search for alternative arenas of participation by members to address their groups' political limitations and the sometimes wrinkly relationship that emerges as a result, and accounts of Indo-Caribbean class and cultural discomforts with SALGA. I use the idea of cross-connections to capture the intrusions, precariousness, and possibilities for new conversations posed by gender, class, cultural, and national divides among members of SALGA and MASALA. In the 1980s in Kolkata, India, before the era of fiber optics, cross-connections were a constant feature of telephone conversations. A two-way conversation would suddenly become a foursome as lines were cross-connected and different conversations were spliced as a result. Callers would overhear each other's conversations and respond with wry humor, sympathetic or flirtatious comments, annoyance, frustration, and impatience. I find these multiple registers of cross-connections, not their accidental and fleeting nature, to be appropriate in describing the conversations that open up in SALGA and MASALA as a result of encounters within and outside. The encounters and the responses they produce call into question the blanket declarations about uncritical queer investments in and perpetuation of oppressive social relations.

POLITICAL LIMITS

The gender politics of both SALGA and MASALA represent one area of friction and debate. At the time I did my fieldwork men outnumbered women in both groups. The sexism of the gay and lesbian movement in the United States has been well documented. The broad-ranging contributions of lesbians to the movement, and their emotion and care work as gay communities were ravaged by AIDS, are routinely marginalized in accounts of the movement. Clearly, sexual dissidence does not automatically produce a consciousness about patriarchal gender relations. While SALGA's and MASALA's work with Sakhi and SAWA, respectively, is premised on an opposition to sexism, differing levels of awareness among gay men in both organizations about sexism and feminism generate confrontations and discussions about gender inequality and the resulting differences in gay and lesbian experiences despite cultural commonalities.

The first members of SALGA, who were all men, felt that "men and women [have] very different concerns and cannot work together" (Niraj 1995, 1). Although they were correct about recognizing that men and women have different issues, they were wrong about the impossibility of an alliance. As women joined the group, however, it was left to lesbians to raise the collectively relevant question of gender as it informed sexuality. Ray-Chaudhuri, reflecting on gender relations within SALGA, pointed out that the organization provided a valuable opportunity for gay men, particularly first-generation gay men, to be exposed to lesbians. Interestingly, since SALGA had few first-generation lesbians, the question of unequal gender relations, brought up by second-generation lesbians, was reframed as the differences between immigrants born and raised in the United States and those who were new arrivals. By subsuming gender difference under generational and cultural difference, gay men missed the chance to examine their sexist and culturalist assumptions. This displacement interfered with gay men clearly articulating an antisexist position.

In MASALA, lesbians noted that interventions by observant gay men during meetings helped address the sexism they sometimes felt. As Fernandopulle pointed out, "Some of the men have some interest in observing gender dynamics. Yeah, like sometimes we've had discussions and a [male] member has noticed that it has been all men speaking and suggested, 'Why don't we let some of the women speak? I'd like to hear from some women.' And that's just nice, you know. Because, the women of course notice and they are like [she rolls her eyes and both of us laugh]. But you know some iota of gender consciousness helps." However, giving lesbians permission to speak does not shift power relations because men continue to think that they control the space and conversation. Despite this fact, neither Fernandopulle nor Goyal felt that the male privilege that surfaced at meetings was translated into an unfair division of labor within the organization. Fernandopulle stressed that affective politics, built through strong friendships, held MASALA together as a co-gender organization and allowed men and women to work cooperatively.

At the same time, Fernandopulle emphasized the importance of making MASALA a space where lesbians could share their experiences, reflect on them, and talk to each other because of some key differences between them and gay men in naming their sexuality. She linked sexuality with the gender discrimination in pay that continued to enforce women's dependence on men and patriarchal families. In her view, South Asian men are more able than women to come out to their families because of their better socioeconomic standing and their relative privilege as sons that allowed them to move away and explore their sexuality. As an organization MASALA needed to understand and respond to these gender specificities if it wanted to recruit and retain women.

Unlike the lesbian MASALA members, MASALA men had little exposure to the ways in which radical women of color had linked sexuality with gender and race.[13] Often, their idea of queer politics was restricted to an assertion and celebration of gay pride. This limitation caused tensions between gay MASALA members and SAWA—where some members of which also belonged to MASALA. A prime example of the disjuncture between feminist and gay politics was the last-minute effort by MASALA to cancel an all-women SAWA-MASALA performance of a narrative poem at a MASALA benefit for Gay Pride in June 1996.

A few weeks before Gay Pride, a number of SAWA members of MASALA had performed co-member Sunu Chandy's narrative poem "Inheritance" at Toronto's Desh Pardesh, an annual celebration of the work of South Asian artist-activists. The poem, initially set in Chicago, invokes an "inherited culture" in which a brother reassures his sister long distance that her family would survive the crisis created by unemployment and depression. Opening up with subjects that are taboo among South Asian immigrants, Chandy moves back and forth between the United States and India and among multiple, rarely articulated inheritances—Indian women's defiance, love and humor, family ties, violence and sexual harassment, the bitter taste of U.S. racism, the brunt of compulsory heterosexuality, and the elusive longing for "home." In Toronto, the performance had moved an audience of over three hundred people to laugh, cry, rage, and commiserate.

On the evening of the Boston performance, some of the MASALA men started to have misgivings about the match between the content of the performance and the spirit of the evening, which they felt should be celebratory. They feared that the intensity of the poem, despite its humor, would dampen the party. After some wrangling, the SAWA-MASALA members went ahead with their performance, the power of which moved the Boston audience as deeply as it had in Toronto. The sudden opposition to the content of the performance was not unexpected, since the lesbians in the group had long noted the ways in which the fluid boundaries between the political and social limited gay men's engagement with the intersections of homophobia, sexism, and xenophobia, thereby interfering with their politicization.

While the gay men I interviewed in both organizations had a range of difficulties in examining the issue of sexism in queer activism, they did gender what members wanted out of their involvement by arguing that while men wanted to be social, women had a greater need to be "political." They attributed the turnover in women's membership to this need and they tried to respond to it programmatically rather than politically. Both organizations have tried to address the problems of recruiting and retaining women by involving their lesbian members in the day-to-day running of the groups and in organizing events that directly speak to lesbians. While lesbian members in both organizations recognize these efforts and continue to have a strong sense of belonging, they also have been drawn into overtly political work with other progressive organizations.

COLLABORATIONS

The collaborations of SALGA and MASALA, often initiated by women, broaden the definition and perception of queer politics connecting them to immigrant rights, health care for people of color, labor organizing, and South Asian feminism. Through these efforts SALGA and MASALA members demand that their work become intelligible to their organizations as queer politics. The SALGA member Javid Syed testified to this process when he admiringly observed that though women worked outside of the organization in the city's lesbian health initiatives, the Audre Lorde Project, and labor campaigns, they did so as "SALGA women." While the multiple membership of MASALA and SALGA members is a sign of the political limitations of these groups, it also indicates a trajectory different from the one Joseph (2002, 173–74) observes on her campus where, for example, queer activists do not see the pertinence of labor issues to their struggles. In both organizations, new conversations opened up as members crossed over to other political arenas.

The agenda and political culture of SALGA started to shift in response to the infusion of individual members' experiences in other struggles. As I discuss in the next chapter, Ray-Chaudhuri's pioneering work with the Lease Drivers Coalition (LDC) connected state surveillance of queer communities to the daily exposure of taxi drivers to police brutality. This collaboration continued as SALGA sent volunteers to help the New York Taxi Workers' Alliance (formerly LDC) document the impact on taxi drivers of the events of September 11, 2001.

The alliance of SALGA with Sakhi was neither natural nor immediate but rather built over time through mutual education about each organization's political stance. In describing the process from SALGA's point of view, Syed said: "We see basic connections between sexism and homophobia and this is explicitly discussed in some situations. As a feminist organization, Sakhi, at one point, was not that queer friendly and has been struggling with becoming increasingly responsible. This shows in the way Prema Vohra [at that time Sakhi's program director] now talks to us about participating in the India and Pakistan Day Parades." The participation by SALGA in Sakhi events made homophobia visible to Sakhi, as in the case of a Sakhi-sponsored talk by India's first woman inspector-general, Kiran Bedi, whose negative reaction to gays and lesbians troubled SALGA. While Bedi represented a form of feminism for both Sakhi and SALGA members, Syed, in recounting the event, recalled: "She was someone who we might look upon as an ally because of all this work she has done but [she] is still homophobic on many levels and needed to be called out." On being informed by SALGA of its reservations about Bedi, Sakhi supported SALGA's questions to Bedi about the contradictions between her achievements as a woman and her position on gays and lesbians. According to Syed, through such opportunities for new conversations, the two groups developed "a level of goodwill and a level of investment in each other's causes and a definite acknowledgment of the overlaps and connections." "Similarly," he added, "they call on us when they do protests against wife batterers," thus helping SALGA see the various faces of institutionalized violence.

Many SALGA members, gay and lesbian, had the foresight to work with the Audre Lorde Project (ALP) from its earliest days. ALP is a progressive Brooklyn-based community organization devoted to issues confronting queers of color. When I did my fieldwork in 1996, the ALP was a fledgling center looking for a physical location. But in attending SALGA general meetings it became clear to me that a segment of the membership had thrown its energies behind the project and was working to drum up support from others who were not aware of the life and work of Audre Lorde. The project is dedicated to Lorde, a black lesbian feminist organizer, poet, and theorist, whose untiring work for social justice chalked a new path for building solidarity by tackling rather than erasing difference. Syed, who worked closely with ALP, felt "it was a constant source of inspiration and enthusiasm because here are these incredible folks making connections around issues that affect queer communities of color and working toward a progressive agenda!" The engagement by SALGA members as South Asians with Audre Lorde's vision of radical change marks a significant moment in South Asian space-making politics, and it lays the groundwork for cross-racial coalitions around queer issues.

Through individual members' cross-membership, SALGA grew aware of the role of immigration in shaping queer realities, thus nudging the organization, in Tim Baran's view, toward taking explicitly political positions. Syed's work as a staff member of the Asian & Pacific Islander Coalition on HIV/AIDS (APICHA) and as a volunteer with ALP and South Asian AIDS Action (SAAA) introduced the politics of immigrant health care to SALGA. As a result, SALGA was drawn into working with the larger South Asian, Asian American, African American, and Caribbean communities. In testifying to the cross-pollination of ideas, Syed felt that the "painful experiences" of clients in his paid work with APICHA "fueled" his HIV/AIDS activism in SALGA. At the time I talked with him, APICHA was reconceptualizing itself as a community service agency rather than an agency narrowly devoted to HIV/AIDS because the delivery of services was intrinsically linked with the immigrant realities of limited English and the lack of access to well-paid jobs, which translated into a lack of health insurance and concomitantly a lack of good health care. Thus, in APICHA's view, work such as offering classes in English as a second language, job training, legal defense, and domestic violence education was as urgent as services that focused on HIV/AIDS treatment and prevention. In explaining why attending to immigration and immigration status was so necessary, Syed stated: "There are specific issues that immigrants face whether they are documented or undocumented . . . . [These are] things that mainstream organizations don't take into consideration and, therefore, there is a huge barrier to [health care] access. The people who started APICHA were Asian Americans. It was obvious to them that a lot of the issues that make access such a problem are issues of immigration, whether it is language access, conceptualizing health care in a different way, paranoia of deportation or *realities* of deportation, having undocumented status and what that means in this country." Such innovative thinking around health parallels Manavi's reimaginings of services appropriate for immigrant survivors of violence against women.

While SALGA does not provide direct services, it does define queer sexuality as part of a healthy sexuality. The work done by APICHA introduced it to links between the quality of queer immigrant life and the barriers posed by immigration laws and English-only services not attuned to cultural and immigration needs. In talking about the significance of such exposure for citizen second-generation SALGA members who were unaware of the perils faced by non-citizens, Ray-Chaudhuri remarked: "For second-generation people it was important to see first-generation people and the kinds of struggles they have to deal with. Dealing with coming out to your family is not just a simple matter because it threatens your immigration status." Further, SALGA's involvement with SAAA—a short-lived organization started by progressives, mostly heterosexual, to do HIV/AIDS education among South Asian immigrants—also helped it realize that health care issues, including conceptualizing a healthy sexuality, became far more meaningful when connected to immigration problems. As Syed observed, while these outreach efforts did not significantly increase SALGA's membership, they were successful in sparking conversations in SALGA about its accessibility as a community organization. As a result, SALGA has become more open to people who identify as hijra and khusra—vernacular sexual categories. The organization continuously struggles to create a pluralistic environment that recognizes—to quote Syed—that "a lot of recent immigrants do not have access to the same privileges that we do and are not comfortable in English and need to have other sorts of interactions where their lack of English does not make them seem uncommunicative." In sum, the positive outcomes of cross-connections become most audible in members' accounts of collaboration.

In Boston, MASALA members networked with several of the area's mainstream queer groups on organizing the annual Gay Pride march and on issues such as gay marriage. Over time, it developed strong ties with the Queer Asian Pacific Alliance (QAPA) and the Massachusetts Asian AIDS Prevention Project (MAAPP), and SAWA. In 1996, the women in MASALA—who like the SALGA women sought political channels outside of the group—wanted to create a forum for lesbians of color in the area to talk about the issues they found most urgent. Cross-membership between SAWA and MASALA led these women to host an early spring weekend conference (which I attended as an ally) to identify priorities for lesbians of color. It provided a unique opportunity for African American, Latina, and Asian American women to meet each other, become familiar with their organizations' work, and exchange a rich variety of experiences, including the impacts of discrimination, invisibility, and cultural isolation on the different groups as they negotiated racially segregated cities, racism in the mainstream queer groups, and the erasure of lesbians in health services. This heartwarming event resulted in the formation of the Coalition of Queer Women of Color bringing together an African American group, Girlfriends; a Latina organization, Luna; and lesbian members of QAPA, MASALA, and SAWA.

The Coalition of Queer Women of Color identified two projects. One project focused on bringing pressure to bear on community health centers in Boston to provide adequate health services for queers of color, particularly lesbians. The SAWA-MASALA member Serena Sundaram recounted the effectiveness of the coalition in an internal report to SAWA: "We found that one health establishment tried to play one group [which was now part of the coalition] against the other, failing miserably when the second group came out in full support of the first. As a coalition meeting with them, we were so much stronger: a force to be dealt with." Thus, political desires that could not be fulfilled within MASALA led to their convergence with those expressed by other groups.

The other project, aimed at feeding the sense of community created at the weekend conference, was developed through sharing creative work such as political poetry, prose, and music. The first public event, held in March 1996 in downtown Boston, was the Annual International Women's Day Celebration for Queer Women of Color and Allies. While the celebration was an enormous success, SAWA members, who co-organized the event, were reminded of the fragility of community. After spending all day cooking large pots of *sambar* (food we had volunteered to provide for the event) and then hauling the pots downtown on an icy evening, some of our members were treated dismissively by some members of the coalition. We were not treated as part of the event because, we learned later, these members had never encountered South Asians in queer spaces. That night we soothed our sore hearts with the wonderful poetry and music created by our sisters. At the next coalition meeting, we were pleasantly surprised at how responsibly the underlying issues of invisibility were treated, teaching us that community is contingent and processual. As Sundaram wrote in her report: "This was a group dedicated to becoming political allies. . . . There was a misunderstanding [at the Women's Day event]. It was raised. Responsibility was immediately taken and after open discussion . . . , we were able to move on. None of us were afraid that the problems were insurmountable." The recognition that coalitions can only be built through substantively engaging with difference was in contrast to the painful, though eventually rewarding, negotiation with the pan-Asian battered women's shelter in Boston that I discussed in chapter 4. Even though the coalition was short lived, its multiracial context and its lessons about enacting political commitments were formative for MASALA and SAWA members.

Having discussed how feminist, labor, and anti-racist politics are incorporated into queer activism, I want to ask how movements that ally themselves with queers and benefit from their labor understand queer politics. How are queer efforts in feminist or labor organizations understood and represented? My analyses of South Asian women's organizations and labor organizations show that they subsume the work of queer activists, who are renamed as feminist or labor activists. This move absorbs queer participation and does not theoretically develop the connection between capitalism, heterosexuality, and patriarchy. In chapter 4, I discussed SAWA's move to privatize lesbian sexuality in representing its organizational culture by calling itself queer friendly rather than part queer. In the next chapter, I question the erasure of lesbian contributions to the Lease Drivers Coalition. Many on the Left cannot fathom SALGA's interest in a labor organization beyond outreach to queer taxi drivers. But SALGA's imagination transcends such a view. The alliance was actually based on the connections it made among the state-driven mechanisms that criminalize queers and working-class men traversing public space.

Here I focus on SALGA's relationship with Sakhi to illustrate a larger problem in U.S. and international feminisms, which tend to conflate gender with sexuality (Butler 1999; Calhoun 1994; see also Gopinath 2002, 157–58). This view allows little room to consider sexuality outside of heterosexual relations of dominance and subordination that socially reproduce patriarchy. Since sexuality has little autonomy outside of gender relations, women's groups struggle awkwardly with homosexuality in trying to respond to lesbians and sexual identity-based movements.

An effort to devise outreach programs and services for South Asian lesbian survivors of partner violence has been one such awkward response on the part of Sakhi and Manavi as organizations that address violence against women. Ray-Chaudhuri's response, when I asked her about these methods, is telling. She said that in the event of partner abuse members would turn to SALGA rather than Sakhi because their network in that group was stronger and safer. In acknowledging Sakhi's "pro-sex attitude" and its commitment to free desire from patriarchal reproductive control, Ray-Chaudhuri marked a fundamental problem in dealing with lesbianism that is not only applicable to Sakhi but also to other women's groups. She said, "It's not a theoretical thing. There is a real discomfort that people feel; it tests something about your politics." Lesbian sexuality and the intimacy among women (not just between lesbians) that conversations about sexual autonomy open up is neither explored within these groups nor is there a careful understanding of heterosexuality as a system of privilege from which straight women benefit. At a certain level, the women's groups have failed to imagine what lesbian women would need beyond (necessary) services for lesbian survivors of domestic violence. And even then, why would lesbians trust in services designed by women who have not subjected to a radical analysis heterosexuality and their implication in it?

When I asked Annanya Bhattacharjee of Sakhi to comment on the organization's image as a straight space, she remarked: "This is not only an outside perception. . . . People within Sakhi have voiced it. It is not clear to everybody what the problem is. But we realize that it is getting to a point where we have to figure it out. . . . That we are totally against the exploitation of gays and lesbians has to be ingrained in our language and spirit in an everyday way beyond Sakhi's mission. We have to do outreach with regard to domestic violence in lesbian relationships." A commitment to ending the discrimination against gays and lesbians that results from the enforcement of heterosexuality by every institution in society is quickly recast as addressing violence in lesbian relationships. In this translation, the perceived reworking in lesbian relationships of patriarchal models of power and control with which women's groups are most familiar is foregrounded. The inability (again, not particular to Sakhi) to pin down the problem—unexamined practices of normative heterosexuality—parallels the bafflement on the part of SALGA and MASALA men with the needs of the lesbians in their groups. In both cases, scrutinizing their / our own contradictory investments in systems of power such as heterosexuality and patriarchy becomes the first politically necessary step.

Despite these drawbacks, Sakhi's culture did allow open, if fractious, discussions about how organizationally to implement its commitment to support queer struggles. Syed and Bhattacharjee's assessment of Sakhi—one from the outside and one inside—confirms the sincerity of these efforts. One such contentious moment came when Sakhi debated how best to support SALGA once the latter was banned from the Pakistan Day Parade in 1996. The Pakistan Day Parade organizers gave Sakhi permission to march but banned SALGA through a display of unabashed homophobia. Sakhi's Pakistani members, understandably, wanted to utilize the permission as an opportunity to march in the parade as activists who opposed violence against women in their communities. If in solidarity with SALGA Sakhi decided not to march, it would mean disregarding the wishes of its Pakistani members. In that case, could it claim to be a "South Asian" organization? This core question reveals the constructedness of a South Asian identity, which appears seamless and self-evident at moments when India Day Parade organizers ban Sakhi on the pretext that it is South Asian, not Indian.

Even though Sakhi's board members, in recommending that Sakhi officially march in the Pakistan Day Parade, came up with several constructive strategies to show their solidarity with SALGA, its general membership reversed by a margin of one vote the board's decision to march (Abraham 2000, 193–94). Criticizing the reversal and calling for a pragmatic rather than an ideological and ultimately divisive approach, Abraham comments: "In reality such an outcome was not helpful substantively either for our alliance or for the organization. In a way, the organizers of the parade had won, for they no longer had to contend publicly with gays and lesbians or domestic violence. So in demonstrating the strength of our alliance, we had in fact silenced an important minority, those Pakistani women who wanted to march in the parade and show their community that domestic violence existed and that individually and collectively we can fight it" (194).

Curiously, Sakhi's repeated decision to stand on the margins with SALGA in protest during the India Day Parade even in years when it could have participated is not interpreted in the same way. In that case, standing with SALGA does not excise a feminist and queer critique from that parade. Thus, the most important (and, in my view, valid) issue for Abraham seems to be Sakhi's ability to accommodate its Pakistani members. Yet, she assumes that these members always already inhabit stable heterosexual identities, thus prohibiting us from imagining Pakistani women marching as feminists and lesbians. The Pakistan Day Parade organizers, in inviting Sakhi, constructed women's identity and women's issues as essentially heterosexual. Abraham's analysis falls into this trap. She subsumes the rights of sexual minorities under Sakhi's commitment to women's rights by suggesting that had Sakhi marched the Pakistani community would have had to deal with feminism and homosexuality and this would have been a pragmatic solution to SALGA's exclusion. For heterosexuals, even progressive ones, it is always pragmatic to accept and thereby reproduce their secure place in the sex-gender system and its rewards. So, instead of framing the debate over Sakhi's alliance with SALGA as too ideologically charged, it would be more productive to see it as Sakhi's efforts to grapple seriously with the intersection of sexuality and gender in ways that do not reduce one to the other.

DIASPORA

The navigation by Sakhi and SALGA of multiple identity claims, discussed above, invites questions about how such organizations construct a South Asian identity in the diaspora. In the New York–New Jersey area SALGA was the only group I studied that examined its transnational self-presentation in the context of Indo-Caribbean communities. While Francophone and Anglophone Caribbean drivers are members of the NYTWA that evolved from a view of itself as primarily South Asian to that of a multiracial alliance, I did not come across the kinds of debates I encountered in SALGA. I speculate that SALGA's focus on desire, embodiment, and its commitment to creating a transnational culture through social functions gives it the analytical tools and a greater flexibility compared to the explicitly political groups. Indeed, SALGA realized that constructing a South Asian space went beyond attracting members from various South Asian nations. It needed to make space for South Asian diasporic communities created by colonial labor export policies in places like Trinidad and Guyana and by postcolonial displacements.

Coalitions formed by SALGA with New York's Indo-Caribbean communities have included fundraising for Caribbean gay groups, marching in the Queens Pride Parade, and doing outreach in straight Indo-Caribbean clubs by staging surprisingly well-received drag shows. Yet, it has constantly struggled with low Indo-Caribbean participation as members in the organization. The problem, as Baran notes, reveals itself this way: "When we have functions like parties, you see Indo-Caribbeans come out en masse. They want to go to the parties but they don't want to be part of the planning committee or . . . discussions within SALGA." How is this stark difference explained? Baran offered a nuanced analysis of the structural barriers that stood in the way of Indo-Caribbean membership in a space primarily defined for South Asians from South Asia. Disparities in education between immigrants from the Caribbean and first- and second-generation immigrants from South Asia, the dominance of (northern) South Asian languages, and, ironically, SALGA's political agenda around queer visibility were some of the reasons.

From an Indo-Caribbean perspective, evidently, SALGA was a class-marked space. Education and cultural capital, not so much actual income, registered the class differences between Indo-Caribbeans and South Asians. When Indo-Caribbeans attended SALGA meetings, they felt out of place because they could not take for granted either the levels of education or the career trajectories that shaped SALGA's culture. In talking about how intimidating he found the difference with South Asians when he first joined SALGA and the shifts he has witnessed since, Baran said:

> I was intimidated the first time I came in and I saw how vastly educated everyone was. . . . I think that's what happens with Indo-Caribbeans because I tell you, if you go to college and graduate with a bachelor's degree, that really is an accom-

plishment. With Indians or South Asians who come over here—that's only a stepping stone to other stuff.[14] In SALGA, even now you can see that. I did have a bachelor's and I was working on my master's but even then I was intimidated. . . . We are starting to represent different education [Baran interrupts himself]. You know, it's very hard for Indo-Caribbeans to recognize the whole caste system in India . . . and it's educational differences, and it's the color of your skin—all those kinds of things. . . . SALGA has come to a point where vocal members are comfortable enough to say we need to be representative of the whole cross-section of South Asians.

Baran's narrative as an Indo-Guyanese in New York in a South Asian space pries open the memory not just the sign of multiple diasporas. As the historian Madhavi Kale reminds us: "In the British Caribbean, to be Indian was to be first a sugar worker. . . . Secondarily, to be Indian was to be a migrant, an alien from a space made known and accessible through British industry and enterprise" (1998, 134). The Indo-Caribbean presence in contemporary New York intimates South Asians from South Asia of a plantation history of indenture that has been excised from postcolonial narratives of Indian history—at least in the school and college texts taught in India. It is marginal to Indian and British labor history, as Kale shows, even though discourses about these indentured men and women were foundational to the category "labor." Writing out this particular working-class history fragments our memory as South Asians. What connections might this forgetting have to the representation of these workers by all parties involved—nineteenth- and early-twentieth-century colonists, planters, recruiters, social reformers—as submissive and industrious or untrustworthy, weak, and depraved or duped and victimized?

In another diaspora and in another era of mass migration, Indo-Caribbeans in New York confront those of us from South Asia with our amnesia about who those indentured workers were, why they left, and what happened to them in the far-away places where they labored. The effort to unlock these histories is being made by activists such as Riti Sachdeva, a former SAWA-MASALA member, and Lisa Seepaul in their performance Kalapani—The Crossing. Baran's seemingly sudden reference to caste in a discussion about class cannot be easily dismissed when post-1965 Hindu immigrants unreflectively cash in on their centuries-long upper-caste monopoly on land ownership and in the nineteenth and twentieth century on education and white-collar employment.[15] And what echoes might we hear of a plantation past that was riddled with migrant anxieties about losing caste; migrant strategies to keep their caste even when taboos on intercaste and interreligion contact were broken in the labor depots at ports, on ships, and in plantations; aggressive colonial policies to manage the caste question; and the argument made by some Caribbean commentators about trade mobility among these migrants as a result of the loosening grip of caste? (Kale 1998).

Differences among Indo-Caribbean and South Asian communities erupted openly over language and culture. At certain moments, members created group solidarity and intimacy through the use of vernacular as well as South Asia–specific cultural references. In a twist to earlier discussions about the dominance of English in SALGA that left out ESL speakers, Baran offered another take on language use: "There are *enormous* cultural differences. Just simple things like language, for example. In 1995 about fifteen of us went up to the Catskills for a weekend. It was just a *brilliant* time. . . . *But* if you didn't speak Hindi or Urdu, then you couldn't be involved in every conversation, and then, even if you did speak the language but grew up here, you still can't relate because of the jokes and the references that were made. And I happened to be the only Indo-Caribbean in that group. . . . I didn't get it."

These cross-connections have generated further conversations in SALGA about the needs it would have to address if it were to diversify its membership beyond a South Asia–centered base. Syed indicated that redefining SALGA as a space that would reflect a multilingual South Asia also meant considering those who had never been to South Asia and their relationship to it. Moreover, SALGA members would have to examine how they related to those whose national and cultural identities were tied to nations in Africa, Europe, or the Caribbean and not directly to South Asia. Turning momentarily to MASALA, I wonder whether Imtiyaz Hussein found the understanding he so desired of his transnational Ismaili queer identity or whether as the only Ismaili in the group he once again had to relegate his Tanzanian roots and faith to the margins.

The social functions of SALGA have allowed for an exploration of encounters among distinct national/regional cultures. Indo-Caribbeans have transformed SALGA as a space by Caribbeanizing its parties and, in the process, redefining South Asianness for members like Ray-Chaudhuri. Elaborating on this development, Baran said: "I think SALGA does provide a space for Indo-Caribbeans even if it is only on a social basis. . . . Indo-Caribbeans are noted for bacchanal—having a good old time. When there is a party—it is so interesting—and there is bhangra music and all this Hindi music, then they are like, 'Hey, where is the soca, calypso, and reggae?' So they want to hear it. SALGA is getting more exposure to that music in Indo-Caribbean culture and they are enjoying it." Had SALGA been a purely political space, this kind of intervention would not have been possible.

In explaining the reluctance of Indo-Caribbeans to become members of SALGA despite their high attendance at social events, Baran pointed out that SALGA's increasing visibility in New York City makes it difficult for Indo-Caribbeans who are not out to their families or communities: "SALGA is quite political. . . . And it seeks out publicity. If we are going to do a protest or something, *we* solicit the media. The Indo-Caribbeans . . . who want to be part of SALGA now recognize that they have to be at least a part of the stuff and if you're closeted, god forbid, you won't be able to do that." The deterrents were homophobia in Caribbean communities and the fact that many young Indo-Caribbean gay men lived with their parents, especially if they were attending school. A social space that stops short of being a counterpublic allowed Indo-Caribbeans to enter and participate in SALGA, even shift its culture, without the fear of disclosure that lurks in more visible and public activities.

From these accounts, we see that fractures, instability, and difference attend the process of community building, flying in the face of romantic versions of seamless and intrinsically anti-institutional communal action. When exclusionary practices within groups open up collaborations, they too are fragile, open to risks, and contentious. But these divisions are not necessarily threatening or divisive. Instead, they can clarify a group's political direction and social intent.

Conclusion

This chapter has traced the issues and interests that emerge when South Asian organizers center nonnormative sexuality in their activism. The relative neglect of queer organizing in recent accounts of South Asian activism reflects a tendency in South Asian Left politics to either fold questions of sexuality into sexism or treat them as marginal to analyses of political economy and race relations. Sexuality-based movements do the crucial work of exposing the social construction of desire by locating it in institutional practices. They show how sexuality, far from being private, is public business. They examine social institutions ranging from families and religious bodies to a nation's laws and courts that invent and enforce ideas about normalcy and deviance. As part of the movement, SALGA and MASALA specify the transnational workings of these institutions in the lives of immigrant queers. Centering the public mechanisms through which queers are penalized allows the two organizations to shift the terrain of rights struggles away from citizenship toward transnational claims. This institutional approach helps SALGA, for example, to find common cause with taxi drivers who are also publicly policed. It enables the organization to forcefully articulate the ramifications of Hindu nationalism in the diaspora.

The dynamics of immigrant family and community formation as well as the intense heterosexism of immigration law inform SALGA and MASALA's efforts to provide a space where their members find support, referrals to resources, affection, sex, fun, and a sense of belonging. These impulses seem similar to those that animate the larger LGBT movement, but Euro-American homonormative constructions of gayness and gay culture have discounted South Asian sexual subjectivities, thus engendering autonomous organizations like SALGA and MASALA. Just as the South Asian women's organizations in this study redefine shelters, support groups, and counseling in order to suit South Asian survivors, so do SALGA and MASALA put the touchstones of LGBT organizing— such as public spectacles, visibility, and community—to work in ways that respond to their membership's cultural and immigration needs. They based these needs in a transnational framework of rights rather than in dominant LGBT models of consumer citizenship.

The two organizations make culture by queering the everyday protocols and practices that scaffold social life. In this way, they intervene in the cultural reproduction of South Asian immigrant communities and the racism in mainstream LGBT cultural and political spaces. Such culture-making activities fuse the social with the political. The two organizations directly utilize social activities for political purposes. Their attention to definitions of culture and identity makes it possible for them to deal with destabilizations such as those posed by Indo-Caribbeans, who excavate a different journey than that made by South Asians migrating directly to the United States. Again, like the emergence of Hindu nationalism as a queer issue (beyond the obvious fact of SALGA's exclusion from performances of national identity), the eruption of excised histories in the context of queer organizing is not accidental. Queer politics' treatment of sexuality as a force that shapes all social relations facilitates such engagements, thus complicating and deepening the analyses of culture, kinship, exclusive forms of nationalism, and state practices that are offered by the women's and labor organizations in this study.

The social work of culture and community building must be placed in the forefront by SALGA and MASALA, unlike the case in women's or labor organizing in which social activities, despite their cementing role, recede to the background. The absence of a strict "party line" in SALGA and MASALA is related to the primacy of social activities. Both groups treat them as central to affording a safe space to South Asian queers. This stance has made both of these groups resilient, thus drawing in new participants. Even though the differing levels of politicization among members of these groups has led some SALGA and MASALA stalwarts to complain about having to go over the same ground with new initiates, these limits pull members into other types of struggles, which infuse their groups with new issues and analyses.

One of my driving concerns in this chapter has been to reexamine recent criticisms leveled at queer politics in the United States for its uncritical implication in capitalism, which in turn damages a holistic vision of social justice that can address poverty and racism. Indeed, SALGA's and MASALA's existence bears out the severe limits of a queer politics that is constructed only around sexual identity at the expense of its interrelation with race and class. However, these organizations' work also represents tendencies in queer politics. A more hopeful though by no means pure account surfaces when we consider SALGA's and MASALA's reformulations of queer politics in the dual context of a predominantly white LGBT movement and the conservative thrust of South Asian immigrant communities. In the pessimistic evaluations of queer politics, we are faced with the irrevocable logic of capitalism and modernity. While capitalism, nationalism, and state regulatory practices are indeed versatile, they do not inevitably overpower, absorb, or co-opt resistance. Identity and community, as strategies, do not have to erase difference and enact violent exclusions or take such a culturalist turn that they disengage with the state and the economy. In fact, SALGA and MASALA members adopt both strategies but without a corollary investment in consumer-citizenship. This means that they find ways to hold South Asian states and the United States accountable for their category construction—hetero/homo, normal/deviant, citizen/immigrant, authentic/inauthentic. Positioned as queer immigrants in the United States, they offer political directions that do not play into assimilationist discourses, thereby contradicting claims that such moves are strategically necessary to wrest support from the state (see Berlant and Freeman 1992).

The work of the two queer organizations also contests the characterization of queer politics as being disconnected from struggles against globalization and labor exploitation. The critics, in their valorization of labor activism, seem to forget that labor organizing also has to navigate the "consumers' republic," which contained insurgency by reinventing workers as a prime group of consumers for the very goods they mass produced. Members of SALGA and MASALA do cross over to ally themselves with labor struggles. They do so because they are familiar with the structures of power that expose immigrant queers and workers to public policing and hate crimes. Today, immigrant labor, displaced through neoliberal policies and working in sweatshop conditions in the United States, has to contend with the legacies of the "consumers' republic" for labor unions. As I describe in the next chapter, immigrant labor struggles have had to find new paths and new organizational structures to bypass these legacies, especially at a time when the entitled citizen-consumers of the neoliberal state hold immigrant workers like taxi drivers and domestics hostage to publicly enforced servility.

CHAPTER 6

"Know Your Place in History": Labor Organizations

On a hot and hazy afternoon in July 2001, more than a hundred South Asian, Caribbean, Latino, East Asian, and white yellow-cab drivers gathered on a small, empty lot at the corner of Houston and Lafayette streets in lower Manhattan. They held banners asking the city to approve an extra fifty cents on the taxi fare meter to help them cope with spiraling gas prices. Their slogans were strong and forceful, even though the exhaustion of a day that started at 3 or 4 AM was etched deep on the faces of those who had just finished their shift. Night drivers, freshly shaved and crisply dressed, had started their day early so that they could head out to pick up their cabs right after the demonstration. In between slogans and chants, driver after driver went onto a makeshift stage to address their fellow workers. In a variety of English dialects they spoke radical words asking for worker solidarity and economic justice. They even appealed to the ring of cross-armed, poker-faced police officers who fringed the rally. At shift change they yelled out to drivers, filling up at a station across the street, to join them. As traffic stopped at the light, New Yorkers, momentarily jerked out of their boredom, looked with bemusement at the banner-wielding, slogan-shouting men and women of color, who for a few hours had claimed a public space as theirs. The air throbbed not only with asphalt heat but also with the energy and excitement of working-class people speaking out against their exploitation. Bhairavi Desai, a key organizer of the New York Taxi Workers Alliance (NYTWA), which had put together the event, ended the rally with a rousing speech. She asked the drivers to know their place in history. They were immigrant workers in the United States demanding what has been long denied to them: economic justice, rights, and dignity. Backing them was their courageous history of anticolonial struggle. At this historic moment, they were agents who were shaping a new labor movement.

In the United States, working-class labor organizing emerged in the early 1990s among post-1965 South Asian immigrants. For two decades, solidly middle-class professionals and technicians had dominated this immigrant group until in the 1980s it started to become diversified along class lines. Among South Asians, domestic workers and yellow cab drivers in New York City have pioneered class-based organizing. The group Andolan (which means "to agitate") and the NYTWA broke away from their founding organizations—Sakhi for Women and the Coalition against Anti-Asian Violence (CAAAV)—in the late 1990s to become autonomous entities focused on labor issues.

Taxi driving and domestic work, in many ways, cannot be more different. Taxi drivers are mobile, and their workplace—the streets of New York—is very public. In contrast, domestics work sequestered in the private sphere. Yet taxi drivers and domestic workers also have a lot in common. The taxi industry and paid domestic work both draw heavily on immigrants, whose entitlements to basic labor protections are few and under persistent attack. Both occupations require long hours of work under grueling conditions where workers face high levels of physical and psychological violence. The deplorable conditions of work in both contexts are related to the simultaneous retreat of the state from its welfare commitments and its punitive encroachment on the lives of these workers on the grounds that they are immigrants. Both types of work are gendered, with women predominantly doing care work and men driving taxis. Further, neither occupation is organized around a central place, such as a factory floor, and thus the immigrants working in these situations are isolated from other workers. In both occupations, rights of consumers are privileged over rights of workers.

Neither domestic workers nor taxi drivers have the right to unionize, and yet they have found ways to demand rights due to workers. They confront a lack of formal recognition for their workplaces, a loophole that leads to the abuse of power at these sites. Their struggles redefine what counts as "work" as well as who counts as "labor" and what kinds of rights these workers can claim. Feminist principles inform both types of organizing in revaluing low-paid service work and redefining violence to include economic hardship. Taxi drivers question their conversion from unionized workers into independent entrepreneurs. Domestic workers demand labor protections in order to define reproductive labor as work and private households as places of employment. They strip the veneer of the familial to expose the unequal economic relationship between them and their employers. All these aspects of domestic work and taxi driving require innovative labor organizing tactics that are very different from those used on a factory floor.

Often, working-class activists are credited with action rather than reflection. They are asked to speak experientially rather than analytically. This chapter is based on analyses offered by working-class activists, who are among the most brilliant labor leaders in a movement that has come to recognize the crucial importance of organizing immigrants. In this chapter I intervene in discussions by the South Asian Left regarding South Asian labor organizing in the United States as lagging behind developments in Britain (see, for example, Prashad 1998, 2000, 98–101), where South Asian and African Caribbean factory workers allied with each other to fight class and race oppression at work and in their neighborhoods in the 1960s and the 1970s.[1] I rescue the narration of South Asian working-class struggles in the United States from these apologetic renditions and situate the emergence of two labor organizations, Andolan and the NYTWA, in historically distinct social and political formations that led to class stratification among South Asians.

By the time the United States started to import skilled labor from South Asia, Britain already had, beginning in 1962, clamped down on immigration through overtly racist policies (Sivanandan 1981/82). Unlike Britain, which deskilled the labor it imported after 1948 by segregating the workers, according to A. Sivanandan, "in the dirty, ill-paid jobs that white workers did not want" (112), the United States had started its new phase of labor importation with professionals. Though the first post-1965 South Asian immigrants to the United States were underemployed and underpaid, they occupied white-collar positions. But the global restructuring of capital, as it manifested itself in the United States, could not be fed simply by skilled labor. The domestic economy needed immigrant labor in low-wage and hazardous jobs with little security and no benefits. South Asian immigrants who worked these jobs entered the United States starting in the 1980s through a variety of sanctioned and unsanctioned methods.

The shape and form of South Asian labor struggles at the turn of the twenty-first century, then, must be located in the regimes that cheapen immigrant labor by differentiating it on the basis of gender, ascribed race, and citizenship status, both in the legal and ideological sense. As Lisa Lowe observes: "One of the distinct features of the global restructuring of capital is its ability to profit not through homogenization but through differentiation of specific resources and markets that permit the exploitation of gendered and racialized labor within regional and national sites" (1996, 161). This also means that class struggles have to engage with exploitation based on race, gender, and nationality.

Economic restructuring in the United States since the late 1960s has posed fundamental challenges to labor organizing (Bonacich 1996; Bonacich and Appelbaum 2000; Brecher and Costello 1998; Lipsitz 1994; López-Garza and Diaz 2001; Ong, Bonacich, and Cheng 1994).[2] It is not only remarkable that South Asian workers are organizing but also that they are organizing at a time when assaults on labor in the United States have reached historic proportions. The state and corporations blame the very struggles for hour-wage protections and benefits, which once gave workers some sense of power, for making American labor less competitive and causing capital to flee overseas (Lipsitz 1994). From the perspective of workers, this new phase of globalization and economic restructuring has meant deindustrialization and deunionization. In 2000, only 13.5 percent of workers belonged to unions (Bacon 2001). In addition, unions face a new landscape. The reemergence of certain forms of labor extraction such as part-time work, temp work, home work, piece work, and underpaid domestic work escape the factory-floor models of labor organizing and the bureaucratized methods of labor-management negotiations. Until recently, traditional unions have been frustrated with the reappearance of immigrant workers, a chronic thorn in the flesh of organized labor.

Between the mid-nineteenth century and the early twentieth, organized labor actively and successfully opposed Asian immigration, Asian employment in factories, mills, and mines, and Asian membership in unions (Kwong 1997, 139–59; R. Lee 1999, 51–82; Saxton 1971). The craft unions of that time were virulently opposed to "coolie labor," a racialized term that evoked the horrors of a degenerate and unfree swarm (see Roediger 1991 on Free Labor, 23–36, 85–87). Early-twentieth-century Punjabis working in lumber mills in the Pacific Northwest were regularly run out of town by white workers (Jensen 1988, 42–56). Unions consistently argued that Asian labor competed with white workers to bring down wages and lengthen the workday. They used this rhetoric despite the fact that Asian workers agitated for higher pay and a shorter workday. During this period, Asian immigrants in factories, construction sites, and plantations staged protests, went on strike, rioted, and lodged court cases.[3] As unions managed to force the various Asian immigrant groups out of the open labor market and into ghettoized self-employment or farm work, Asian farm workers organized themselves into the Japanese-Mexican Labor Association (1903) and the Filipino Labor Union (1933) (Chan 1991, 86, 88). These unions were barred from joining the American Federation of Labor (AFL). The AFL's then president, Samuel Gompers, was staunchly anti-Asian, and it was not until 1936 that the AFL started to charter Asian-led unions (Chan 1991, 86–87, 89). Protectionist union politics that see immigrants as a threat to domestic labor still survive today. Until 2000, the AFL-CIO supported the 1986 Immigration and Reform Control Act's (IRCA) sanctions discouraging employers from hiring immigrant labor (Bacon 2001). However, the vision, energy, and militancy that immigrant workers have brought to organizing have begun to persuade traditional labor of the importance of immigrant rights as workers' rights.

Andolan and the NYTWA represent many of the hopeful trends seen in nontraditional labor organizing. In contrast to the powerlessness that the sociologists Edna Bonacich and Richard Appelbaum (2000) diagnose among workers in the garment industry, Andolan and the NYTWA operate on the basis that workers have power and that this power is realized through organizing. For them, this is the case despite the crushing and terrifying conditions of their twelve- to eighteen-hour workday. These workers know full well that New York City would grind to a halt if they stopped caring, cleaning, and providing taxi rides to the millions who require these services each day.

Dignifying Domestic Work

An estimated six hundred thousand domestic workers keep upper- and middle-class households in New York City running, and 90 percent of these workers are immigrants from Third World countries. For a century after the failure of post–Civil War reconstruction in the United States, African American women were overrepresented in paid domestic work (Amott and Matthaei 1996; Dill 1994; Glenn 1992). In the last decade, feminists who study the commodification of social reproduction in the United States have drawn our attention to the market shift to migrant women as domestic workers (Carty 2000, forthcoming; Chang 2000; Hondagneu-Sotelo 2001; Parrenas 2001).[4] Along with Caribbean, Mexican, and Filipina women, South Asian women migrate great distances to take care of other people's homes and families in the United States. These women from India, Pakistan, Bangladesh, and Sri Lanka make as little as $200 per month for eighteen-hour days seven days a week.

The American state's retreat from its welfare commitments has created a crisis in care work, which it manages by making the super-affordable labor of immigrant women available to middle-class homes. These middle-class households are made up of productive, contributing, and consuming "citizens." Among the deserving citizens are those South Asian immigrants who are able to execute their role as model minorities. South Asian immigrant women pick up the slack at home while their compatriots—professionals or small entrepreneurs—chase success, acquire property, and buy consumer goods. A well-kept secret behind the immigrant success story is the grossly underpaid labor of South Asian domestics. A deeply gendered project that enables South Asian households' dependence on women, who are imported for the express purpose of doing domestic work, undergirds the extremely divisive project of portraying South Asians as successful minorities. This dependence clearly demonstrates the interlocking gendered, classed, and sexualized dimensions of the model minority myth.

In New York City, South Asian domestic workers have started to organize themselves to demand rights. In their efforts, they follow in the footsteps of African American women who against severe odds unionized themselves from the 1930s onward to ask for higher pay, better work conditions, and dignity of labor, along with engaging in a series of daily resistances (Amott and Matthaei 1996, 171, 174–76; Foner 1979; Jones 1985; Kelley 1994).[5] Domestic workers today, like their African American sisters earlier in the twentieth century, still do not have the right to collective bargaining under the National Labor Relations Act (NLRA)—reflecting lawmakers' understanding of domestic work as a one-to-one arrangement. Since federal law defines a workplace as one with at least fifteen employees, households employing domestic workers rarely get formal recognition.[6]

The first project to organize South Asian workers, undertaken by Sakhi in 1994, challenged exactly this privatization of domestic work. According to Sakhi's founder-member Anannya Bhattacharjee, soon after Sakhi established its domestic violence project in 1989 it started to receive calls from the city's South Asian domestic workers, who reported abuses that paralleled South Asian women's experiences of domestic violence. Like abusive husbands, employers used such intimidation tactics as impounding women's passports, restricting their mobility, and threatening them with deportation. Sakhi established the Domestic Workers Committee (DWC) to organize domestic workers in an effort to address the problems of working-class women who were also being abused within a domestic and privatized space.

The DWC emphasized collective action and Sakhi members wanted the domestic workers themselves to provide leadership. While individual members received one-to-one legal counseling, especially when back payment was involved or their passports were withheld, the women strategized by sharing their experiences and educating each other about their legal rights and seeking solutions. In elaborating on these goals the first coordinator of the committee, Neela Trivedi, said: "The DWC was primarily focused on organizing the workers. They learn to fight for rights; we educate them about their rights and provide them with a space to come together, meet other women like them. This way they develop skills to resist exploitation." The DWC's tactics were aimed at overtly challenging structures of power and holding abusers publicly accountable.

The women often demonstrated in front of their employers' homes. In doing so, the DWC undid the boundaries between public and private. Marking the difference between Sakhi's domestic workers' project and its domestic violence project, Bhattacharjee explained how the demonstrations made households visible as workplaces: "The domestic workers' project helps to change the home into a space that can be readily challenged. Women's relationship to their family is different from women and their relationship with their employers. They [domestic workers] can demonstrate in front of her employer's home. For battered women, this is not an easy thing to do—the relationship is an intimate, emotional one, very much tied into the definition of home. Domestic workers do not have the same emotional connection. The domestic workers' project has helped us see the home as a place that we can demonstrate in front of and slander in public." The readiness of domestic workers as compared to survivors of domestic violence to challenge the home and its association with privacy and noncommercial relations led many Sakhi members to invest their hopes for a tranformative politic in the DWC.

Conflicts between the goals of Sakhi's domestic violence project and the domestic workers' project, however, led to the dissolution of the DWC (see chapter 4). Domestic workers increasingly felt that they had little autonomy in setting committee goals. Many also felt that they were expected to follow middle-class women's perception of working-class priorities. The committee's coordinator, Nahar Alam, a Bangladeshi woman who was herself a domestic worker and who is a passionate organizer, founded Workers Awaaz (or the Workers' Voice) in 1997. This organization split further in 1998 when Alam and several other women formed Andolan. I focus here on Andolan because of its emphasis on self-sufficiency and workers' leadership and also because Alam, who was the first worker to be appointed as coordinator of the DWC, represents a link between Sakhi and Andolan. At present, Andolan is a small nonhier- archical organization that receives little funding. Its fiscal sponsor is the Coali- tion against Anti-Asian Violence (CAAAV). Having learned from the earlier mistakes in the DWC of relying on middle-class women, Andolan is a worker- run organization. It has forty to forty-five members, of whom twenty-five are active. It also has two volunteers, who are not domestic workers. Andolan focuses on organizing South Asian women and the few men who work in this occupation. Most of the workers are employed in South Asian homes.

South Asian workers end up in South Asian households for a number of structural and cultural reasons. Many are recruited directly from South Asia or through ethnic newspapers in the New York–New Jersey area.[7] South Asian employers often prefer women from their homelands because they can pay them less than domestic workers of other nationalities. Many domestic workers apply to South Asian employers because they feel that they are less particu- lar about legal documentation than are non-South Asian Americans. These women often seek households where they can speak their vernacular and have their dietary needs met. In an interview with the Samar Collective (1994, 14), one woman said, "I am from Bangladesh and my favorite food is Bangladeshi food. If I stay with an American family they won't know that I need to eat rice three times a day." These needs on the part of workers as well as recruitment patterns and pay differentials have led to one class of South Asians employing another.

Not all South Asian domestic workers are immigrants. Some of them are U.S. citizens but have not fared any better than the women from abroad. When asked why this was so, Alam pointed to a complex set of reasons as well as gender ideologies that push women into this feminized form of work. Giving the example of a citizen who made fifty-five cents an hour, she said: "Her problem is that she does not know English. She does not know what rights she has: rights to at least minimum wage whether you have papers or not. . . . This is why women like her get afraid. . . . If you don't have education [in the United States and in English], it is difficult to get a job. It does not matter that you are a citizen or have a green card."[8] In addition to these disadvantages, she noted that women often start working as domestics because they have been socialized into thinking that housework and looking after children are jobs that they can always find: "In our countries these types of work are imposed on us. Our husbands never help us. Our parents tell us, 'You have to do this; you have to learn this work.' Society also reinforces this idea. As a result we have this feeling that housekeeping and babysitting are what we can do. This is why women take up these jobs. But at the same time we feel so much shame to say, 'I do babysitting.'" In giving her example, Alam points out how women's labor is cheapened through multiple layers of devaluation with the resultant effects of the shame- and fear-induced reluctance about asking for better pay or better conditions.

South Asian women, who are recruited to work as domestics in the United States from abroad, come from a range of socioeconomic backgrounds. On one end of the continuum, some women held higher education or professional degrees and white-collar jobs in their home countries or came from reasonably well-off families just like many Latina, Filipina, and Caribbean domestic workers. On the other end were poor rural women whose poverty had forced them to work since childhood and had kept them out of school. Conflicts due to these disparities in class, status, education, and literacy came up from time to time at Andolan meetings. Domestic workers who used to be middle class and might have themselves employed maids back home sometimes expressed classist assumptions about poor rural women. The politicized Andolan members recognized that many domestic workers experienced the shift in their class status as contradictory (see also Parrenas 2001, 150–96). They tried to address these divisions by fostering a common working-class consciousness. They encouraged their members to see that regardless of what they used to be in their home countries or what they did there, they now shared common issues and interests as domestic workers in the United States.

To mobilize domestic workers, Andolan combines collective action with legal services and job certification workshops. Rights education, advocacy, and events such as demonstrations are part of its collective action. In the last few years, Andolan has forged a transnational rights regime that draws on international conventions on migrant workers as well as U.S. federal and state labor laws. Unlike Sakhi, it does not see a contradiction between organizing for rights and providing services that meet women's practical needs such as legal aid to file for back pay or to adjust their immigration status. Its classes to certify women as babysitters are reminiscent of the efforts of black domestic workers in the post–World War II period to negotiate for better pay through training and certification (Amott and Matthaei 1996, 173). While Andolan's South Asian membership is a reflection of language-based organizing, some of its members' limited English does not prevent the organization from working in coalition with Filipina, Thai, African, and Caribbean domestic workers.[9]

THE DOUBLE CRISIS OF CARE WORK AND DISPLACEMENT

The entry of South Asian women as domestic workers in the United States is relatively new compared to the presence of Filipina, Caribbean, and Mexican women whose countries of origin have been historically enmeshed in relations of subordination forged by U.S. colonialism and neocolonialism. South Asian domestic workers in New York City are recruited locally and from their homelands through methods that seem to depend on individual networks and the market forces of supply and demand. These methods obscure the structural forces that proletarianize these women and make them available for domestic work. These same forces also create the demand for paid reproductive work in U.S. homes. The appearance of South Asian domestic workers in U.S. homes coincides with three structural developments. First, the aggressive liberalization of South Asian economies led by the International Monetary Fund and the World Bank in the late 1980s and 1990s deepened the crisis in sustainability among the poor and precipitated downward mobility among the middle-class. Second, the continuing restructuring of the U.S. economy created unskilled low-wage service jobs as well as high-skilled and relatively well-paid jobs in information technology, banking, and investment. At the household level, service sector professionals depend on low-wage immigrants to carry out the work of social reproduction.[10] Third, the exclusion of noncitizens who are permanent residents from an array of public programs with the passage of the 1996 Illegal Immigration Reform and Immigrant Responsibility Act has meant that these green card holders have had to find ways to take care of their elderly and children. The state takes no responsibility for them and no private insurance is available for the nonresident elderly parents of these immigrants. South Asian domestic workers are thus a convenient answer to these problems at no cost to the state and relatively little cost to the private employers.

A severe drop in the standard of living related to structural adjustment programs (Chang 2000, 1997) has pushed South Asian women to seek domestic work abroad. According to one South Asian domestic worker-organizer, "Poverty, domestic violence, inability to raise children properly on the family income back in South Asia, widowhood, and abandonment by the family" are some of the chief reasons that compelled women to find work thousands of miles away from home (Alam 1997, 16). The majority of South Asian women working as domestics in the New York metropolitan area are from Bangladesh and India. The rest are from Pakistan, Nepal, and Sri Lanka. The artificial devaluation of South Asian currencies against the dollar as well as austerity measures implemented through cutbacks in government-subsidized social programs in these countries have made the money that women make at home count for less, and the money they can earn by going abroad count for more. To sustain their families in the midst of these enormous economic pressures, women who either have the resources or are offered the opportunity choose to immigrate (Samar Collective 1994, 11).

The U.S. state creates a double crisis through its adoption of neoliberal policies and its globalization of those policies with the help of supranational agencies in the name of structural adjustment. On the one hand, neoliberalism creates a crisis in sustainability for certain sections of South Asian women. On the other hand, it creates a crisis in carrying out the work of social reproduction for middle-class families in the United States. The state manages the domestic crisis in care work by replacing the public programs it cuts with women's labor made available as a result of the deepening crisis in the economic South. Once these crises are set in motion, private employers and agencies can be left to recruit, transport, and place dislocated Third World women in labor-hungry households in the United States. Although the United States does not have a formal program to import domestic workers like Canada, Hong Kong, or Singapore, it ensures the supply of super-affordable labor through a set of privatizing strategies.

PRIVATIZING STATE POWER

Like the native-born African American women working for white employers in Bonnie Thornton Dill's study (1994), South Asian workers in South Asian homes find their labor privatized, informalized, and devalued. But their situation is greatly complicated by their employers' use of immigration status as a way of intimidating workers and systematically cheapening their labor. The severe exploitation that domestic workers suffer because they are immigrant, a codification that is intimately tied to state sovereignty, cannot be seen simply as the malpractices of individual employers. The state and individual employers mutually benefit from the arrangement by constructing these women as a particularly rightless group of people on the grounds that they are immigrant and often undocumented.

In 1986, the IRCA made employers responsible for securing and checking their employees' work authorization. Without such authorization an immigrant cannot be legally employed. While the law incriminates unauthorized workers as well as employers who hire undocumented immigrants, in practice it turns employers into gatekeepers. As I discussed in chapter 3, through the IRCA the state—in a classic neoliberal move—successfully outsourced its surveillance functions to individual employers while retaining and exercising its power to codify immigrants according to the manner and purpose of their entry. At that moment of categorization, women who are brought in by their employers under visas that do not permit them to work are criminalized (Alam 1997, 16). Employers can then use the unauthorized status of their employees to keep them isolated, ill paid, and overworked. For the state to solve successfully the crisis in care work for middle-class families, it must depend on inducing in workers the fear of enforcement rather than on the actual enforcement that would bar unauthorized workers. In this context, collective action against the very fears that silence and immobilize domestic workers becomes a key organizing tool.

The ways in which private employers start to operate like quasi immigration officers are revealed in what domestic worker-organizers identify as common employer practices such as demanding access to their employees' passport and immigration papers, partially mandated by the IRCA. According to the organizers, employers who fly in with their newly recruited employees from their home countries routinely seize the women's passports once they pass through immigration at the airport. This infringes upon not only the women's right to private property but, more importantly, their right to mobility. To forestall complaints to authorities or sympathetic outsiders, employers instill in women, from the moment they board the plane, the all too real fear of the police and the INS. According to Alam, while the message is attuned to the level of their employees' education, it is the same: "Do not talk to strangers"; "People in America are bad"; "If anyone asks you anything, say you are a relative." The employer practice of impounding their employees' passports is not restricted to women brought in from abroad. Workers recruited locally also report having to surrender their papers to their employers. Employers use the threat of INS intervention, arrest, and eventual deportation—all state functions—to hold these women captive in intolerable situations.

Even workers whose employers promise them legal residency can be locked into low-wage work for a very long time because adjusting their immigration status takes an average of eight to ten years (see also AALDEF and NELP, 21). Since these workers are sponsored for permanent residency by their employers, they are tied to their sponsors for those years. Adjusting their status through employer sponsorship institutionally prolongs the discriminatory conditions under which these women must work.

The state also criminalizes employers who hire undocumented workers under the IRCA. However, the sanctions against employers—a fine and/or criminal charges—are asymmetrical relative to what an undocumented worker faces under immigration law. A domestic worker without the right papers faces deportation—a devastating prospect for that woman's dependent household. Furthermore, in keeping with its neoliberal character, the state makes employers individually responsible for ascertaining the work authorization status of the employee. In practice, employers have successfully passed the burden of proof to employees.

Recognizing this burden, domestic worker advocates remind women who are hired locally that they have a right not to answer questions about their immigration status and need only to provide a copy of one of many documents (passport, social security card, temporary resident or permanent resident or employment authorization card, birth certificate, or refugee travel document) if asked for work authorization (AALDEF and NELP 2001, 4, 8–9). Andolan and other domestic worker groups raise both worker and employer consciousness about the IRCA's sanctions against employers to deter them from using the threat of the INS to abuse their employees (21). This strategy directly intervenes on the workers' behalf by stressing that employers who hire undocumented workers break the law and can be punished for doing so.

FIGHTING BACK

South Asian domestic workers bear the consequences of these privatized exercises of state power in the form of poor wages, a lack of benefits, and a lack of labor protections. While these conditions characterize the entire industry, the market is stratified along racial, national, and linguistic lines. The stark gap between market wages and what South Asian women receive from their immigrant employers exemplifies that stratification. The average income of a South Asian live-in nanny-housekeeper is $200 per month. In contrast, a survey by the Asian American Legal Defense and Education Fund (AALDEF) and the National Employment Law Project (NELP) found the average rate for a nanny who takes care of one child and does no housekeeping to be $450 per week (AALDEF and NELP 2001, 11). According to an Andolan organizer, "No South Asian domestic worker can expect to make more than $350 a month." Neither citizenship nor higher education brings these women better work conditions because they are deskilled immigrant women of color (Espiritu 1997, 68–69; Man 2002). The discrepancy in pay shows how deeply underground South Asian women's labor has been driven. In Andolan's experience, the combined devaluation of reproductive labor and immigrant labor have led women to realize that switching to more formalized workplaces such as restaurants or hotels does not protect them from exploitation.

The pay received by South Asian domestic workers is for an eighteen-hour workday, and overtime pay is not common. Quite often, domestic workers report the steady escalation of their duties without a matching pay raise. This form of employment does not come with paid vacation, health benefits, or retirement funds. In addition to being overworked and grossly underpaid, the women often suffer from daily indignities in the hands of their employers; acute isolation and alienation; and mental, physical, and sexual abuse. Most South Asian workers tend to be live-ins because of their poor pay and because they usually do not have relatives or friends with whom they can share an apartment. As live-ins, they sometimes do not have their own space and thus are forced to sleep in unheated basements even in the dead of winter. Alam recounted many stories of women who developed chronic illnesses as a result of their living conditions. Like Latina workers in the sociologist Pierrette Hondagneu-Sotelo's study (2001), South Asian women are often asked to eat leftovers or rotting food. In many instances, they are not allowed to use the telephone, thus cutting them off from their families in South Asia as well as the world outside their work. Beating and verbal abuse are not uncommon. Neither is sexual abuse, which has historically accompanied domestic work. In talking about the silence that shrouds the issue, Alam said, "Sexual harassment is common. But it is also common that people don't talk about it because in our society, in our community, it has a stigma. People blame women, leaving out the men. If I speak out, then it is my shame. The news will travel home; this news will reach my family." To complicate matters, Title VII—which makes any form of employment discrimination, including sexual harassment, illegal—does not apply to private households because they are not recognized as workplaces (NOW Legal Defense and Education Fund 1997, 3).

The isolated nature of domestic work done behind the walls of a privatized space is compounded by the multiplicity of employment arrangements, which fragments and stratifies the workforce. Each arrangement is associated with levels of protection that domestic workers can legally demand under state labor laws. This creates a situation where workers, unless organized, are confused about their rights. Part-time babysitters and companions to sick or elderly people do not even enter the definition of an employee according to federal and New York labor laws and, therefore, do not receive protection (AALDEF and NELP, 34). The next most vulnerable group is live-in domestic workers, who have fewer rights under the law than those who do not live in. The law mandates a work week of forty-four hours for live-ins, whereas those who do not live in have a forty-hour week. Though New York State authorizes overtime for live-ins, this is not the case in the adjacent states of New Jersey and Connecticut, where some of Andolan's members work (NOW Legal Defense and Education Fund 1997).

Given these tremendously oppressive conditions, we might ask how it is possible for these forcibly isolated workers to organize. Just as there are historical continuities in conditions there is continuity in worker struggles, which are responsible for many of the labor protections that do exist in this occupation. It must be remembered that in the United States domestic workers were not entitled to labor protections afforded under the Fair Labor Standards Act (FLSA) until 1974. Andolan organizers do not stop at asking for better enforcement of existing labor laws, which continue to restrict unemployment insurance, workers' compensation, and disability to documented immigrants. They draw on the 1990 U.N. Migrant Rights Convention (Office of the High Commissioner for Human Rights 1990), which came into force in 2002, to demand basic entitlements for undocumented and documented workers. These entitlements include the right of workers to move freely across borders through expanded authorizations; to reunite with their families (from which immigrants can remain separated for years because of their temporary or undocumented status); and to economic security in their countries of employment.

Through rights education, Andolan ensures that workers know they have the rights to minimum wage regardless of their immigration status, payment for overtime under state guidelines, a weekly day off, disability insurance, workers' compensation, and a safe work environment. The group is engaged in securing health insurance paid for workers by their employers, paid vacation, and wages when the employer goes on vacation. Andolan also demands privacy for live-ins, and, to enable women to live outside their employers' homes Alam has been trying to raise money to acquire housing.

The first step toward organizing has been to find ways to reach domestic workers sequestered in suburban homes or in upper-class neighborhoods in Manhattan and the other boroughs. The DWC, Workers Awaaz, and Andolan, besides advertising in local ethnic newspapers, all do outreach in Jackson Heights, New York's "Little India," a neighborhood where employers bring the women they hire to help with shopping or to keep an eye on children. Organizers distribute fliers that describe employers' legal responsibilities toward their employees and contact information for their organizations. Just as black women organized on bus rides to work, and Latina and Caribbean women in parks where they take the children in their care, so do South Asian women use these excursions to reach out to others like them.

Once a domestic worker manages to reach Andolan, a member usually meets the woman and shows her how to use public transportation to get to a meeting so that the next time she can do it herself. Alam describes the impact of these meetings on new members: "Coming to the first meeting is often a powerful experience for a worker. . . . This step, although very common in other organizing efforts, has a special meaning for this especially isolated community" (1997, 17). At these meetings, women train each other in labor and immigration law to learn their rights. They also teach each other how to interview for a job, negotiate work conditions with a prospective employer, and demand changes in existing work conditions (18). This process dispels the sense of powerlessness that the state promotes among poorly paid immigrant workers through its immigration laws and poor enforcement of labor laws (Bonacich 1996, 322).

These methods build women's confidence and self-reliance. To illustrate the will to fight back that the collective process nurtures, as well as the accompanying risks, Alam offered the following example: "We had a case of a woman who had done an MBA from India and got a job as a domestic worker in a house here. . . . Because she was educated, on joining us she quickly caught on—she understood and fought for her rights. She started talking back to her employers: asking for more money, for a five-day week. They were surprised. How come she was talking back? She was given an ultimatum. If she wanted to stay, she needed to obey them or she needed to leave immediately. That was midnight! She called me but I was not home. She sat at a train station all night until a friend came to pick her up in the morning. That is how she survived." Through Andolan, the woman learned how to ask for better work conditions, and when this backfired she used Andolan's support network to get out of the situation and file a case against her employers in order to retrieve her passport and personal belongings.

As empowering as this strategy is for domestic workers, Andolan realizes that it leaves the task of enforcing labor protections to employees who have little structural power in a privatized situation. As part of the multiracial and multiethnic coalition Domestic Workers Union (DWU), Andolan has demanded an industry-wide standard contract. The standard contract drafted by AALDEF and NELP, in addition to making wage and hour protections binding on employers, introduces workers' entitlement to two weeks of paid vacation every year, one week's worth of paid sick leave, payment for the time employers are away on vacation, and medical insurance. By writing these benefits into the contract, the advocates advanced their dual goals of enforcing federal standards at state and local levels and addressing the severe gaps in the standards themselves. The campaign for a standard contract gathered momentum with local media coverage on the inhuman treatment of domestic workers, as well as with worker-led public demonstrations. In March 2002, the lobbying, demonstrations, and testimonies led to the introduction of a bill and a resolution sponsored by eighteen members of the New York City Council.

As workers negotiated with the state for regulations that would protect them, the state remobilized its neoliberalism while seemingly conceding to those demands. The New York City Council's conversion of the DWU's demand for an industry-wide standard contract to a bill proposing a code of conduct is an example of a working out of its neoliberal logic. The code left it up to a new set of subcontractors—employment agencies—to enforce labor laws. On top of excluding half of the 600,000 domestic workers and the majority of South Asian domestics who do not go through employment agencies, the proposed code continued to operate within the same logic that led the state to previously outsource its regulatory functions to individual employers.

The bill and the resolution are rhetorically progressive. The bill recognizes that "the majority of domestic or household employees in New York City are immigrant women of color who, because of race and sex discrimination, language barriers, and immigration status, are particularly vulnerable to unfair labor practices" (New York City Council 2002). Organizers read this legislative action with all of its limitations as a sign of their growing visibility and leverage.[11] But to what extent do they change the privatized mechanisms through which the state severely depresses women's paid reproductive labor? First, the bill leaves out those women who, like many of the South Asian workers organized by Andolan, are recruited through informal methods. These women are likely to be among those who are the most underpaid and, therefore, the most attractive for many employers. Second, the fact that the bill makes no provision for a process to monitor the implementation of the code once the worker disappears into the employer's household or to register a grievance in case of infractions, puts the responsibility back on the worker to take action if exploitative conditions were to continue. Even those who are placed by employment agencies and are likely to benefit from the bill do not have better recourse to justice in case of violations. Third, what becomes punishable in this proposed legislation is the failure of employment agencies to inform their consumers (employers of domestic workers) about their responsibilities under federal and state laws. In effect, the bill turns a labor protection issue into a consumer issue, conflating the conflictual interests of employers and employees. The Department of Consumer Affairs, which under the bill is supposed to oversee the employment agencies and track compliance, itself has resisted this confusion by pointing out that enforcing labor laws is the business of the Department of Labor (Lee 2002).

The bill does not require the state to change its practices or become accountable. Perhaps the most telling statement of the state's neoliberal move was the one made by the Democratic councilwoman Gale Brewer in favor of the proposal: "We're in a budget crunch and this bill doesn't cost anything," she declared (quoted in Tsai 2002). Indeed, the state can look benevolent without having to invest in services or enforcement that domestic workers need to free themselves of exploitation and violence.

Andolan constructs its campaigns around labor rights within a larger gendered analysis of immigration policies, which punish exploited workers instead of their exploitative employers and systematically undercut labor protections to which workers are entitled regardless of their immigration status. In recognizing that neither organizing its constituency nor its demands could succeed unless domestic workers' situations are placed in the entire context of their lives and the political economy of feminized labor migration, Alam (1997, 16) reminds us, "It is impossible to organize domestic workers without also understanding the many ways in which they have been oppressed not just as workers but also as women, immigrants and non-English speaking people." No organizing effort can be successful without recognizing and addressing the harmful contradiction between labor and immigration laws. Andolan insists that the transnationalization of women's labor must come with the universal recognition of the value of their labor and their rights as migrant workers. It assembles a transnational rights complex by drawing on New York State and U.S. federal laws as well as U.N. guidelines about the rights of migrant workers to demand fair and safe work conditions and to resist the criminalization of those who are undocumented.

Andolan's demands for better enforcement of federal and state hour-wage protections, health benefits, paid vacation, and respect from employers reflect what immigrant domestic workers have been asking for in other regions. But these measures, if put in place, will do more than simply "upgrade" the occupation, which is how Hondagneu-Sotelo (2001, 210–43) interprets the organizing efforts of the domestic workers she studies in Los Angeles. Andolan's approach entails revaluing the work of social reproduction—both paid and unpaid—and immigrant women's labor. It exposes the state's neoliberal practices. In asking for better application of federal and state laws it does not mistake the state to be a protector. It understands that the state is implicated in and gains from the cheapening of immigrant women's labor through the specious distinction between native and nonnative workers and documented and undocumented workers. Andolan's tactics teach us the difference between holding the state accountable for its labor practices and depending on the state for protection.

Sweatshop on Wheels

In Manhattan, below Ninety-Sixth Street, it is relatively easy to hail a yellow cab at any time of the night or day. Six times out of ten, the driver will be from Bangladesh, Pakistan, or India. The reason one can hop into a cab at 2 AM to go from, say, the Village to Park Slope in Brooklyn at minimal expense is that the taxi industry is organized around immigrant labor and twelve-hour shifts. Therefore, New Yorkers can avail of ceaseless service and, perhaps, what was until the 2004 fare hike the cheapest taxi ride in the world. The NYTWA organizes drivers to transform the grueling conditions under which they work. Rank-and-file driver-members assert their rights to economic justice, safety, and dignity in the face their hegemonic construction as immigrant workers who have no rights. In their struggles, we see a return of labor militancy in the form of successful strikes and demonstrations.

While the NYTWA targets "local" administration and business, its campaigns for rights are intrinsically tied to the transnational mobility of capital and labor. The deunionization of the taxi industry and its resultant turn to immigrant labor to perform the least desirable jobs in the lower end of the new service economy in the metropoles has to be understood as a manifestation of this recent phase of globalization, which began in the 1970s. By 1979, the state had stamped out taxi workers' rights won by a unionized workforce through a simple move: converting workers into self-employed business people.

The assault on unionization and workers' rights, however, cannot be understood simply as a retreat by the state from its welfare commitments.[12] In the case of the taxi industry, the state advanced rather than simply retreated because it started to regulate, monitor, and punish drivers with greater intensity on the grounds that they were immigrants. The NYTWA's demands for economic justice come out of the material effects of the state's representational politics that constructed drivers as threatening aliens. The battle on the streets for immigrant drivers is between two sets of rights: on the one hand are the rights of the non-riding "public" and paying customers who are the entitled citizen-consumers, and on the other hand are the rights of drivers-turned-immigrant service workers. Valorizing passengers and pedestrians in this way parallels the move to define employers of domestic workers as consumers. In both contexts there is a pattern in which consumers emerge as citizens deserving quality service.

The NYTWA began as the Lease Drivers Coalition (LDC), which was established in 1992 as the first workers' project of the Coalition Against Anti-Asian Violence (CAAAV) in New York City. Second-generation middle-class South Asian women—mostly bisexuals and lesbians—were involved in CAAAV as staff, board members, or volunteers. They proposed the project as a way of addressing the high exposure of these workers to police and passenger violence. Debi Ray-Chaudhuri, a South Asian Lesbian and Gay Association (SALGA) member and one of the women who initiated the project, remembered leafing through local newspapers with a CAAAV program director to find out that in 1992 South Asians comprised 43 percent of yellow cab drivers and more than fifty South Asian drivers had been killed on the job that year. For her, the dire need for an institutionalized base and organized response became evident when, she notes, "looking at the number of deaths, which was pretty stark, we got a sense that even from a traditional safety standpoint this was a very *urgent* situation."

From these investigations it became clear to the LDC founders that the violence directed at drivers was embedded in institutionalized racism. The project matched CAAAV's goals to fight racially motivated hate crimes and police brutality. "Drivers deal right away with people's ideas about race," Ray-Chaudhuri pointed out. "First of all, they are demonized in the media as ignorant immigrants and then victimized by the police *specifically* because they are South Asian more than if they were black or Caribbean. . . . Drivers taste that, feel that everyday." As the majority, South Asians have been more visible than other people of color in the industry. The goal was to transform this visceral experience of racialized violence into action.

Drivers, like domestic workers, often migrated from their countries to cope with the devastating effects of liberalization policies there. Unlike domestic workers, however, they did not migrate specifically to work in the taxi industry. Many left home in the hope of improving their ability to support their families with remittances in foreign currencies. Most of the South Asian drivers I spoke to financially provided for their families at home. Many drivers had a history of multiple migrations, having worked in the Middle East and Europe before making their way to the United States. Marginalized as immigrants of color, they were unable to find jobs despite their education, skills, or professional training. They temporarily turned to driving taxis to get through school or to escape jobs at gas stations, convenience stores, or restaurants where the pay was worse and they had little autonomy. As with domestic workers, their depressed earnings in the industry, more often than not, locked them into it.

From its inception, the LDC founders were aware of the historic importance of organizing workers, who were a new and marginalized presence in South Asian communities, from the "ground up," to use Ray-Chaudhuri's words.[13] The LDC's mandate of creating a workers' movement, beyond organizing taxi drivers against the single issue of racist violence, ultimately led the staff and members of the project to split off from CAAAV to form their independent organization, the New York Taxi Workers Alliance, in January 1998. The organizational structure and philosophy of CAAAV, which encouraged vanguardism with middle-class organizers in decision-making roles, its case-by-case approach to violence, and its emphasis on community organizing, along with the LDC's own leaning toward service provision for a few years, interfered with the autonomy that drivers needed to address their daily realities. Between 1996 and 1997, the LDC under its new staff organizer, Bhairavi Desai—a working-class second-generation Indian American woman—started to move toward mass-based organizing to address drivers' primary concern about low earnings. The focus of the project could no longer be the police. Rather, it was the entire complex represented by the city, the Taxi and Limousine Commission (TLC), the garages and brokers with whom taxi drivers did business, the New York Police Department (NYPD), and passengers. Having found a superb strategist and fearless organizer in Desai, the LDC left CAAAV.

The NYTWA, on breaking away from CAAAV, became a multiracial worker-led organization.[14] In addition to South Asians, there are African, Caribbean, Latino, East Asian, European, white, and African American drivers who are members of the NYTWA. As the name suggests, it now organizes all strata of yellow cab drivers, not just lease drivers. As a result, in 2003 the NYTWA had 4,800 members. The membership presents a mix of citizens, permanent residents, and undocumented immigrants. Many of its driver-organizers had been politicized in anticolonial or democratization movements in the Third World or in the U.S. civil rights movement. With vigorous outreach, Desai has been able to attract women drivers who, in her estimate, form about 1 percent of the industry and have specific needs as women workers. While nondriver members continue to play a vital role as volunteers, decision making is in the hands of the driver-members.

The NYTWA has kept its structure very simple. It has a small paid staff and an organizing committee but no executive director or board. The ethnically diverse organizing committee operates democratically through discussion and debate to decide on organizational and budgetary priorities, campaigns, strategies, and internal policies. Monthly membership meetings provide a forum for defining campaigns and deciding on policy issues. The group had three paid full-time members on its staff in 2002. Out of its tiny office in Manhattan the NYTWA carries on its day-to-day tasks of contesting tickets, providing legal aid, faxing city council members, taking a flood of calls from beleaguered taxi drivers, doing publicity, and holding meetings. The organization supports itself through membership fees ($10 per month) and grants from private foundations.

The presence of South Asian women in organizing working-class men surprises people both inside and outside of the industry because it is interpreted as breaking gender and class taboos. Desai and the lesbian, bisexual, and straight women who founded the LDC refused to buy into the image that working-class men were particularly sexist or more prone to harassing women than were middle-class men. The strong lesbian/bisexual presence in LDC had to do with these women's ability to relate to the legitimized violence directed at marginalized groups of people in public spaces (Advani 1997, 217). Their route to labor organizing through feminism has been crucial to the organization's awareness of gender inequality, masculinity, and sexism as core issues. Before Desai applied for the staff position at the LDC, she volunteered with Manavi. She has consistently confronted (not without pain and personal cost) sexist attitudes toward women and women's leadership when these issues have surfaced in the NYTWA. Her efforts have made it possible for women to be taken seriously as organizers and outreach workers in a male-dominated industry. It is important that the key role of women in shaping the NYTWA not become a repressed part of its history.[15]

AN "IMMIGRANT JOB":
RESTRUCTURING THE TAXI INDUSTRY

The NYTWA confronts problems that stem from the restructuring of the taxi industry in the 1970s. This reorganization was part of a larger economic restructuring that attacked unions and led to the whittling away of benefits and job security. During the 1970s, drivers in the industry were converted from unionized workers with benefits to independent contractors or small business owners (see Matthews 2005, 49–55, 57–69). The restructuring has fragmented the industry and set up a hierarchy among various ownership arrangements. The deunionization was marked by a racial recomposition of the workforce, which used to be majority white. With longer hours of work, the removal of benefits, increased workplace hazards, and the shift to leasing, taxi driving has evolved into an "immigrant job." At present, 90 percent of the drivers are immigrants and 60 percent of the entire workforce is made up of Bangladeshis, Pakistanis, and Indians.

The restructuring posed enormous challenges for organizing. Independent contractors are technically not employees and therefore do not fall under labor and occupational safety laws. In not being workers they do not have the right to bargain collectively, and this is why the NYTWA is neither technically a union nor affiliated with one.[16] Just as there are no "workers," there also is no identifiable "management." The various layers and components of the industry make it difficult for those aggrieved to identify a party with which to negotiate. Garages are not factory floors and drivers cannot be organized in that space. Like Andolan, the NYTWA has had to find alternative spaces such as the taxi line at airports, restaurants, and gas stations to reach out to drivers. It continues to find it difficult to track new drivers because of the industry's mobile and decentralized nature. The dream of small business ownership is such a powerful capitalist mythology (with its American twist of the ideology of hard work and individual achievement) that many drivers do not think of themselves as workers, even though they work in poor conditions for poor returns.

In the 1960s, drivers who worked on a commission system unionized themselves into Local 3036 to secure health benefits, paid vacation, and retirement funds. [17] According to the veteran driver-organizer Kevin Fitzpatrick, under the commission system drivers worked forty-five hours a week and negotiated to keep nearly 50 percent of the metered fare. Within a decade of winning these gains, workers lost them in keeping with the national trend. In reflecting on this moment when labor lost what it had gained through long struggle, Lipsitz states: "But sometimes what seems to be a sunrise can really be a sunset. We were not witnessing a dawn of a new movement for democracy in U.S. industry in the early seventies, but rather the beginnings of a new era of inequality and injustice ushered in by deindustrialization and economic restructuring" (1994, 7). In 1979, New York City—in collusion with union leaders who went against the rank-and-file sentiments—returned to the leasing system that had been made illegal in 1937.

Legalizing leasing has led to a highly stratified industry organized along corporate lines. To use Kevin Fitzpatrick's analysis, the "financial instrument" of this new corporate presence is the medallion—a number issued by the city that turns a vehicle into a cab. In 2003, a medallion was worth about $250,000 on average. Since the 1970s, garages and brokers have been able to buy most of the limited number of medallions that the city issues and lease them out to drivers. Of a total of 12,187 medallions, 8,287 were owned by garages and private non-driver individuals and leased out.[18] Brokers lease medallions to drivers who are in the process of buying their cars. Garages lease out both the medallion and the car to drivers on a daily or weekly basis. Of the 45,000 licensed drivers in New York City—18,000 to 24,000 of whom are on the road on any given day—only 8 to 12 percent of full-time drivers own medallions (Desai 2002). This organization stratifies the industry by placing lease drivers at the bottom, car owners/broker leasees on the next rung, and owner-drivers on the top. Within each layer, there is a maze of subcontracting arrangements between drivers.

The Taxi and Limousine Commission (TLC) oversees this complex industry. It was formed by the city in 1971 to regulate and license yellow cabs, for-hire vehicles, certain kinds of vans, and limousines. In 1995, then-mayor Rudolph Giuliani transferred the enforcement of rules to a newly created taxi unit of the New York Police Department (NYPD). This transfer meant a direct extension of state power over drivers in their day-to-day work.

From the drivers' perspective the shift to leasing increased their vulnerability to exploitation. The terms and conditions of leasing are not governed by a standard contract across the industry. Like the one-to-one agreements between domestic workers and their employers, drivers enter arrangements with the leasing garage or broker on an individual basis leading to a range of complications. Under leasing, drivers have to pay up front for their lease and other expenses like gas. Depending on the shift and the day of the week, lease drivers pay anywhere between $100 and $115 per shift for their lease and between $16 and $20 for gas (which has increased significantly since 2005). This means that drivers start their shifts with a negative income. During the shift, drivers first have to recover their lease money and then try to make money for themselves (see Matthews 2005, 42–48). While car owners/broker leasees and owner-drivers make monthly payments, they too have to make sure that they earn enough to cover their payments. As a result, most drivers work all twelve hours of the shift and usually seven days a week. On a good shift without tickets and time in court, a driver might take home $80 to $100. These earnings of $6–$8 an hour hardly befit their status as independent contractors. Through the system of upfront payments, leasing effectively transfers the risks of business fluctuations to drivers. As the NYTWA points out, whether drivers had a slow shift or not, garages and brokers make their money.

UNITING DRIVERS FOR ECONOMIC JUSTICE

Through its campaigns the NYTWA addresses how the switch to leasing, with its attendant fragmentation, has increased worker vulnerability to economic exploitation and state violence. For the NYTWA the structural position of the majority of drivers as immigrants of color is inseparable from the work conditions and violence to which they are subjected. The NYTWA's economic justice campaign uses innovative methods to win back the protections that drivers lost during the 1970s restructuring. Pragmatically, the NYTWA recognizes that, in itself, leasing is not immediately reversible. The group understands that demanding better labor laws and better enforcement of these laws is not going to bring change because drivers are not workers. What can be transformed, by organizing drivers to claim the fruits of their labor, are the existing relations of power in the industry. Through well-organized membership drives, political education, and mobilization, the NYTWA has transformed a fractured group of workers into a visible presence ready to come out in force and exercise its power. Since 1997, the industry and the city have had to contend with this organized collective.

Each of the NYTWA's demands for economic justice—an increase in fares, enforcement and decrease of lease caps, a surcharge to compensate for spiraling gas prices, an industry-wide standard contract, and an end to unfair ticketing practices—is directed at the TLC. Rather than wage its battle garage by garage and broker by broker, the NYTWA has identified the TLC as its target because of its policymaking and regulatory functions. Though the taxi industry is private, its role in offering a "public service" has opened it up to increased state regulation. Its ever-expanding role in regulating drivers (while failing to curb the corrupt practices of garages and brokers) in recent years has led to deep incursions by the state into the industry.

The work of transforming the TLC into a space where drivers can publicly argue their case started in the LDC under Desai's leadership. The TLC meetings used to be dominated by the TLC commissioners, the NYPD's taxi unit representatives, politicians with vested interests in the taxi industry, and three organizations representing the interests of garages, brokers, and private nondriver owners. While the drivers also were supposed to send their representatives, the TLC marginalized them by holding its meetings during the morning rush hour, which is peak business for drivers. Neither the day drivers nor the exhausted night-shift drivers could attend these meetings in large numbers. Under these circumstances, it was easy to brush aside the protests of the lone driver who made a meeting. In addition, before the LDC-turned-NYTWA gathered strength, drivers did not have a single organization representing them.

Since 1998, the NYTWA has been a persistent presence at TLC meetings and a compelling force at the TLC's public hearings on policy proposals like new rules, fare hikes, or lease caps. The organization has accomplished this stance by familiarizing itself with the TLC's procedures. In preparation for these events, the NYTWA builds momentum by researching the issue at hand, surveying drivers, educating council members, and raising media awareness. In recent years, drivers have turned out for key TLC meetings in record numbers. Between 200 and 300 drivers attend public hearings at which designated drivers present powerful testimonies. The NYTWA has achieved a goal it had set during its LDC days to "not only attend, but really contribute and drastically change the [TLC] space," to quote Desai. This transformation in driver participation in TLC policy proceedings has secured media attention for drivers and has increased the NYTWA's legitimacy.

As in the case of domestic workers, unifying drivers has not been easy for the NYTWA, though for different reasons. The fragmenting practices of leasing lead drivers to believe that the problems they face are personal. The NYTWA thus has had to develop an institutional analysis so that drivers can see that the violation of their rights is a shared condition. The lack of a standard contract that governs the entire industry means that leasing arrangements vary among garages and brokers. In pointing to the uncertainty about the terms of leasing and the isolation that these nonstandard practices produce among drivers, Desai said, "Different garages charge different leases: in terms of money and conditions, one driver is told one thing, another something else. . . . The driver is told one thing the first day and another thing the third day. This creates a psychological feeling that rights are in a state of confusion. . . . They are going to accept the changes after awhile because of the exhaustion from the amount of work, and [technical] language issues in the lease agreement." Some garages illegally charge lease drivers for repairs, make drivers pay for tickets served on owners, and renege on verbal assurances and written agreements. The NYTWA routinely renders services to drivers whose garages or brokers flagrantly violate TLC rules and their lease agreements. It also intervenes when garages intimidate drivers by bringing criminal charges against them. Until drivers started organizing, they had no way of knowing which practices were irregular. Since 1998, the NYTWA has been formulating a campaign to have the New York State attorney general's office investigate corrupt garages and brokers.

Similarly, the crushing weight of multiple tickets for traffic violation and TLC standards individualizes a systemic problem. For each ticket, drivers are summoned to the TLC's court, thus putting them in crisis mode. Their need for immediate service in fighting these tickets overwhelms the benefits of collective organizing. As one driver-organizer pointed out in speaking to drivers at a membership meeting: "While we are helping one driver to fight his ticket, there are ten others who are getting the same tickets. We're being distracted. What we should do is bring those eleven together and put pressure on the top; show people who are giving these summons, how they are killing us; show them we are going to fight back, we're not going to take it!" Fighting back not individually but collectively has been one of the NYTWA's core principles. According to

Desai, translating the power that drivers have as workers into collective action was the "simple concept that we live by on a day-to-day basis."

To build this collectivity, the NYTWA had to midwife a transnational alliance that would enable Pakistanis, Bangladeshis, and Indians to work together across the political and ethnic tensions that crackle among them. Its success has depended on these groups coming together—because South Asians together form the majority. Pakistani drivers constitute the largest South Asian group, although Bangladeshis represent a growing community that might outstrip Pakistanis in a few years.

In New York, far from home, South Asian drivers have re-created nationally bound spaces with Pakistanis, Bangladeshis, and Indians all leasing from specific garages and eating and socializing at specific restaurants. These symbolic borders reflect South Asia's geopolitics. For example, Bangladeshi drivers carry with them the vivid memories of living through the 1971 liberation war to end Pakistan's oppressive rule over its eastern territory. In Desai's first years of outreach she noticed that Bangladeshis had understandable reservations about an organization that, until 1997, was dominated by Pakistanis. Betrayal, torture, and war cast a long shadow on efforts to bring Bangladeshi and Pakistani drivers together.

Immigrants from India form the oldest of the South Asian groups in the industry. Their numbers, however, are relatively small. Until the late 1990s, Sikhs tended to outnumber Hindus. Sikhs came to the United States as political asylum seekers in the 1980s during the height of the separatist Khalistani movement in Punjab and its occupation by the Indian military. This particular ethnic-national configuration of Indians and Pakistanis has contributed to a relationship between them that is less fraught, even though India and Pakistan bitterly vie for power in South Asia. Desai speculated that one reason for the relative amity between Indians and Pakistanis could be that many of the drivers were from divided Punjab. Though the partition of British-occupied India at independence placed them in two different nations, they shared a common language and culture, and in some cases, the same ancestral villages. The Indian government's harsh military rule in Punjab in the 1980s also led many Pakistanis to perceive Sikhs as people who shared a common critique of the Indian nation-state. Unlike Bangladeshis and Pakistanis, Indians and Pakistanis shared space, often doing business with the same garages, frequenting the same restaurants, and living in the same neighborhoods. Despite the frequent escalations of conflict between India and Pakistan in recent years, NYTWA members have consistently resisted factionalism along national-religious lines.[19]

Organizing Bangladeshis is one of the NYTWA's priorities because among the groups of drivers they are one of the newest and most disenfranchised. However, they are also the most receptive to being mobilized because of their relatively recent history of national liberation struggle. As the Pakistani driver-organizer Rizwan Raja noted, "Bangladeshis are more politically aware. They think, 'If I do this, then things can be changed through political struggle' because they got their independence through recent political struggle."[20] To pull in Bangladeshi drivers, NYTWA organizers initially had to meet them in their territory—Bangladeshi restaurants in Manhattan and Queens.

In order to increase Bangladeshi membership and Bangladeshi leadership in the organizing committee, NYTWA organizers quickly realized that these antagonisms had to be openly addressed through mediated dialogue and a greater vigilance about exclusionary practices. For example, at the meetings I attended in 1996 and 1997, members checked themselves and each other when, in the heat of the moment, some of them in the presence of Bangladeshi drivers would disrupt the process of translation by erupting into a volley of fast exchanges in Urdu or Punjabi. This reflexivity came from the awareness that the imposition of Urdu on Bengali-speaking East Pakistanis was one of the factors that led to the liberation war. Strategically, the NYTWA did not simply insist on the common language of exploitation to build solidarity, nor did it use the rhetoric of inclusion. Rather, it paid careful attention to the deep rifts between these groups and tried to understand them in historical context. As a result, Bangladeshi membership and leadership in the NYTWA has been translated from a goal to a reality.

The LDC and NYTWA in its earlier days constantly negotiated the allegiance of Pakistanis, Bangladeshis, and Indians to their respective nation-states. At the same time, it utilized the critiques of nation-states that came out of the drivers' involvement with the self-determination movements in Punjab, the liberation movement in Bangladesh, and the democratization movements that have challenged military rule in Pakistan and Bangladesh. This political experience, which entailed confrontations with postcolonial nation-states, informs the organization's analysis of the place of immigrant workers within the U.S. national body and the economy. People crossing borders for work gave rise to the need for an organization like the NYTWA. In turn, it has found it necessary to cross other borders, also dangerous, in order to translate into unity the predominance in the taxi industry of drivers from three neighboring countries in South Asia. Without these early lessons in creating a transnational space through daily engagements with national difference, it would not have been possible for the NYTWA to grow into a well-knit multinational, multiracial, and multilingual organization.

These efforts at building unity have put the NYTWA in a position to negotiate with the TLC.[21] In 2001, the TLC raised the flat rate for John F. Kennedy airport rides from $30 to $45 in response to the NYTWA's economic justice petitions and the resulting hearings. In 2004, drivers received their first fare increase since 1996. Between 2002 and 2003, the NYTWA battled with the TLC not only to increase the fare but also to decrease the lease caps so that an increase in leases did not cancel out the benefits of a fare increase.[22] The restructuring of the fares and leases to address the exploitation of drivers is at the core of NYTWA's struggle for economic rights. It continues to campaign for a standard contract between drivers and leasers or brokers, a fuel surcharge, and changes in fines for small equipment violations. It has pushed the TLC to explore the question of providing health insurance for drivers. In a survey of 200 drivers, it found that 77 percent of them were uninsured. The drivers' long hours at work can lead to heart and kidney disease, diabetes, and severe back pain, while the occupational hazards range from asthma from pollution to physical injury from police and passenger violence (Ramirez 2002, 4).

THE PUNITIVE STATE:
PASSENGER ENTITLEMENT AND POLICE BRUTALITY

The NYTWA's campaign for economic rights is integrally tied to its campaign against the racist and xenophobic violence that drivers face from police and passengers. Abusive encounters severely impact drivers' earnings because they involve a loss of time at work, which amounts to an economic loss. While the rules governing taxi drivers grew more elaborate after Giuliani came to office in 1994, drivers have been exposed to higher levels of workplace violence ever since the industry turned to immigrant labor. During the twelve hours that drivers spend in public space, they risk being charged with violating traffic rules, being robbed and shot, and being beaten and cursed by police and passengers. Though the state offered no protection to these racialized immigrants, it had by no means withdrawn from their lives. In fact, the state has expanded its direct power over these immigrants, criminalizing them through abusive police surveillance and fines.

The city's need to closely regulate yellow cab drivers stems directly from a perception that immigrant drivers are rude, irresponsible, reckless, and unmanageable. The drivers' brown bodies, language, and ethnic practices, just by being what they are, have been seen as posing a threat to law and order. The racialization of these bodies as threatening is deeply gendered. The difficulty in coding these South Asian bodies as docile, feminized, and compliant—attributes often ascribed to East Asian men—leads to their representation as hypermasculine and therefore dangerous and belligerent.

The city, the TLC, and the police together form a complex that jointly assaults drivers and their income. According to a NYTWA educational flyer, the TLC generates $2.5 to $3 million per month in fines and fees. A large portion of these revenues comes from the yellow cab industry, which over time has become the most strictly regulated of all the services that the TLC oversees. With the NYPD entering the scene as the TLC's enforcement agency, the efforts in ticketing and collecting fines have become more aggressive. This was the police force that the Mollen Commission, established under Mayor David Dinkins, found in its 1994 report to be using excessive force particularly toward poor people of color (Human Rights Watch 1998). In 1996, the National Asian Pacific American Legal Consortium noted that the NYPD was "the major perpetrator in New York City" of anti-Asian violence (CAAAV 1996, 4).

Taxi passengers were turned into entitled consumers under Giuliani's law-and-order platform and his "Quality of Life" program. These policies explicitly defined taxi driving as service work. The TLC, the NYPD, and the city constructed passengers as needing to be protected from discourteous and racist drivers who threatened public safety. The enshrinement of consumer rights in the taxi industry in New York City expresses one of the contradictory ways in which citizenship has been redefined under neoliberalism (see Evans 1993 for his analysis of the United Kingdom under Thatcher). Consumers become entitled citizens worthy of protection as a result of their participation in the "free" market. However, the very state that wants to eliminate state controls to restore the free play of market forces steps in aggressively to protect consumers against these foreign, unreliable, and ever-threatening service providers.

The NYTWA realized that to effect any meaningful change in the lives of drivers it needed to confront the nexus among the three punitive agents: the TLC, the NYPD, and the passengers. While the leasing structure fragments drivers, the TLC's use of the police and the passengers to enforce its regulations integrates the workplace in a way such that it comes to resemble a factory floor. In making the connections between the city, the TLC, the police, and the passengers, Desai pointed out: "[For] drivers, their factory floor is out on the street. Who's their supervisor? The cops. Who's their secondary supervisor? It is the passenger in the back of the cab who tells them what to do. Who has armed them? The city. The city has armed both sets of people to make sure that this group of workers follows all the rules just like any good worker would in one controlled geographic location, right? That's one thing about the history of the enforcement against the taxi industry. . . . Police brutality is historically a tool which has been used by property-owning white people to control non-white people, primarily working class and poor non-white people, which also includes immigrants. So we need to contextualize these experiences in a historical framework." The enforceable right to a particular quality of service ties customers to the police and the TLC. The TLC, through an eleven-item passengers' bill of rights, defines the standards that the service must meet. The police and the TLC handle customer complaints, which are heard in closed TLC courts where drivers rarely win a case.

The bill of rights is posted inside each cab. It informs passengers that they have the right to a clean cab, "smoke and incense-free air," a "radio-free (silent) trip," and a polite English-speaking driver who knows his or her way around the city (Taxi and Limousine Commission 2002). The entitlements associate immigrant drivers with poor English, dreadful manners, filth, and bothersome smells. An attempt by a *New York Times* commentator to humorously characterize her cab ride is representative of how passengers see their drivers. Even when trying to make friendly small talk with cabbies she finds that they only "mumble and curse at other cars and speak into microphones [probably CB radios] in strange tongues" (Birsh 1995). As the Asian American writer-activist Helen Zia (2000, 201) observes, nearly everyone has a New York City "taxi from hell" story in which drivers are portrayed as offensive, manic, and alien. Offended customers are encouraged to call the police or the TLC, the number for which is posted in several places in the cab, or to go to the TLC's Web site to fill out a form with a convenient checklist of violations. Reminiscent of anti-Asian laws of the nineteenth century and the early twentieth, the standards of service turn xenophobic racism into public policy.

Police brutality toward drivers takes the form of physical assault, verbal abuse in racist and xenophobic language, revictimization of drivers robbed or in the danger of being robbed, and indifference to their calls for help. In their day-to-day work, drivers stomach epithets like "stupid Indian" or "stupid cab drivers." These words have been hurled at them by police not only when they were being ticketed but also when they call the police for help. Saleem Osman, a Pakistani taxi driver and a former LDC staff organizer, writes about the workings of police intimidation of immigrant drivers: "Seat dirtied by a passenger? Show us your immigration papers! Complaints by a racist drunken man? We'll deport you (especially if you don't speak the language well enough to defend yourself)" (1995, 7). Any protest against unfair treatment by police invites physical violence and criminal charges. Osman himself was wrongfully charged after being assaulted by police for intervening in a dispute between a driver and a white motorcyclist. As he was being beaten up, the police officer told him "Go back to your own country," and followed with "There's no black mayor in New York any more—so you better watch out" (Davar 1995, 12). With the passage of the 1996 Anti-Terrorism and Effective Death Penalty Act, criminal convictions against noncitizens, even minor ones, are grounds for deportation (Williams 1996; Volpp 2003), and this possibility has made drivers even more vulnerable in encounters with the police or passengers. Further, post-9/11 homeland security measures have made drivers even more anxious regarding the possibility of deportation.

The taxi industry has one of the highest workplace homicide rates, and drivers are sixty times more likely to be killed than other workers, including police officers (Occupational Safety and Health Administration 2002). Because taxi driving is a cash business, night drivers are in constant danger of being robbed and shot. Delays in the response by police to drivers' calls for assistance and the routine dismissal of drivers' grievances contribute to these high homicide rates. The driver-organizer Raja expressed well the irony of police presence when he said, "When you don't need them, they'll be all over you. You run a red light and they'll be there! When you need them, you call them, "'I'm being mugged,' they won't be there. They will come fifteen minutes later." Such delays have often cost drivers their lives or have led to debilitating injuries. The extent to which the police devalue drivers' lives is reflected in one officer's unabashed statement that he "hate[s] these immigrant cabdrivers" and feels "no emotion whenever one of them is killed" (CAAAV 1996, 3).

The normalization of violence against drivers sends out the message that they have no rightful place in their country of residence and no basis on which they can claim their basic rights to safety against theft and violence. Drivers recognize that the pressures under which they work are designed to make them forget their rights. In commenting on the pervasiveness of racism in drivers' encounters with law enforcement, Raja noted: "If you look at the makeup of this industry, the laws of this industry are made *totally* in a way thinking that these guys are immigrants and they have no rights. You might have some rights in Pakistan but if you are driving a cab here, you don't have any rights." While drivers like Raja enjoyed few rights in Pakistan under military rule, many felt they had none at all in the United States. Talking about the effects of the public reinforcement of the sense of illegitimacy on the streets of New York, Desai pointed out: "How can a South Asian driver who is told, 'you shouldn't even be working here,' how the hell is he going to feel comfortable changing the conditions of work, if he's not even feeling comfortable being here?" Since South Asians were inordinately targeted by law enforcement agencies as a result of their concentration in the industry, the LDC started off by addressing that sense of displacement and disentitlement.

From the very beginning, the LDC protested the racism underlying police brutality and police callousness regarding the deaths of South Asian drivers. The group organized several powerful demonstrations against the deaths, beatings, and wrongful arrests (Advani 1997; Zia 2000, 203–4). These public protests, during which drivers held up banners such as "South Asians demand end to police brutality," allowed them to become visible and occupy public space as immigrant workers demanding social justice on an issue that affects numerous communities of color in New York City. Between 1992 and 1995, the LDC demanded better driver-safety laws. Its first campaign, Operation Safe Cab, was successful in getting the TLC to once again require taxis to install a bullet-proof partition between the driver and the back seat. In addition, the TLC agreed to equip cabs with trouble lights for the drivers to use to signal patrolling police cars. The LDC acted as the drivers' advocates in the numerous cases of police brutality and offered its members free court representation, other forms of legal aid, and translators (Davar 1995, 11).

Under the NYTWA, drivers have linked their fight against police brutality to the NYPD's relentless ticketing, which adds to their economic woes. Police often issue anywhere from two to ten tickets to a single driver in a given week. For each traffic violation, drivers used to get two tickets, one returnable to the Department of Motor Vehicles (DMV) and the other to the TLC. Each time they are pulled over, drivers can get multiple tickets for violations in addition to the one for which they were stopped. Under Giuliani's beautification project, the TLC could fine a driver even if a passenger refused to take a receipt and left it in the car or if a passenger left a seat belt tucked under the seat without the driver's knowledge. Since 1998, fines have been increased and new fines have been added to an already onerous list. Tickets can cost a driver $300 to $1,000 per month. But the story does not end with paying the ticket. Drivers have to appear in court for all tickets and complaints, which amounts to time lost from work and lawyers' fees. In response, the NYTWA has systematized legal aid as part of its membership benefits. Even at the discounted rates the NYTWA offers to its members, drivers spent $60 to $100 for each DMV ticket and $100 to $200 for each TLC ticket, depending on the type of offense.

The NYPD's rampant and violent abuse of ticketing also promotes the idea that immigrant drivers are multiple offenders who are beyond correction and restraint, and thus cuts deeply into drivers' earnings in ways that are not immediately apparent. Connecting economic exploitation and police brutality, Desai said: "Looking at the issue of police brutality: for a driver that's an economic issue. It isn't just about a cop beating you, which is incredibly heinous. . . . He does it in the middle of the time you're making the money you need to pay off your lease. It's a workers' issue. It happens when your mental state is that of a worker. . . . Whatever issue we look at, we look at it as these guys experiencing it as workers, as marginalized, economically exploited people." Though Desai uses the specific example of physical violence, she and the other NYTWA members do not restrict their understanding of brutality to assault. For them, the economic hardship and insecurity inflicted through ticketing is also a form of violence. By putting workers at the center of her analysis, Desai articulates the simultaneity of racism, class exploitation, and poverty that has been key to grasping how oppression works in the lives of people of color. She insists on the impossibility of separating racist violence from a driver's subject position as a worker. By framing violence as an issue of economic justice, the NYTWA resists the isolation of racism as a single concern and situates it firmly in the drivers' daily experience.

The NYTWA deploys a combination of tactics—direct militant action, legal action, consumer education, and publicity—against these grave injustices. Among the direct action tactics, the 1998 taxi strikes against Giuliani were a resounding success in terms of participation and attracting public attention. Since the NYTWA has yet to set up a strike fund, strikes cannot be used as the only direct action tool. The organization prepares its workers for massive mobilization by building momentum through a series of rapid public actions such as the large-scale distribution of fliers, demonstrations, public meetings, and motorcades. Some of these are, of course, traditional union strategies.

Since 1998, the NYTWA has worked closely with the Asian American Legal Defense Fund and the immigrant rights clinic at New York University's law school to take class action measures rather than fighting violations solely on a case-by-case basis. Eliminating certain ticketing practices and license suspensions that violated due process through courts has been among its victories. The NYTWA has petitioned the TLC to eliminate fines for small equipment violations and replace them with the correction notices received by drivers of private cars and other commercial vehicles. It has also consistently protested the TLC's closed court process on the grounds that it violates basic civil rights.

The NYTWA's use of consumer education is growing. Just as organizers in the garment industry have learned to use the energies of anti-sweat consumers (Bonacich 1996), so does the NYTWA understand that it needs the support of passengers. Since Giuliani and the print media played up consumer fears by portraying drivers as reckless, poorly trained, accident-prone, and racist, the NYTWA encourages its members to win over passengers by giving them informational postcards about conditions in the industry and by surveying them.

In an age when strikes are increasingly rare as a result of union busting and worker intimidation, the NYTWA staged two strikes in May 1998 against fresh rules that increased across the board the burden of penalties on drivers. The rules proposed in late April by Giuliani to the TLC raised fines for a variety of already existing offenses and defined new penalties. They also instituted tougher insurance requirements, which made even garages sympathize with strikers. The rules, according to the mayor's office and the TLC, were proposed to safeguard public interest, which was increasingly threatened by drivers who "break the law and think it is okay to do so" in the words of a TLC official (Strozier 1998a). The drivers went on strike on 13 and 21 May. The 13 May strike, which had a support rate of 98 percent, was considered to be one of the most successful in the city's recent history. On 21 May, twenty thousand drivers participated in the second strike (Prashad 2000; Strozier 1998a; Zia 2000; Matthews 2005, 11–37).

The new rules made taxi driving more risky than ever before. Twelve of the rules specifically targeted drivers while the other five applied to all types of owners including garages and brokers. Ten of the rules were new. Fines on existing violations were more than doubled. In some case, the increase was 600 percent, as in the case of drivers who were found to be threatening toward TLC representatives and employees. Needless to say, this rule could be easily applied to drivers who stood up for their rights. Offenses that used to lead to license suspensions now qualified for license revocations. The TLC's points system was revised to set an impossible standard that applied only to yellow cabs. Six points, which is equal to two traffic violations in eighteen months, meant a thirty-day license suspension. As the NYTWA pointed out, such a standard was unrealistic given the long hours that drivers were forced to work, police harassment in the form of tickets, and the TLC's arbitrary closed-court process through which drivers were often found guilty. In addition to fines and points, drivers would also have to pay out-of-pocket for drug tests and defensive driving courses.

Outraged, drivers fought back with work stoppages. Their strategies show how they utilized a combination of direct and legal action to fight the city and the TLC. The extraordinary driver participation in the 13 May strike could be partly attributed to the sweep of the rules that cut across ownership arrangements. By cracking down on all types of drivers, Giuliani's proposal had the unplanned effect of uniting the workforce. Not surprisingly, when word spread of the impending strikes, the Giuliani administration tried several strike-breaking tactics. As an "emergency" measure, the city announced that it would permit livery cars to pick up street hails, which are legally the monopoly of yellow cabs. Livery cabs, however, declined and showed solidarity with yellow cab drivers. To increase the pressure on the city, the NYTWA called another strike on 21 May. On the same day, the owner-driver led United Yellow Cab Association planned a motorcade to City Hall without consulting the NYTWA. On the day of the motorcade, as foreseen by the NYTWA, the city deployed hundreds of police officers. The police commissioner at the time, Howard Safir, justified this show of force in his infamous statement equating protesting drivers with terrorists: "It's no different than if we discovered a terrorist threat and we moved to stop the terrorists from carrying out their act" (Strozier 1998b). Safir's equation, presented as common sense, underlines the specificity of how South Asian working-class men are raced in the United States. According to their plan the cab drivers drove over the Fifty-Ninth Street bridge to enter Manhattan from Queens, but they were stopped by police. The two taxi organizations appealed this obstruction in federal court on the grounds that the drivers' First Amendment right to peaceful protest was being violated. A week later, on 28 May, drivers held their motorcade after having been cleared by a federal judge. That day, the TLC voted to pass fifteen of the seventeen proposals; however, in violation of their own rules they took the vote after a closed-door meeting. The NYTWA challenged the vote on procedural grounds in the state supreme court. Even though the court admitted that the TLC had indeed breached its procedure, it upheld fifteen of the seventeen rules. The court did, however, require the TLC to pay the lawyers representing the drivers as a fine for its violation.

The success of the strike needs to be assessed in terms of the drivers' undeniable impact on New Yorkers and on tourists, the ability of the drivers to unite a divided workforce, and the new media visibility they brought to their work. For the first time, the drivers' interests and perspectives received media time. The NYTWA began to see both the importance of and payback for its efforts to reach out to media. The coverage of the strike was undoubtedly groundbreaking. However, without context it made the mobilization look spontaneous and ephemeral, hiding from view the long, systematic, and backbreaking organizing that the LDC and then NYTWA had done since 1992. Though media reports on the taxi industry since the strike do incorporate the NYTWA's point of view as a result of its intervention and education, they continue to disregard movement building. A glaring example of this is the framing of Operation Refusal.

Near Columbia University on a late October evening in 1999 several cabs whizzed past the Hollywood actor Danny Glover, his daughter, and her room-mate, refusing to stop for them. Deeply frustrated, Glover filed a complaint with the TLC and held a press conference. Glover's complaint led to a swell of support from the city's African American and Hispanic communities long underserved by yellow cabs. African American leaders such as Rev. Al Sharpton and ex-mayor David Dinkins spoke out. The issue quickly became framed as the racism of one group of people of color toward another, with newspapers running headlines like "New York's cabbies show how multi-colored racism can be" (Luek 1999). What was missing in all this was the fact that the cab drivers themselves had thought about the problem of refusal and had uncovered its structural roots in residential segregation.

Then-mayor Giuliani promptly stepped in to save African Americans from racist immigrants. This was, of course, the same mayor whose policies un-leashed greater police violence in African American, Puerto Rican, and Domin-ican communities, withdrew critical services and funding, and pushed them out of their neighborhoods through gentrification. The mayor's office and the TLC launched Operation Refusal on 10 November 1999. A driver caught refusing a street hail by undercover TLC inspectors or police officers had his taxi confis-cated and his license suspended on the spot. Within a month, the NYTWA reported that forty-nine drivers had been suspended and were awaiting court hearings. Through its own research, it found that most of the refusal cases were based on destination rather than race. However, the two issues coincided be-cause of race-based residential segregation (New York Taxi Workers Alliance 2001a). Materially, the weeks-long license suspension meant that the drivers could not make a living. Legally, they were treated as guilty before the alleged refusal came to trial. On appeal, the federal court ruled that the on-the-spot suspensions indeed violated due process of law and were unconstitutional. In addition to taking legal action, the NYTWA publicly resisted the ideological underpinnings of Operation Refusal.

One of LDC's founding goals had been to address the racism of South Asian drivers toward African Americans. According to Ray-Chaudhuri, the idea was for South Asians to recognize that "our position is not independent of African American and Latino struggles." In recalling the kinds of conversations that the LDC wanted to stimulate in the South Asian drivers' community, she said, "One of the functions the LDC serves is to discuss South Asian perceptions about black Americans—their fears about poverty and their racist assumptions. For the first time we could talk about racism toward African Americans and how that relates to racism toward South Asians." While the discussions sometimes got mired in the ethics of nondriver volunteers raising the consciousness of drivers who put their lives on the line in dangerous neighborhoods (Bald 1996), the LDC's anti-racist stance was successful in defeating the move by Pak Brothers, a drivers' association, to get the city council to pass a "right of refusal" as part of the driver safety campaign (Advani 1997, 218–19).

Under the NYTWA, the terms of the debate over drivers' racism toward African Americans changed. While the group continued to encourage members to examine how racism played one exploited group against another, it started to question the distribution of transportation services in the city. It linked the areas that yellow cabs preferred to serve to the pressures of covering the lease. Choked bridges and tunnels, which connect Manhattan to the outer boroughs, made trips out to the Bronx or Brooklyn financially unfeasible, especially when cabs often return empty from these areas. Linking residential segregation by race to cab and livery services, the NYTWA pointed out: "The city government forced yellow cab drivers into serving a primarily middle and upper class white constituency by restructuring the business and simultaneously created a different segment of the industry—liveries—to service people of color areas. . . . The racist profiling of African Americans by yellow cab drivers is thus neither simply a matter of economics nor is it a simple case of prejudice. It is instead a product of a systematic creation of differential services for different people—redlining in short. It is what has long been identified as 'systemic and institutionalized racism'" (New York Taxi Workers Alliance 2001a). Redlining, in this context, takes the form of the black cars serving Wall Street, the yellow cabs serving white middle-class Manhattan, and the liveries serving the poorer neighborhoods where people of color lived.

For the NYTWA, diversity training for drivers perceived as being ignorant, hide-bound Third World immigrants was not going to solve the structural problems of residential segregation. According to a NYTWA position paper on solutions to refusal, dialogue and education had to hinge on understanding that, "[neither] working class immigrant drivers nor African Americans had anything to do with the way the system was constructed. It is therefore critical that both communities come together to understand the systematic way in which this industry has been set up to create conditions ripe for both exploitation and discrimination." The shift to an analysis of residential segregation by race and the economics of taxi driving under leasing resisted simplistic readings of South Asian racism toward African Americans.

At the same time that the NYTWA offered all the communities involved a way to think structurally about refusal, it asked its driver-members to question their uncritical acceptance of the hegemonic images of African Americans and Latinos as well as their desire to gain legitimacy by distancing themselves from these groups. One driver who watched a black couple and their child being passed by four empty cabs on a cold winter evening raised a series of soul-searching questions for fellow drivers in a piece he wrote in the wake of Operation Refusal: "Some drivers say black people 'understand' why cabs don't pick them up. Do you think this family 'understood' that they couldn't get a NYC yellow cab to stop for them? Do you think they 'understood' that they are 2nd class citizens? . . . Our children attend the same rotten schools and play in the same run down parks. . . . Do we need to make our neighbors our enemies?" (New York Taxi Workers Alliance 2001b). One of the long-term issues in the NYTWA's political education, which I have seen members impart in an organic way at meetings, has been to ask drivers to examine their desires for assimilation, how they themselves are racialized on the streets of New York, and how they share the problem of police brutality with African American and Hispanics who are similarly criminalized.

The analysis and solutions put forward by the NYTWA have evolved out of nine years of consistent work on issues of race and racism. In describing how race politics works on the streets during his day-to-day work, Raja shred the mask of the state's benevolent posture in rescuing African Americans from racist immigrant drivers when he described how he and his African American passenger waited in Flatbush, a predominantly black neighborhood in Brooklyn, for police to respond to their complaints about each other. His account makes clear that African Americans are not among the chosen citizen-consumers whose entitlements the state zealously steps in to protect.

During a nightshift in 1998 Raja was refused his fare by an African American passenger on the grounds that he had "an attitude." The passenger tried to grab at Raja's hack license and then snatched his rate card under the instruction of his girlfriend who claimed to work for the TLC. He also called 911 for help. Raja, warning his passenger that taking his rate card was theft of property and refusing to pay his fare was theft of services, also called 911. In response to the passenger's threats about having him arrested, Raja pointed out to his passenger that he too was just as likely to get arrested because as a black man he had a high possibility of having a criminal record. When police did not arrive even after forty-five minutes, Raja laid out the situation for his passenger.

RAJA: Where is the police now?

PASSENGER: I don't know.

RAJA: I'll tell you. With your accent, they [the police] knew it was a black man sitting in a cab and they knew that there will be a problem because you don't want to pay. They perceive you as guys who don't pay and they want you to run away with my money. Now I'm calling up with my accent. They can tell it is an immigrant. So who cares about an immigrant? They don't care about you. They don't care about me. What are we waiting for? There's no police to help out. If you are two colored men—*men*—they allow you to fight so that they can come and arrest you.

The conversation ended with both men exchanging apologies and Raja receiving the money for his fare. As the story shows, neither immigrant drivers nor African American consumer-passengers are seen as deserving the protection of the state's law-and-order platform. Both groups, in fact, are seen as the very people who were responsible for the law-and-order problem and who needed to be punished. Both were targets of racism—but as Raja pointed out, they were targets in ways that were specific to their racialization. Raja's antiracist stance was crafted in the midst of his day-to-day work charged with the fear of losing his fare, not making his lease, getting injured in a fight, and having criminal charges lodged against him. What served him that evening was his experience as a driver who had taught himself to read the racial vocabulary of his encounters with passengers and police as well as his experience as an organizer.

The NYTWA is able to intervene so effectively in the framing of drivers' refusal of passengers of color because of its sustained engagement with the race issues that drivers face every day. The powerful testimonies by South Asian drivers at a public hearing on the issue of refusals introduced the much-needed complexity into the debate, which convinced members of the African American and Hispanic communities, as well as Danny Glover himself, that punitive action against the drivers was an inappropriate response. So compelling was the NYTWA's argument that the report on the problem of refusals from the Manhattan borough president's office incorporated many of the group's recommendations. The organization's public exposure of Operation Refusal's divisive effects paid off when Rev. Al Sharpton came out in support of the demonstrations and rallies against the ruthless beating of driver Hisham Amer in the hands of TLC officers in December 2000.[23] The anti-racism and cross-racial coalition work of the NYTWA were not abstract mission statements but rather lived practices that allowed it to clearly articulate the structural position of immigrant workers vis-à-vis the poor communities of color in the city.

Conclusion

Andolan and the NYTWA have reinvented immigrant workers—both undocumented and documented—into subjects who demand rights that they are routinely denied. In doing so, they devise labor strategies for the twenty-first century. The two organizations have reformulated workers' rights so that they can apply to immigrants regardless of their immigration status. Such a position rejects the distinction between "legal" and "illegal" workers while addressing how that distinction, so central to maintaining a nation-state's identity as sovereign, is a constant source of vulnerability in the lives of many workers. For domestic workers, the weakness of labor protections to which they are technically entitled lies in the dual devaluation of reproductive work and immigrant labor. Despite the formal separation of wage-hour protections from a worker's immigration status, both the immigration laws and the discursive construction of the immigrant as someone who has no rightful place within U.S. borders undercut labor laws. For their part, taxi drivers are not even entitled to labor protections because they are no longer considered to be workers. Both organizations claim rights in the face of impossibilities that naturalize the criminalization of undocumented workers, stigmatize working-class immigrants, and convert workers into so-called entrepreneurs.

The organizations' rights discourse draws on local, state, and federal laws as well as on international conventions. This discourse configures a transnational complex of rights that helps us to reimagine what workers need as they cross borders. Instead of insisting that workers be defined solely by their class position, both organizations demonstrate how the hierarchies of gender, nation, and race facilitate worker exploitation. Just as Andolan and the NYTWA refuse to see workers solely as products of class inequality, they also do not believe that legalizing undocumented workers would single-handedly solve the problems they address. Sections of the labor movement, engaged in pushing for amnesty for undocumented workers and arguing that the legalization of immigrants has to be an ongoing process, are coming to a similar realization (Quiroz-Martinez 2001). The demand for legalization needs to be accompanied by demands to end the earning differentials that workers face because they do not speak fluent English; because they are seen as immigrants even though they might be naturalized U.S. citizens; and because they are women and men who do some of society's most undesirable jobs.

That neither Andolan nor the NYTWA rely on citizenship marks the difference between place-taking and space-making politics. These labor organizations' sustained engagement with various government agencies is reminiscent of the platform of civic engagement established by the Association of Indians in America as it went about in the 1970s seeking protection, primarily in the workplace, against discrimination based on race, nationality, and gender. But the goal of labor organizations in demanding an end to the discriminatory and exploitative conditions in their workplaces by approaching city and state officials and by collaborating with experts on labor, immigration, or human rights is not the attainment of abstract liberal citizenship. Both organizations have members whose U.S. citizenship does not translate into better pay or better work conditions. Both organizations clearly understand the contradictory workings of the state that needs their labor and yet both reviles them and retreats from responsibility for them while extending its punitive power in their lives. The activists understand that as poor working-class immigrants they are far from being the universal and entitled American citizens in whose image middle-class place-taking politics try to cast South Asians. Andolan and the NYTWA exemplify— though as representatives of a laboring class of immigrant workers and not all South Asians or Asian Americans—the argument by the literary critic Lisa Lowe that Asian American subjectivities, communities, and struggles constitute "alternatives to liberal citizenship in the political sphere" (1996, 156).

Both Andolan and the NYTWA broke away from organizations run by middle-class South Asian and Asian American progressives. This assertion of autonomy raises questions about the possibility of cross-class solidarity (see Zia 2000, 200, 209; Prashad 1998, 2000). As is evident from the painful debates in Sakhi and CAAAV between 1996 and 1997, middle-class activists are far more conflicted about how they can go about supporting working-class struggles than are the working-class activists themselves, who are clear about running and leading their organizations. Thus, the core question about cross-class solidarity does not hinge so much on how middle-class progressives can support working-class people. Rather, for structural change to occur middle-class activists need to honestly examine their own dependence on low-wage service workers in countless instances. Then they might be able to transform that relationship with the knowledge of how one set of invisible ill-paid workers sustains another set of better-paid and relatively privileged workers in advanced capitalism. To move away from the paralyzing effects of guilt, middle-class activists need to understand that what is at stake is the radical revaluation of reproductive and service work, both on their own part and on that of others.

The lived experience of domestic workers and taxi drivers with global economic restructuring as they switch to other workplaces only to find that those, too, are low-paying, dead-end service sector jobs underlines the importance of workers organizing themselves in these other sites. The narrative of initial suffering and eventual upward mobility sustains many immigrants, yet it rings hollow over time. Those to whom I spoke often mentioned that they were ultimately persuaded to organize even at the risk of losing their jobs because they had come to see that standing up for their rights was the only sustainable answer to their hardship. As the two organizations arrived at a better understanding of their fragmented workplaces and their connection to other types of service work, they started to work in multiethnic and multiracial contexts. The NYTWA—after successfully bringing together Bangladeshis, Indians, and Pakistanis in a transnational alliance—expanded to organizing with other ethnic groups in the taxi industry. Andolan, while still a South Asian organization, campaigns in alliance with women who come from other parts of the world but share similar conditions of work. Thus, to construct a more complete history of South Asian labor organizing we need to look beyond South Asian organizations to multiracial contexts where South Asians work with other people of color (though not always in direct contact) in home health care, hospitals, airports, gas stations, newspaper stands, agriculture, and, on the high end, in the information technology industry.

The two labor organizations embody and enact the oft-repeated mantras of the Left. They work in multiracial and multiethnic coalitions. They organize across borders. They build worker solidarity. They do anti-racist, anticapitalist, and feminist work. They translate the power that workers have into something real and executable. Through their work they teach us why and how the calls to action become necessary if workers are to live with dignity. What makes them so successful are the sweat, tears, the bitter gall of fear and humiliation, the frustration of being beaten back, the elation of winning a campaign, mutual support, love, laughter, deep compassion, the unrewarding, unnoticed, and unglamorous work of building strategies step by step, and most importantly, an unwavering belief in their cause.

Conclusion

The urgency of documenting contemporary South Asian contributions to movements for social transformation first struck me after I attended the "Black Women in the Academy: Defending Our Name" conference held at MIT in 1994. More than two thousand attendees had gathered to reflect on the sensationalized public attacks on Anita Hill and Lani Guinier and the quotidian practices that delegitimized black women's scholarship and activism in the academy (see White 1999, 257–65). During this historic conference, the term "black women" became a contested and contentious category: Who could claim to be black women and on what basis? For some panelists and attendees, the presence of Asian American women, including South Asians, was indecipherable because some African American women had only encountered Asians as model minorities. It was at this event that the feminist scholar-activist M. Jacqui Alexander called for research that would allow people of color in the United States to become conversant in each other's histories. Such fluency would require a familiarity with those histories that had yet to become part of U.S. academic and activist repertoires of struggles against ethnic-racial oppression.

When two years later I embarked on the project that led to this book, I wanted my rendition of South Asian feminist, queer, and labor organizing to provide a transnational vocabulary that would allow South Asian immigrants and other minoritized groups in the United States to enter into conversation with each other about social justice. The urgency I felt in doing my research was greatly influenced by the preoccupations in the 1990s of U.S. scholar-activists with the issue of cross-racial alliance building for change and with developing analyses that could capture the inseparability of race, class, gender, and sexuality. I wanted to center on the needs and visions of immigrants to enrich accounts of progressive politics led by people of color. My work in this book has been driven by my belief that black, East Asian, Latina/o, and Chicana/o organizers can learn as much from the efforts I describe here as South Asians can learn from them. Because South Asians are perceived as a homogenously privileged group, they are asked to learn and not teach. This work has mapped heterogeneous interests within South Asian communities to make the case that South Asian feminist, queer, and labor activists contribute to the social analyses emerging from people of color movements. They complicate the black-white framework of race relations and construct a transnational complex of rights to contend with the daily power of borders in the lives of immigrants.

Throughout this book I have argued that a South Asian identity signals a particular politics of social change that cannot be generalized to all immigrants of South Asian origin. The identity represents space-making politics, which part ways from place-taking strategies. A South Asian identity makes available those kinds of political possibilities that are not contingent on nation-based citizenship. Space-making politics do not replace place-taking politics or political enactments of national, language-based, and intranational regional identities. Place-taking and space-making politics operate concurrently but in tension with each other. Unlike calls issued by place takers as well as the South Asian Left for a politically united community, in this book I insist that the two types of politics reflect incompatible interests and social locations. In my mind, accounting for these differences and addressing them are tasks that are central to the social change endeavors led by South Asians in alliance with other people of color.

Based on my activism and my own encounters with immigration regulations I realized that in order to tell this story effectively I needed to engage citizenship as an analytical category that intersects with—and is as potent as—social hierarchies constructed by gender, sexuality, race, and class. To become fluent in each others' histories as racialized minorities, we would need to understand the ways in which citizenship dictates access to rights not only for second-class citizens in the United States but also for immigrants who are not citizens. The terms of entry and residence that structure immigrant lives are so naturalized in the name of law that they are rarely questioned. In contrast, the activists in this study offer a new lexicon and, beyond that, a paradigm that frees rights from the conceptual prison of citizenship.

I hope that the unruly immigrants whose work I have documented here open up my readers' imaginations in ways that help them question lived or idealized forms of citizenship as the only path to rights. The participants in my study ask activists and scholars to imagine possibilities at which most balk: that rights do not have to be contained within borders; that claims can crisscross national borders and draw on different rights regimes; that national membership does not have to be the coveted goal; and that migrant rights are precisely that—rights particular to people who cross borders. Over the last three decades, we have been able to denaturalize gender, race, and sexuality so that we can see them as principles that organize power relations in society. I ask that we start to think about citizenship and its correlate—national borders—as similar structures of power. Like race, gender, and sexuality, citizenship structures the daily realities of both those who formally have it and those who don't. Yet, those who have it rarely question the legitimacy of borders and the hierarchies that national belonging sets up through its disciplinary mechanisms.

My subjects' healthy skepticism about locating rights in citizenship has profound implications for the way in which minority rights have been conceptualized in the U.S. academy, particularly in the different types of ethnic studies. To scrutinize the language of full citizenship, through which the histories of excluded minority groups are told, means that we start to critically examine the civil rights framework within which the ideologies of full citizenship are embedded. We set much store in the belief that if only minoritized groups had access to citizenship, their rights needs would be met. This is thinking as usual.

In my new location in Hawai'i, the debates within the Native Hawaiian sovereignty movement and between prosovereignty Asian Americans and Native Hawaiians have impressed on me further the need for a language of rights that does not depend on full citizenship (Fujikane 2005, forthcoming; Trask

2000). In post-statehood Hawai'i, East Asian Americans, who form the largest ethnic group in a planter-engineered multiracial society, have advanced their rights through claims on full citizenship. Such an investment in citizenship—though understandable in the context of systematic efforts on part of the territorial government to deprive the nisei of their rights (see Glenn 2002, 190–235)—ignores the U.S. colonization of Hawai'i and the unilateral imposition of U.S. citizenship and Americanization programs on Native Hawaiians. The discourse of civil rights and full citizenship pits immigrant rights against indigenous rights and harms Native Hawaiian demands for self-determination: freedom from U.S. political, military, and cultural domination. In order to respond to the damaging conflict between indigenous and immigrant rights that arises out of the civil rights paradigm's tacit reliance on citizenship, those of us who study ethnic minorities would do well to explore frameworks that imagine subjects of rights other than the citizen. Indigenous and immigrant activists tackling the nation-state both inside and outside of the United States are conceiving such blueprints (see, for example, Smith 2005, 128–31). As I have shown in this book, space makers—in order to solve the crisis in migrant rights—traverse multiple nation-based rights regimes and multiple nation-building projects to craft a transnational complex without turning to citizenship. They do not deny that states continue to be the primary guarantors of rights but they resist the brute power of borders as the defining feature of state sovereignty and national identity.

Denaturalizing citizenship has become essential in the post-9/11 phase of U.S. militarization and empire building. Immigrant rights advocates search for new strategies to confront the unabashed assault on civil liberties. These developments, far from being unprecedented, are historically continuous with the incarceration of both issei and nisei after the bombing of Pearl Harbor. But the contemporary rights violations are more appropriately dealt with through transnational strategies than through asking for rights rooted in citizenship as the nisei had during their interment. As long as we see these current and historical episodes as lapses from what citizenship can be, we continue to confine ourselves to nationalist thinking. We fail to recognize that citizenship is a violent mechanism through which the state creates legitimate and illegitimate members of the national body (see Sharma 2006).

The South Asian and Muslim immigrant communities have been wracked by special registration laws developed after 9/11, incarceration without habeus corpus, and deportation through expedited removal. These measures remain underanalyzed if cast solely as civil rights abuses. The enshrinement of national security above the protection of civil rights, which theoretically are due to all U.S. residents whether they are citizens or not, informs the impunity with which these measures are executed at the expense of immigrants. Because the activists discussed in this book have looked beyond conventional channels of political empowerment, they have been able to respond meaningfully to local South Asian communities terrorized by violence (see Das Gupta 2004) and to FBI raids in the wake of 9/11. By this time, South Asian social justice groups had institutionalized alternative modes of organizing, had developed alternative conceptions of rights, and had already worked with highly exploited groups who were most at risk after 9/11. Instead of being cowed, they continue to advocate the rights of immigrant citizens and noncitizens alike. Since the late 1990s the New York-based group Desis Rising Up and Moving (DRUM) has been directly organizing against the detention and deportation of low-income South Asians. Its foresight in identifying anti-immigrant enforcement as an issue in South Asian communities readied it to defend the rights of post-9/11 targets of state terror. Its excellent work needs documentation.

The implication of these groups and their development of a transnational framework through which to articulate rights is not that they "lack power but . . . [that they] have presence"—to quote Saskia Sassen (1998, xxi) in her discussion of new immigrant actors in global cities. The unruly immigrants who are the subject of this book instruct us in the inventive thinking that is produced at sites of resistance. They enable conceptual shifts so that we may think outside the confines of citizenship or the insipid reworkings of nationalist frameworks in such notions as the "international civil society of global citizens" or human rights, which even advocates lament are notoriously weak (for a transnational feminist critique, see Grewal 1998). The activists provoke us to envisage rights for multiply displaced people who have the greatest need and the fewest entitlements. At a time when those of us on the Left despair at the acute injustices executed by the U.S. warfare state (Gilmore 2002), I offer this book up with much hope. I trust that the activists' passion for a just world and the methods through which they translate their visions into a roadmap for change will fuel emancipatory struggles in the midst of reincarnated crises.

NOTES

Introduction

1. After September 11, 2001, the Immigration and Naturalization Service (INS) was reorganized. It is now called the U.S. Citizenship and Immigration Services (USCIS) and operates under the newly formed Department of Homeland Security. Despite the name change, in this book I call the agency "INS" because of its popular usage and resonance.

2. I take up post-9/11 South Asian organizational strategies in my 2004 and 2005 work that documents the disastrous economic and social impact of the street-level "war on terror" on taxi drivers in New York City. Because 9/11 has unavoidably thrust the question of immigrant rights into public debates, the new project continues to trace immigrant-centered framings of rights.

3. An expanding body of interdisciplinary scholarship has taken a transnational approach to immigrant realities. This approach entails tracing circulations of goods, people, capital, money, images, and ideas across national borders in order to map new social and political fields that spill out of nationally enclosed spaces (Abelman and Lie 1995; Appadurai 1993; Basch, Schiller, and Szanton Blanc 1994; Das Gupta 1997; Espiritu 2003; Grewal and Kaplan 1994; Hondagneu-Sotelo and Avila 1997; Itzigsohn 2000; Portes 1996).

4. My participants often identified as "queer" and talked about the "queer movement" or "queer politics." They also used the terms "gay" and "lesbian" and referred to the "lesbian, gay, bisexual, and transgender" (LGBT) movement. I use "queer" in this book to discuss SALGA and MASALA's organizing in order to capture the range of non-normative desires, pleasures, and identities that exceed the homo/hetero binary and that cannot always be collapsed into "LGBT."

5. The terms *place takers* and *space makers* developed in my conversations with Becky Thompson and Diane Harriford.

6. In the literature distributed by the organizations, South Asia includes Afghanistan, Bhutan, Burma, Maldives, Nepal, and Tibet.

7. The philosopher Martha Nussbaum has traced cosmopolitanism to Stoic thought, which proposes the idea (also presented by Emanuel Kant) that "we should give our first allegiance to *no* mere form of government, no temporal power, but to the moral community made up by the humanity of all human beings" (1994, 4). The intellectual historian David Hollinger (1995, 93–95), in calling for a cosmopolitanism more compatible with pluralist visions of American culture and society, goes back to the early-twentieth-century writer Randolph Bourne to retrieve his vision of a deprovincialized United States. For the sociologist Craig Calhoun (2003), the image of the cosmopolitan at ease everywhere resonates with Richard Sennett's discussion in the 1970s of eighteenth- and nineteenth-century urban life. Each of these versions goes back in history to access a particular formulation of cosmopolitanism.

8. In recent years, South Asians have challenged the historically informed association of the term "Asian" with East Asians. This challenge has led to the inclusion of South Asians in the category "Asian American," though not without a critical examination on their part of the terms and political contingency of that incorporation (Shankar and Srikanth 1998).

1. *Terms of Belonging*

1. The notion of abstract liberal citizenship is central to (capitalist) democracies (Marx 1978, 40–46). These democracies, in granting the "rights of man," require that subjects, as members of the political state, shed their particularities, including those that stem from their material conditions, and step into the political sphere to exercise their equal rights. Marx theorized the compartmentalization of the political subject from the nonpolitical member of civil society as a central contradiction of liberal democracies.

2. Naturalization laws after the fourteenth amendment specified that all other immigrants applying for citizenship would have to be white, in keeping with the 1790 law passed by the first Congress that restricted naturalization to "free white" aliens (Jensen 1988, 247).

3. For the role of the census in constructing race, see Anderson 1988; Anderson and Fienberg 2000; Choldin 1986; Espiritu 1992; Lee 1993; Rodriguez 2000.

4. The 1940 census (U.S. Bureau of the Census 1943, 5, table 1) counted only 2,405 "Hindus." The 1950 and 1960 censuses could have dropped the separate category for South Asians from its short form because of their small numbers. The two censuses had eliminated the category for Koreans because there were too few of them (Espiritu and Omi 2000, 49).

5. The Bracero Program, which brought in an estimated 350,000 temporary agricultural laborers annually from Mexico to work in the fields in the Southwest between 1942 and 1964, was an exception to the restrictions on immigration imposed by the 1924 national origins quotas (Calavita 1992; Fitzgerald 1996, 218; Tichenor 2002, 172–75, 208–11). As a Western Hemisphere nation, Mexico was exempt from the quotas and converted into a source of labor when agricultural interests in the Southwest pressured the federal government to establish a migrant workers' program during World War II in order to address what they claimed to be a chronic labor shortage.

6. The 1996 Illegal Immigration Reform and Immigrant Responsibility Act made permanent residents, regardless of their length of stay in the United States, ineligible for two federally funded programs, supplemental security income and food stamps. This exclusion legislated a crucial difference between citizens and resident aliens in terms of their entitlements. Resident aliens, despite their economic and social contributions, were denied access to welfare measures.

7. In the context of the 1986 Immigration Reform and Control Act, the socialist feminist scholar Grace Chang (2000) notes the ways in which the state, through Immigration and Naturalization Service advertisements, discouraged undocumented Latinas seeking amnesty from accessing social programs to which they and their children were entitled. While the Indian immigrants who were agitating for minority status in the 1970s cannot be compared with poor, undocumented Latina women, what can be compared are state tactics. The state, through informal mechanisms, establishes differential access to rights for immigrants—citizens or not—and still reproduces itself as a welfare state committed to racial justice.

8. In an e-mail exchange dated 17 December 1997, Manoranjan Dutta clarified that the AIA's 1980 census campaign was motivated by principles of civic participation and disagreed with scholars like Maxine Fisher who cast the AIA's efforts as opportunistic. He wrote, "The emuneration in the decennial census of the country is a basic civic duty. I am proud to have been involved in this successful effort in 1980. . . . Maxine and others betrayed their lack of understanding of the issues involved."

9. Manoranjan Dutta, phone interview with author, 1 August 1996, Boston. All subsequent quotes are from this interview.

10. Many have deplored the rejection by South Asians of any form of identification with blacks so as to distance themselves from the disadvantages that the latter suffers (Prashad 2000; Mazumdar 1989b). However, neither the AIA nor the ILA officially expressed such reservations. When I asked Dutta whether the AIA had considered "black" as a suitable category for South Asians, he said that the organization had felt that such a demand would not be entertained by federal officials and that the group had a better chance of success if it pushed to have people of Indian heritage included as Asians. He also showed a keen awareness that slavery set apart blacks from other minoritized groups by suggesting that the insertion of South Asians into that category would be inappropriate because they did not share that history.

11. Unlike Dutta, however, Pian was arguing for a summary Asian-Pacific category rather than a separate listing of the various groups (U.S. House of Representatives 1976, 32).

2. Contests over Culture

1. Sujata Warrier, interview with author 24 July 1997, New York City. All subsequent quotes are from this interview.

2. For exemplary political critiques of the model minority image by Asian American scholars, see Abelman and Lie 1995, 148–80; Aguilar-San Juan 1994; Chang 1999, 48–60; Lee 1999, 145–203; Omatsu 1994, 62–65; Prashad 2000; and Shah 1997. For the relationship of South Asian immigrants to the model minority image and progressive South Asian interventions see Bhattacharjee 1992; Prashad 2000; Sethi 1994; and Shah 1994. Extensive empirical work has also been done to challenge the unadjusted statistical averages that portray Asian Americans as economically successful, to show income disparities between older East Asian groups and more recent refugee populations from South East Asia, and to reveal the costs of scholastic achievements for Asian American youth (see Barringer, Gardner, and Levin 1995; Cabezas and Kawaguchi 1988; Fong 2002; Kim 1994; Lee 1994; Ong and Hee 1994; U.S. Commission on Civil Rights 1992).

3. Newer work is beginning to articulate the connections between the model minority myth and U.S. constructions of gender, sexuality, and nation. The Asian Americanist Robert Lee (1999) traces the myth to cold war America, dating it past the 1966 write-ups by the *New York Times Magazine* and *U.S. News and World Report*, to argue that the trope of ethnic assimilation ascribed to Asian Americans managed not only racial anxieties but also anxieties about gender and sexuality in the shadows of the 1950s "red menace." However, such an analysis focuses on the hegemonic gender, nationalist, and sexual politics of representation, not the politics of Asian American self-representation. More recently, Susan Koshy (2004) has coined the term "sexual model minority" to mark the post-1965 resignification in literary representations of Asian American women as ideal family-centered yet sexy partners in marriage for white men.

4. Kavita Goyal, interview with author 12 March 1996, Boston. All subsequent quotes are from this interview.

5. Imtiyaz Hussein, interview with author 22 March 1996, Boston. All subsequent quotes are from this interview.

6. Anonymous SALGA member, interview with author 20 August 1996, New York City. All subsequent quotes are from this interview.

7. Javid Syed, interview with author 21 August 1996, New York City. All subsequent quotes are from this interview.

8. Anushka Fernandopulle, interview with author 31 July 1997, Boston. All subsequent quotes are from this interview.

9. The National Labor Relations Act does not recognize domestic workers as "employees" who have the right to collective bargaining (NOW Legal Defense and Education Fund 1997). This exclusion points to the dominant understandings of domestic work as a privatized, one-to-one arrangement.

3. Law and Oppression

1. The argument that U.S. laws protect women against domestic violence, used quite uncritically by many advocates of battered immigrant women, erases two historical contexts. First, laws against domestic violence in the United States came out of a long struggle in which feminists worked to get this sort of long-privatized violence recognized as a social problem. Second, the fact that these laws emerged from political struggle obviously indicates that the United States has had its share of resistance from traditional forces that naturalize male domination in families.

2. This pattern cannot be generalized to all Asian immigrant women. Filipinas, for example, often emigrate independently to fill U.S. labor market shortages through the Philippines' overseas workers' programs.

3. It is not uncommon to hear about the abuse of South Asian women who sponsor their husbands. The fact that men's dependence on women for immigration status does not necessarily give women power in the relationship demonstrates the mutually reinforcing role of familial and state patriarchy.

4. The waiting period can be longer than two years of marriage because it begins on the date on which the INS approved the couple's petition for conditional status. The next round of joint applications asking the INS to remove the conditional status and make the sponsored spouse's status permanent needs to be initiated within ninety days of the date on which the conditional residency ended.

5. In 2000 VAWA was reauthorized for five years. Other than creating the T-visa and U-visa for victims of trafficking and of certain form of criminal activities that include violence against women, provisions related to women's immigration status and entitlements remained unchanged. Congress passed the Violence Against Women Act again in 2005 (see National Task Force to End Sexual and Domestic Violence Against Women 2005; National Alliance to End Sexual Violence 2005 for an overview of the provisions of the act). Since President Bush signed the VAWA 2005 Reauthorization into law on January 5, 2006, it was not possible to assess its impact on immigrant survivors.

6. Women's reluctance to press charges against their husbands is often wrongly interpreted as cultural, unhealthy, and irrational. If a permanent resident husband is convicted of domestic violence and the immigration authorities find out about the conviction, under the 1996 laws, which have been strengthened since 9/11, the husband loses his residency and is automatically deported. Such state action jeopardizes transnational families, making immigrant women wary about filing charges. Those

who focus solely on the interpersonal dimensions of abuse in the domestic violence movement need to attend to state violence when they push immigrant women to take action that further extends the state's power over their lives.

7. In 2001, the Women's Immigrant Safe Harbor Act (WISH) was introduced in the House of Representative to remove the 1996 restrictions on the use of public assistance by immigrant survivors of domestic violence, who have legal status. The act was never put to a vote and, since then, other pieces of legislation like the VAWA 2005 reauthorization and the Temporary Aid for Needy Families reauthorization, have incorporated the act but failed to push it through (e-mail correspondence with Jonathan Blazer, National Immigration Law Center; Amanda Baran, Legal Momentum; and Jennifer Ng'andu, National Council of La Raza, 29 November 2005).

8. Congress' fears about Hawai'i did not materialize. In 1998, 69 percent of Hawai'i's voters approved an amendment to the state constitution restricting marriage to opposite-sex couples.

9. Since this section focuses on the emergence of a South Asian labor force that is not professional, I do not discuss the most recent trend in U.S. labor policy to import skilled temporary workers under its H-1B visa program. A high percentage of workers who are admitted under this program are from India and work in the information technology industry. Though these workers are highly skilled, the structure of this transnational industry and labor practices in it resemble that of the garment industry and service industries that rely on immigrant deskilled labor.

10. Neela Trivedi, interview with author 28 August 1996, New York City. All subsequent quotes are from this interview.

11. Bhairavi Desai, interview with author 2 March 1997, New York City. All subsequent quotes are from this interview.

4. "Owning Our Lives": Women's Organizations

1. In 1993, Sakhi formally recognized six women as "founders" on the basis of their level of involvement in and contribution to building the organization in its first few years.

2. Shamita Das Dasgupta of Manavi delivered the lecture "Women's work or feminist activism: A South Asian woman's perspective" on 15 April 1994 at Brandeis University, Waltham, Massachusetts.

3. This example was also recounted at Manavi's cultural sensitivity workshop on 22 November 1996.

4. According to Manavi's Shamita Das Dasgupta, the laws of the countries of origin come into play when either the abuser or the survivor is in that country or when a batterer goes back to that country and files for the restitution of conjugal, property, or custody rights. For example, if a case is filed in an Indian court it may deny or not implement a settlement made in U.S. courts, and it is not bound to recognize a U.S.

divorce and its terms. It is important to remember that the property involved could be owned in the country of origin or transferred there by the abuser. While both men and women could reopen a case in the country of origin, Das Dasgupta points out that "women rarely do this—men often do" (e-mail correspondence with the author, 30 November 2004).

5. Anannya Bhattacharjee, interview with author 8 November 1996, New York City. All subsequent quotes are from this interview.

6. Julia Sudbury (1998, 82–86, 121–26) in her study of black women's organizations in Britain warns against the blanket dismissal of state funding as necessarily dangerous. Among the organizations she studied, many found that central funding (or federal funding in U.S. terms) protected them from local authorities. Others used what Sudbury calls "dissimulation"—that is, meeting state requirements for funding on paper while continuing to do their work (84–85). She also argues that if the state's only intention in funding black community organizations is to co-opt them, then funding for these organizations would be more available than it actually is (83).

7. Tula Goenka, interview with author 2 July 2001, Syracuse, New York.

8. Anonymous Sakhi board member, interview with author 6 November 1996, New York City. All subsequent quotes are from this interview.

9. Indian feminists, speaking at a conference organized in Boston by the Women's Rights Network in summer 1997, talked about the effectiveness of public shaming to curb batterers in urban and semi-urban communities in southern India.

10. Riti Sachdeva, interview with author 6 November 1996, Boston. All subsequent quotes are from this interview.

11. According to the 1990 census data the total Chinese population in the central city was 51,439 and that of Asian Indians was 18,209. Vietnamese and Cambodians constituted the next most populous communities with totals of 14,333 and 13,594, respectively.

12. Most of these women were born in South Asia but had moved to the United States with their families at a very young age. They were not U.S. citizens by birth and, therefore, not technically "second-generation" immigrants. However, I prefer using the term "second-generation" to the more accurate label, "1.5-generation," because both sets of immigrants, despite the difference in their citizenship status, share the struggles of growing up in the United States.

13. Kalpana Subramanian, interview with author 25 August 1997, Boston. All subsequent quotes are from this interview.

14. Serena Sundaram, interview with author 21 December 1996, Auburn, Maine. All subsequent quotes are from this interview.

15. The first forum was organized by SAWA and held on 28 October 1995. Titled "What's Going On?" its aim was to discuss issues arising from local attempts at cross-cultural alliance work, and thus all progressive Asian groups were invited to the discussion. The outcomes of the forum were discussed within SAWA and in meetings with ASIA

and AARW. It resulted in SAWA publishing its position in the ASIA newsletter and online at the SAWA Web site (http://way.net/sawa).

16. It is important to note the tensions between politics and culture embedded in the label "Asian American." The term "Asian American" was born out of political struggles that began with the black liberation movement of the late 1960s (Omatsu 1994) and continued to be developed as a strategic identity for political empowerment (Espiritu 1992). The increasing tendency since the 1970s to treat "Asian American" as a cultural rather than a sociopolitical identity that is rooted in an analysis of power relations and liberatory vision stands in the way of the political consciousness that is so necessary to fight the ways in which Asian Americans find themselves oppressed in the United States (see also Aguilar-San Juan 1994; Prashad 1998).

17. I am indebted to Richard Rath for this insight.

18. Guerrero (1997) theorizes the United States as an advanced colonial and capitalist state that creates violent contradictions for Native American women by pitting Native American sovereignty against civil rights that reduce indigenous people to racial minorities and ask them to forward their rights claims within the framework of U.S. citizenship.

19. The premises underlying domestic violence work and labor organizing are different. The domestic violence movement treats a survivor as someone who has to be empowered. In contrast, the starting point of building a labor movement is the recognition that workers have power because they supply labor. Bhairavi Desai, who organizes taxi drivers for New York Taxi Workers Alliance, talks about the fact that workers have power but are not in power until they organize.

20. Mohanty discusses the possibilities of cross-border organizing in the context of women workers located in different nations and their ability to resist the current tendencies of global capital, which utilizes local ideologies about gender, caste, class, sexuality, and race to devalue their work and render it invisible.

5. Subverting Seductions

1. In keeping with her argument that community and capitalism are actually related and this reliance on each other is supplementary, Joseph warns that resistance cannot be imagined outside of capitalist relations and its logic.

2. The assertion that gay and lesbian issues stand apart from analyses of racism, imperialism, and capitalism informs the emergence of a visible gay and lesbian movement in the United States in the 1970s and its contemporary white middle-class pro-establishment character. The Gay Activists Alliance of New York (GAA) broke off from the Gay Liberation Front (GLF) in 1969 in order to focus solely on securing gay and lesbian rights through the existing political system. It disagreed with the GLF's anticapitalist stance, its association with the Black Panthers, and the movement

against the war in Vietnam. The GAA itself was challenged in 1973 when lesbians, protesting the group's gay-dominated structure and agenda, walked out to form the Lesbian Feminist Liberation.

3. Transgender people have been a recent addition. The SALGA charter (1995) named only gays, lesbians, and bisexuals.

4. The discussions I have seen do not touch on erotic relations between women but rather focus on men who have sex with men. Sexual identities such as kothi, panthi, and hijra are seen to escape Western definitions of "gay." Kothis are men who are said to take on a feminine gender identity and, while having sex with panthis (hyper-masculine men), are penetrated by them. However, in actual practice kothis can and do penetrate their male sexual partner (O. Khan 2001). Hijras are often called the third sex and are seen as homosexuals. The feminist sociologist Jyoti Puri (2004) challenges this ascription of hijra sexuality on the grounds that if hijras indeed es-caped the bigender categorization then their desires also need to be reformulated and cannot be returned to a homo/hetero schema that recognizes only two sexes.

5. Debi Ray-Chaudhuri, interview with author 10 November 1996, New York City. All subsequent quotes are from this interview.

6. Lesbian relationships between SAWA members were never organizationally acknowl-edged despite the fact that these partnerships produced some of SAWA's best projects. The erotic energy of these relationships, the support that lesbian and straight mem-bers individually gave to these couples, as well as the sadness of breakups remained undercurrents in SAWA. In documenting the history of multiracial feminism Becky Thompson (2001, 186–94) notes the dangers of rendering lesbian relationships in-visible in organizational histories. Though she makes her remarks in the particular context of interracial relations and anti-racist coalitions, feminists of color need to openly confront the heterosexist politics of the kind of erasures that played out in SAWA.

7. There is some debate over whether Guyana could be considered part of the Caribbean since it is not an island and part of South America. The sociologist Mary Waters (1999, 56) found evidence in her study in New York City of some Guyanese immi-grants who rejected their association with the Caribbean, as well as others who justified their Caribbean identity on the grounds of a shared history and culture with the islands. Also, when considering Indo-Guyanese and Baran's identification of himself as "Indo-Caribbean," we need to remember that colonial labor allotment policies in the British Caribbean, which included British Guiana, connected the histories of the 430,000 Indian indentured workers brought to these colonies be-tween 1837 and 1917 (Kale 1998).

8. Tim Baran, interview with author 1 March 1997, New York City. All subsequent quotes are from this interview.

9. In the eighty years of colonial labor recruitment, over 240,000 Indians arrived in

Guyana to work in the sugar plantations and thousands of others migrated from other Caribbean colonies to seek work in Guyana. The turn to Indian indentured labor in the British Caribbean was designed to punish emancipated Afro-Caribbeans, from whom the planters wished to be "freed" (Kale 1998, 144–47), thus creating tensions between Indians and Afro-Caribbeans despite a common plantation history and hybridization of the two cultures. According to the Guyanese sociolinguist John Rickford: "The indentured immigrants certainly often shared the same kinds of oppression and suffering that their African predecessors had experienced as slaves. Indeed, it was the slaves themselves who described the treatment of the very first batches of indentured Indians in horrendous terms before a Commission of Enquiry in 1839. . . . But common oppression was not necessarily sufficient to produce a common identity" (1987, 65–66). While Indian indentures picked up Afro-Guyanese creole, and there is evidence of African creoles and Indians adopting and adapting each other's cultural practices, the two groups maintained distinct identities. Tensions between them ran deep. Drawing on Walter Rodney's history of Guyanese working people, Rickford situates the tensions historically in African creoles' protest against the importation of indentured labor because it not only lowered their wages and put up barriers to free land holdings but also because it required that they be taxed to meet a third of the immigration costs. Imprints of these divisions survive in the contemporary relations between Guyanese of African and Indian descent.

10. Here it is worth recalling my account in chapter 1 of the AIA's India-centric approach to proposing a census category for people from South Asia and its diaspora to recognize the entrenched resistance among mainstream ethnic groups to a transnational identity.

11. I am indebted to Kathy Ferguson for suggesting the term "nested nationalisms" to capture the interplay of Indian and American nationalisms at the parade.

12. In late 1998 *Fire*, a film about the unfolding sexual relationship between two sisters-in-law, provoked calls for a ban on its screening in India. The Shiv Sena, a militant arm of the Hindu nationalist Bharatiya Janata Party, which was elected to power at the national level that same year, spearheaded the call. To foreground the transnational reproduction of discourses about sexuality and national cultural integrity, Gopinath (2002) connects the FIA's ban on SALGA and its progressive allies' participation in New York's India Day Parade to the Hindu Right's casting of *Fire* as a threat to national identity.

13. Nayan Shah (1993, 116–17) notes the key role of feminism in South Asian women's articulations of their lesbian identities. In comparison, narratives of politicization did not accompany gay men's reflections on their sexual identity.

14. Interestingly, model minority discourses also construct Caribbean immigrant communities. Unlike South Asian immigrants for whom race becomes a salient category only on migration (see chapter 1), Caribbean people have to renegotiate racial identities that

were crafted in multiracial and creolized Caribbean societies. Within a U.S. bipolar model of race relation, Caribbeans of African descent in New York City insist on a separate "West Indian" identity, distinguishable from an African American one, as Waters (1999) has found. In this context, the comparative racialization of South Asians and Indo-Caribbeans needs further research.

15. Expert and nonexpert views on caste, often articulated by caste Hindus, reject a straightforward correlation between caste and class. While it is true that caste Hindus can fall anywhere in the class spectrum, it is also true that they were never systematically prevented from education, dignified forms of employment, or land ownership in the ways in which the lowest castes were and are. To draw an analogy, an analysis of white privilege does not mean that there are no poor whites. It means that whiteness structures society in a way that reserves basic resources and opportunities for whites. This is definitely the case for Indian society where, despite postcolonial efforts at affirmative action or "reservation" policies, we still see caste Hindus dominate politics, education, and all sectors of employment that are not seasonal, poorly paid or unpaid, or hazardous.

6. "Know Your Place in History"

1. For a history of Asian and African Caribbean militancy and coalition in Britain during this period, see Sivanandan 1981/82; for Asian women's participation in strikes, see Wilson 1978; for Asian and black Marxist feminist analyses in the 1970s, see Sudbury 1998, 162–69. In Britain, the term "Asian" refers to South Asians from that region and from East Africa.

2. Economic restructuring since the late 1960s has come to stand for the shift from industrial production to a service-oriented economy dominated by information technology. This shift has created high-end jobs in banking, investment, management, telecommunication, and information technology. It has also opened up low-wage, casualized service and manufacturing jobs that depend on immigrant labor (Sassen 1998, 46). Downsizing, flexible production, subcontracting, part-time and temporary work, and decentralized production managed through highly integrated information networks are the hallmarks of this phase of economic restructuring.

3. For example, Chinese workers struck in 1867 against the Central Pacific Railroad in the high Sierras; in 1875 at a salmon cannery in Oregon; in 1874 at a laundry in New Jersey; and in 1876 at shoe factories in San Francisco. Chinese shoe manufacturers, hired to break a strike at the Simpsons shoe factory in Massachusetts in 1873, rioted within a few months of their hire (Kwong 1997, 142–46; Lee 1999, 64–66). Chinese workers in post–Civil War southern plantations and railroad projects contested violations of their contract and demanded back pay (Lee 1999, 65). Among anti-Asian white unions were the Knights of Labor, the Secret Order of St. Crispin, California

Workingman's Party, the International Workingman's Association, and the AFL. Japanese and, later, Filipino plantation workers in Hawai'i unionized and after 1909 staged a number of successful strikes (Beechert 1985; Kerkvliet 2002; Jung 2003; Takaki 1983). With regard to South Asians, antagonism from white labor quickly isolated the 5,000-odd immigrants into farm work in California (Jensen 1988; Leonard 1992). While there is some scattered evidence of Indian students, who worked in the fields during the summer like their Japanese and Filipino counterparts, arriving at an awareness of class oppression through racial segregation, there is no account of South Asian involvement in unionizing. South Asian farmers were far more interested in circumventing the Alien Land Law through proxy ownership than in identifying with farm workers, even though many Punjabis had Mexican spouses whose family members did such work (Leonard 1992).

4. Marx calls the labor required to sustain workers "reproductive labor" or the work of social reproduction. As the socialist feminist Evelyn Glenn details, "Reproductive labor includes activities such as purchasing household goods, preparing and serving food, laundering and repairing clothing, maintaining furnishing and appliances, socializing children, providing care and emotional support for adults, and maintaining kin and community ties" (1992, 1). Feminists have theorized the gendered dimensions of unpaid and paid reproductive labor—the significance of which Marx did not grasp. Androcentric scholarship dismisses reproductive labor because it is carried out by women within their families and is seen as a labor of love rather than labor that needs to be compensated. Along with unpaid reproductive labor, feminists have also examined paid domestic work carried out by outsiders in order to understand its commodification, feminization, racialization, and devaluation.

5. Both the Wagner Act of 1935, which is credited with improving the lot of labor, and the Social Security Act of 1935 excluded domestic workers as beneficiaries, with the full knowledge that black women were overrepresented in domestic work. This meant that domestic workers could not access welfare state protections and their unions had no legal status. Women who were unionizing could be legally fired by their employers.

6. The NOW Legal Defense and Education Fund quotes the NRLA's reason for excluding domestic workers on the grounds that "there never would be a great number suffering under the difficulty of negotiating with the actual employer and there would be no need for collective bargaining and conditions leading to strikes would not obtain" (1997, 3). Such a determination underscores the invisibility of paid domestic work and its extent, as well as doubts in the minds of legislators, lawyers, and judges about whether domestic work counts as real work (see also Hondagneu-Sotelo 2001).

7. These methods of recruiting South Asian domestic workers are less formalized than the methods for Filipinas, whose outmigration is coordinated and overseen by the Philippines state through its Overseas Employment Administration.

8. Nahar Alam, interview with author 24 July 2001, New York City. All subsequent

quotes are from this interview. When I interviewed Nahar Alam she had left Workers Awaaz to found Andolan. As a result, this section focuses on Andolan's work. My interview with Alam was conducted in Bengali and English. The excerpts quoted here and elsewhere are my translation.

9. Among the groups with which Andolan regularly demonstrates and builds its campaigns are Workers' Awaaz, CAAAV, Damayan Domestic Workers Association, Filipino Workers' Center, Asian American Legal Defense and Education Fund (AALDEF), and the National Employment Law Project (NELP).

10. For example, in New York City the services offered by immigrants—such as laundries, twenty-four-hour delis, take-out restaurants, day care, home health care, housecleaning, babysitting, and dog walking—support the hours and work culture of service sector professionals.

11. The bill, Introduction 0096-2002, "Standards and Conduct of Employment Agencies" (New York City Council 2002) was signed into law by Mayor Michael Bloomberg in March 2003.

12. I am indebted to Colin Danby for this insight on the contradictory workings of the neoliberal state.

13. The LDC's commitment to building a South Asian organization from the "ground up" set it apart from the existing nation-based drivers' groups, like Pak Brothers and United Yellow Cab Association, which tended to depend on the politics of patronage and favors from city officials and politicians.

14. I have been able to keep in touch with NYTWA throughout the process of writing this book because of the organization's openness to my continued involvement with it.

15. Prashad 2000, for example, represents the NYTWA as an organization of working-class men.

16. The Service Employees International Union (SEIU) and the AFL-CIO aggressively courted the NYTWA after its successful 1998 strikes. It rejected these overtures in order to continue to operate legitimately, autonomously, and democratically without submitting to the highly bureaucratized and top-down ways in which conventional unions still function. Along with the technicality of drivers being independent contractors, the refusal to join a union is also informed by the 1970s betrayal of rank-and-file drivers by their union. That history has left many old-time drivers scarred and distrustful of formal unions.

17. While Local 3036 still exists, its members are retirees who participated in rolling back what the union had won.

18. In 2004, the TLC announced the sale of 300 new medallions every year for three years. As a result, the current number of medallions has gone up to 12,487.

19. Issues such as the communalized politics of India's nuclear build-up since 1998; military action in Kashmir; and, since 9/11, India's dire warnings to Pakistan about spreading terrorism reverberate through the driver community, creating anxieties among

Indians and Pakistanis about political instability and economic hardship in their home countries.

20. Rizwan Raja, interview with author 5 August 2002, New York City. All subsequent quotes are from this interview.

21. The fare and lease campaign represents long-standing demands on part of the NYTWA. However, the campaign has taken on a special urgency in the wake of 9/11. A discussion of NYTWA's campaigns related to 9/11 is beyond the scope of this chapter; see Das Gupta 2005 for an analysis of the severe economic loss that drivers suffered after 9/11 and the NYTWA's efforts to address those losses.

22. Fares went up by 26 percent and leases by 8 percent. The NYTWA was instrumental in countering efforts on the part of brokers and garages to cancel out the increase in fares by proportionally increasing the lease.

23. An Egyptian driver, Hisham Amer, was viciously beaten on 13 December 2000 when he took "too long" to show his license to four TLC officials who had stopped him to inspect his cab (Liu 2001; New York Taxi Workers Alliance 2001c). Among the groups that joined the NYTWA in protesting the violence against Amer were the Haitian American Alliance (which had mobilized against the NYPD's brutalization of a Haitian immigrant, Abner Louima), the Asian American Legal Defense and Education Fund, the Workers Awaaz, the Coalition for American Islamic Relations, the Rev. Al Sharpton's National Action Network, the Forum of Indian Leftists, the National Employment Law Project at New York University School of Law's Immigrant Rights Clinic, and South Asians against Police Brutality.

WORKS CITED

AALDEF (Asian American Legal Defense and Education Fund) and NELP (National Employment Law Project). 2001. *Rights Begin at Home: Protecting Yourself as a Domestic Worker*. New York: AALDEF and NELP.

Abelman, Nancy, and John Lie. 1995. *Blue Dreams: Korean Americans and the Los Angeles Riots*. Cambridge, Mass.: Harvard University Press.

Abraham, Margaret. 1995. "Ethnicity, Gender, and Marital Violence: South Asian Women's Organizations in the United States." *Gender and Society* 9 (4): 450–68.

——. 2000. *Speaking the Unspeakable: Marital Violence among South Asian Immigrants in the United States*. New Brunswick, N.J.: Rutgers University Press.

Acker, Joan. 1995. "Feminist Goals and Organizing Processes." In *Feminist Organizations: Harvest of the New Women's Movement*, edited by M. M. Ferree and P. Y. Martin. Philadelphia: Temple University Press.

Advani, Anuradha. 1997. "Against the Tide: Reflections on Organizing New York City's South Asian Taxicab Drivers." In *Making More Waves: New Writing by Asian American Women*, edited by E. H. Kim, L. V. Villanueva, and Asian Women United of California. Boston: Beacon Press.

Agarwal, Priya. 1991. *Passage from India: Post-1965 Indian Immigrants and Their Children: Conflicts, Concerns and Solutions*. Palos Verdes, Calif.: Yuvati Publications.

Agnew, John. 1999. "Mapping Political Power beyond State Boundaries: Territory, Identity, and Movement in World Politics." *Millennium: Journal of International Studies* 28 (3): 499–521.

Aguilar-San Juan, Karin. 1994. "Linking the Issues: From Identity to Activism." In *The State of Asian America: Activism and Resistance in the 1990s*, edited by K. Aguilar-San Juan. Boston: South End Press.

Alam, Nahar. 1997. "Domestic Workers Do Their Homework." *Samar* 8 (summer/fall): 15–20.

Alba, Richard. 1990. *Ethnic Identity: The Transformation of White America.* New Haven: Yale University Press.

——. 1999. "Immigration and the American Realities of Assimilation and Multiculturalism." *Sociological Forum* 14 (1): 3–25.

Alexander, G. P. 1997. *New Americans: The Progress of Asian Indians in America.* Cypress, Calif.: P & P Enterprises.

Alexander, M. Jacqui. 1994. "Not Just (Any) Body Can Be a Citizen: The Politics of Law, Sexuality, and Postcoloniality in Trinidad and Tobago and the Bahamas." *Feminist Review* 48 (autumn): 5–23.

——. 1997. "Erotic Autonomy as the Politics of Decolonization: An Anatomy of Feminist and State Practice in the Bahamas Tourist Economy." In *Feminist Genealogies, Colonial Legacies, Democratic Futures,* edited by M. J. Alexander and C. T. Mohanty. New York: Routledge.

——. 1998. "Imperial Desire/Sexual Utopias: White Gay Capital and Transnational Tourism." In *Talking Visions: Multicultural Feminism in a Transnational Age,* edited by E. Shohat. New York: New Museum of Contemporary Art; Cambridge, Mass.: MIT Press.

Alexander, M. Jacqui, and Chandra Talpade Mohanty. 1997. "Introduction: Genealogies, Legacies, Movements." In *Feminist Genealogies, Colonial Legacies, Democratic Futures,* edited by M. J. Alexander and C. T. Mohanty. New York: Routledge.

Altman, Dennis. 1996. "Rupture or Continuity? The Internationalization of Gay Identities." *Social Text* 14 (3): 77–94.

Amott, Teresa, and Julie Matthaei. 1996. *Race, Gender and Work: A Multicultural Economic History of Women in the United States.* Rev. ed. Boston: South End Press.

Ancheta, Angelo N. 1998. *Race, Rights, and the Asian American Experience.* New Brunswick, N.J.: Rutgers University Press.

Anderson, Margo J. 1988. *The American Census: A Social History.* New Haven: Yale University Press.

Anderson, Margo, and Stephen E. Fienberg. 2000. "Race and Ethnicity and the Controversy over the US Census." *Current Sociology* 48 (3): 87–110.

Anzaldúa, Gloria. 1987. *Borderlands/La Frontera: The New Mestiza.* San Francisco: Aunt Lute Books.

Appadurai, Arjun. 1993. "Patriotism and Its Futures." *Public Culture* 5 (3): 411–29.

Appelbaum, Richard P. 1996. "Multiculturalism and Flexibility: Some New Directions in Global Capitalism." In *Mapping Multiculturalism,* edited by A. F. Gordon and C. Newfield. Minneapolis: University of Minnesota Press.

Appiah, Anthony K. 1998. "Cosmopolitan Patriots." In *Cosmopolitics: Thinking and Feeling beyond the Nation,* edited by P. Cheah and B. Robbins. Minneapolis: University of Minnesota Press.

Arnold, Gretchen. 1995. "Dilemmas of Feminist Coalitions: Collective Identity and Strategic Effectiveness in the Battered Women's Movement." In *Feminist Organizations: Harvest of the New Women's Movement*, edited by M. M. Ferree and P. Y. Martin. Philadelphia: Temple University Press.

Asian Women United of California. 1989. *Making Waves: An Anthology of Writings by and about Asian American Women.* Boston: Beacon Press.

Ayuda. 1996. "An Advocate's Primer on Immigration Law, Welfare and Battered Immigrant Women and Children." Washington, D.C.: Ayuda, Inc.

Bacchetta, Paola. 1999. "When the (Hindu) Nation Exiles Its Queers." *Social Text* 17 (4): 141–66.

Bacon, David. 2001. "Labor Fights for Immigrants." *Nation*, 21 May, 15–18.

Bacon, Jean. 1996. *Life Lines: Community, Family, and Assimilation among Asian Indian Immigrants.* New York: Oxford University Press.

Bahri, Deepika. 1998. "With Kaleidoscopic Eyes: The Potential (Dangers) of Identitarian Coalitions." In *A Part, Yet Apart: South Asians in Asian America*, edited by L. D. Shankar and R. Srikanth. Philadelphia: Temple University Press.

Bald, Vivek. 1996. "Taxi Meters and Plexiglass Partitions." In *Contours of the Heart: South Asians Map North America*, edited by S. Maira and R. Srikanth. New York: Asian American Writers' Workshop.

Bannerji, Himani. 2000. *The Dark Side of the Nation: Essays in Multiculturalism, Nationalism and Gender.* Toronto: Canadian Scholars' Press.

Barnett, Bernice McNair. 1995. "Black Women's Collectivist Movement Organizations: Their Struggles during the "'Doldrums.'" In *Feminist Organizations: Harvest of the New Women's Movement*, edited by M. M. Ferree and P. Y. Martin. Philadelphia: Temple University Press.

Barringer, Herbert, Robert Gardner, and Michael Levin. 1995. *Asian and Pacific Islanders in the United States.* New York: Russell Sage Foundation.

Basch, Linda, Nina Glick Schiller, and Cristina Szanton Blanc. 1994. *Nations Unbound.* Langhorne, Pa.: Gordon and Breach.

Beechert, Edward D. 1985. *Working in Hawaii: A Labor History.* Honolulu: University of Hawai'i Press.

Berlant, Lauren, and Elizabeth Freeman. 1992. "Queer Nationality." *boundary 2* (spring): 149–80.

Bhattacharjee, Anannya. 1992. "The Habit of Ex-Nomination: Nation, Woman, and the Indian Immigrant Bourgeoisie." *Public Culture* 5 (1): 19–43.

——. 1996. "Sakhi Demonstrated against Batterer Mohammed Mohsin." *Sakhi Quarterly* 1 (summer): 1–2.

——. 1997a. "The Public/Private Mirage: Mapping Homes and Undomesticating Violence Work in the South Asian Immigrant Community." In *Feminist Genealogies, Colonial Legacies, Democratic Futures*, edited by M. J. Alexander and C. T. Mohanty. New York: Routledge.

——. 1997b. "A Slippery Path: Organizing Resistance to Violence against Women." In *Dragon Ladies: Asian American Feminists Breathe Fire*, edited by S. Shah. Boston: South End Press.

Birsh, Judith. 1995. "The Way to a Cabbie's Heart." *New York Times*, 30 April, 19.

Bonacich, Edna. 1972. "A Theory of Ethnic Antagonism: The Split Labor Market." *American Sociological Review* 37 (5): 547–59.

——. 1996. "The Class Question in Global Capitalism: The Case of the Los Angeles Garment Industry." In *Mapping Multiculturalism*, edited by G. Avery and C. Newfield. Minneapolis: University of Minnesota Press.

Bonacich, Edna, and Richard P. Appelbaum. 2000. *Behind the Label: Inequality in the Los Angeles Apparel Industry*. Berkeley: University of California Press.

Brecher, Jeremy, and Tim Costello. 1998. "Labor's Day: The Challenge Ahead." *Nation*, 21 September, 11–13, 16–17.

Breines, Wini. 2002. "What's Love Got to Do with It? White Women, Black Women, and Feminism in the Movement Years." *Signs* 27 (4): 1095–133.

Butler, Judith. 1999. *Gender Trouble: Feminism and the Subversion of Identity*. New York: Routledge.

CAAAV (Coalition against Anti-Asian Violence). 1996. "Police Brutality in Asian Communities." *CAAAV Voice* 8 (1): 3.

Cabezas, Amado, and Gary Kawaguchi. 1988. "Empirical Evidence for Continuing Asian American Income Inequality: The Human Capital Model and Labor Market Segmentation." In *Reflections on Shattered Windows: Promises and Prospects of Asian American Studies*, edited by G. Okihiro, S. Hune, A. Hansen, and J. Lius. Pullman: Washington University Press.

Calavita, Kitty. 1992. *Inside the State: The Bracero Program, Immigration, and the I.N.S.* New York: Routledge.

Calhoun, Cheshire. 1994. "Separating Lesbian Theory from Feminist Theory." *Ethics* 104 (April): 558–81.

Calhoun, Craig. 2003. "Ethnicity in the Cosmopolitan Imaginary." Paper presented at the East-West Center, Honolulu, Hawai'i, 20 February.

Carty, Linda. 1994. "African Canadian Women and the State: 'Labour Only Please.'" In *We're Rooted Here and They Can't Pull Us Up: Essays in African Canadian Women's History*, edited by P. Bristow. Toronto: University of Toronto Press.

——. 1999. "The Discourse of Empire and the Social Construction of Gender." In *Scratching the Surface: Canadian Anti-Racist Feminist Thought*, edited by E. Dua and A. Robertson. Toronto: Women's Press.

——. 2000. "Hard Work and Possible Choices: Caribbean Domestic Workers in New York City." Paper presented at the African American Studies Colloquium, Syracuse University, 22 February.

——. Forthcoming. *Caribbean Domestic Workers in New York and Toronto: Transnational Capitalism Circulating Cheap Labor*.

Center for Immigrant Rights. 1998. "The Rights of Battered Immigrant Women and Children: A Fact Sheet." New York: Center for Immigrant Rights.

Champagne, John. 1999. "Transnationally Queer? A Prolegomenon." *Socialist Review* 27 (1–2): 143–64.

Chan, Sucheng. 1991. *Asian Americans: An Interpretive History.* Boston: Twayne Publishers.

Chang, Grace. 1997. "The Global Trade in Filipina Workers." In *Dragon Ladies: Asian American Feminists Breathe Fire*, edited by S. Shah. Boston: South End Press.

——. 2000. *Disposable Domestics: Immigrant Women Workers in the Global Economy.* Cambridge, Mass.: South End Press.

Chang, Robert S. 1997. "A Meditation on Borders." In *Immigrants Out! The New Nativism and Anti-Immigrant Impulse in the United States*, edited by J. F. Perea. New York: New York University Press.

——. 1999. *Disoriented: Asian Americans, Law, and the Nation-State.* New York: New York University Press.

Cheah, Pheng, and Bruce Robbins, eds. 1998. *Cosmopolitics: Thinking and Feeling beyond the Nation.* Minneapolis: University of Minnesota Press.

Chicago Cultural Studies Group. 1994. "Critical Multiculturalism." In *Multiculturalism: A Critical Reader*, edited by D. T. Goldberg. Cambridge, Mass.: Basil Blackwell.

Cho, Milyoung. 1994. "Overcoming Our Legacy as Cheap Labor, Scabs, and Model Minorities: Asian Activists Fight for Community Empowerment." In *The State of Asian America: Activism and Resistance in the 1990s*, edited by K. Aguilar-San Juan. Boston: South End Press.

Choldin, Harvey. 1986. "Statistics and Politics: The 'Hispanic Issue' in the 1980 Census." *Demography* 23 (3): 403–18.

Chopra, Karen McBeth. 1995. "A Forgotten Minority: An American Perspective: Historical and Current Discrimination against Asians from the Indian Subcontinent." *Detroit College of Law Review* (winter): 1269–348.

Chow, Esther Ngan-Ling. 1993. "The Feminist Movement: Where Are All the Asian American Women?" In *Feminist Frameworks*, edited by A. M. Jagger and P. S. Rothenberg. New York: McGraw-Hill.

Cohen, Lizabeth. 2003. *A Consumers' Republic: The Politics of Mass Consumption in Postwar America.* New York: Vintage Books.

Collins, Patricia Hill. 1986. "Learning from the Outsider Within: The Sociological Significance of Black Feminist Thought." *Social Problems* 33 (6): 14–32.

——. 1991. *Black Feminist Thought.* New York: Routledge.

Combahee River Collective. 1983. "A Black Feminist Statement." In *This Bridge Called My Back: Writings by Radical Women of Color*, edited by C. Moraga and G. Anzaldúa. New York: Kitchen Table Press.

Crenshaw, Kimberlé. 1995. "Mapping the Margins: Intersectionality, Identity Politics, and Violence against Women of Color." In *Critical Race Theory: The Key Writings That*

Formed the Movement, edited by K. Crenshaw, N. Gotanda, G. Peller, and K. Thomas. New York: New Press.

Cvetkovich, Ann. 2003. *An Archive of Feelings*. Durham, N.C.: Duke University Press.

Darien-Smith, Eva. 1995. "Law in Place: Legal Mediations of National Identity and State Territory in Europe." In *Nationalism, Racism, and the Rule of Law*, edited by P. Fitzpatrick. Brookfield, Vt.: Dartmouth Publishing Company.

Das Dasgupta, Shamita. 1994. "Sexuality: The Unexamined Factor in Domestic Violence Work." *Manavi Newsletter* 6 (1): 3–4.

——. 1998. *A Patchwork Shawl: Chronicles of South Asian Women in America*. New Brunswick, N.J.: Rutgers University Press.

——. 2000. "Violence Against Women." Paper presented at the Conference "Migrant Visions: The Other Face of South Asians in North America." Syracuse University, 28 April.

Das Dasgupta, Shamita, and Sujata Warrier. 1997. *In Visible Terms: Domestic Violence in the Asian Indian Context: A Handbook for Intervention*. 2nd ed. Union, N.J.: Manavi.

Das Gupta, Monisha. 1997. "'What Is Indian about You?' A Gendered, Transnational Approach to Ethnicity." *Gender and Society* 11 (5): 572–96.

——. 2004. "A View of Post-9/11 Justice from Below." *Peace Review* 16 (2): 141–48.

——. 2005. "Of Hardship and Hostility: The Impact of 9/11 on New York City Taxi Drivers." In *Wounded City: The Social Impact of 9/11*, edited by N. Foner. New York: Russell Sage Foundation.

Dasgupta, Sathi. 1989. *On the Trail of an Uncertain Dream*. New York: AMS Press.

Dasgupta, Sayantani, and Shamita Das Dasgupta. 1993. "Journeys: Reclaiming South Asian Feminism." In *Our Feet Walk the Sky: Women of South Asian Diaspora*, edited by Women of South Asian Descent Collective. San Francisco: Aunt Lute Books.

Davar, Tamina. 1995. "What Is the Lease Drivers Coalition?" *Peela Paiya* (summer): 10–13.

Davies, Jill. 1997. "The New Welfare Law: State Implementation and Use of the Family Violence Option." Washington, D.C.: National Resource Center on Domestic Violence and the National Network to End Domestic Violence.

Davis, F. James. 1991. *Who Is Black? One Nation's Definition*. University Park, Pa.: Pennsylvania State University.

Davis, Tracy J. 1999. "Opening the Door of Immigration: Sexual Orientation and Asylum in the United States." *Human Rights Brief* 6 (3): 19–20.

Desai, Bhairavi. 2002. "New York Taxi Drivers Need Disaster Relief." *New York Times*, 2 March, A15.

Dhaliwal, Amarpal. 1995. "Gender at Work: The Renegotiation of Middle Class Womanhood in a South Asian-Owned Business." In *Reviewing Asian America: Locating Diversity*, edited by W. L. Ng, S. Y. Chin, J. Moy, and G. Okihiro. Pullman: Washington State University Press.

Dill, Bonnie Thornton. 1994. *Across the Boundaries of Race and Class: An Exploration of Work and Family among Female Domestic Servants*. New York: Garland.

Dutt, Ela. 1990. "Fewer Professionals Coming?" *India Abroad*. 16 March, 15.

Dutta, Manoranjan. 1980. "Asian/Pacific American Employment Profile: Myth and Reality—Issues and Answers." In *Civil Rights Issues of Asian Pacific Americans: Myths and Realities, May 8–9, 1979, Washington, D.C.: A Consultation Sponsored by the United States Commission on Civil Rights*, edited by U.S. Commission on Civil Rights. Washington, D.C.: U.S. Government Printing Office.

———. 1982. "Asian Indian Americans: Search for an Economic Profile." In *From India to America: A Brief History of Immigration; Problems of Discrimination; Admission and Assimilation*, edited by S. Chandrasekhar. La Jolla, Calif.: Population Review.

Eisenstein, Zillah R. 1994. *The Color of Gender: Reimaging Democracy*. Berkeley: University of California Press.

Elkhanialy, Hekmat, and Ralph W. Nicholas. 1976a. "An Overview." In *Immigrants from the Indian Subcontinent in the U.S.A.: Problems and Prospects*, edited by H. Elkhanialy and R. W. Nicholas. Chicago: India League of America.

———. 1976b. "Racial and Ethnic Self-Designation, Experiences of Discrimination, and Desire for Legal Minority Status Among Indian Immigrants in the U.S.A." In *Immigrants from the Indian Subcontinent in the U.S.A.: Problems and Prospects*, edited by Elkhanialy and Nicholas. Chicago: India League of America.

Equal Employment Opportunity Commission. 1977. "Equal Employment Opportunity Commission: Government-Wide Standard Race and Ethnic Categories." *Federal Register* 42 (64): 17900.

Espiritu, Yen Le. 1992. *Asian American Panethnicity: Bridging Institutions and Identities*. Philadelphia: Temple University Press.

———. 1997. *Asian American Women and Men: Labor, Laws and Love*. Thousand Oaks, Calif.: Sage.

———. 2003. *Home Bound: Filipino American Lives across Cultures, Communities, and Countries*. Berkeley: University of California Press.

Espiritu, Yen Le, and Michael Omi. 2000. "'Who Are You Calling Asian?' Shifting Identity Claims, Racial Classifications, and the Census." In *Transforming Race Relation: A Public Policy Report*, edited by P. M. Ong. Los Angeles: LEAP Asian Pacific American Public Policy Institute and UCLA Asian American Studies Center.

Evans, David. 1993. *Sexual Citizenship: The Material Construction of Sexualities*. New York: Routledge.

Federal Interagency Committee on Education. 1975. "Report of the Ad Hoc Committee on Racial and Ethnic Definitions." Washington, D.C.: Federal Interagency Committee on Education.

Ferguson, James, and Akhil Gupta. 2002. "Spatialized States: Toward an Ethnography of Neoliberal Governmentality." *American Ethnologist* 29 (4): 981–1002.

Ferguson, Roderick. 2003. *Aberrations in Black: Toward a Queer of Color Critique*. Minneapolis: University of Minnesota Press.

Fernandes, Jorge. 2002. "Return of the Native." Ph.D. dissertation, University of Hawai'i.

Fernandez, Marilyn. 1998. "Asian Indian Americans in the Bay Area and the Glass Ceiling." *Sociological Perspectives* 41 (1): 119–49.

Ferree, Myra Marx, and Patricia Yancey Martin. 1995a. "Doing the Work of the Movement: Feminist Organizations." In *Feminist Organizations: Harvest of the New Women's Movement,* edited by M. M. Ferree and P. Y. Martin. Philadelphia: Temple University Press.

——, eds. 1995b. *Feminist Organizations: Harvest of the New Women's Movement.* Philadelphia: Temple University Press.

Fisher, Maxine P. 1980. *The Indians of New York City: A Study of Immigrants from India.* Columbia, Mo.: South Asia Books.

Fitzgerald, Keith. 1996. *Face of the Nation: Immigration, the State, and the National Identity.* Stanford, Calif.: Stanford University Press.

Foner, Philip Sheldon. 1979. *Women and the American Labor Movement: From Colonial Times to the Eve of World War I.* New York: Free Press.

Fong, Timothy P. 2002. *The Contemporary Asian American Experience: Beyond the Model Minority.* 2nd ed. Upper Saddle River, N.J.: Prentice Hall.

Fornaro, Robert. 1984. "Asian Indians in America: Acculturation and Minority Status." *Migration Today* 12 (3): 29–32.

Foss, Robert J. 1994. "The Demise of the Homosexual Exclusion: New Possibilities for Gay and Lesbian Immigration." *Harvard Civil Rights–Civil Liberties Law Review* 29 (summer): 439–75.

Foucault, Michel. 1990. *The History of Sexuality. Volume I: An Introduction.* New York: Vintage Books.

Frankenberg, Ruth. 1993. *White Women, Race Matters: The Social Construction of Whiteness.* Minneapolis: University of Minnesota Press.

Franklin, Cynthia G. 1997. *Writing Women's Communities: The Politics and Poetics of Contemporary Multi-Genre Anthologies.* Madison: University of Wisconsin Press.

Fuchs, Lawrence H. 1990. *The American Kaleidoscope: Race, Ethnicity, and the Civic Culture.* Hanover, N.H.: University Press of New England.

Fujikane, Candace. 2005. "Foregrounding Native Nationalisms: A Critique of Anti-nationalist Sentiment in Asian American Studies." In *Asian American Studies after Critical Mass,* edited by K. A. Ono. Malden, Mass.: Blackwell.

——. Forthcoming. "Introduction: Asian Settler Colonialism in the U.S. Colony of Hawai'i." In *Asian Settler Colonialism in Hawai'i,* edited by C. Fujikane and J. Y. Okamura. Honolulu: University of Hawai'i Press.

Gabaccia, Donna. 1997. "Liberty, Coercion, and the Making of Immigration Historians." *Journal of American History* 84 (2): 570–75.

Gall, Susan B., and Timothy L. Gall, eds. 1993. *Statistical Record of Asian Americans.* Detroit: Gale Research Inc.

Gans, Herbert. 1979. "Symbolic Ethnicity: The Future of Ethnic Groups and Cultures in America." *Ethnic and Racial Studies* 2 (1): 1–20.

———. 1992. "Second-Generation Decline: Scenarios for the Economic and Ethnic Futures of the Post-1965 American Immigration." *Ethnic and Racial Studies* 15 (2): 171–92.

Gee, Jennifer. 2003. "Housewives, Men's Villages, and Sexual Respectability: Gender and the Interrogation of Asian Women at the Angel Island Immigration Station." In *Asian/Pacific Islander Women: A Historical Anthology*, edited by S. Hune and G. M. Nomura. New York: New York University Press.

Gerstle, Gary. 1997. "Liberty, Coercion and the Making of Americans." *Journal of American History* 84 (2): 524–58.

Gilmore, Ruth. 2002. "Terror, Structural Adjustment, and the Warfare State." In *Race, Gender and the War on Terror* (videorecording). Berkeley: Center for Race and Gender, University of California.

Glazer, Nathan, and Daniel P. Moynihan. 1970. *Beyond the Melting Pot*. 2nd ed. Cambridge, Mass.: MIT Press.

Glenn, Evelyn Nakano. 1992. "From Servitude to Service Work: Historical Continuities in the Racial Division of Paid Reproductive Labor." *Signs* 18 (1): 1–43.

———. 2000. "Citizenship and Inequality: Historical and Global Perspectives." *Social Problems* 47 (1): 1–20.

———. 2002. *Unequal Freedom: How Race and Gender Shaped American Citizenship and Labor*. Cambridge, Mass.: Harvard University Press.

Gluckman, Amy, and Betsy Reed. 1997. "The Gay Marketing Moment." In *Homo Economics: Capitalism, Community, and Lesbian and Gay Life*, edited by A. Gluckman and B. Reed. New York: Routledge.

Gopinath, Gayatri. 1996. "Funny Boys and Girls: Notes from a Queer South Asian Planet." In *Asian American Sexualities: Dimensions of the Gay and Lesbian Experience*, edited by R. Leong. New York: Routledge.

———. 1998. "Homo-Economics: Queer Sexualities in a Transnational Frame." In *Burning Down the House: Recycling Domesticity*, edited by R. M. George. Boulder: Westview Press.

———. 2002. "Local Sites/Global Contexts: The Transnational Trajectories of Deepa Mehta's *Fire*." In *Queer Globalizations: Citizenship and the Afterlife of Colonialism*, edited by A. Cruz-Malavé and M. F. Manalansan IV. New York: New York University Press.

———. 2005. *Impossible Desires: Queer Diasporas and South Asian Public Cultures*. Durham, N.C.: Duke University Press.

Gordon, Milton. 1964. *Assimilation in American Life: The Role of Race, Religion, and National Origins*. New York: Oxford University Press.

Grewal, Inderpal. 1998. "On the New Global Feminism and the Family of Nations: Dilemmas of Transnational Feminist Practice." In *Talking Visions: Multicultural Feminism in a Transnational Age*, edited by E. Shohat. New York: New Museum of Contemporary Art; Cambridge, Mass.: MIT Press.

Grewal, Inderpal, and Caren Kaplan, eds. 1994. *Scattered Hegemonies: Postmodernity and Transnational Feminist Practices*. Minneapolis: University of Minnesota Press.

Guerrero, Marie Anna Jaimes. 1997. "Civil Rights versus Sovereignty: Native American Women in Life and Land Struggles." In *Feminist Genealogies, Colonial Legacies, Democratic Futures*, edited by M. J. Alexander and C. T. Mohanty. New York: Routledge.

Gupta, Sangeeta R., ed. 1999. *Emerging Voices: South Asian American Women Redefine Self, Family, and Community*. Walnut Creek, Calif.: AltaMira Press.

Handlin, Oscar. 1951. *The Uprooted*. Boston: Little, Brown.

Haney-López, Ian. 1996. *White by Law: The Legal Construction of Race*. New York: New York University Press.

Hansen, Marcus Lee. 1987. *The Problem of the Third Generation Immigrant*. Republication of the 1937 address, edited and with an introduction by Peter Kivisto and Oscar Handlin. Rock Island, Ill.: Swenson Swedish Immigration Research Center and Augstana College Library.

Harvey, David. 1990. *The Condition of Postmodernity: An Enquiry into the Origins of Cultural Change*. Cambridge, Mass.: Blackwell.

Helweg, Arthur, and Usha Helweg. 1990. *An Immigrant Success Story*. Philadelphia: University of Pennsylvania Press.

Hennessy, Rosemary. 2000. *Profit and Pleasure: Sexual Identities in Late Capitalism*. New York: Routledge.

Hing, Bill Ong. 1993. *Making and Remaking Asian America through Immigration Policy, 1850–1990*. Stanford, Calif.: Stanford University Press.

Hochschild, Arlie Russell. 1997. *The Time Bind: When Work Becomes Home and Home Becomes Work*. New York: Metropolitan.

Hollinger, David A. 1995. *Postethnic America*. New York: Basic Books.

——. 1997. "National Solidarity at the End of the Twentieth Century: Reflections on the United States and Liberal Nationalism." *Journal of American History* 84 (2): 559–69.

Hondagneu-Sotelo, Pierrette. 2000. "Feminism and Migration." *Annals of the American Academy of Political & Social Science* 571: 107–20.

——. 2001. *Doméstica: Immigrant Workers Cleaning and Caring in the Shadows of Affluence*. Berkeley: University of California Press.

Hondagneu-Sotelo, Pierrette, and Ernestine Avila. 1997. "'I'm Here, but I'm There': The Meaning of Latina Transnational Motherhood." *Gender and Society* 11 (5): 548–71.

Human Rights Watch. 1998. "Shielded from Justice: Police Brutality and Accountability in the United States" [cited 19 June 2003], http://www.hrw.org/reports98/police/.

International Gay and Lesbian Human Rights Commission. 1997. "Asylum from Persecution Based upon Sexual Orientation" [cited 30 July 2001]. http://www.iglhrc.org/news/factsheets/9704-asylum.html.

Islam, Naheed. 1993. "In the Belly of the Multicultural Beast I Am Named South Asian." In *Our Feet Walk the Sky: Women of the South Asian Diaspora*, edited by Women of South Asian Descent Collective. San Francisco: Aunt Lute Books.

Itzigsohn, Jose. 2000. "Immigration and the Boundaries of Citizenship." *International Migration Review* 34 (4): 1126–154.

Jacobson, David. 1996. *Rights across Borders: Immigration and the Decline of Citizenship.* Baltimore: Johns Hopkins University Press.

Jasso, Guillermina, and Mark R. Rosenzweig. 1995. "Do Immigrants Screened for Skills Do Better Than Family-Reunification Immigrants?" *International Migration Review* 29 (1): 85–111.

Jayawardena, Kumari. 1986. *Feminism and Nationalism in the Third World.* New Delhi: Kali for Women.

Jenkins, Carol, Greg Pappas, and Yassir Islam. 2001. "Letters in Response to 'A Rose by Any Other Name . . . ?'" *Pukaar* 32 (January): 4.

Jensen, Joan. 1988. *Passage from India: Asian Indian Immigrants in North America.* New Haven: Yale University Press.

Jha, Chandra K. 1976. "Forward." In *Immigrants from the Indian Subcontinent in the U.S.A.: Problems and Prospects,* edited by H. Elkhanialy and R. W. Nicholas. Chicago: India League of America.

Jones, Jacqueline. 1985. *Labor of Love, Labor of Sorrow: Black Women, Work, and the Family from Slavery to the Present.* New York: Basic Books.

Joseph, Miranda. 2002. *Against the Romance of Community.* Minneapolis: University of Minnesota Press.

Jung, Moon-Kie. 2003. "Interracialism: The Ideological Transformation of Hawai'i's Working Class." *American Sociological Review* 68 (3): 373–400.

Kale, Madhavi. 1998. *Fragments of Empire.* Philadelphia: University of Pennsylvania Press.

Kallen, Horace M. 1956. *Cultural Pluralism and the American Idea.* Philadelphia: University of Pennsylvania Press.

Keating, Analouise. 2002. "Charting Pathways, Marking Thresholds . . . A Warning, an Introduction." In *This Bridge We Call Home,* edited by G. Anzaldúa and A. Keating. New York: Routledge.

Kelley, Robin D. G. 1994. *Race Rebels: Culture, Politics, and the Black Working Class.* New York: Free Press.

Kerber, Linda K. 1997. "The Meanings of Citizenship." *Journal of American History* 84 (3): 833–54.

Kerkvliet, Melinda Tria. 2002. *Unbending Cane: Pablo Manlapit, a Filipino Labor Leader in Hawai'i.* Honolulu: Office of Multicultural Student Services, University of Hawai'i at Manoa.

Khan, Owais. 2001. "A Rose by Any Other Name . . . ? Gay Vs MSM." *Pukaar* 32 (January): 3, 24.

Khan, Shivananda. 2001. "Kothis, Gays and (Other) MSMs." *Pukaar* 32 (January): 4–5, 23.

Khandelwal, Madhulika. 1995. "Indian Immigrants in Queens, New York City: Patterns of Spatial Concentration and Distribution, 1965–1990." In *Nation and Migration: Politics of Space in the South Asian Diaspora,* edited by P. Van der Veer. Philadelphia: University of Pennsylvania Press.

———. 2002. *Becoming American, Being Indian*. Ithaca: Cornell University Press.

Kibria, Nazli. 1997. "The Construction of 'Asian American': Reflections on Intermarriage and Ethnic Identity among Second-Generation Chinese and Korean Americans." *Ethnic and Racial Studies* 20 (3): 523–44.

———. 1998. "The Racial Gap: South Asian American Racial Identity and the Asian American Movement." In *A Part, Yet Apart: South Asians in Asian America*, edited by L. D. Shankar and R. Srikanth. Philadelphia: Temple University Press.

Kim, Pan Suk. 1994. "Myth and Realities of the Model Minority." *Public Manager* 23 (3): 31–35.

King, Katie. 2002. " 'There Are No Lesbians Here': Lesbianisms, Feminisms, and Global Gay Formations." In *Queer Globalizations: Citizenship and the Afterlife of Colonialism*, edited by A. Cruz-Malavé and M. F. Manalansan IV. New York: New York University Press.

Koshy, Susan. 1998. "Category Crisis: South Asian Americans and Questions of Race and Ethnicity." *Diaspora* 7 (3): 285–320.

———. 2004. *Sexual Naturalization: Asian Americans and Miscegenation*. Stanford, Calf.: Stanford University Press.

Kwong, Peter. 1997. *Forbidden Workers: Illegal Chinese Immigrants and American Labor*. New York: New Press.

Lacey, Marc. 1996. "House Passes Immigration Bills." *Boston Globe*, 22 March, 3.

Laguerre, Michel S. 1999. "State, Diaspora, and Transnational Politics: Haiti Reconceptualised." *Millennium: Journal of International Studies* 28 (3): 633–51.

Lee, Chinsun. 2002. "Women Raise the City." *Village Voice*, 13–19 March, http://www.villagevoice.com/issues/0211/lee.php.

Lee, Erika. 2003a. *At America's Gates: Chinese Immigration during the Exclusion Era, 1882–1943*. Chapel Hill: University of North Carolina Press.

———. 2003b. "Exclusion Acts: Chinese Women during the Chinese Exclusion Era, 1882–1943." In *Asian/Pacific Islander Women: A Historical Anthology*, edited by S. Hune and G. M. Nomura. New York: New York University Press.

Lee, Rachel. 2000. "Notes from the (Non)Field: Teaching and Theorizing Women of Color." *Meridians: Feminism, Race, Transnationalism* 1 (1): 85–109.

Lee, Robert G. 1999. *Orientals: Asian Americans in Popular Culture*. Philadelphia: Temple University Press.

Lee, Sharon M. 1993. "Racial Classification in the US Census: 1890–1990." *Ethnic and Racial Studies* 16 (1): 75–94.

Lee, Stacey J. 1994. "Behind the Model Minority Stereotype: Voices of High- and Low-Achieving Asian American Students." *Anthropology and Education Quarterly* 25 (4): 413–29.

Leonard, Karen. 1985. "Punjabi Farmers and California's Alien Land Laws." *Agricultural History* 59 (4): 549–62.

———. 1992. *Making Ethnic Choices: California's Punjabi Mexican Americans*. Philadelphia: Temple University Press.

———. 1997. *The South Asian Americans*. Westport, Conn.: Greenwood Press.

Lesbian and Gay Immigration Rights Task Force. 2001. "HIV and Immigration Law" [cited 2 August], http://www.lgirtf.org.

Lessinger, Johanna. 1990. "Asian Indians in New York: Dreams and Despair in the Newsstand Business." *The Portable Lower East Side* 7 (2): 73–87.

———. 1995. *From the Ganges to the Hudson: Indian Immigrants in New York City*. Needham Heights, Mass.: Allyn and Bacon.

Lewis, Martin W., and Kären E. Wigen. 1997. *The Myth of Continents: A Critique of Metageography*. Berkeley: University of California Press.

Lin, Margaretta Wan Ling, and Cheng Imm Tan. 1994. "Holding up More Than Half the Heavens: Domestic Violence in Our Communities, a Call for Justice." In *The State of Asian America*, edited by K. Aguilar-San Juan. Boston: South End Press.

Lipsitz, George. 1994. *Rainbow at Midnight: Labor and Culture in the 1940s*. Urbana: University of Illinois Press.

Liu, Michael. 2001. "Taxi Drivers Demand Justice in Beating" [cited 16 June 2003], www.aamovement.net/immigrant_labor/nytwa.html.

López-Garza, Marta, and David R. Diaz, eds. 2001. *Asian and Latino Immigrants in a Restructuring Economy: The Metamorphosis of Southern California*. Stanford, Calif.: Stanford University Press.

Lorde, Audre. 1984. *Sister/Outsider*. Freedom, Calif.: Crossing Press.

Lowe, Lisa. 1996. *Immigrant Acts: On Asian American Cultural Politics*. Durham, N.C.: Duke University Press.

Luek, Thomas. 1999. "No Fare: New York's Cabbies Show How Multi-Colored Racism Can Be." *New York Times*, 7 November, sec. 4, p. 3.

Luibhéid, Eithne. 2002. *Entry Denied: Controlling Sexuality at the Border*. Minneapolis: University of Minnesota Press.

Luthra, Punam. 1993. Pati Dev. In *Our Feet Walk the Sky: Women of the South Asian Diaspora*, edited by Women of South Asian Descent Collective. San Francisco: Aunt Lute Books.

Lynch, Caitrin. 1994. "Nation, Woman, and the Indian Bourgeoisie: An Alternative Formulation." *Public Culture* 6: 425–37.

Lyons, Matthew. 1997. "'Very Cruel and Mischievous': Race Categories and U.S. Law." Unpublished manuscript.

Maher, Kristen H. 2002. "Who Has a Right to Rights? Citizenship's Exclusions in an Age of Migration." In *Globalization and Human Rights*, edited by A. Brysk. Berkeley: University of California Press.

Maira, Sunaina. 2002. *Desis in the House: Indian American Youth Culture in New York City*. Philadelphia: Temple University Press.

Maira, Sunaina, and Rajini Srikanth. 1996. *Contours of the Heart: South Asians Map North America*. New York: Asian American Writers' Workshop.

Man, Guida. 2002. "Globalization and the Erosion of the Welfare State: Effects on Chinese Immigrant Women." *Canadian Woman Studies/Les Cahiers de la Femme* 21/22 (4/1): 26–32.

Manalansan IV, Martin F. 2003. *Global Divas: Filipino Gay Men in the Diaspora*. Durham, N.C.: Duke University Press.

Manavi. 1990. "Reflections. *Manavi Newsletter* 2 (1): 1.

——. 1992. "A few Thoughts on Resources." *Manavi Newsletter* 4 (2): 4–6.

Mandaville, Peter. 1999. "Territory and Translocality: Discrepant Idioms of Political Identity." *Millennium: Journal of International Studies* 28 (3): 653–73.

Mandell, Betty Reid. 1997. "Downsizing the Welfare State." *New Politics* [cited 17 March 2006]. http://www.wpunj.edu/newpol/issue22/mandel22.htm.

Mani, Lata. 1993. "Gender, Class, and Cultural Conflict: Indu Krishnan's *Knowing Her Place*." In *Our Feet Walk the Sky: Women of the South Asian Diaspora*, edited by Women of South Asian Descent Collective. San Francisco: Aunt Lute Books.

Marshall, Thomas Humphrey. 1950. *Citizenship and Social Class, and Other Essays*. Cambridge: Cambridge University Press.

Martin, Patricia Yancey, Diana DiNitto, Diane Byington, and M. Sharon Maxwell. 1992. "Organizational and Community Transformation: The Case of a Rape Crisis Center." *Administration in Social Work* 16 (3–4): 123–45.

Martinez, Elizabeth. 1998. "Seeing More Than Black and White: Latinos, Racism and the Cultural Divides." In *Race, Class and Gender: An Anthology*, edited by M. L. Andersen and P. H. Collins. Belmont, Calif.: Wadsworth Publishing Company.

Marx, Karl. 1978. "On the Jewish Question." In *The Marx-Engels Reader*, edited by R. C. Tucker. New York: Norton.

MASALA (Massachusetts Area South Asian Lambda Association). 2005. "Mission Statement" [cited 4 May 2005]. http://www.bostonmasala.org/about.

Mathew, Biju. 2000. "Byte-Sized Nationalism: Mapping the Hindu Right in the United States." *Rethinking Marxism* 12 (3): 108–28.

——. 2005. *Taxi! Cabs and Capitalism in New York City*. New York: New Press.

Mathew, Biju, and Vijay Prashad. 2000. "The Protean Forms of Yankee Hindutva." *Ethnic and Racial Studies* 23 (3): 516–35.

Matthews, Nancy. 1995. "Feminist Clashes with the State: Tactical Choices by State-Funded Rape Crisis Centers." In *Feminist Organizations: Harvest of the New Women's Movement*, edited by M. M. Ferree and P. Y. Martin. Philadelphia: Temple University Press.

Matute-Bianchi, Maria. 1991. "Situational Ethnicity and Patterns of School Performance among Immigrant and Nonimmigrant Mexican-Descent Students." In *Minority Status and Schooling: A Comparative Study of Immigrant and Involuntary Minorities*, edited by M. Gibson and J. Ogbu. New York: Garland.

Mazumdar, Sucheta. 1989a. "General Introduction: A Woman-Centered Perspective on Asian American History." In *Making Waves: An Anthology of Writing by and about Asian American Women*, edited by Asian Women United of California. Boston: Beacon Press.

——. 1989b. "Racist Responses to Racism: The Aryan Myth and South Asians in the United States." *South Asia Bulletin* 9 (1): 47–55.

McLaren, Peter. 1994. "White Terror and Oppositional Agency: Towards a Critical Multiculturalism." In *Multiculturalism: A Critical Reader*, edited by D. T. Goldberg. Cambridge, Mass.: Basil Blackwell.

Mignolo, Walter D. 2000. "The Many Faces of Cosmo-Polis: Border Thinking and Critical Cosmopolitanism." *Public Culture* 12 (3): 721–48.

Min, Pyong Gap. 1995. "Major Issues Relating to Asian American Experiences." In *Asian Americans: Contemporary Trends and Issues*, edited by P. G. Min. Thousand Oaks, Calif.: Sage Publications.

Mitchell, Don. 1997. "State Restructuring and the Importance of 'Rights-Talk.'" In *State Devolution in America: Implications for a Diverse Society*, edited by L. A. Staeheli, J. E. Kodras, and C. Flint. Thousand Oaks, Calif.: Sage Publications.

Mogelonsky, Marica. 1995. "Asian-Indian Americans." *American Demographics* 17 (August): 32–39.

Mohanty, Chandra Talpade. 1993. "Defining Genealogies: Feminist Reflections on Being South Asian in North America." In *Our Feet Walk the Sky: Women of the South Asian Diaspora*, edited by Women of South Asian Descent Collective. San Francisco: Aunt Lute Books.

——. 1997. "Women Workers and Capitalist Scripts: Ideologies of Domination, Common Interest, and Politics of Solidarity." In *Feminist Genealogies, Colonial Legacies, Democratic Futures*, edited by M. J. Alexander and C. T. Mohanty. New York: Routledge.

Moraga, Cherríe, and Gloria Anzaldúa. 1983. *This Bridge Called My Back: Writings by Radical Women of Color*. New York: Kitchen Table Press.

Moran, Rachel. 1998. "Unrepresented." In *Race and Representation: Affirmative Action*, edited by R. Post and M. Rogin. New York: Zone Books.

Motihar, Kamala. 1996. "Who Are Asian Indian Americans?" In *Reference Library of Asian America*, edited by S. Gall and I. Natividad. Detroit: Gale Research.

Nagar, Richa. 2000. "Saboteurs? Or Saviors? The Position of Tanzanian Asians." *Samar* 13 [cited 5 May 2005]. http://www.samarmagazine.org/text/article.php?id=10.

Narayan, Uma. 1997. "Toward a Feminist Vision of Citizenship: Rethinking the Implications of Dignity, Political Participation, and Nationality." In *Reconstructing Political Theory: Feminist Perspectives*, edited by M. L. Shanley and U. Narayan. University Park, Pa.: Pennsylvania State University Press.

National Alliance to End Sexual Violence. 2005. "Resources: VAWA 2005 Short Summary" [cited 28 November 2005], http://www.naesv.org/Resources/VAWA2005ShortSummary.html.

National Health Law Program. 1996. "Health Related Provisions in the Illegal Immigration Reform and Immigrant Responsibility Act of 1996" [cited 4 June 2003], http://nhelp.org/pubs/19961008immigrant.html.

National Task Force to End Sexual and Domestic Violence against Women. 2005. "The Violence against Women Act Reauthorization 2005" [cited 28 November 2005], www.vawa2005.org/overview.pdf.

New York City Council. 2002. "Int. No. 96" [cited 17 January 2003], http://www.council.nyc.us/textfiles/Int%200096-2002.htm.

New York Taxi Workers Alliance. 2001a. "NYTWA Proposal to Address Service Refusal." *Shift-Change*, April, 2.

——. 2001b. "Facing Up to the Refusal Issue." *Shift-Change*, April, 10.

——. 2001c. "NYC Taxi Drivers Rise to Support Brother Hisham." *Shift-Change*, April, 1, 6.

Niraj. 1995. "A Brief History of SALGA-NY." *SALGA* 2 (2): 1.

Nobles, Melissa. 2000. *Shades of Citizenship: Race and the Census in Modern Politics.* Stanford, Calif.: Stanford University Press.

Novak, Michael. 1979. "The New Ethnicity." In *America and the New Ethnicity*, edited by D. R. Colburn and G. E. Pozzetta. New York: Kennikat Press Corp.

NOW (National Organization of Women) Legal Defense and Education Fund. 1997. "Out of the Shadows: Strategies for Expanding State Labor and Civil Rights Protections for Domestic Workers." New York: NOW Legal Defense and Education Fund.

Nussbaum, Martha C. 1994. "Patriotism and Cosmopolitanism." *Boston Review* (October/November): 3–5.

Occupational Safety and Health Administration. 2002. "Workplace Violence" [cited 21 September 2002], http://www.osha.gov/oshinfo/priorities/violence.html.

Office of the High Commissioner for Human Rights. 1990. "International Convention on the Protection of Rights of All Migrant Workers and Members of Their Family" [cited 17 January 2003], http://193.194.138.190/html/menu3/b/m_mwctoc.htm.

Office of Management and Budget. 1977. "Directive No. 15: Race and Ethnic Standards for Federal Statistics and Administrative Reporting (as Adopted on May 12, 1977)" [cited 27 May 2005], http://www.learner.org/channel/workshops/primarysources/census/docs/office.html.

Okihiro, Gary. 1994. *Margins and Mainstreams: Asians in American History and Culture.* Seattle: University of Washington Press.

Omatsu, Glenn. 1994. "The 'Four Prisons' and the Movement of Liberation: Asian American Activism from the 1960s to the 1990s." In *The State of Asian America: Activism and Resistance in the 1990s*, edited by K. Aguilar-San Juan. Boston: South End Press.

Omi, Michael. 1996. "Racialization in the Post–Civil Rights Era." In *Mapping Multiculturalism*, edited by A. Gordon and C. Newfield. Minneapolis: University of Minnesota Press.

Omi, Michael, and Dana Y. Takagi. 1998. "Situating Asian Americans in the Political Discourse on Affirmative Action." In *Race and Representation: Affirmative Action*, edited by R. Post and M. Rogin. New York: Zone Books.

Omi, Michael, and Howard Winant. 1994. *Racial Formation in the United States: From the 1960s to the 1980s.* 2nd ed. New York: Routledge.

Ong, Paul M., ed. 2000. *Transforming Race Relations: A Public Policy Report.* Los Angeles: LEAP Asian Pacific American Public Policy Institute and UCLA Asian American Studies Center.

Ong, Paul, Edna Bonacich, and Lucie Cheng, eds. 1994. *New Asian Immigration in Los Angeles and Global Restructuring.* Philadelphia: Temple University Press.

Ong, Paul, and Suzanne Hee. 1994. "Economic Diversity." In *The State of Asian Pacific America: Economic Diversity, Issues and Policy*, edited by P. Ong. Los Angeles: LEAP Asian Pacific American Public Policy Institute and UCLA Asian American Studies Center.

Osman, Saleem. 1995. "Unite for Hope!" *Peela Paiya* (summer): 5–7.

Pardo, Mary. 1995. "Doing It for the Kids: Mexican American Community Activists, Border Feminists?" In *Feminist Organizations: Harvest of the New Women's Movement*, edited by M. M. Ferree and P. Y. Martin. Philadelphia: Temple University Press.

Park, Robert Ezra. 1950. *Race and Culture.* Vol. 1. Glencoe, Ill.: Free Press.

Parrenas, Rhacel Salazar. 2001. *Servants of Globalization: Women, Migration, and Domestic Work.* Stanford, Calif.: Stanford University Press.

Pateman, Carole. 1988. *The Sexual Contract.* Stanford, Calif.: Stanford University Press.

Pellegrini, Ann. 2002. "Consuming Lifestyles: Commodity Capitalism and Transformations in Gay Identity." In *Queer Globalizations: Citizenship and the Afterlife of Colonialism*, edited by A. Cruz-Malavé and M. F. Manalansan IV. New York: New York University Press.

Pendleton, Gail. 1998. "Update on Immigration Law and Applications for Battered Immigrants under the Violence against Women's Act (VAWA)." Boston: National Immigration Project of the National Lawyers Guild.

Perea, Juan F. 2000. "The Black/White Binary Paradigm of Race." In *Critical Race Theory: The Cutting Edge*, edited by R. Delgado and J. Stefancic. Philadelphia: Temple University Press.

Pollock, Sheldon. 2000. "Cosmopolitan and Vernacular in History." *Public Culture* 12 (3): 591–625.

Poore, Grace. 1996. "Three Movements in A Minor: Lesbians and Immigration." *Off Our Backs* 12–13: 22.

Portes, Alejandro. 1996. "Transnational Communities: Their Emergence and Significance in the Contemporary World." In *Latin America in the World Economy*, edited by R. P. Korzeniewicz and W. C. Smith. Westport, Conn.: Greenwood Press.

Portes, Alejandro, and Min Zhou. 1993. "The New Second Generation: Segmented

Assimilation and Its Variants." *Annals of the American Academy of Political and Social Science* 530 (November): 74–96.

Prashad, Vijay. 1998. "Crafting Solidarities." In *A Part, Yet Apart: South Asians in Asian America*, edited by L. D. Shankar and R. Srikath. Philadelphia: Temple University Press.

———. 2000. *Karma of Brown Folk*. Minneapolis: University of Minnesota Press.

———. 2001. *Everybody Was Kung Fu Fighting: Afro-Asian Connections and the Myth of Cultural Purity*. Boston: Beacon Press.

Puar, Jasbir K. 1998. "Transnational Sexualities: South Asian (Trans)Nationalisms and Queer Diasporas." In *Q&A: Queer in Asian America*, edited by D. L. Eng and A. Y. Hom. Philadelphia: Temple University Press.

———. 2002. "Introduction." Special issue on Queer Tourism: Geographies of Globalisation. *GLQ: Journal of Lesbian and Gay Studies* 8 (1–2): 1–6.

Puri, Jyoti. 2004. "Inconsistencies and Complicities of the 'Global Gay.'" In *Occasional Papers Series on Gender and Globalization in Asia and the Pacific*. Honolulu: Women's Studies Program, University of Hawai'i at Manoa.

Purkayastha, Bandana. 2005. *Negotiating Identities: Second-Generation South Asians Traverse a Transnational World*. New Brunswick, N.J.: Rutgers University Press.

Quiroz-Martinez, Julie. 2001. "A Fair and Just Amnesty." *Nation*, 21 May, 18, 20–22.

Ramirez, Margaret. 2002. "Cabbies' Lifestyle a Wheel Struggle; Face Health Hazards without Insurance." *New York Newsday*, 8 March, A4.

Rangaswamy, Padma. 2000. *Namasté America: Indian Immigrants in an American Metropolis*. University Park: Pennsylvania State University Press.

Ratti, Rakesh. 1993. *A Lotus of Another Color: An Unfolding of the South Asian Gay and Lesbian Experience*. Boston: Alyson Publications.

Rayaprol, Aparna. 1997. *Negotiating Identities: Women in the Indian Diaspora*. Delhi: Oxford University Press.

Reagon, Bernice Johnson. 1983. "Coalition Politics: Turning the Century." In *Home Girls: A Black Feminist Anthology*, edited by B. Smith. New York: Kitchen Table Press.

Reddy, Chandan. 2003. "They Cannot Represent Themselves; They Must Be Represented: A Queer of Color Critique of Neo-Liberal Citizenship and the Discourse on Family." Paper presented at the Association of Asian American Studies, San Francisco, 9 May.

Reed, Cynthia. 1996. "When Love, Comity, and Justice Conquer Borders: INS Recognition of Same-Sex Marriage." *Columbia Human Rights Law Review* 28 (fall): 97–134.

Reimers, David M. 1985. *Still the Golden Door: The Third World Comes to America*. New York: Columbia University Press.

Reinelt, Claire. 1995. "Moving into the Terrain of the State: The Battered Women's Movement and the Politics of Engagement." In *Feminist Organizations: Harvest of the New Women's Movement*, edited by M. M. Ferree and P. Y. Martin. Philadelphia: Temple University Press.

Richmond, Anthony H. 1994. *Global Apartheid: Refugees, Racism, and the New World Order*. Toronto: Oxford University Press.

Rickford, John R. 1987. *Dimensions of a Creole Continuum: History, Texts, and Linguistic Analysis of Guyanese Creole*. Stanford, Calif.: Stanford University Press.

Rimmerman, Craig A. 2002. *From Identity to Politics: The Lesbian and Gay Movement in the United States*. Philadelphia: Temple University Press.

Rodriguez, Clara E. 2000. *Changing Race: Latinos, the Census, and the History of Ethnicity in the United States*. New York: New York University Press.

Roediger, David R. 1991. *The Wages of Whiteness: Race and the Making of the American Working Class*. London: Verso.

Rudrappa, Sharmila. 2004. *Ethnic Routes to Becoming American: Indian Immigrants and the Cultures of Citizenship*. New Brunswick, N.J.: Rutgers University Press.

Rushin, Donna Kate. 1983. "The Bridge Poem." In *This Bridge Called My Back*, edited by C. Moraga and G. Anzaldúa. New York: Kitchen Table Press.

Sachdeva, Riti. 1993. "Who Is South Asian?" *Desiaspora*, 5.

Sachdeva, Riti, Ramani P. Sripada-Vaz, and Monisha Das Gupta. 1996. "Pan-Asian Coalition Building: How Do We Do It?" [cited 23 May 1999], http://www.way.net/sawa/desiaspora/o2coal.html.

SALGA (South Asian Lesbian and Gay Association). 1995. "SALGA-NY Charter." *SALGA* 2 (2): 1.

———. 1996. "Independence Day Parades/Moments of Oppression?" *SALGA* (October): 1, 4.

Samar Collective. 1994. "One Big, Happy Community? Class Issues within South Asian Homes." *Samar* 4 (winter): 10–15.

———. 2002. "Is This the Desi Future?" *Samar* 15 (summer/fall).

Sandoval, Chela. 1991. "U.S. Third World Women: The Theory and Method of Oppositional Consciousness in the Postmodern World." *Genders* 10 (spring): 1–24.

Saran, Paramatma. 1985. *The Asian Indian Experience in the United States*. Cambridge, Mass.: Schenkman.

Sassen, Saskia. 1996. *Losing Control? Sovereignty in an Age of Globalization*. New York: Columbia University Press.

———. 1998. *Globalization and Its Discontents: Essays on the Mobility of People and Money*. New York: New Press.

———. 2001. *The Global City: New York, London, Tokyo*. 2nd ed. Princeton, N.J.: Princeton University Press.

SAWA (South Asian Women for Action). 1993. "SAWA (Formerly Indian-Subcontinent Women's Alliance for Action)." *Désiaspora*, 1.

Saxton, Alexander P. 1971. *The Indispensable Enemy: Labor and the Anti-Chinese Movement in California*. Berkeley: University of California Press.

Schiller, Nina Glick, and Georges E. Fouron. 1999. "Terrains of Blood and Nation: Haitian Transnational Social Fields." *Ethnic and Racial Studies* 22 (2): 340–66.

Schmitt, Eric. 1996. "Panel Votes for Worker Visas for 250,000." *New York Times*, 6 March, A14.

Scott, Ellen. 2000. "Everyone against Racism: Agency and the Production of Meaning in the Anti-Racism Practices of Two Feminist Organizations." *Theory and Society* 29: 785–818.

Sekhri, Priya. 1996. "A 'Nest' in the Making." *Manavi Newsletter* 8 (3): 1–2.

Sethi, Rita Chaudhry. 1994. "Smells Like Racism: A Plan for Mobilizing against Anti-Asian Bias." In *The State of Asian America: Activism and Resistance in the 1990s*, edited by K. Aguilar-San Juan. Boston: South End Press.

Shah, Nayan. 1993. "Sexuality, Identity, and the Uses of History." In *A Lotus of Another Color: An Unfolding of the South Asian Gay and Lesbian Experience*, edited by R. Ratti. Boston: Alyson Publications.

Shah, Purvi. 1996. "Literacy." *Sakhi Quarterly* 1 (summer): 7.

——. 1997. "Redefining the Home: How Community Elites Silence Feminist Activism." In *Dragon Ladies: Asian American Feminists Breathe Fire*, edited by S. Shah. Boston: South End Press.

Shah, Sonia. 1994. "Presenting the Blue Goddess: Toward a National, Pan-Asian Feminist Agenda." In *The State of Asian America: Activism and Resistance in the 1990s*, edited by K. Aguilar-San Juan. Boston: South End Press.

——, ed. 1997. *Dragon Ladies: Asian American Feminists Breathe Fire*. Boston: South End Press.

Shah, Svati P. 2001. "Out and Out Radical: New Directions for Progressive Organizing" [cited 11 October 2004], http://www.samarmagazine.org/archive/article.php?id=60.

Shankar, Lavina Dhingra, and Rajini Srikanth, eds. 1998. *A Part, Yet Apart: South Asians in Asian America*. Philadelphia: Temple University Press.

Sharma, Nandita. 2002. "Travel Agency: Feminist Strategies for Survival in a Global World." Paper presented at the Women's Studies Colloquium Series, at University of Hawai'i at Manoa, 6 December.

——. 2006. *Home Economics: Nationalism and the Making of "Migrant Workers" in Canada*. Toronto: University of Toronto Press.

Sheth, Manju. 1995. "Asian Indian Americans." In *Asian Americans: Contemporary Trends and Issues*, edited by P. G. Min. Thousand Oaks, Calif.: Sage Publications.

Sheth, Pravin. 2001. *Indians in America: One Stream, Two Waves, Three Generations*. Jaipur: Rawat Publications.

Sinha, Sumantra Tito. 1998. "From Campus to Community Politics in Asian America." In *A Part, Yet Apart: South Asians in Asian America*, edited by L. D. Shankar and R. Srikanth. Philadelphia: Temple University Press.

Sivanandan, A. 1981/82. "From Resistance to Rebellion: Asian and Afro-Caribbean Struggles in Britain." *Race and Class* 23 (2/3): 111–52.

Small Business Administration. 1982. "Minority Small Business and Capital Ownership

Development Assistance; Designation of Minority Group Eligibility of Asian Indian Americans." *Federal Register* 47 (163/23 August): 36743.

Smith, Andrea. 2005. "Native American Feminim, Sovereignty, and Social Change." *Feminist Studies* 31 (1): 116–32.

Smith, Barbara. 1983. *Home Girls: A Black Feminist Anthology.* New York: Kitchen Table Press.

——. 1998. "Doing It from Scratch: The Challenge of Black Lesbian Organizing." In *The Truth That Never Hurts: Writings on Race, Gender, and Freedom.* New Brunswick, N.J.: Rutgers University Press.

Smith, Neil. 1992. "Contours of a Spatialized Politics: Homeless Vehicles and Production of Geographical Scale." *Social Text* 33: 55–81.

Song, Min. 1998. "Pakhar Singh's Argument with Asian America: Color and the Structure of Racial Formation." In *A Part, Yet Apart: South Asians in Asian America,* edited by L. D. Shankar and R. Srikanth. Philadelphia: Temple University Press.

South Asian Citizens Web. 1999. "Action Alert" [cited 11 October 2004], http://bridget .jatol.com/pipermail/sacw_insaf.net/1999/000218.html.

Soysal, Yasemin Nuhoglu. 1994. *Limits of Citizenship: Migrants and Postnational Membership in Europe.* Chicago: University of Chicago Press.

Sripada, Ramani. 1993. "Why Stand Alone? The Importance of Coalition Building." *Desiaspora,* 3.

Stasiulis, Daiva, and Abigail B. Bakan. 1997. "Negotiating Citizenship: The Case of Foreign Domestic Workers in Canada." *Feminist Review* 57 (autumn): 112–39.

Strobel, Margaret. 1995. "Organizational Learning in the Chicago Women's Liberation Union." In *Feminist Organizations: Harvest of the New Women's Movement,* edited by M. M. Ferree and P. Y. Martin. Philadelphia: Temple University Press.

Strozier, Matthew. 1998a. "Manhattan's Streets Strangely Empty as Taxis Went on Strike over New Rules." *India in New York,* 22 May, 20.

——. 1998b. "Blocked on Bridge, Yellow Cab Drivers Protest on Foot." *India in New York,* 29 May, 22.

Stychin, Carl F. 1998. *A Nation by Rights: National Cultures, Sexual Identity Politics, and the Discourse of Rights.* Philadelphia: Temple University Press.

Sudbury, Julia. 1998. *"Other Kinds of Dreams": Black Women's Organizations and the Politics of Transformation.* London: Routledge.

Takaki, Ronald T. 1983. *Pau Hana: Plantation Life and Labor in Hawaii, 1835–1920.* Honolulu: University of Hawai'i Press.

——. 1989. *Strangers from a Different Shore: A History of Asian Americans.* Boston: Little, Brown.

Taxi and Limousine Commission. 2002. "Taxicab Rider Bill of Rights" [cited 9 November 2004], http://www.nyc.gov/html/tlc/html/passenger/taxicab_rights.shtml.

Thompson, Becky. 2001. *A Promise and a Way of Life: White Antiracist Activism.* Minneapolis: University of Minnesota Press.

Tichenor, Daniel J. 2002. *Dividing Lines: The Politics of Immigration Control in America.* Princeton: Princeton University Press.

Trask, Haunani-Kay. 2000. "Settlers of Color and 'Immigrant' Hegemony of 'Locals' in Hawai'i." *Amerasia Journal* 26 (2): 1–24.

Tsai, Michelle. 2002. "Proposed Law Would Protect Nannies, Others," http://www.womensenews.org/article.cfm/dyn/aid/877/context/cover/.

U.S. Bureau of the Census. 1921. *Fourteenth Census 1920: Population General Report and Analytical Tables.* Washington, D.C.: Department of Commerce.

———. 1933. *Fifteenth Census of the United States: 1930: Population: General Report Statistics by Subject.* Vol. 2. Washington, D.C.: Department of Commerce.

———. 1943. *Sixteenth Census of the United States: 1940: Population: Characteristics of the Nonwhite Population by Race.* Washington, D.C.: Department of Commerce.

———. 1952. *Census of Population 1950: Characteristics of the Population: Part 5: California.* Vol. 2. Washington, D.C.: Department of Commerce.

———. 1953. *Census of Population: 1950: Characteristics of the Population.* Vol. 2. Washington, D.C.: Department of Commerce.

———. 1964. *Census of Population: 1960: Characteristics of the Population: Part 1: United States Summary.* Vol. 1. Washington, D.C.: Department of Commerce.

———. 1973. *1970 Census of Population: Characteristics of the Population: Part 1: United States Summary: Section 2.* Vol. 1. Washington, D.C.: Department of Commerce.

———. 1982. *Census of Population and Housing: Users' Guide: Part A: Text.* Washington, D.C.: Department of Commerce.

———. 1993. *1990 Census of Population: Social and Economic Characteristics: Massachusetts (CP-2–23).* Vol. 1. Washington, D.C.: U.S. Government Printing Office.

U.S. Commission on Civil Rights. 1980. *Civil Rights Issues of Asian and Pacific Americans: Myths and Realities: May 8–9, 1979, Washington, D.C.: A Consultation Sponsored by the United States Commission on Civil Rights.* Washington, D.C.: U.S. Government Printing Office.

———. 1992. *Civil Rights Issues Facing Asian Americans in the 1990s.* Washington, D.C.: U.S. Government Printing Office.

U.S. Department of Justice. 1997. "Fact Sheet: Illegal Immigration Reform and Immigrant Responsibility Act of 1996 Summary" [cited 4 June 2003], www.immigration.gov/graphics/publicaffairs/factsheet/955.htm.

U.S. House of Representatives. 1976. *Committee on Post Office and Civil Service. 1980 Census. Hearings before the Subcommittee on Census and Population.* 94th Cong., 2d. Sess. Washington, D.C.: U.S. Government Printing Office.

———. 1977. *Committee on Post Office and Civil Service. 1980 Census.* 95th Cong. 1st Sess. Washington, D.C.: U.S. Government Printing Office.

——. 1979. *Committee on Post Office and Civil Service. Oversight Hearings on the 1980 Census Part VII—Los Angeles, Calif.: Hearing before the Subcommittee on Census and Population. 96th Cong. 1st Sess.* Washington, D.C.: U.S. Government Printing Office.

——. 2001. "Permanent Partners Immigration Act of 2001" (Introduced in House of Representatives). Washington, D.C.: Government Printing Office.

Vaid, Jyotsna. 1989. "Seeking a Voice: South Asian Women's Groups in North America." In *Making Waves: An Anthology of Writings by and about Asian American Women*, edited by Asian Women United of California. Boston: Beacon Press.

——. 1999/2000. "Beyond a Space of Our Own: South Asian Women's Groups in the U.S." *Amerasia Journal* 25 (3): 111–26.

Vanita, Ruth. 2002. "Introduction." In *Queering India: Same-Sex Love and Eroticism in Indian Culture and Society*, edited by R. Vanita. New York: Routledge.

Varadarajan, Tunku. 1998. "The Spoilers." *New York Times*, 19 April, 96.

Visweswaran, Kamala. 1997. "Diaspora by Design: Flexible Citizenship and South Asians in U.S. Racial Formation." *Diaspora* 6 (1): 5–29.

Volpp, Leti. 2003. "The Legal Mapping of U.S. Immigration, 1965–1996." In *Crossing into America*, edited by L. Mendoza and S. Shankar. New York: New Press.

Warner, Michael. 2002. *Publics and Counterpublics*. New York: Zone Books.

Waters, Mary C. 1990. *Ethnic Options: Choosing Identities in America*. Berkeley: University of California Press.

——. 1999. *Black Identities: West Indian Immigrant Dreams and American Realities*. New York: Russell Sage Foundation; Cambridge, Mass.: Harvard University Press.

White, Deborah G. 1999. *Too Heavy a Load: Black Women in Defense of Themselves, 1894–1994*. New York: Norton.

Williams, Lena. 1996. "Terrorism Law Being Used to Deport Immigrants." *New York Times*, 16 July, http://www.nytimes.com/yr/mo/day/front/ny-immigrants.html.

Wilson, Amrit. 1978. *Finding a Voice: Asian Women in Britain*. London: Virago Press.

Women of South Asian Descent Collective, ed. 1993. *Our Feet Walk the Sky: Women of the South Asian Diaspora*. San Francisco: Aunt Lute Books.

Woo, Deborah. 2000. *Glass Ceilings and Asian Americans: The New Face of Workplace Barriers*. Walnut Creek, Calif.: AltaMira Press.

Yamada, Mitsuye. 1983. "Asian Pacific American Women and Feminism." In *This Bridge Called My Back: Writings by Radical Women of Color*, edited by C. Moraga and G. Anzaldúa. New York: Kitchen Table Press.

Yanagisako, Sylvia. 1995. "Transforming Orientalism: Gender, Nationality, and Class in Asian American Studies." In *Naturalizing Power: Essays in Feminist Cultural Analysis*, edited by S. Yanagisako and C. Delaney. New York: Routledge.

Young, Judy. 2003. "'A Bowlful of Tears': Lee Puey You's Immigration Experience at Angel Island." In *Asian/Pacific Islander Women: A Historical Anthology*, edited by S. Hune and G. M. Nomura. New York: New York University Press.

Yuval-Davis, Nira. 1997. "Women, Citizenship and Difference." *Feminist Review* 57 (autumn): 4–27.

——. 1999. "The 'Multi-Layered Citizen': Citizenship in the Age of 'Glocalization.'" *International Feminist Journal of Politics* 1 (1): 119–36.

Zia, Helen. 2000. *Asian American Dreams: The Emergence of an American People.* New York: Farrar, Straus and Giroux.

INDEX

AALDEF (Asian American Legal Defense and Education Fund), 221, 224–25, 244, 273 n.9

Abelmann, Nancy, and John Lie, 106

Abraham, Margaret, 84, 128, 131, 200

abstract liberal citizenship, 53–54, 252, 262 n.1

advocacy, 139–44, 149–50, 153

affirmative action, 30, 33, 37–39, 42, 51, 271 n.15. *See also* civil rights

African Americans: cross-racial organizing and, 45; as domestic workers, 213, 219; model minority image and, 28, 34, 58–59; racialization and, 43, 255; South Asians and, 263 n.10; taxi drivers and, 247–51; women, 213, 219, 255. *See also* black/white paradigm

agricultural workers, 79, 101–2, 263 n.5

AIA (Association of Indians in America), 28–30, 35–40, 42–48, 137, 252

Alam, Nahar, 8, 16–17, 18, 125, 215, 216, 218, 220, 222, 223–24, 226, 272 n.8

Alba, Richard, 76

Alexander, M. Jacqui, 92, 151, 179, 255, 267

ALP (Audre Lorde Project), 193, 194

Amer, Hisham, 274 n.23

American Federation of Labor (AFL), 212, 273 n.16

Andolan: CAAAVL and, 215; coalition building and, 273 n.9; community outreach and, 223–24; economic restructuring and, 25–26; home-country histories and, 80; intra-community class struggles and, 253–54; membership, 215, 217, 224; organizational growth/vision and, 209, 215, 217, 223–25; Sakhi and, 8, 209; transnational complex of rights and, 217, 252–54; transnational law and, 26. *See also* Alam, Nahar; Domestic Workers Committee (DWC); labor organizations

Annual International Women's Day Celebration for Queer Women of Color and Allies, 197

anticitizenship, 24, 34, 53

antidowry campaign, 143, 157

Anti-Terrorism and Effective Death Penalty Act, 241

antiviolence activism, 25, 61–67, 69, 78, 124, 155

Anzaldúa, Gloria, 4

APAAC (Asian Pacific American Agenda Coalition), 143–47
API (Asian and Pacific Islanders), 50
APICHA (Asian & Pacific Islander Coalition on AIDS), 194
Apna Ghar (shelter), 64–65, 66, 68, 89, 117–18
Appelbaum, Richard, 14, 106, 212
ASAP (Asian Shelter and Advocacy Project), 141–42
Asha, 89
Ashiana (shelter), 118–19
ASIA (Asian Sisters in Action), 148
Asian American Legal Defense and Education Fund (AALDEF), 221, 224–25, 244, 273 n.9, 274 n.23
Asian Americans: Asian and Pacific Islanders (API), 50; Asian Indians, 20–23, 32–36, 41, 43, 45–46, 50–52, 53, 77–78; black/white paradigm and, 52, 59; coalition building and, 148; domestic violence organizations and, 18; East Asians and, 262 n.8; ethnicity paradigm and, 268 n.16; feminism and, 110; gay tourism and, 179; genealogy of term, 268 n.16; immigration status and, 50, 100, 145; labor discrimination and, 100; legal/illegal discourse and, 50, 144–45, 147; model minority image and, 58–59, 264 nn.2–3; Native Hawaiʻians and, 257–58; panethnicity and, 141; racialization and, 39, 51; sexuality and, 179; small businesses and, 79; South Asians and, 136, 137, 141, 148–50, 262 n.8; unionization and, 231
Asian & Pacific Islander Coalition on AIDS (APICHA), 194
Asian and Pacific Islanders (API), 50
Asian Indians, 20–23, 32–36, 41, 43, 45–46, 50–52, 53, 77–78
Asian Pacific American Agenda Coalition (APAAC), 143–47
Asian Shelter and Advocacy Project (ASAP), 141–42

Asian Sisters in Action (ASIA), 148
assimilation, 20, 53–54, 59–61, 206–7. See also cultural adaptation discourse; model minority image
Association of Indians in America (AIA), 28–30, 35–40, 42–48, 137, 252
asylum: cultural imperialism and, 91–92, 94, 95, 96, 98, 107; gender and, 17, 95, 107, 119–20, 125; political, 236; restrictions of, 96; sexuality and, 92, 95–96, 107
Audre Lorde Project (ALP), 193, 194

Bangladeshi immigrants, 218, 236–38
Baran, Tim, 75, 163, 175–76, 194, 201–4
Barnett, Bernice, 110
Basch, Linda, Nina Glick Schiller, and Cristina Szanton Blanc, 155
Bedi, Kiran, 193
Bhattacharjee, Anannya, 54, 63, 87, 122–23, 126–27, 129, 131, 133, 198–99, 214
blacks. See African Americans; Indo-Caribbean immigrants; West Indians
black/white paradigm: affirmative action and, 30, 33, 37–39, 42, 51, 271 n.15; Asian Americans and, 52, 59; blackness, 255; civil rights and, 30, 38; feminism and, 110–11; minoritization and, 38; Operation Refusal and, 246–51; race and, 30, 255; racialization and, 30, 43–48, 48–51; racism and, 22, 30, 52; South Asian identity and, 43–48, 136, 256, 263 n.10; transnational complex of rights and, 256; women and, 136, 255. See also racialization
Black Women in the Academy (conference), 255
Bollywood, 181–85
Bonacich, Edna, and Richard Appelbaum, 212
borders: border consciousness, 4; globalization and, 13; nationalism and, 12–13; nation-building and, 70, 258; nation-

states and, 12–14, 16, 18–19, 257–58; sovereignty, 13; state-building and, 26, 258; transnational complex of rights and, 108, 257–58; transnationalism and, 12, 17–18, 157. *See also* state-building

Bourne, Randolph, 262 n.7

Bracero Program, 101–2, 263 n.5

Brewer, Gail, 226

Bureau of the Census (United States), 43–44, 45, 48–52, 262 n.4. *See also* Subcommittee on Census and Population

CAAAV (Coalition against Anti-Asian Violence), 7, 209, 215, 228–29, 252

Calhoun, Craig, 262 n.7

Campaign for Lesbian Rights, 74, 188

Canada, 71, 72, 74, 113, 145–46, 161–63, 191–92, 219

Canadian immigrants, 71, 72, 74, 113, 145–46, 161–63, 191–92, 219

capitalism: abstract liberal citizenship and, 53–54, 252, 262 n.1; consumerism and, 25–26, 163, 165, 172–73, 177, 178–80, 209; domestic workers and, 25–26; gays and lesbians and, 163, 268 n.2; labor market needs and, 101–2; reproductive labor and, 272 n.4

care work, 63, 131, 134, 209, 213, 217–19, 219–20

Caribbean immigrants, 40, 72, 74–75, 163, 171, 175–76, 182, 189, 200–203, 213, 270 n.14

census (U. S. Bureau of the Census), 43–44, 45, 48–52, 262 n.4. *See also* Subcommittee on Census and Population

Census Bureau (India), 36

Chandy, Sunu, 191–92

Chang, Grace, 102, 263 n.7

Chang, Robert, 51, 83

Chinese immigrants, 34, 45, 50, 77, 267 n.11, 271 n.3

Choldin, Harvey, 49

citizenship: abstract liberal, 53–54, 252, 262 n.1; as analytical category, 256–57; consumerism and, 206–7; cosmopolitanism and, 11; cultural authenticity and, 60; denaturalization of, 256–59; feminist critiques of, 15–16; immigrant status and, 54–55; legal/illegal discourse and, 258; migration and, 12–16; nationalism and, 12–13, 26, 163, 184–85, 188–89; nation-state and, 12–14, 16, 18–19, 257–58; neoliberalism and, 164, 165, 179, 185, 239–40; race and, 262 n.2; racialization and, 23, 29–30, 39, 52, 53–55; rights discourse and, 12–16, 26, 30, 156, 257; sexual, 165, 185–89; sovereignty and, 268 n.18; transnational complex of rights and, 18–19, 26, 156, 185–89; transnationalism and, 13. *See also* full citizenship; immigration status; legal/illegal discourse

civil rights: abuses, 258–59; affirmative action and, 30, 33, 37–39, 42, 51, 271 n.15; black/white paradigm and, 30, 38; discrimination and, 29–30, 33–35, 41, 45; full citizenship and, 14–15, 30, 37, 39, 257–58; immigration status and, 37; nationalism and, 188–89, 258–59; nation-state and, 258–59; racialization and, 29, 37; sovereignty and, 268 n.18; whiteness and, 29–30

Civil Rights Act, 41

class: caste and, 202–3, 271 n.15; -based organizing, 209; cross-class organizing, 122, 253–54; cultural adaptation discourse and, 23–24; gender and, 111–12; internal conflicts and, 7; intracommunity, struggles, 76–78, 102, 105–7; mobility, 59–61, 76, 77–78; nation-state and, 13; sexuality and, 191; volunteerism and, 133–34. *See also* elite-class immigrants; professionals; working-class immigrants

Coalition against Anti-Asian Violence (CAAAV), 7, 209, 215, 228–29, 252

coalition building: AIA and, 10, 44, 45; antiviolence organizations and, 128–29; Asian
Americans and, 148; cross-class organizing, 122, 253–54; cross-racial, 28, 255–56;
cross-racial alliances and, 236–38, 247–51,
274 n.23; funding and, 112; labor organizations and, 253–54; legal/illegal discourse
and, 143–47; missed opportunities for,
44; model minority image and, 28;
NYTWA and, 253–54; queer organizations
and, 148, 172, 192–200; racial solidarity
and, 44, 45; taxi drivers, 253–54; women's
organizations and, 111, 128–29, 130, 138–
39, 141–43, 147–53, 155–56, 273 n.9
Coalition for American Islamic Relations,
274 n.23
Coalition of Queer Women of Color, 196
collective action: activism and, 8, 9, 56, 133,
189, 200, 214, 217, 236; domestic workers
and, 214; social change organizations and,
8, 9, 56, 133, 189, 200, 214, 217, 236; space-
making politics and, 56–57; taxi drivers
and, 26, 231, 233–38, 244–46. See also
unionization
Collins, Patricia Hill, 13
colonization, 10, 74, 149, 162–63, 258
Combahee River Collective, 153
Commission on Civil Rights (U.S.), 86,
100
community, 81, 128, 163–65, 171–74, 206–7
Concerned Asian-American and Pacific-
American People's Task Force, 51
consumerism: capitalism, 25–26, 163, 165,
172–73, 177, 178–80, 209; citizenship and,
206–7; consumer rights, 26, 209, 238–41,
244–46; cultural production and, 179;
domestic workers and, 25–26, 209; gays
and lesbians and, 163, 164–65, 178–79,
206–7; queer organizations and, 25, 165,
172–73, 205, 206–7; race and, 249–51;
sexual citizenship and, 185–89; structural
marginalization and, 246–51; taxi drivers

and, 25–26, 209, 238–41, 244–46; transnationalism and, 177, 179–80
Convention on Migrant Workers, 18, 223
cosmopolitanism, 11–12, 262 n.7
Crenshaw, Kimberlé, 85, 86, 154
criminalization, 89, 219–21
cross-connections, 189–90
cross-racial alliances, 28, 44, 192–94, 217,
236–38, 247–51, 251–56, 274 n.23
cultural adaptation discourse, 21, 23–24,
59–61, 183–89. See also model minority
image
cultural authenticity: assimilation model and,
59–61; citizenship and, 60; class and, 76,
77–78; cultural adaptation discourse and,
21, 23–24, 59–61, 183–89; domestic violence and, 62–69, 83; domestic workers
and, 62; family values and, 60, 63–65;
gender roles, 57, 62, 64–66, 83; identity
formation and, 81; immigration status
and, 64–66; model minority image and,
57–61; nationalism and, 10–12, 66, 69–
70, 74; place-taking politics and, 57–61;
religion and, 66; sexuality and, 69–75,
71–75, 168–69; social change organizations and, 81; social mobility and, 76–77;
space-making politics and, 57; transnationalism and, 72–73
curry queens, 177–81
Cvetkovich, Ann, 173

Damayan Domestic Workers Association,
273 n.9
Danby, Colin, 273 n.12
Das Dasgupta, Shamita, 67–68, 89, 115, 117,
118, 120–21, 151, 266 nn.2, 4
Defense of Marriage Act (DOMA), 92, 96–98
Department of Homeland Security (U.S.),
241, 261 n.1
deportation: domestic violence and, 86, 87–
88, 89, 91, 94, 102, 120–21, 214, 220–21,
265 n.6; taxi drivers and, 241, 258–59

Desai, Bhairavi, 104–5, 209, 229, 230, 234–36, 240, 242, 243–44, 268

Desh Pardesh, 191–92

Desis Rising Up and Moving (DRUM), 259

differential access, 13, 14, 21, 247–51, 263 n.7. *See also* discrimination

Dill, Bonnie Thornton, 219

Dinkins, David, 247

Directive 15 (FICE), 37

discrimination: civil rights and, 29–30, 33–35, 41, 45; differential access and, 13, 14, 21, 247–51, 263 n.7; ethnicity paradigm and, 21, 48–52; gender and, 21, 29, 100, 191, 225–26, 248–49; immigration status and, 100; job-market, 23, 37, 53, 100, 191, 222, 225–26, 248–49, 252; nationality-based, 29, 31, 33–34, 37–39; race-based, 21, 23, 29, 34, 37–39, 45–47, 53–54; racialization and, 37–39; sexuality and, 191, 199

Diwali Festival (South Street Seaport), 63, 68, 128

DOMA (Defense of Marriage Act), 92, 96–98

domestic violence, 83–91, 114–29, 140–43; advocacy, 139–43, 149–50, 153; community and, 67, 128; criminalization of, survivors, 89; cultural adaptation discourse and, 21, 23–24; cultural authenticity and, 62–69, 83; cultural sensitivity and, 118–19, 142, 149–50, 154–55; definitions of, 114–15, 116–19; deportation and, 86, 87–88, 89, 91, 94, 102, 120–21, 214, 220–21; domestic workers and, 122, 124, 129–35, 214, 222; empowerment narratives, 117–19; family values and, 63–65; feminism and, 63, 64–65, 110, 116, 265 n.1; gender and, 116, 125; home-country and, 57, 65–66, 119–21, 266 n.4; immigration status and, 90, 116, 121; intracommunity class struggles and, 142; labor organizing and, 268 n.19; language and, 88, 117–18; lesbians and, 198–99; men and, 64–65, 84–87, 89–90, 91; model minority image and,

63–64; nation-state and, 63, 65, 70; place-taking politics and, 57; public policy and, 140–43, 265 n.5, 266 n.7; religion and, 66, 68–69, 119; shelters, 64–65, 66, 68, 89, 117–19; social services and, 117–19, 125, 129, 142, 266 n.7; space-making politics and, 116–19; spousal sponsorship and, 83–84, 86–90, 142; survivor advocates, 139–40, 149–50, 153; violence against women and, 153–55. *See also* Manavi; Sakhi for South Asian Women; South Asian Women for Action (SAWA); women's organizations

domestic workers, 212–27; African American, 213, 219; background of, 215–17; Bangladeshi, 17; capitalism and, 25–26; care work and, 63, 131, 134, 209, 213, 217–19, 219–20; citizenship and, 14, 141, 216; class and, 67, 216–17; consumerism and, 25–26, 209; cross-racial alliances, 217; cultural authenticity and, 62; definitions of work and, 24–25, 210; domestic violence and, 122, 124, 129–35, 214, 222; economic restructuring and, 217–19; employers, 102–3, 218; family reunification and, 223; gender and, 102–3, 216, 218; globalization and, 217–18; health care and, 103; immigration status, 102–3, 215–17, 219–21; intracommunity class struggles, 67, 78–79, 102, 130–35, 213, 214, 216–17; labor activism of, 9–10, 26, 209–10, 224–27; Mexican immigrants, 213, 217; migration and, 213, 220–21; model minority image and, 213; NLRA and, 18, 213, 272 n.6; private sphere and, 209, 214–15, 219–21; recruitment of, 217–19; reproductive labor and, 272 n.4; sexual abuse and, 222; social services and, 125, 131–35; transnational complex of rights and, 217, 223, 226; unionization and, 18, 209; violence against women and, 122; women's organizations and, 24–25, 62, 121–22, 124, 129–35, 154;

domestic workers (*continued*)
workplace conditions and, 18, 102, 103, 209, 221–23, 224–25. *See also* Andolan; Domestic Workers Committee (DWC); labor organizations

Domestic Workers Committee (DWC): collective action and, 214; community outreach and, 223–24; domestic space and, 214–15; intracommunity class struggles and, 130, 131, 133, 214; Sakhi and, 7, 8, 114, 129–30, 131–32, 213. *See also* Andolan

Domestic Workers Union (DWU), 224

DRUM (Desis Rising Up and Moving), 259

dual citizenship, 15–16

Dutta, Manoranjan, 29, 36–37, 40, 41, 42–43, 263 nn.8, 10, 264 n.11

DWC. *See* Domestic Workers Committee (DWC)

DWU (Domestic Workers Union), 224

Eilberg Act, 99

electoral politics, 15, 138–39, 147

elite-class immigrants: cheap labor and, 78–79; domestic violence and, 142; domestic workers and, 67, 102, 213; family reunification and, 105; immigration law and, 98–100; intracommunity class struggles and, 105–7, 132–34; labor exploitation and, 132–34; legal/illegal discourse and, 144; model minority image and, 27–28, 105; occupation-based preferences and, 99–100; small businesses and, 78–79; volunteerism and, 133–34; women's organizations and, 111–12; worker exploitation and, 131. *See also* professionals

employers, 99–101, 100, 124, 219–21

Equal Employment Opportunity Commission (EEOC), 39

Espiritu, Yen, 42, 83, 141

ethnicity paradigm, 20, 21, 22–23, 42, 48–52, 54, 60, 268 n.16

Evans, David, 165, 185

Fair Labor Standards Act, 103, 223

family reunification: class and, 38–39, 76–80, 101, 105–6; DOMA and, 96–98; domestic workers and, 223; legal/illegal discourse and, 143–46; migrant workers and, 18; occupation-based visas vs., 38–39, 77–78, 99–101, 105; Permanent Partners Immigration Bill and, 97–98; preferences, 84; sexuality and, 92, 93, 96–98, 186; working-class immigrants and, 38–39, 77, 101, 105–6; youth and, 144. *See also* marriage

family values, 63–65

Federal Aviation Administration (FAA), 2, 3

Federal Interagency on Culture and Education (FICE), 37–39

Federation of Indian Associations (FIA), 128, 184, 187

feminism (South Asia): antidowry campaign and, 143, 157; sexuality and, 74, 170 n.13, 267 n.9, 270 n.13; women's resistance and, 64–65

feminism (United States): antiviolence work and, 155–56; Asian Americans and, 110; black/white paradigm and, 110–11; critiques of citizenship and, 15–16; domestic violence and, 63, 64–65, 110, 116, 265 n.1; ethnicity paradigm critique and, 22–23; expanded notions of, 110–11; heterosexism and, 197–200; immigrant rights and, 13, 110–11; intersectionality and, 13, 154; labor organizations and, 210, 226, 230–31; minoritization and, 110–11; naming of culture and, 22–23; nation-states and, 111, 153; queer organizations and, 25; racism and, 109–11, 147–48; reproductive labor and, 272 n.4; second-wave, 110–11, 157–58; sexuality and, 25, 197–200; Third World, 13, 115, 147–48; transnational complex of rights and, 156–57; women of color and, 22, 152–53, 158; women's organizations and, 63, 109–11, 115, 136–37, 139, 144, 151

Ferguson, James, and Akhil Gupta, 17

Ferguson, Kathy, 270 n.11

Fernandes, Jorge, 11

Fernandopulle, Anushka, 75, 172, 180, 182, 191

Ferree, Myra, and Patricia Martin, 156

FIA (Federation of Indian Associations), 128, 184, 187

FICE (Federal Interagency on Culture and Education), 37–39

Filipina/o immigrants, 15, 32, 45, 50 52, 149, 212, 213, 265 n.2, 272 n.3, 7

Filipino Labor Union, 212

Filipino Workers' Center, 273 n.9

Fire (Mehta), 74, 188, 270 n.12

Fisher, Maxine, 263 n.8

Fitzpatrick, Kevin, 232

food stand workers, 78, 183–84

Forum of Indian Leftists, 274 n.23

Fourteenth Amendment, 44, 262 n.2

Frankenberg, Ruth, 43, 47

full citizenship: civil rights discourse and, 14–15, 30, 37, 39, 257–58; critiques of, 257–58; home-country histories and, 29; nation-state and, 29, 257–58; place-taking politics and, 53–55; racialization and, 23, 29–30, 39, 52, 53–55; second-class citizenship vs., 14–15, 29; sexuality and, 163–64, 185–86, 187; space-making politics and, 257–58; transnational complex of rights and, 16–20. *See also* citizenship

Fullilove vs. Klutznick, 52

GAA (Gay Activists Alliance of New York), 168, 181, 268 n.2

GAO (General Accounting Office) study, 100

Gay Activists Alliance of New York (GAA), 168, 181, 268 n.2

Gay Liberation Front (GLF), 268 n.2

gays and lesbians: asylum and, 92, 95–96; capitalism and, 163, 268 n.2; community and, 165–67; consumerism and, 206–7, 163, 164–65, 178–79; cosmopolitanism and, 11; cultural authenticity and, 71–75; family unification and, 92, 93; HIV/AIDS and, 93–94; home-country persecution and, 95–96; marriage and, 92, 94, 96–98; noncitizenship of, 163–64; "permanent" same-sex partners and, 92; politics of naming and, 168–71; racism and, 268 n.2; as skilled workers, 94–95; South Asian identity and, 168–71; spousal sponsorship and, 94, 96–98; transnational complex of rights and, 163–64; transnationalism and, 159–60, 162–63; visibility and, 165–67. *See also* lesbians; Massachusetts Area South Asian Lambda Association (MASALA); queer organizations; sexuality; South Asian Lesbian and Gay Association (SALGA)

gay tourism, 178–79

gender: asylum programs and, 17, 95, 107, 119–20, 125; care work and, 63, 131, 134, 209, 213, 217–19, 219–20; class and, 79, 111–12; criminalization and, 28; cultural adaptation discourse and, 21; cultural authenticity and, 57, 62, 64–66, 83; cultural imperialism and, 83–86, 87, 90–91; discrimination and, 21, 29, 100, 191, 225–26, 248–49; domestic violence and, 116, 125; domestic work and, 102–3, 216, 218; drag and, 184–85, 201; generational differences and, 111; Hindu nationalism and, 63, 66, 74; immigration status and, 102–3; intracommunity class struggles and, 111; labor exploitation and, 132–34; labor organizations and, 226, 230–31, 273 n.15; model minority image and, 59, 264 n.3; nationalism and, 63, 66, 74; nation-state and, 13, 63; professionals and, 79; queer organizations and, 189–92; reproductive labor and, 272 n.4; sexuality and, 167–68, 189–92, 198–200; social services and, 119, 125; South Asian identity and, 128, 270 n.13; spousal sponsorship

gender (*continued*)
and, 84, 85–88; transnational complex of
rights and, 119–21; volunteerism and, 133–
34; women's organizations and, 113–14,
135–36, 139–40, 157–58. *See also* men;
sexual citizenship; sexuality; women
General Accounting Office study, 100
generational conflict, 7, 111, 114, 115, 121, 137–
38, 157, 167, 267 n.12
Girlfriends (black lesbian organization), 196
Giuliani, Rudolph, 232, 238, 243–47
Glazer, Nathan, and Daniel Patrick
Moynihan, 54
Glenn, Evelyn Nakano, 13, 15, 272 n.4
GLF (Gay Liberation Front), 268 n.2
globalization: borders and, 13; citizenship
and, 26; domestic workers and, 217–18;
economic citizenship and, 12, 271 n.2; economic restructuring and, 13, 18, 211, 218,
227; gay tourism and, 178–79; labor
migration and, 210–11; neoliberalism and,
13, 218, 273 n.12; sexuality and, 168–69,
207; unions and, 211
Glover, Danny, 247, 251
Goenka, Tula, 124
Gompers, Samuel, 212
Gopinath, Gayatri, 70, 169, 181, 185–88, 270
n.12
Gordon, Milton, 60
Goyal, Kavita, 70, 75, 174–75, 191
green card holders. *See* immigration status
Guamanian immigrants, 50, 52
Guerrero, Marie, 268 n.18
guest worker programs, 101–2. *See also* Bracero Program
Gupta, Akhil, and James Ferguson, 17
Guyanase immigrants, 175–76, 201, 269
nn.7, 9

Haitian American Alliance, 274 n.23
health care, 42, 93–94, 99, 103, 125, 143–44,
194–95, 196

Health Professions Education Assistance
Act, 99
Helweg, Arthur, and Ulsa Helweg, 21, 105
Hennessy, Rosemary, 164, 172, 173, 179
hetero/homo binary, 96, 261 n.4
heterosexuality, 59, 96, 150–51, 197–200. *See
also* gender; patriarchal structures
hijra, 73, 169, 170, 269 n.4
Hindu nationalism: cultural authenticity and,
11, 66; domestic violence and, 66; gender
roles and, 63, 66, 74; nation-building and,
188; racialization and, 47–48; sexuality
and, 70, 73–74, 84, 163, 187–88, 205–6,
270 n.12; xenophobia and, 68, 70
HIV/AIDS, 93–94, 194–95
Hochschild, Arlie Russell, 134
Hollinger, David, 262 n.7
homophobia, 9, 24, 71–75, 173, 193–94,
204
homosexuality: domestication of, 98; heterosexual privilege and, 92; home-
country views on, 72–73, 95–96;
homophobia and, 9, 24, 71–73, 74–75,
173, 193–94, 204; marriage and, 92, 96–
98; naturalization of, 96; "sexual deviation" disqualifications and, 92–93. *See also*
hetero/homo binary; heterosexuality;
sexuality
Hondagneu-Sotelo, Pierrette, 110–11, 222, 227
hotel/motel businesses, 101, 104
human rights discourse, 15–16, 19, 120, 252,
259. *See also* civil rights; transnational
complex of rights
Hussein, Imtiyaz, 71, 161–63, 170–72, 176,
203

IIRIRA (Illegal Immigration Reform and
Immigrant Responsibility Act), 84–85,
146, 218, 263 n.6
illegal immigrants. *See* immigration status;
legal/illegal discourse
Illegal Immigration Reform and Immigrant

Responsibility Act, 1996 (IIRIRA), 84–85, 146, 218, 263 n.6

IMFA (Immigration Marriage Fraud Amendments), 84, 85–88, 90

Immigrant Women's Task Force (report), 85

Immigration and Nationality Act (INA), 33–35, 84, 92–93, 99–101

Immigration and Naturalization Service (INS), 1, 17, 91, 97–98, 261 n.1, 263 n.7

immigration law, 83–107; domestic violence and, 86–91; heterosexual contract and, 91–98; marriage and, 83–86; model minority image and, 82–83; neutrality of law and, 87–91; public assistance programs and, 90–91; sexuality and, 91–98; subordination of women and, 83–86; worker's rights and, 98–107

Immigration Marriage Fraud Amendments (IMFA), 84, 85–88, 90

Immigration Reform and Control Act (IRCA), 87, 91, 99–101, 100, 112, 212, 219, 220, 263 n.7

immigration status: citizenship and, 54–55; civil rights and, 37; criminalization and, 107–8; cultural authenticity and, 64–66; discrimination and, 100; domestic violence and, 90, 116, 121; domestic workers and, 102–3, 215–17, 219–21; family reunification and, 143–44; gender and, 102–3; heterosexual privilege and, 91–92; hierarchy of rights, 14, 156; labor organizations and, 251–54; legal/illegal discourse and, 50, 107–8, 119–21, 144–46; naturalization of, 13–14; privatization and, 219–21; public assistance programs and, 91; racial identity and, 31–35; rights and, 54–55, 143–46; sexuality and, 92–93; social mobility and, 34; social welfare programs and, 90–91; taxi drivers and, 103–5, 106, 107; transnational complex of rights and, 108, 143–47; women and, 84,

102–3. See also legal/illegal discourse; marriage

INA (Immigration and Nationality Act), 33–35, 84, 92–93, 99–101

Independence Day Parade (India), 128

independent contractors, 79–80, 104–5, 231–33, 273 n.16

India, 9, 10, 11, 15, 29, 95–96, 128

India Day Parade (New York), 11, 70, 73–74, 75, 167, 183–89

India League of America (ILA), 35, 40–42

Indian Subcontinent Women's Alliance for Action, 114, 136. See also South Asian Women for Action (SAWA)

Indo-Caribbean immigrants, 7, 10, 163, 175–76, 200–204, 205, 270 n.14

INS (Immigration and Naturalization Service), 1, 17, 91, 97–98, 261 n.1, 263 n.7

inter-ethnic relations, 7, 10, 110–11, 144–53, 200–201, 236–38, 255, 271 n.3

intersectionality, 13, 154

intracommunity class struggles: class and, 76–78, 102, 105–7, 111–12, 132–34; domestic violence organizing and, 130, 131, 133, 142, 214; domestic workers and, 67, 78–79, 102, 130–35, 131, 133, 213, 214, 216–17; gender and, 111; labor organizations and, 107, 130, 131, 133, 214, 253–54; middle class immigrants and, 132–34; professionals and, 76–78, 102, 105–7; queer organizations and, 170; social change organizations and, 132–34; South Asian diaspora and, 202–3; taxi drivers and, 76, 253–54; women and, 107, 111–12, 132–34; women's organizations and, 132–34, 138, 157, 253–54; worker exploitation and, 107, 132–34; working-class immigrants and, 76–80, 105–7, 132–34

Iranians, 50

IRCA (Immigration Reform and Control Act), 87, 91, 99–101, 112, 212, 219, 220, 263 n.7

Irish-American Gay, Lesbian and Bisexual Group of Boston, 187
Islam, Naheed, 10

Japanese and Korean Exclusion League, 40
Japanese immigrants, 34, 50, 79, 149, 212, 271 n.3
Japanese-Mexican Labor Association, 212
Jha, Chandra, 41
Johnson, Lyndon, 34
Joseph, Miranda, 164, 173, 174, 179, 193, 268 n.1

Kalapani (Sachdeva and Seepaul), 202
Kale, Madhavi, 202
Khush, 162, 169, 177
khusra, 169, 170
Kibria, Nazli, 76, 77
Korean immigrants, 40, 43, 50, 51, 52, 77, 106, 149, 262 n.4
Koshy, Susan, 42, 47, 264 n.3

labor market needs, 98–101, 102–3, 105, 106
labor organizations, 208–54; American Federation of Labor (AFL), 212; British, 210; class-based organizing and, 209; collective action and, 214; cross-racial alliances and, 236–38, 247–51, 274 n.23; domestic violence and, 268 n.19; economic restructuring and, 211; feminist principles and, 210, 226, 230–31; gender and, 226, 230–31, 273 n.15; history of organizing, 209; home-country histories and, 80; immigration status and, 251–54; intra-community class struggles and, 107, 130, 131, 133, 214; organizing strategies and, 209–10; queer politics and, 197–200; racism in, 211–12; unionization and, 80; women and, 129–35, 226; Workers Awaaz, 8, 78, 103, 215, 223, 273 nn.8–9, 274 n.23. *See also* Andolan; Domestic Workers Committee (DWC); New York Taxi Workers Alliance (NYTWA)

Latina/o immigrants, 28, 147, 179, 216, 223–24, 263 n.7
Lease Drivers Coalition (LDC), 6, 184, 197–98, 228–29, 249, 273 n.13. *See also* New York Taxi Workers Alliance (NYTWA)
Lee, Erika, 83
Lee, Robert, 264 n.3
legal/illegal discourse, 50, 107–8, 119–21, 144–46
Lehman, William, 48
Lesbian and Gay Immigration Rights Task Force (LGIRTF), 93, 95–96
lesbian, gay, bisexual, and transgender (LGBT) mainstream movements: community-building and, 163–65, 172–73, 181; consumerism and, 163–65, 268 n.2; critiques of, 9, 163–65; cultural authenticity and, 71–72; mainstream, 9; queer immigrants and, 9; racialization and, 164–65; racism and, 25, 71–72, 176–77, 268 n.2; social/cultural work and, 205; use of "queer" and, 261 n.4; visibility and, 172–73. *See also* Massachusetts Area South Asian Lambda Association (MASALA); queer organizations; South Asian Lesbian and Gay Association (SALGA)
lesbians, 189–90, 196–97, 198–99, 270 n.13
Lessinger, Johanna, 106
LGIRTF (Lesbian and Gay Immigration Rights Task Force), 93, 95–96
Lie, John and Nancy Abelmann, 106
Lipsitz, George, 232
Lorde, Audre, 8
Lotus (Ratti), 175
Lowe, Lisa, 39, 81, 211, 252
Luibhéid, Eithne, 92–93
Luna (queer Latina organization), 196
Lynch, Caitrin, 64, 65

Maitri, 89
Malaysia, 10, 137
Manalansan, Martin, 165–66, 169

Manavi, 114–21; Bridging the Gap workshop and, 119; class diversity and, 113, 115–16, 121; community-building and, 67–68; cultural authenticity and, 62, 65–66; cultural sensitivity training and, 119; domestic violence and, 24, 64, 89, 154; feminist principles and, 109–11, 115; funding and, 67, 113, 116, 121, 123, 155; generational diversity and, 115, 121; membership, 113, 121; national origin diversity and, 113–14, 121; organizational growth/vision and, 112–13, 115–16, 155; Project Zamin and, 120; religious diversity and, 115–16, 119; Sakhi and, 122; social services and, 88–89, 118–19; transitional housing and, 118–19; VAWA and, 116; violence against women and, 62, 114–15, 154

Mann, Hardeep, 136

marriage: domestic partners and, 97–98; fraud, 85–88, 94; gays and lesbians and, 92, 94, 96–98; heteronormativity and, 98; heterosexual privilege and, 91–92; legal dependency and, 90, 98, 265 nn.4,6; spousal sponsorship and, 83–90, 94, 96–98, 142; VAWA and, 88, 90. *See also* domestic violence

Martin, Patricia, 156

Massachusetts Area South Asian Lambda Association (MASALA), 159–208; antiracist organizing and, 25; coalition-building and, 148, 172, 196–97; community-building and, 25, 160–61, 165, 171–74, 174–75, 182, 191–92; consumer capitalism and, 25, 165, 206–7; cultural authenticity and, 69–70; curry queens and, 177, 179, 180–81; feminist organizing and, 25; funding, 168; gender and, 167–68, 190–92; lesbians and, 190–92; membership, 168, 177–78, 180, 203; nationalism and, 165; organizational growth/vision and, 162, 167–68; political work of, 172–74, 191–92; queer theorizing and, 191–92; SALGA

and, 162; SAWA and, 160–61, 191–92; sexuality vs. sexual practice and, 170–71; social/cultural work, 172–74, 203, 205–6; South Asian diaspora and, 72, 74–75; use of "queer" and, 261 n.4; visibility and, 25, 165–66. *See also* queer organizations; South Asian Lesbian and Gay Association (SALGA)

Massachusetts Asian Pacific American Agenda Coalition (APAAC), 143–47

Mazumdar, Sucheta, 47, 107, 111

Mehta, Deepa, 74, 188, 270 n.12

men: cultural authenticity and, 64–65; domestic violence and, 84–87, 89–90, 91; men who have sex with, 269 n.4; spousal sponsorship and, 84, 85–88. *See also* gender; patriarchal structures

methodology, 5–6, 8–9, 131–32, 215

Mexican immigrants, 33, 43, 101, 144, 145, 212, 213, 217, 263 n.5, 271 n.3

middle-class immigrants: cross-class organizing and, 253–54; domestic violence and, 142; domestic workers and, 213; intracommunity class struggles and, 132–34; labor exploitation and, 131, 132–34; legal/illegal discourse and, 144; volunteerism and, 133–34; women's organizations and, 111–12

migration: agricultural workers and, 263 n.5; Bracero Program and, 263 n.5; citizenship and, 12–16; Convention on Migrant Workers and, 18, 223; domestic workers and, 213, 220–21; feminism and, 13; home-country elections and, 15; Mexican immigrants and, 263 n.5; mobility of rights and, 19–20; rights and, 12–16, 257; space-making politics and, 258–59; structural adjustment programs (SAP) and, 13; temporary workers and, 266 n.9; transnational complex of rights and, 4, 19–20, 108, 143–47, 223; transnationalism and, 4; women and, 220–21

minoritization, 29–30, 41–42, 60, 268 n.18

model minority image: African Americans and, 28, 34, 58–59; Asian Americans and, 58–59, 264 nn.2, 3; Caribbean immigrants and, 270 n.14; class and, 27–28, 34, 105; coalition building and, 28; constructions of criminality vs., 28; cross-racial alliances and, 28; cultural adaptation discourse and, 23–24; cultural authenticity and, 57–61; domestic violence and, 63–64; domestic workers and, 213; gender and, 59, 264 n.3; legal/illegal discourse and, 144–45; legislation and, 82–83; myth of immigrant success and, 79–80, 103–5, 106, 107; place-taking politics and, 57–58; race and, 28; sexuality and, 42, 47, 59; skin color and, 27, 28; small business and, 104, 106; South Asians and, 27–28, 57–61, 142; structural assimilation and, 60; women's organizations and, 111

Mohanty, Chandra, 268 n.20

Mollen Commission, 239

Mootoo, Shani, 72

Moran, Rachel, 38

Moynihan, Daniel Patrick, 54

multiculturalism, 60

Nagar, Richa, 161

Narayan, Uma, 16, 54–55

National Action Network, 274 n.23

National Asian Pacific American Legal Consortium, 239

National Association of Americans of Indian Descent, 35–36, 52

National Employment Law Project, 221, 224–25, 273 n.9, 274 n.23

National Federation of Indian Associations, 35–36

nationalism: borders and, 12–13; citizenship and, 12–13, 26, 163, 184–85, 188–89; civil rights discourse and, 188–89, 258–59; cul-

tural authenticity and, 10–12, 66, 69–70, 74; ethnicity paradigm and, 54; gender and, 63, 66, 74; nested, 270 n.11; postcolonial, 10–11; religion and, 11, 63, 66, 69–70, 73–74, 76, 84, 115–16, 163, 187–88, 205–6, 270 n.12; sexuality and, 63, 70, 73–74, 84, 163, 184–85, 187–88, 205–7, 270 n.12; transnationalism and, 10–11, 13, 162–63, 182. See also Hindu nationalism; nation-building; nation-states; state-building

National Labor Relations Act (NLRA), 18, 213, 265 n.9, 272 n.6

nation-building, 70, 188, 257–58

nation-states: colonization and, 10, 74, 149, 162–63, 258; deterritorialization of, 12; domestic violence and, 63, 65, 70; feminism and, 111, 153; full citizenship and, 257–58; intersectionality and, 13; legalization of hierarchies and, 13; queer sexuality and, 70; scale/scope and, 17; sovereignty and, 13; space-making politics and, 257–58; transnational complex of rights and, 4, 18–19, 20–21, 259; women and, 65, 70. See also nation-building; state-building

Native Hawai'ians, 257–58

neoliberalism: citizenship and, 164, 165, 179, 185, 239–40; consumerism and, 179, 185, 207, 239–40; economic restructuring and, 24–25, 100, 163–64, 218–19, 272 n.2; globalization and, 218, 273 n.12; privatization and, 219–21, 225–27; sexuality and, 163–64; social welfare programs and, 218–19; women and, 218–19

Nepali immigrants, 218

New York Taxi Workers Alliance (NYTWA): antiblack racism and, 247–249; antiviolence campaign and, 243–46; Bangladeshi drivers and, 10, 236–38; Coalition against Anti-Asian Violence (CAAAV) and, 209; coalition building and, 253–54; collective action and, 26, 231, 233–38, 244–46; consumer rights and, 209,

239–42, 244–46; cross-racial alliances and, 236–38, 247–51, 274 n.23; direct action and, 244–46; diversity of, 229–30, 233–34, 236–38; economic restructuring and, 25–26; gender and, 230–31, 273 n.15; home-country histories and, 80; inter-ethnic relations and, 7, 10, 200–201, 236–38; intracommunity class struggles and, 253–54; July 2001 rally and, 209; language diversity and, 237; Lease Drivers Coalition (LDC) and, 6, 184, 197–98, 228–29, 273 n.13; legal strategies and, 244; membership, 229–30, 233–34, 236–38, 273 n.13; multiracial organizing and, 253–54; Operation Refusal and, 247–51; Operation Safe Cab and, 242–43; organizational growth/vision and, 229–31, 273 nn.13, 16; outreach efforts and, 230, 233–38; Pakistani drivers and, 236–38, 273 n.19; police brutality and, 228, 239–44, 246; political education and, 244–45, 249–51; "Quality of Life" campaign and, 239–51; recognizing South Asian racism, 28, 249; religious diversity and, 236–37; Sikh drivers and, 236–38; strike actions and, 244–46, 273 n.16; Taxi and Limousine Commission (TLC) and, 229, 232–33, 238, 239, 273 n.18; transnational complex of rights and, 252–54; transnationalism and, 237–38; workplace conditions and, 104–5
NLRA (National Labor Relations Act), 18, 213, 265 n.9, 272 n.6
NOW Legal Defense and Education Fund, 272 n.6
Nussbaum, Martha, 262 n.7
NYTWA. See New York Taxi Workers Alliance (NYTWA)

occupation-based immigration, 38–39, 77–78, 99–101, 102, 105, 112, 210–11, 219, 220
Omi, Michael, 20, 42; and Howard Winant, 20

Operation Refusal, 247–51
Operation Safe Cab, 242–43
Osman, Saleem, 241

Pacific Immigration Act, 31
Pak Brothers, 248, 273 n.13
Pakistan, 11, 95–96
Pakistan Day Parade (New York), 11, 128, 199–200
Pakistani immigrants, 218
Parmar, Pratibha, 72
patriarchal structures, 59, 63, 80–81, 83–84, 86, 116–17, 125–26, 190–92, 198–99, 265 n.3. See also gender; sexuality
Pellegrini, Anne, 164–65
Permanent Partners Immigration Bill, 97–98
permanent residents. See immigration status
Personal Responsibility and Work Opportunity Reconciliation Act, 90–91
Petersen, William, 34
Pian, Canta, 45, 264 n.11
place-taking politics: assimilation and, 23–24, 53–54; citizenship and, 23, 80; class and, 80; cultural authenticity and, 57–61, 63, 64, 68, 80–81; defined, 9; domestic violence and, 63, 70–71; full citizenship and, 53–55; model minority image and, 57–58; NYTWA and, 80; racialization and, 23; role of the family and, 60; social networks and, 60; South Asian diaspora and, 22; space-making politics and, 22, 54–55, 57, 252, 256; violence against women and, 121. See also space-making politics
pluralism, 20, 262 n.7
police brutality, 58, 88, 193, 205, 228, 239–44, 246
political education, 126–27
Poore, Grace, 94
Prashad, Vijay, 22, 60, 153, 273 n.15
professionals: cultural authenticity and, 77; gender and, 79, 113, 115; global restructuring and, 210–11; "illegal" immigration and,

professionals (*continued*)
114; intracommunity class struggles and,
76–78, 102, 105–7; job market discrimination, 23, 34, 52; model minority image
and, 34; occupation-based preferences
and, 99, 210–11; racial classification and,
23, 34, 42, 52; service sector and, 218, 273
n.10; small businesses and, 79–80;
women's organizations and, 111–14;
worker exploitation and, 79–80, 102, 131,
133–34, 213, 218
Project Zamin (legal clinic), 120
Puar, Jasbir, 73
Punjabi immigrants, 104, 212, 237, 271 n.3
Puri, Jyoti, 269 n.4

QAPA (Queer Asian Pacific Alliance), 97, 148,
196
queer, use of term, 261 n.4
Queer Asian Pacific Alliance (QAPA), 97, 148,
196
queer of color critique, 165
queer organizations, 159–208; affective life of
politics and, 171–74, 204–7; antiracist
activism and, 25, 163; assimilationist discourses and, 206–7; belonging and, 171–
74; class and, 206–7; coalition building
and, 148, 192–200; community-building
and, 163, 171–74, 181–83, 205–6; consumerism and, 25, 165, 172–73, 205, 206–7;
feminist organizing and, 25; gender
dynamics and, 189–92; globalization and,
207; Hindu nationalism and, 73–74, 163,
205–6; immigration and, 194–95; India
Day Parade (New York) and, 11, 68, 70,
73–74, 75, 167, 183–89; Indo-Caribbean
immigrants and, 10, 75, 163, 175–76, 194,
201–4, 205; interracial dating and, 177–
80; labor activism and, 25, 207; LGBT
organizing and, 205; membership in, 177–
80; national identity and, 181; Pakistan
Day Parade (New York) and, 11; politics

of naming, 168–71; race and, 206–7; sexism within, 189–92; sexual citizenship,
183–89; social/cultural work of, 160, 181–
83, 196–97, 205–6; South Asian diaspora
and, 161–63, 200–204; transnational
complex of rights and, 163–64, 185–89,
205; transnationalism and, 25, 72–73, 75–
76, 159–60, 162–63, 168–71; visibility
and, 163, 171–74, 204. *See also* Massachusetts Area South Asian Lambda
Association (MASALA); South Asian Lesbian and Gay Association (SALGA)
quotas, 32, 34, 92, 101, 263 n.5

race: black/white paradigm, 30, 255; construction of, 262 n.3; consumerism and,
249–51; criminalization and, 28; ethnicity
paradigm and, 48–52; national identity
and, 153; nation-state and, 13; Operation
Refusal and, 246–51; racial solidarity and,
45; unionization and, 231; whiteness vs.,
43–48
racialization, 27–55; African Americans and,
43, 255; Asian Americans and, 39, 51;
black/white paradigm, 30, 43–51; citizenship and, 23, 29–30, 39, 52, 53–55, 256–
57; civil rights and, 29, 37; discrimination
and, 37–39; Hindu nationalism and, 47–
48; Indian immigrants and, 31–35; naming strategies and, 39–43; place-taking
politics of, 23; racial ambiguity and, 30; of
South Asian identity and, 28–29, 37–39,
42, 55; whiteness and, 43–48; women
and, 255
racism: antiblack, 247–49; anti-immigrant,
110, 153; antiracism activism, 10, 30, 138,
144–46, 147–50, 153; black/white paradigm and, 22, 30, 52; feminism and, 109–
11, 147–48; labor organizations and, 107,
211–12; LGBT mainstream movements
and, 25, 71–72, 163, 173–74, 176–77;
minoritization and, 38, 48, 59; model

minority discourse and, 77, 106; nativistic, 22, 30; sexuality and, 151, 164, 177–79, 180, 268 n.2; social mobility and, 52, 58–59, 106; by South Asians, 28, 249; taxi drivers and, 228, 240, 241, 246, 247–51; xenophobic, 21, 31, 35, 68, 70, 241

Raja, Rizwan, 237, 241–42, 249–51

Rath, Richard, 268 n.17

Ray-Chaudhuri, Debi, 173, 174, 182, 190, 193, 195, 198, 203, 228, 229

Reagon, Bernice Johnson, 148

Refugee Act, 92, 95

Reinelt, Claire, 156

religion: cultural authenticity and, 66; domestic violence and, 66, 68–69, 119; gay Muslims, 71–72, 161–62, 203; Ismaili, 71, 161–62, 203; Muslims, 66, 68, 69, 71–72, 73, 116, 161–62, 181, 203, 258–59; nationalism and, 11, 63, 66, 69–70, 74, 76, 115–16; sexual identity and, 71–72, 161–62, 203; Sikhs, 236–37; social service providers and, 119; women's organizations and, 113, 115–16, 119. *See also* Hindu nationalism

resident aliens. *See* immigration status

restaurant workers, 78, 101, 102–3

rights: capitalism and, 262 n.1; citizenship and, 12–16, 26, 257; civil, 14–15, 29–30, 37, 38, 39, 258–59, 271 n.5; consumer, 26, 209, 238–41, 244–46; human, 15–16, 19, 120, 252, 259; migration and, 12–16, 18, 223, 257; sexuality and, 163–64, 185–89, 205. *See also* transnational complex of rights

Rodney, Walter, 269 n.9

Rudrappa, Sharmila, 60, 66, 117–18

SAAA (South Asian AIDS Action), 184, 194

Sachdeva, Riti, 135–36, 138–40, 201

Safir, Howard, 246

Saheli: in Massachusetts, 68; in Texas, 89

Sakhi for South Asian Women, 121–35; activism vs. social services and, 124–27,

130–31, 133–34; coalition building and, 128–29, 130; community and, 68, 124, 127–29; cross-class organizing and, 122; cultural authenticity and, 62, 64, 65–66; domestic violence and, 17, 24, 64, 89, 121–22, 124; domestic workers and, 24–25, 62, 121–22, 124, 129–35, 154; DWC and, 7, 8, 24–25, 114, 129–30, 213; economic justice project, 125, 129–30, 134; feminist principles and, 109–11; funding, 113, 123–24, 130, 155; Indian Day Parade and, 68, 184; internal conflicts and, 7–8; intracommunity class struggles and, 130–35, 253; literacy services and, 125, 126, 134; Manavi and, 122; membership, 113–14, 123, 124; national identity and, 113–14; organizational growth/vision and, 113–14, 121–24, 129–31, 133–34, 155, 266 n.1; Pakistan Day Parade (New York) in, 68, 199–200; religion and, 113–14, 128; SALGA and, 128–29, 198–200; sexuality and, 193; social services and, 88–89, 125, 126, 134; South Asian identity and, 122–23; transnational complex of rights and, 17–18; urban issues and, 122; volunteerism and, 133–34; working-class women and, 24, 129–35. *See also* Andolan; women's organizations; Workers Awaaz

SALGA. *See* South Asian Lesbian and Gay Association (SALGA)

Samar Collective, 79, 102, 215

same-sex marriage, 96–98

Sandoval, Chela, 111

Sassen, Saskia, 13, 259

Seepaul, Lisa, 202

self-employment, 79–80, 104–7, 212. *See also* Andolan; labor organizations; New York Taxi Workers Alliance (NYTWA); small businesses

Selvadurai, Shyam, 72

Sennett, Randolph, 262 n.7

September 11, 2001, 4, 258–59, 261 n.1

Service Employees International Union (SEIU), 273 n.16
service sector work, 79, 252
sexual citizenship, 165, 185–89
sexuality: affective life of politics and, 204–7; Asian Americans and, 179; asylum and, 92, 95–96, 107; class status and, 191; constructions of criminality and, 28; cultural adaptation discourse and, 21, 23–24, 183–89; cultural authenticity and, 69–75, 168–69; feminism and, 25, 197–200; full citizenship and, 163–64, 185–87; gender and, 167–68, 189–92, 198–200; globalization of, 168–69; heterosexual privilege and, 91–92; home-country histories and, 72–73, 95–96; immigration status and, 92–93; Indo-Caribbean immigrants and, 163, 200–204, 270 n.14; internal conflicts and, 7; men who have sex with men, 269 n.4; national identity and, 187; queerphobic xenophobia and, 73, 85, 145, 179, 186; sexual practice vs., 170–71; skilled workers and, 94–95; social group membership and, 95–96; South Asian diaspora and, 74–75, 201–2; transnational complex of rights and, 163–64, 185–89, 205; visibility and, 165–67, 204; whiteness and, 177. See also heterosexuality; homosexuality; queer organizations
"Shades of Brown" (Boston University conference), 27–28
Shah, Nayan, 69, 73, 270 n.13
Shah, Purvi, 129
Shah, Sonia, 136
Shah, Svati, 188
Sharpton, Al, 247, 251, 274 n.23
Sikhs, 236–37
Sivanandan, A., 210
skilled workers, 13, 94–95, 105–6, 210–11
small businesses: Asian Americans and, 79; immigration status and, 103–7; legal/ille-

gal discourse and, 144; model minority image and, 104, 106; myth of immigrant success and, 79–80, 103–5, 106, 107; social mobility and, 79–80; women and, 79–80; worker exploitation and, 79–80, 106–7
Smith, Barbara, 152
social change organizations: advocacy and, 140–43; antiviolence work and, 155–56; citizenship and, 26; collective action and, 8, 9, 56, 133, 189, 200, 214, 217, 236; community-building and, 67; cultural authenticity and, 61, 81; home-country histories and, 15, 57, 65–66, 72–73, 80, 95–96, 119–21, 165–66; intracommunity class struggles and, 132–34; organizational growth/vision and, 7–8, 26, 152–53, 159–60; service provision and, 112; sexism vs. sexuality and, 204–5; social services and, 71, 124–27, 129, 133, 194–96; social transformation and, 5–6; South Asian mobilization and, 4–7, 9–11; space-making politics of, 9; transformative activism and, 5–6, 109, 111, 131; transnational complex of rights and, 16–18, 259; volunteerism and, 133–34. See also labor organizations; queer organizations; women's organizations
social mobility: anticitizens and, 34; Asian Americans and, 58–59; cultural authenticity and, 76–77; immigrant status and, 34; racism and, 52, 58–59, 106; small businesses and, 79–80; wage workers and, 79
social services: activism and, 124–27, 129, 194–96; advocacy vs., 140–43; cosmopolitanism and, 11; cultural sensitivity training, 119; domestic violence and, 117–19, 125, 129, 142; gender and, 119, 125; legal/illegal discourse and, 143–47; as political education, 126–27; women's organizations and, 118–19
social welfare programs: differential access

and, 263 n.7; domestic workers and, 213; emergency assistance, 91; HIV screening, 93–94; IIRIRA and, 263 n.6; immigration status and, 90–91, 143–46, 218; INS and, 263 n.7; IRCA and, 91, 263 n.7; neoliberalism and, 218–19; permanent residents and, 218; women and, 90–91, 263 n.7

South Asian AIDS Action (SAAA), 184, 194

South Asian diaspora: affective life of politics and, 171–74; Britain and, 202, 210; Canada and, 71, 72, 74, 113, 145–46, 161–63, 191–92, 219; cultural authenticity and, 74–75; Guyana and, 175–76, 201, 269 nn.7, 9; homophobia and, 25; Indo-Caribbean, 7, 10, 163, 200–204, 270 n.14; inter-ethnic relations, 7, 10, 200–201, 236–38; intracommunity class struggles, 202–3; labor organizing and, 210; Malaysia and, 10, 137; nation-based identity and, 10; place-taking politics and, 22; queerness and, 174–77; sexuality and, 72, 161–63, 197–200, 201–2; social/cultural differences and, 203–4; space-making politics, 22; Tanzania and, 161, 162–63, 171, 182, 203; Trinidad and Tobago and, 202–3

South Asian identity: affirmative action and, 30, 33, 37–39, 42, 51, 271 n.15; black/white paradigm and, 43–48, 136, 256, 263 n.10; critique of panethnicity and, 42; definitions of, 10, 51–52, 137, 262 n.6; gender roles and, 128, 270 n.13; identity formation and, 10–12; model minority image and, 27–28, 57–61, 142; nationalism and, 10–11, 162–63; nation-based identity and, 10, 256, 270 n.10; place-taking politics and, 256; racialization and, 28–29, 37–39, 42, 55; sexuality and, 72–73, 160–61, 162, 187, 199–200, 270 n.13; space-making politics and, 136–37, 256; transnationalism and, 10–11, 162–63. See also cultural authenticity

South Asian Lesbian and Gay Association

(SALGA), 159–208; antiracist organizing and, 25; class diversity and, 170; community and, 25, 160–61, 165, 171–74, 175–76; consumer capitalism and, 25, 165; curry queens and, 177–81; funding for, 167; gender and, 190–92; generational diversity and, 167; Hindu nationalism and, 73–74, 163; immigration and, 194–95; India Day Parade (New York) and, 11, 68, 70, 73–74, 75, 167, 183–89; Indo-Caribbeans and, 10, 74–75, 163, 175–76, 194, 201–4; intracommunity class struggles and, 170; labor organizing and, 25; language diversity and, 170; MASALA and, 162; membership, 167, 177–80; nationalism and, 165; organizational growth/vision and, 159–60, 167; Pakistan Day Parade (New York) and, 68, 75, 199–200; political work and, 172–74; queer visibility and, 25; Sakhi and, 128–29, 198–200; sexual asylum and, 96; sexuality and, 195–96; social/cultural work and, 172–74, 205–6; social services vs. social justice activism and, 167; South Asian diaspora and, 72, 74–75; transgender people and, 269 n.3; transnational complex of rights and, 185–89; as transnational organization, 25; use of "queer" and, 261 n.4; visibility and, 165–66. See also Massachusetts Area South Asian Lambda Association (MASALA); queer organizations

South Asians Against Police Brutality, 274 n.23

South Asian Women for Action (SAWA), 135–52; coalition-building and, 138–39, 141–43, 147–53, 155–56, 267 n.15; college campus relations and, 136; community and, 68; cultural authenticity and, 61–62, 65–66; domestic violence and, 24, 64, 114, 140–43; electoral politics and, 138–39; feminist principles and, 109–11, 136–37, 139, 144, 151; funding for, 114, 138–39, 152, 155–56; gender and, 114, 135–36, 139–40;

South Asian Women for Action (*continued*)
generational diversity, 114, 137–38; heterosexism and, 150–51; immigrant rights
advocacy and, 143–46; intracommunity
class struggles and, 138; legal/illegal discourse and, 143–47; lesbians and, 269 n.6;
MASALA and, 151, 160–61, 191–92; membership, 136–38, 152; organizational
growth/vision and, 114, 135–40, 150–53,
155; outreach efforts and, 137–38, 144;
queer alliances and, 148; sexual politics
and, 150–51; social services vs. social justice activism and, 139, 154, 155–56; South
Asian diaspora and, 137–38; space-
making politics and, 139–40; survivor
advocacy and, 139–40, 149–50, 153; transnational complex of rights and, 139; violence against women and, 139
space-making politics: activism vs. social services and, 131; community and, 67, 81; cultural authenticity and, 57, 64, 80–81;
defined, 9; full citizenship and, 257–58;
home-country histories and, 57, 80; low-
wage workers and, 24; migrant rights and,
258–59; place-taking politics and, 54–55,
57, 252, 256; queers and, 24; transnational
complex of rights and, 108, 163–64;
women and, 24
spousal sponsorship, 83–84, 85–90, 94, 96–
98, 142. *See also* marriage
Sri Lankan immigrants, 218
Sripada, Ramani, 148
state-building: colonization and, 10, 74, 149,
162–63, 258; sovereignty, 13, 156, 219, 257–
58, 268 n.18. *See also* colonization
Strobel, Margaret, 152
structural adjustment programs, 13, 218
Subcommittee on Census and Population, 43
Subramanian, Kalpana, 137, 140
Sudbury, Julia, 158, 267 n.6
Sundaram, Serena, 138, 139, 149, 196, 197
Swami, Ratnam, 51

Syed, Javid, 72, 169–70, 191, 193–94, 195–96,
203

Tanzanian immigrants, 161, 162–63, 171, 182,
203
Taxi and Limousine Commission (TLC), 229,
232–33, 238, 239, 273 n.18
taxi drivers: African Americans and, 247–51;
consumerism and, 25–26, 209, 238–41;
cosmopolitanism and, 11; cross-racial
alliances and, 236–38, 247–51, 274 n.23;
deportation and, 241, 258–59; hierarchy
of rights and, 14; homicide rates and, 10,
241; immigration status and, 103–5; independent contractor status and, 79–80,
104–5, 210, 231–33, 273 n.16; industry
restructuring and, 231–33; inter-ethnic
relations and, 7, 10, 200–201, 236–38;
intracommunity class struggles and, 76,
253–54; labor organizing and, 26, 228–
29, 231–38; Operation Refusal and, 247–
51; organizing strategies and, 9–10, 209–
10; police brutality and, 228, 239–44, 246;
public space and, 209; racism and, 228,
240, 241, 246, 247–51; strikes and, 244–
46; transnationalism and, 127–28; unionization and, 26, 127–28, 209, 231; wages
and, 232–33; workplace conditions, 104–
5, 209, 210, 228, 238–42. *See also* labor
organizations; New York Taxi Workers
Alliance (NYTWA)
Thadani, Giti, 160
Thind, Bhagat Singh, 31, 45
Thompson, Becky, 110, 262 n.5, 269 n.6
Time Bind (Hochschild), 134
TLC (Taxi and Limousine Commission), 229,
232–33, 238, 239
transformative activism, 5–6, 109, 111, 131. *See
also* social change organizations; space-
making politics
transnational complex of rights: black/white
paradigm and, 256; borders and, 108,

257–58; citizenship and, 18–19, 26, 156, 185–89; defined, 16–20; domestic workers and, 217, 223, 226; feminism and, 156–57; gender and, 119–21; human rights discourse and, 19, 259; immigration status and, 108, 143–47; legal/illegal discourse and, 119–21, 143–47, 155–56; migration and, 4, 19–20, 108, 223; nation-state and, 4, 18–19, 20–21, 259; queer organizations and, 163–64, 185–89, 205; sexuality and, 163–64, 185–89, 205; social justice and, 259; space-making and, 108, 163–64; transnational social justice organizations and, 16–20, 259; women and, 112, 119–21, 139, 156–57; workers and, 251–54

transnationalism: borders and, 12, 17–18, 157; consumerism and, 177, 179–80; cultural authenticity and, 72–73; identity formation and, 10–11; immigrant realities and, 261 n.3; nationalism and, 10–11, 13, 270 n.12; sexuality and, 72–73, 75–76, 159–60, 168–71, 270 n.12; taxi drivers and, 127–28. See also transnational complex of rights

Trikone, 54, 159–60, 162, 169, 177

Trinidadian and Tobagan immigrants, 202–3

Trivedi, Neela, 102–3, 129–30, 214

TWA. See New York Taxi Workers Alliance (NYTWA)

unionization, 18, 26, 80, 127–28, 209, 211–13, 224–27, 231, 271 n.3, 273 n.6

United States Citizenship and Immigration Services (USCIS), 261 n.1. See also Immigration and Naturalization Service (INS)

United Yellow Cab Association, 246, 273 n.13

USCIS. See United States Citizenship and Immigration Services (USCIS)

Vaid, Urvashi, 72

VAWA (Violence Against Women Act, 1994), 84–85, 88, 89, 90, 116, 265 n.5

violence against women: antiviolence activism, 25, 61–67, 69, 78, 124, 155; community support against, 123–24; deportation and, 121; domestic workers and, 122; institutional violence and, 9; lesbians and, 198–99; place-taking politics and, 121; sexual abuse and, 119, 222; space-making politics and, 119–21; transformative analysis of, 114–15, 116–19. See also domestic violence; Manavi; Sakhi for South Asian Women

Violence Against Women Act (VAWA), 84–85, 88, 89, 90, 116, 265 n.5

Vohra, Prema, 193

voting rights, 15, 138–39, 147

Warrier, Sujata, 58, 62, 64, 67, 115, 116, 117, 121

Waters, Mary, 269 n.7, 270 n.14

West Indians, 270 n.14. See also Caribbean immigrants; Indo-Caribbean immigrants

whiteness, 29–30, 43–48, 71–72, 177, 237–38, 262 n.2. See also racialization

Winant, Howard, and Michael Omi, 20

WISH (Women's Immigrant Safe Harbor Act), 266 n.7

women: African American, 213, 219, 255; black/white paradigm and, 136, 255; care work and, 63, 131, 134, 209, 213, 217–20; class status and, 113, 115, 129–35; cultural authenticity and, 57, 62–63, 70–71; deportation and, 86, 87–88, 89, 91, 94, 102, 120–21, 214, 220–21; domestic violence and, 86–91, 116; generational differences and, 111; Hindu nationalism and, 63, 66; immigration legislation and, 83–86; immigration status and, 84, 102–3; India Day Parade (New York) and, 11; intracommunity class struggles and, 107, 111–12, 132–34; labor exploitation and, 102–3, 132–34; labor organizing and, 230–31; lesbians, 189–90, 196–97, 198–99, 270 n.13; marriage and, 83–86, 90, 91, 142;

women (*continued*)

Mexican immigrants, 213, 217; migration and, 220–21; mobility and, 220–21; model minority image and, 264 n.3; neo-liberalism and, 218–19; Pakistan Day Parade (New York) and, 11; queer organizations and, 190–92; racialization and, 255; religious diversity and, 119; reproductive labor and, 272 n.4; sexuality and, 197–200; small businesses and, 79–80; social services and, 125; social welfare policies and, 90–91, 263 n.7; South Asian identity and, 128; transnational complex of rights and, 112, 119–21, 139, 156–57. *See also* domestic workers; gender; queer organizations; women's organizations

Women Aware, 118

Women's Immigrant Safe Harbor Act (WISH), 266 n.7

women's organizations, 109–58; antiracism activism and, 10, 30, 138, 144–50, 153; antiviolence work and, 155–56; Apna Ghar, 64–65, 66, 68; Asha, 89; class diversity and, 112–14, 157; coalition building and, 111, 128–29, 130, 138–39, 141–43, 147–53, 155–56, 273 n.9; community outreach and, 123–24; cross-class organizing and, 122; cultural sensitivity and, 154–55; domestic violence and, 24, 88, 112, 153–55; feminism and, 63, 109–11, 115, 136–37, 139, 144, 151; feminist principles and, 109–11; funding concerns and, 112, 113, 114, 116, 155–56, 267 n.6; gender and, 157–58; generational differences and, 157; heterosexism and, 150–51, 197–200; home-country histories and, 65–66; immigrant rights and, 112; institutionalization and, 112, 155–56; inter-ethnic relations and,

110, 111; intracommunity class struggles and, 132–34, 138, 157, 253–54; lesbians and, 269 n.6; Maitri, 89, 91; membership diversity and, 111–12, 113–14; model minority image and, 111; multiracial coalitions, 110–11; queer politics and, 197–200; religious diversity and, 113, 115–16, 119; sexuality and, 112, 150–51, 157, 193, 197, 198–99; social services and, 112, 118–19; social services vs. social change and, 124–27; South Asian diaspora and, 137–38; South Asian identity and, 122–23; the state and, 156; transformative activism and, 109; transnational complex of rights and, 112, 139, 156–57; Women Aware, 118; working-class women and, 24. *See also* Manavi; Sakhi for South Asian Women; South Asian Women for Action (SAWA)

Workers Awaaz, 8, 78, 103, 215, 223, 273 nn.8–9, 274 n.23

working-class immigrants: cross-class organizing and, 253–54; cultural authenticity and, 77; educational attainment of, 105–6; family reunification and, 77, 105; immigration law and, 98, 100–102, 103, 105; India Day Parade (New York) and, 11; intracommunity class struggles and, 76–80, 105–7, 132–34; as labor activists, 210; Pakistan Day Parade (New York) and, 11; women's organizations and, 24, 129–35

xenophobia: queerphobic, 73, 85, 145, 179, 186; race and, 21, 31, 35, 68, 70

Yaar (community-based organization), 184

Yanagisako, Sylvia, 79–80

Monisha Das Gupta is an assistant professor of ethnic studies and women's studies at the University of Hawai'i.

Library of Congress Cataloging-in-Publication Data
Das Gupta, Monisha, 1961–
Unruly immigrants : rights, activism, and transnational South Asian politics in the United States / Monisha Das Gupta.
p. cm.
Includes bibliographical references and index.
ISBN-13: 978-0-8223-3858-1 (cloth : alk. paper)
ISBN-10: 0-8223-3858-0 (cloth : alk. paper)
ISBN-13: 978-0-8223-3898-7 (pbk. : alk. paper)
ISBN-10: 0-8223-3898-x (pbk. : alk. paper)
1. South Asian Americans—Civil rights. 2. South Asian Americans—Societies, etc. 3. South Asian Americans—Politics and government. 4. Immigrants—United States—Social conditions. 5. Political activists—United States. 6. Civil rights movements—United States. 7. Citizenship—United States. 8. Social change—United States. 9. Transnationalism. 10. United States—Race relations. I. Title.
E184.S69D37 2006   305.891'4073—dc22
2006014493